David's Walk with God

Lonny E. Young

WESTBOW
PRESS®
A DIVISION OF THOMAS NELSON
& ZONDERVAN

WestBow Press books may be ordered through booksellers or by contacting:

WestBow Press
A Division of Thomas Nelson & Zondervan
1663 Liberty Drive
Bloomington, IN 47403
www.westbowpress.com
1 (866) 928-1240

ISBN: 978-1-9736-6011-8 (sc)
ISBN: 978-1-9736-6010-1 (e)

Print information available on the last page.

WestBow Press rev. date: 04/11/2019

"And when He had removed him (Saul), He raised up for them David as king, to whom also He gave testimony and said, 'I have found David the son of Jesse, a man after My own heart, who will do all my will. '" (Acts 13:22)

FORWARD

While I was working on my last book, THE PATH, I discovered a mystery that I determined to solve. I became fascinated with the life of King David. Why was he called "a man after God's own heart"? After all, he did make several bad mistakes. So, what made him different? I determined to dig into the passages that spoke of David and his life and circumstances. Try to determine why he was called, "a man after God's own heart".

I don't know about you, but it can be easy to put David on a pedestal. Even with his serious mistakes with Bathsheba and Tamar, God still used him in a great way. He was not superhuman. He was a person just like you or I, again, the question.

I hope this "searching the scriptures" will help you get a more intimate look at David and maybe discern his heart and thus, why God loved him so. Enjoy the journey with me. Have an open mind and an open heart to listen to God speak through the life of this ordinary man that God used greatly!

Dedicated to these godly men in my life
who have invested their time and encouragement
to help me grow as a Christian.

Sam Anderson	Jeff Glassford	Ray Molt
Bill Armstrong	Henry Green	Earl Morley
Butch Aubuchon	Ron Hammontree	Donnie Nichols
Ed Bell	Jim Henson	Sing Oldham
Don Brockman	Ronnie Hicks	Charlie Phillips
Ronnie Buckallew	Ron Huff	Clint Sims

Don Burt   Dennis Huskisson   Larry Smith

Roger Carrender   Dave Jungeblut   John Starr

Jack Cook   Marvin Kennon   Robert Strong

Al Dancy   Quinn McConnell   Paul Trussler

Johnny Deakins   Randy McKinley   Tim Whitehead

Craig Dyer   Bill McKinney   Mike Windsor

Wayne Geiger   Fred Merrill   Lewis Wolfe

Earl Young

I want to thank the three churches I have been privileged to serve in:

Anchor Point Baptist Church, Independence, Mo.
Freeman Baptist Church, Freeman, Mo.
First Baptist Church, Grain Valley, Mo.

Introduction

"But now your kingdom shall not continue. The Lord has sought for Himself a man after His own heart, and the Lord has commanded him to be commander over His people, because you have not kept what the Lord commanded you." (1 Samuel 13:14) (NKJV)

"And when He had removed him (Saul), He raised up for them David as king, to whom also He gave testimony and said, 'I have found David the son of Jesse, a man after My own heart, who will do all my will.'" (Acts 13:22) (NKJV)

Why was David called, "A man after God's own heart?" That is the premise of this treatise. The more I read Samuel and Kings the more curious I became. What was it about David that God would say he was a man after His own heart? He sure wasn't perfect as we will see. He made mistakes just as we have. So, what made him different?

David reminds me a lot of Peter in the New Testament. With Peter, his mouth got him in more trouble than did David. Peter was always saying or doing the wrong thing, but after Jesus straightened him out, he preached a powerful message at Pentecost in the book of Acts. God used him in a great way, in the early church.

I mentioned the book of Kings earlier. This was long past the reign of David and Solomon but look at some of these verses:

"And to his son I will give one tribe, that My servant David may always have a lamp before Me in Jerusalem, the city which I have chosen for Myself, to put My name there. (1 Kings 11:36) (NKJV)

And he (Abijam) walked in all the sins of his father, which he had done before him; his heart was not loyal to the Lord his God, as was the heart of his father David. Nevertheless, for David's sake the Lord his God gave him a lamp in Jerusalem, by setting up his son after him and by establishing Jerusalem. (1 Kings 15:3-4) (NKJV)

Asa did what was right in the eyes of the Lord, as did his father David. (1 Kings 15:11) (NKJV)

And he (Hezekiah) did what was right in the sight of the Lord, according to all that his father David had done. (2 Kings 18:3) (NKJV)

"And I will add to your days fifteen years. I will deliver you and this city from the hand of the king of Assyria; and I will defend this city for My own sake, and for the sake of My servant David." (2 Kings 20:6) (NKJV)

And he (Josiah) did what was right in the sight of the Lord, and walked in all the ways of his father David; he did not turn aside to the right hand or to the left. (2 Kings 22:2) (NKJV)

David was the standard by which subsequent kings were measured. It is my desire, in this study, to examine the scenes in David's life and see if we can determine just what it was that made David, "A man after God's own heart."

1 Samuel 16

And the Lord said to Samuel, How long wilt thou mourn for Saul, seeing I have rejected him from reigning over Israel? Fill thine horn with oil, and go, I will send thee to Jesse the, Beth-lehemite: for I have provided me a king among his sons. (1 Samuel 16:1)

And it came to pass, when they were come, that he looked on Eliab, and said, "Surely the Lord's anointed is before him". But the Lord said unto Samuel, "Look not on his countenance, or on the height of his stature; because I have refused him: for the Lord seeth not as man seeth; for man looketh on the outward appearance, but the Lord looketh on the heart." (1 Samuel 16:6-7)

"Are there al thy children?" And he said, "There remaineth yet the youngest, and, behold, he keepeth the sheep." And Samuel said to Jesse, "Send and fetch him: for we will not sit down till he come hither." And he sent, and brought him in. Now he was ruddy, and withal of a beautiful countenance, and goodly to look to. And the Lord said, "Arise, anoint him: for this is he. Then Samuel took the horn of oil, and anointed him in the midst of his brethren: and the Spirit of the Lord came upon David from that day forward. So Samuel rose up, and went to Ramah. (1 Samuel 16:11-13)

What must have been going through David's mind when one of his brothers shows up in the field and told him that Samuel had requested his presence? Even better, when Samuel anoints him king of Israel. A shepherd? What a resume!

Think about this a minute. Who did God call to free His people from bondage in Egypt? Look at the life of Moses.

And the child grew, and she brought him to Pharaoh's daughter, and he became her son. So, she called his name Moses, saying, "Because I drew him out of the water." (Exodus 2:10) (NKJV)

Moses had spent forty years in the courts of Pharaoh. He learned the ways of the Egyptians, their customs, their gods, their lifestyle. Forty years from his birth, in the lap of luxury. Then God decided to move him.

Now Moses was tending the flock of Jethro his father-in-law, the priest of Midian. And he led the flock to the back of the desert, and came to Horeb, the mountain of God. (Exodus 3:1) (NKJV)

Moses spent another forty years as a shepherd. Learning to care for sheep, learning to guide them, provide for their needs, protect them. In preparation for a far greater calling! The same preparation that David had, though not for forty years.

It is believed that David was in his teens as a shepherd boy. There was still much learning to take place. I want you to notice, at David's anointing the "Spirit of the Lord" came to David (16:13). He will help David through many trying years ahead.

We have seen that one of the "classes" a leader will need, is being a shepherd. There are so many lessons to be learned from watching David, and reflecting on Moses as well. Study the characteristics of a shepherd. Not only must he provide for his flock but he is to protect them and guide them!

There is one more shepherd we want to examine in our trilogy. The Lord Jesus. Look at John chapter 10. I encourage you to read the whole chapter.

"I am the good shepherd. The good shepherd gives His life for the sheep." (John 10:11) (NKJV)

Jesus answered them, "I told you and you do not believe. The works that I do in My Father's name, they bear witness of Me. But you do not believe, because you are not of My sheep, as I said to you. My sheep hear My voice, and I

*know them, and they follow Me. And I give them eternal
life, and they shall never perish; neither shall anyone
snatch them out of My hand." (John 10:25-28) (NKJV)*

The Good Shepherd! Why would Jesus use the analogy of a shepherd? His flock is far beyond our comprehension. His flock is the whole world, to those who hear His voice and obey His commands!

Back to David a minute. You know that David wrote songs, right? Seventy-three of the one-hundred and fifty songs are attributed to David. Songs of praise to the God that David knew out in the fields as he watched over the sheep. Of course, the most famous, Psalm 23.

*The Lord is my shepherd; I shall not want. He makes me
to lie down in green pastures; He leads me beside the still
waters. He restores my soul. He leads me in the paths of
righteousness for His name's sake. (Psalm 23:1-3) (NKJV)*

Have you ever read or sang the hymns of Fanny Crosby? Even though she was blind she must have had a special insight into God's kingdom. Her hymns are so inspiring, so uplifting, so filled with the message of God, it just amazes me. I think the same can be said for David. The many days and nights he spent out in the field with his sheep must have brought him to a special relationship with God.

Look at the words of this psalm. Only someone with a special relationship with God could pen such glorious words. They are also meant to inspire and challenge us to have that intimate relationship with God.

Both in Moses' and David's life there was that time when God needed to get their attention. He did that by getting them away to some quiet place. In the case of Moses, it was the backside of the desert, in David's, out in the field tending sheep.

I would like you to ponder these examples. Do you have a "quiet place" to be alone with God? Do you know God?

In the days' ahead we are going to take a journey. We are going to walk with King David, through the Scriptures and watch him as he deals with his daily trials and triumphs. What influences his decisions? What about the mistakes he makes? How does David deal with his relationship with God when he "messes up"?

We have the great advantage of hindsight. We know how the story ends. Someone once said, "It's not the destination, it's the journey." Join me in this journey and discover with me what it was about David that made him "A man after God's own heart."

After David was anointed there seems to be a gap. There is no way of knowing how much time passed from the day Samuel anointed David and the next scene. That's where this waiting occurs.

Let's imagine you're out in your field shepherding your sheep. Your brother runs out and says that the prophet Samuel wants to see you. You follow him back to the house. Samuel then proceeds to anoint you the next king of Israel.

Judging from the text in verse 13 in chapter 16 it doesn't say that Samuel told David why he was being anointed. We can safely assume David and his family knew what had happened.

That being the case, David goes out and raises an army to depose Saul. Isn't this interesting. What did David do? He went back to his sheep. Waiting for God's time and God's plan. We will see later that David has two opportunities to kill Saul but doesn't do so.

Here are a couple of verses to ponder:

> *But those who wait on the Lord shall renew their strength; they shall mount up with wings like eagles, they shall run but not be weary, they shall walk but not faint. (Isaiah 40:31) (NKJV)*

> *For evildoers shall be cut off; but those who wait on the Lord, they shall inherit the earth.*

> *(Psalm 37:9) Wait on the Lord, and keep His way, and He shall exalt you to inherit the land; when the wicked are cut off, you shall see it. (Psalm 37:34) (NKJV)*

David always had the confidence that God had a plan (Jeremiah 29:11), and that it was his responsibility to wait for God to open the door. Like I said, David could have done a lot of things differently right now. Maybe it was that Spirit that came upon him at his anointing that gave him the peace to wait on God's timing.

How about you? Has God laid on your heart a task, or a vision, or a desire to do something and at the same time has asked you to wait? Maybe it is something you want very badly, but God seems to be keeping the door closed. It's frustrating, isn't it? I know, I've been there. In fact, I even broke down the door only to find a permanent road block. My desire was denied. That was when I learned the importance of waiting on God. It's a tough lesson to learn.

David learned that lesson at a very early age. Maybe he learned it out in the field tending his sheep. It's hard to say. Unruly sheep can teach you, patience, I'm sure.

We are not a patient generation. With technology and fast-food drive-ins and instant gratification we are quickly losing our ability to wait. It was only a generation or two back that waited for the things they wanted. They worked, saved, for years sometimes to achieve their goal. So how do you learn to wait?

Look at Jeremiah 29:11, you would do well to remember this verse!

> For I know the thoughts that I think toward you, says the Lord, thoughts of peace and not of evil, to give you a future and a hope. Then you will call upon Me and go and pray to Me, and I will listen to you. And you will seek Me and find Me, when you search for Me with all your heart. (Jeremiah 29:11-13) (NKJV)

But the Spirit of the Lord departed from Saul, and an evil spirit from the Lord troubled him. (1 Samuel 16:14)

This is unique to the Old Testament. The Holy Spirit in the Old Testament would come and go as God had need of the individual. God would choose certain individuals to accomplish His purpose at certain times. We can see this profoundly in the life of Samson. Remember a few verses back, when David was anointed? He was indwelled with the Spirit of the Lord in verse 13.

In the New Testament, the ministry of the Holy Spirit changed. As it was in the New Testament so it is today. In John 14 and 16 we read:

> If you love Me, keep My commandments. And I will pray the Father, and He will give you another Helper, that He may abide with you forever—the Spirit of truth, whom the

world cannot receive, because it neither sees Him nor knows Him; but you know Him, for He dwells with you and will be in you. (John 14:15-17) (NKJV)

Nevertheless, I tell you the truth. It is to your advantage that I go away; for if I do not go away, the Helper will not come to you; but if I depart, I will send Him to you. And when He has come, He will convict the world of sin, and of righteousness, and of judgment: of sin, because they do not believe in Me; of righteousness, because I go to My Father and you see Me no more; of judgment, because the ruler of this world is judged.
(John 16:7-11) (NKJV)

Saul refused to obey God's leading. Therefore, God removed the Spirit from Saul and has indwelled David with that Spirit. I think the difference between Saul and David was that Saul never repented of his disobedience. He might say he was sorry but God knew his heart.

Notice Saul's life after the Spirit had been removed. The Bible calls it a "spirit of distress." For the king of Israel that is not where you want to be. I think it is interesting that God provided a remedy. The music of a harpist. And of course, by accident, it happened to be David.

Take note here and all throughout the Bible. Nothing, happens by accident. One of my favorite stories is the one told of Joseph in the book of Genesis. One of my favorite verses is in Genesis:

"But as for you, you meant evil against me; but God meant it for good, in order to bring i about as it is this day, to save many people alive." (Genesis 50:20) (NKJV)

"For if you remain completely silent at this time, relief and deliverance will arise for the Jews from another place, but you and your father's house will perish. Yet who knows whether you have come to the kingdom for such a time as this? (Esther 4:14) (NKJV)

David is where God wants him, when He wants him there, for a reason. If you look at the story of Joseph, it took God thirteen years (Gen. 37:2, 41:46) to arrive where God wanted him. God is always at work to accomplish His will in your life. The key is to listen to the prompting of His Holy Spirit.

And it came to pass, when the evil spirit from God was upon Saul, that David took an harp, and played with his hand: so Saul was refreshed, and was well, and the evil spirit departed from him. (1 Samuel 16:23)

> *David was the youngest. And the three oldest followed Saul. But David occasionally went and returned from Saul to feed his father's sheep at Bethlehem. (1 Samuel 17:14-15) (NKJV)*

> *Then Jesse said to his son David, "take now for your brothers an ephah of this dried grain and these ten loaves, and run to your brothers at the camp. And carry these ten cheeses to the captain of their thousand, and see how your brothers fare, and bring back news of them." (1 Samuel 17:17-18) (NKJV)*

Do you remember Joseph? His father sent him to check on his brothers. Jacob didn't see him again for thirteen years.

David's brake with his family was more gradual. He had a temp job with Saul but returned occasionally to tend the sheep. It is my guess that this chore would make the brake permanent. I'm sure his father kept up with David's exploits but that "home" bond would be broken.

Something we need to note here. There was a foundation laid during these early years. Whether in the field with the sheep and writing his songs, or at home under the influence of his father Jesse. There had to be a foundation of a relationship with God taught to David. David didn't just establish his relationship with God on the field with Goliath. That foundation was laid very early in his upbringing.

Do you remember that day you left home? That day you realized that you had to make the decisions now. You no longer could rely on your parent's wisdom, the decisions you made would affect the rest of your life. The realization that you were now accountable to no one but yourself. Let me ask you a question. What foundation was established in your life prior to your leaving home? What truths did you fall back on when you had to make a decision?

David is embarking on the adventure of a lifetime. Much as you will or have when you left home and began building a life for yourself. Judging from David's actions, his father instilled in him a reverence for God. I think his hours and hours in the field with his father's sheep established a relationship with God. It takes both a reverence and a relationship with Almighty God to guide us through our everyday walk with God.

A frustrating thing about walking with God is that God never reveals what's next. Do you think, when David left that morning with lunch for his brothers, that he would become the hero of Israel and the enemy of Saul? I think not. Do you think God knew what was going to happen that day that David left to feed his brothers? Of course, He did. It was all part of God's plan. A plan that unfolds, sometimes hour by hour.

When we seem to be headed down an unknown road. A fork that we had never seen coming. What is your reaction? Why not try "excited"? Excited to see what God is up to. How God is going to make Himself known in the days ahead. Excited to see what God has planned, not what you want to happen but what God's perfect plan is for this adventure. That adventure begins with relying on the godly foundation that was instilled from birth.

1 Samuel 17

And he stood and cried unto the armies of Israel, and said unto them, "Why are ye come out to set your battle in array? Am not I a Philistine, and ye servants to Saul? Choose you a man for you, and let him come down to me. If he be able to fight with me, then will we be your servants: but if I prevail against him, and kill him, then shall ye be our servants, and serve us." (1 Samuel 17:8-9)

Is that not the challenge today? We are bombarded daily with God's name being blasphemed or even greater attempts to remove God from our culture. There have been efforts to remove "In God We Trust" from our currency. The Ten Commandments are effectively removed from the public square. Nothing religious is allowed in our public schools. We are challenged every day to acknowledge our God.

Did you notice how Goliath referred to Israel's army? Goliath called them "Servants of Saul" really? It has become increasingly difficult to stand for our faith in our country today. That was not the case at the founding of our country. The Founders recognized the sovereignty of God in the creation of our nation. The history of Israel is quite the opposite.

The challenge is all around us. So, what can we do? My wife and I make it a practice to pray for each meal, whether at home, or dining out. I carry my Bible to every church service. I am seeing less and less Bibles every day. Now they are on our phones, but not visible! Acknowledge God at every opportunity in our conversations with co-workers and family and neighbors. Don't let the loud voices of the "Goliaths" in our midst drown out God's voice!

Another reminder here. Remember where David came from. He is a shepherd, the youngest in his family with seven brothers. David has a relationship with God. You would think this was Saul's great opportunity to lead his people. Saul was camped under a shade tree, hoping this guy would go away. Is that our situation today?

Think about what, we as Christians, have allowed to become commonplace in our country. I listed a few above. We have allowed the "Goliath's" of this country to silence our voices. To change what we know to be right, to trick us into hiding under a shade tree. That ought not be so.

David was simply taking a lunch to his brothers. He hears this challenge and thinks there should be a response. He looks around. From the leaders on down they are hiding. Does the use of God's name in cursing upset you? It should! Deuteronomy says,

> "You shall not take the name of the Lord your God in vain, for the Lord will not hold him guiltless who takes His name in vain." (Deuteronomy 20:7) (NKJV)

That is the third commandment. God thought it important enough to include in His law. Yet we ignore it today. We like to ignore that last part of that verse as well. Look again!

Look what Jesus said in John 16:33,

> "These things I have spoken to you, that in Me you may have peace. In the world, you will have tribulation; but be of good cheer, I have overcome the world." (John 16:33) (NKJV)

Has God shown Himself sufficient in your life? Has God proved Himself in your walk with Him? Jesus told us what kind of world we will live in two-thousand years ago. He also made us a promise that He has overcome the world. He simply asks that we take a stand for Him. We lift up His name. Let's continue to follow David. He acknowledges that something is wrong. David is willing to take a stand for his God. How about you?

And Eliab his eldest brother heard when he spake unto the men; and Eliab's anger was kindled against David, and he said, "Why camest thou down hither? And with whom has thou left those few sheep in the wilderness? I know thy pride, and the haughtiness of thine heart; for thou art come down that thou mightest see the battle." And David said, "Is there not a cause?" And he turned from him toward another, and spake after the same manner: and the people answered him again after the former manner. (1 Samuel 17:28-30)

I think the Army mentality has invaded the church. Have you ever asked for "volunteers" in the church? It is so hard to get someone to step up and take on a ministry.

I hadn't been saved but about six months. I didn't know Genesis from Revelation. My Sunday School teacher told us that the pastor was teaching a high school boys class. He didn't think the pastor should have to teach. I volunteered to teach the class. I had no idea what I was getting into. That was one of the best decisions I ever made. It forced me into God's word. I went on to teach in one form or another for over thirty years.

One of my favorite stories is when Israel is to finally trust God and enter the Promised land. Look at Joshua:

> *"And it shall come to pass, as soon as the soles of the feet of the priests who bear the ark of the Lord, the Lord of all the earth, shall rest in the waters of the Jordan, that the waters of the Jordan shall be cut off, the waters that come down from upstream and shall stand as a heap." (Joshua 3:13) (NKJV)*

God had brought Israel here before. And they refused to enter the land that God had promised them. This time they will have to take that step of faith, then God will stop the Jordan. If I may let me give one more verse:

> *Then he touched their eyes saying, "According to your faith let it be to you." (Matthew 9:29) (NKJV)*

I would be curious to know just how many blessings we miss from God because we refused to "step into the water." I firmly believe that God is always testing our faith. Not tempting us, but testing us. These tests, if passed, strengthen our faith. Here is another verse:

> *His lord said to him, "Well done, good and faithful servant; you were faithful over a few things, I will make you ruler*

over many things. Enter into the joy of your lord."(Matthew
25:21) (NKJV)

God is always stretching and strengthening our faith. The more He can trust us in the small things, the greater the responsibility in the greater things. It all boils down to trusting God. David had heard and seen Goliath. David didn't know what was ahead. David was willing to trust God and even to put his life in God's hands to do the right thing. A man after God's own heart will trust God and stand up for God and follow God's leading and direction.

Was David "super-human"? David is no different than you or me, except in his faith in God's power and direction!

"Thy servant slew both the lion and the bear: and this uncircumcised Philistine shall be as one of them, seeing he hath defied the armies of the living God". David said moreover, "The Lord that delivered me out of the paw of the lion, and out of the paw of the bear, he will deliver me out of the hand of this Philistine." And Saul armed David with his armour, and he put an helmet of brass upon his head; also he armed him with a coat of mail. And David girded his sword upon his armour, and he assayed to go; for he had not proved it. And David said unto Saul, "I cannot go with these; for I have not proved them. And David put them off him." (1 Samuel 17:36-39)

Did you notice early in these verses where David credits his strength? "The Lord will deliver me." David recognized that God was his strength, not the armor or mail. I'm sure this was one of the reasons David was a man after God's own heart. David also recognized that man-made defenses would not work. His faith was in God!

Look at this verse in Hebrews:

> *But without faith it is impossible to please Him, for he who comes to God must believe that He is, and that He is a rewarder of those who diligently seek Him. (Hebrews 11:6) (NKJV)*

Do you know what I like about this verse? It's the word "diligently". Faith is not a here today, gone tomorrow thing. We have already talked about Matthew 9:29. When was the last time God "tested" your faith? When was the last time you actually put something in God's hands and left it there? We are talking about prayer of course. You prayed and asked God to do something for you. Has He answered your prayer? Is it something that is within the will of God? God will not answer a prayer contrary to His will and plan for your life. Think about your prayer again.

Here is a fantastic way to test God. He even challenges you to trust Him. He dares you to trust Him. Look at this verse:

> *"Bring all the tithes into the storehouse, that there may be food in My house, **and try Me** now in this." Says the Lord of hosts. "If I will not open for you the windows of heaven and pour out for you such a blessing that there will not be room enough to receive it." (Malachi 3:10) (NKJV)*

It took me a long time to try this. When I did, God completely fulfilled His promise. It's a test. He challenges us to trust Him.

David had already seen what God had done in the field against the lion and the bear. David also had a special "peace" in his relationship with God the Father. David trusted God so much that he was willing to face a deadly foe with just a slingshot and five stones, more about that later.

What is your faith in? What are you trusting in? Your physical prowess, your stocks and bonds, your high-paying job, your retirement savings? Seriously! These can all be gone tomorrow. David recognized that in Saul's puny armor and mail. David knew that God was so much more tested that this armor. David relied in God's strength and David's relationship with Almighty God to see him through!

And he took his staff in his hand, and chose five smooth stones out of the brook, and put them in his shepherd's bag which he had, even in a scrip; and his sling was in his hand: and he drew near to the Philistine. (1 Samuel 17:40) (NKJV)

How many times have you heard the story of David and Goliath? Have you ever noticed that he chose FIVE stones? How many times was the number of stones mentioned in a sermon or a Sunday School lesson? I wonder if they really knew why, five stones, or they just skipped over it.

Did David think he might miss and therefore brought some insurance? Remember, David had killed a lion and a bear. You might get the idea it was one of each, the Bible doesn't say. I'm sure if he spent years as a shepherd growing up he saw more than one. So why did he pick up five stones? Look in 2 Samuel 21:

> These four were born to the giant in Gath (Goliath's home), and fell by the hand of David and by the hand of his servant. (2 Samuel 21:22) (NKJV)

Did David have faith in God? Enough to believe that he not only would defeat Goliath but his four sons as well. Just so there is no mistake, look at this verse:

> And a champion went out from the camp of the Philistines, named Goliath, from Gath, whose height was six cubits and a span. (1 Samuel 17:4) (NKJV)

Now how David knew that Goliath had four sons we can only guess. Maybe a rumor in camp, maybe Saul told him, who knows, it's not important. The lesson is "trust God".

It has always been a pet-peeve of mine that people tend to put God in a box. If we can't conceive of it, it isn't possible. If we can't imagine the outcome it can't happen. We limit God's power within the realm of our capabilities.

David had every intention of defeating this giant AND any others that would challenge him. His faith in God's power was amazing. I'm sure this is one of the reasons God said that David was a man after His own heart. David was willing to trust God. We have already talked about faith and its relationship with God.

Think about the measure of faith that Saul exhibited. He was a head taller that his army. He had already won a victory. Read 1 Samuel 14. God had demonstrated to Saul His power early on in his reign. Yet, Saul grew farther and farther away from God. The greater the victory the more Saul thought it was in his power, not God's.

As David grew in his faith, beginning with slaying the lion and bear in the field watching over his father's sheep, David turned to God and trusted God even more. His faith grew.

Have you taken a measure of your faith lately? Has God tested you lately? Has God asked you to do something "out of your comfort zone"? If He has, what was your response?

God could use David in mighty ways because David was willing to trust God. Not just one giant in his life but five! David was willing to take on the whole family to stand up for God's name. To demonstrate the power of God, David was willing to trust God and take that step of faith that was a testimony to all of Israel. We will see later how this victory strengthened the faith of Israel's army and helped win many victories for God!

And when the Philistine looked about, and saw David, he disdained him: for he was but a youth, and ruddy, and of fair countenance. And the Philistine said unto David, Am I a dog, that thou comest to me with staves? And the Philistine cursed David by his gods. And the Philistine said to David, Come to me, and I will give thy flesh unto the fowls of the air, and to the beast of the field. Then said David to the Philistine, Thou comest to me with a sword, and with a spear, and with a shield: but I come to thee in the name of the Lord of hosts, the God of the armies of Israel, whom thou hast defied. This day will the Lord deliver thee into mine hand; and I will smite theee, and take thine head from thee; and I will give the carcases of the host of the Philistines this day unto the fowls of the air, and to the wild beasts of the earth: that all the earth may know that there is a God in Israel. And all this assembly shall know that the Lord saveth not with sword and spear: for the battle is the Lord's, and he will give you into our hands. (1 Samuel 17:42-47)

Do you see where Goliath's faith was? His size and his weapons. No doubt he had been victorious in the past. Have you noticed how long Israel has been fighting with the Philistines? Even back in Samson's days in the book of Judges. It seems God has his special weapons for dealing with unruly children (Israel).

God knows our weaknesses. He knows how to deal with us when we stray from His will. It's gentle at first. It depends on how long it takes for us to repent. A loving father tries to teach his children right from wrong with as little pain as possible. It's up to us just how much "pain" is required.

God is using the Philistines to raise up David and to eliminate Saul. Why? Saul had been infected with that dread disease "pride". Saul had begun to think it was all him that accomplished the deeds God had brought. That is a most deadly combination.

But look at David. David acknowledges from the very beginning that the victory was God's. That David was simply the tool that God chose to use to accomplish His will. When we can adopt that attitude, we will gain the blessing and the power that God has for us. It's all to God's glory.

I wonder if this is where the saying, "The bigger they are, the harder they fall" came from?

Did you notice in verse 42 how Goliath described David, "for he was only a youth"? One of my favorite verses in the New Testament talks about this:

> *But God has chosen the foolish things of the world to put to shame the wise, and God has chosen the weak things of the world to put to shame the things which are mighty. (1 Corinthians 1:27) (NKJV)*

Logically it should have been Saul who confronted Goliath. Saul had the size and the experience, but God had removed Saul's power and authority. The main thing about giving David the opportunity for this victory is that God, not David, will get the glory. David acknowledges that in his rebuke of Goliath. Here's a great quote from Genesis:

> *And the Lord said to Abraham, "Why did Sarah laugh, saying 'shall I surely bear a child, since I am old?'" "Is anything too hard for the Lord? At the appointed time, I will return to you, according to the time of life, and Sarah shall have a son." (Genesis 18:13-14) (NKJV)*

And it came to pass, when the Philistine arose, and came and drew nigh to meet David, that David hasted, and ran toward the army to meet the Philistine. And David put his hand in his bag, and took thence a stone, and slang it, and smote the Philistine in his forehead, that the stone sunk into his forehead; and he fell upon his face to the earth. (1 Samuel 17:48-49)

I ran across a plaque while I was in Branson, Missouri. The plaque read: "If God brings you to a storm, He will bring you through it." When you start running into storms and don't know why your here, just remember this saying. You are here for a purpose! God has a lesson for you to learn. Trust Him!

Let's take a refresher course up to this point. Remember where David was? He was minding his own business in the fields shepherding his father's sheep. He gets a message from one of his brothers, "Samuel wants to see you." Look back to 1 Samuel 16. I just noticed something. When Samuel anointed David it doesn't say that Samuel told David WHY he was anointing him. God told Samuel (16:1). But, it doesn't say that he told David. Interesting.

What does David do after the anointing? David returns to the sheep. Later Saul calls him to play and sing for him. He returns home after his duty was done. It's just by "accident" that David happened to be bringing lunch to his brothers when he hears Goliath's boast and blasphemy. God does nothing by "accident"! Do you wonder sometimes how you happen to be at a certain place at a certain time? My advice would be to pray!

Have you ever seen pictures of Goliath? Did you notice his armor? The point being that where David hit Goliath was the ONLY place he could have killed him. David was used to hitting animals on the ground, nothing nine feet high. David's aim was sure and deadly, because David's strength was in the Lord, not in his right arm!

That was always the downfall for Samson. Samson believed his strength was in his hair. We do the same thing. I think, most of the time, we think our strength is between our ears. The more degrees and diploma's we have the "mightier" we are. Our wall could be covered with such testimonies to our knowledge, but still, without the Spirit of God, we are as dumb as a rock.

David's life would forever change that day. He would no longer return to the fields of the sheep. God had bigger plans. So long as God had David's attention and trust and faith God would work miracles in David's life. One of the key ingredients in being a man after God's own heart is trusting in God. Walk that path, daily trusting God, for the right turns and forks in the road. Turn left, turn right, go straight or stop. God must always be in the lead.

Face any trials or storms lately? What was your response? Did you look for another road? Of course, you had to ask why, we all do. Did you get an answer? I thought not. God doesn't have to explain Himself to no one. That is the challenge! That is where faith comes in. You must trust God to take that next step.

Faith is like a muscle in our arm. The more you use it, trust it, exercise it, the stronger it gets. God wants us to trust Him to strengthen that faith "muscle". The more we lean on God and trust Him the greater God will use us in miraculous ways. The exciting part is watching God work!

1 SAMUEL 18

And it came to pass, when he had made an end of speaking unto Saul, that the soul of Jonathan was knit with the soul of David, and Jonathan loved him as his own soul. And Saul took him that day, and would let him go no more home to his father's house. Then Jonathan and David made a covenant, because he loved him as his own soul. And Jonathan stripped himself of the robe that was upon him, and gave it to David, and his garments, even to his sword, and to his bow, and to his girdle. (1 Samuel 18:1-4)

David would no longer return to the shepherd's field. David moved into the palace with Saul and his new found "soul-mate" Jonathan. I like the term used today, "kindred Spirit." I capitalized Spirit here because I think that was their bond. Ask most Christians and they will tell you that there is a special bond in God's family. Your Spirit bears witness with their spirit that you are children of God. (Romans 8:16).

Some people try to make more of these verses than is here. Evidently, they have never experienced the bond between God's children. Here again, is the contrast between father and son. In the book of Judges, we see a godly king succeeded by an ungodly son and vice-versa. I couldn't understand that. It would be interesting to know Saul's relationship with God. Many theologians wrestle with whether Saul was "saved" or not. His life gives no indication other than his constant disobedience.

On the other hand, Jonathan recognized right off that David was near to God. Even when his father told him that David would steal the throne from Jonathan, the heir to the throne from Saul. Jonathan did everything he could to help David. I wonder how much Jonathan knew about God's plans for David?

One of my fondest memories as a young Christian were the evenings, when a group of pastor's and Christian leaders would gather and talk about the Bible and ministry experiences. I loved the camaraderie. I soaked up as much as I could. I can see this kind of relationship between Jonathan and David. Jonathan saw what God did through David with Goliath. Jonathan wanted that kind of relationship with God.

Isn't it interesting that God gives no details of David meeting Jonathan? He goes from the field of battle to Saul's presence and there he meets Jonathan. Imagine the conflict in David's heart. His bond with Jonathan and his conflict with his father, Saul. David is as confused as we are why this is happening.

Here's something to ponder. Look at the contrast between Jonathan's relationship with God, recognizing David's closeness with God, and Saul's complete disobedience and conflict with God. That is almost the scene today. Those who fight and deny that God exists and those who are obedient and are walking with God. That's the world we live in today. There is no middle ground. Either you are a child of God, or you are lost!

Jonathan begins a new chapter in David's life. We will see how this relationship affects David much later in his life. After David becomes King of Israel. Just remember the name Mephibosheth. It's a great story of a promise kept!

Do you have a Jonathan in your life? A "kindred-Spirit" that shares your struggles and blessings in your walk with God. Someone who is there in your triumphs and disasters. I hope so. God never meant for us to walk alone in ministry. He will always provide a "Jonathan" to those who seek a special relationship with God.

And it came to pass as they came, when David was returned from the slaughter of the Philistine, that the women came out of all the cities of Israel, singing and dancing, to meet king Saul, with tabrets, with joy, and with instruments of music. And the women answered one another as they played, and said, Saul hath slain his thousands, and David his ten thousands. And Saul was very wroth, and the saying displeased him; and he said, They have ascribed unto David ten thousands, and to me they have ascribed but thousands: and what can he have more but the kingdom? (1 Samuel 18:6-8)

I love what Ronald Reagan said once, "It is amazing what can be accomplished, when it doesn't matter who gets the credit." I'm kind of curious. How much has Jonathan told Saul about his relationship with David? Let me venture another question. Was Saul jealous of David because of his victories, or was it because God had taken His hand off him and placed it on David? Something to think about.

How do you respond when it seems God is blessing someone you might feel unworthy? Especially if you think you are the one deserving the blessing. Beware! Jealousy is a cancer that can kill your soul as deeply as cancer can kill the body. It must be one of Satan's greatest weapons to destroy the Christian's testimony.

Satan has so many weapons in his arsenal that it is hard to keep track of them. The strange thing about these weapons is that they are powerless unless we allow them to be effective. God's Holy Spirit dwells within us and He is more than a match for anything that the devil can throw our way. The problem is we tie His hands with our unbelief. We surrender far too easily and think we are powerless. How do we activate this power? We pray! We trust God, and we give it to God to handle.

We can only imagine what Saul might have accomplished if he had listened and obeyed God. There is another weapon Satan likes to use frequently, pride. Remember, at one time, Saul, shortly after he was anointed king, was prophesying. (1 Samuel 10). He had an awareness of God in his life. He later had some victories on the battlefield. At some point Saul began to think it was his power and not God's. This began his fall away from God. At one point Saul even thought he could fulfill the office of priest. (1 Samuel 13:8-10).

One of the worst results of these weapons that Satan uses is the "cancer" effect. It slowly eats away at our testimony, and more importantly, our relationship with God. We grow more and more distant from God. We can see that in Saul. He started so well but slowly drifted further from God. Jonathan tried on several occasions to get through to his dad but he wouldn't listen. Jonathan recognized God's hand on David, and right away acknowledged (David's) right to rule. Jonathan didn't care if he was king or not he only wanted God's will to be done.

I used to struggle with why God was working in some others and my efforts were for naught. Then I realized how much I was trying to "make" it happened. One of the tricks is to ask someone to "pray" about something you want revealed. That's sad and dangerous! You pray, let God know your desires then step back, keep your mouth shut and watch God work it out. Maybe it won't be the way you want it, but it IS the way God wants it! That's important! Too many times we think God needs our input or our help to make something happen. When we begin meddling in God's sovereignty we are looking for trouble! Ask Saul!

And Saul cast a javelin; for he said, I will smite David even to the wall with it. And David avoided out of his presence twice. And Saul was afraid of David, because the Lord was with him, and was departed from Saul. Therefore, Saul removed him from him, and made him his captain over a thousand; and he went out and came in before the people. And David behaved himself wisely in all his ways; and the Lord was with him. (1 Samuel 18:11-14)

Do you see it? The battle that is going on in the world today. The battle between those who are with God, Spirit led, and those who follow the dictates of the flesh.

Did you notice that Saul had thrown a spear at David twice? That's interesting because later, David will have two opportunities to kill Saul. Two opportunities that he refused to take. You don't suppose God had anything to do with Saul's aim, do you? Saul had been in at least two battles prior to this. He is experienced, yet he missed.

The picture and the contrast we are to get from this episode is the battle we face today. Do we do the right thing or do we surrender to the flesh. You might ask, why is the right thing usually the hardest? It is.

You might want to remember the thing that frightens Saul. David is going to take his place. Saul knows that God has taken His hand from him and placed it on David (v. 12). Is Saul praying and asking God why? No, I think Saul knows. Saul knows he is not walking with God. Saul has chosen his own path, his own will, his own purpose, and turned his back on God's leadership. One of the biggest reasons God was hesitant in providing a king for Israel. It has always been, as we will see in the book of First and Second Kings, finding a godly king, a godly leader, to lead God's people.

That is a major challenge for us today. Every four years, after I vote, I watch to see who our nation elects as a President. I use that election to gauge the 'spiritual' condition of our country. What kind of man has our country chosen for its leader?

When God chose Saul as their first king, He did so because Israel had gotten ahead of God. I think it was God's plan to make David the king all along. David was not ready yet. But the people wanted a king now! Again, the contrast between a worldly king and a godly king. It is all in God's timing.

This brief episode is another great example why David was a man after God's own heart. David stayed true to following God. David trust his relationship with God to bring him through this trial. Think about this a minute. If David was getting the cheers of the people, the credit for slaying "ten thousand's" why would Saul make him the captain of a thousand men? It would seem Saul was placing him able to receive more praise. Of course, Saul may have been hoping he would be killed in battle. More likely the latter.

Sometimes we don't understand why God puts us in certain battles. We question God's wisdom. There is a couple of verses in Proverbs that I run through my mind over and over when I don't understand why things are as they are.

> *Trust in the Lord with all your heart,*
> *And lean not on your own understanding;*
> *In all your ways acknowledge Him,*
> *And He will direct your paths.*
> *Proverbs 3:5-6 (NKJV)*

And Michal Saul's daughter loved David: and they told Saul, and the thing pleased him. And Saul said, I will give him her, that she may be a snare to him, and that the hand of the Philistines may be against him. Wherefore Saul said to David, Thou shalt this day be my son-in-law in the one of the twain. (1 Samuel 18:20-21)

This is the second daughter of Saul's that he offered to David. The first ran off with someone else. I think it is interesting how fixed Saul is at destroying David. Even to the point of using his own daughters to trap him.

I wonder how this "change of heart" took place? Let's go back and try to think what went through Saul's mind when God called him to be king. It certainly wasn't something Saul sought. Remember when Samuel announced Saul as their king? They had to drag out from hiding (10:22). Then Saul had a couple of victories, first against the Ammonites in chapter 11 and then against the Amalekites in chapter 15. It was against the Amalekites that Saul disobeyed Samuel and God withdrew His hand.

I'm wondering if these two victories changed Saul's perspective from trusting God to trusting himself? Think about it. As a young pastor, I remember struggling with God's power in our church. It gets very hard to not think that this was all your doing. When you start leaving God out of the power, you begin your downfall. Saul drifted further and further from God and his power got weaker and weaker.

Remember the apostle Peter? In Matthew 14, when Peter gathered enough faith to step out of the boat and walk on the water to Jesus. Peter had the power to walk on water, BUT when he took his eyes off the power that allowed him to do that, he sank! If we know, and acknowledge where our power and authority comes from, God will continue to keep His hand on us, as soon as we think it's all about us—the power leaves!

That is one of the reasons David was a man after God's own heart. Oh, we know that David took his eyes off God on more than one occasion. But David always found his way back to God. Saul just seemed to drift further and further from God. Even to the point of looking up a witch in order to talk to God.

Saul used the affections of his daughter, to try to defeat David. Using other people is another trick Satan likes to use to accomplish his misdeeds. This is especially useful in families. The younger against the older, etc. The sad part is that this is also useful in the church. Every church has an inner circle. Just as Peter, James and John were Jesus' inner circle. This can foster jealousy and resentment if God's Spirit isn't active and working in certain lives. We must always be aware of Satan's devices and his tricks to divide, whether in a church family or the home.

The closer we walk with God, maintain that intimate relationship the easier it is to spot those feelings creeping into our life. The feelings of jealousy or pride. To envy someone else's relationship with someone, or when someone else gets recognition that we think we deserve, etc. When you start feeling those emotions creep into your thoughts start praying! God will open your heart and your eyes and get your focus back on Him. That was Saul's downfall. When he finally realized that God had completely withdrawn His power and that relationship, and His Holy Spirit. . . it was too late!

When we begin feeling our heart turn to stone, pray, and God can change your heart!

And Saul saw and knew that the Lord was with David, and that Michal Saul's daughter loved him. And Saul was yet the more afraid of David; and Saul became David's enemy continually. Then the princes of the Philistines went forth: and it came to pass, after they went forth, that David behaved himself more wisely than all the servants of Saul; so that his name was much set by. (1 Samuel 18:28-30)

I was thinking, it is interesting how Saul has used or ignored his children. First, Jonathan his son rejected Saul's reasoning that he would forfeit the throne unless he hated David. Jonathan had a kindred-spirit in David and they were close friends. Second, Merab, a short relationship. Saul offered his oldest daughter to David in hopes of destroying him by having an ally in David's house. That didn't last long. Third, there is Michal, Saul's second daughter. Again, Saul offered her to David to have a spy in David's house. The problem was Michal was in love with David. All three of Saul's children were used by him to thwart David's growing popularity. It didn't work!

David continued, as David was from the beginning. David trusted God's leadership and timing. Remember, David has been anointed by Samuel. Think about this, in verse 30, David continues to go out and fight the Philistines for Saul. He puts his life on the line for someone who wants him dead. Because David is walking with God not Saul.

We need to be careful in our daily lives who we are walking with or following. Where are our eyes focused? In the future? Here is a trick I like. Put your finger in front of your face about a foot away. Now, focus on your finger. In your peripheral vision what do you see? It's blurry, isn't it? Now focus on something beyond your finger. Is your finger blurry? Of course, it is. It all depends on your focus. Is your focus on God or what is going to happen next week, tomorrow, or next year?

A couple of times David took his focus off God and he got in major trouble! Another reason David is a man after God's own heart. God knew where to find David most of the time, right behind Him. David, for the most part, followed closely behind God's leadership. Of course, we would like to say, "all the time" but then David wouldn't be like us. That is the miraculous thing about David. David is just like you and I, he is human. He makes mistakes, yet God was able to use him in fantastic ways. Is God using you?

It is interesting, Saul had victories on the battlefield as well as David. So why is David different? David never lost sight of the power behind the victories. Saul began to trust in his own prowess, his own strength.

There were three temptations that Jesus endured in the wilderness (Matthew 4). The lust of the flesh (4:3-4). The lust of the eye (4:8-10) and the pride of life (4:6-7). The apostle John also talks about these three temptations in 1 John 2:16. Saul could not deal with the "pride of life". He was king and he ruled supreme, except he forgot the power that put him on that throne. Many times, we have such short memories as to the blessings we receive.

I want us to keep remembering where David came from and how, by trusting God, David became a servant of God, and God used him in fantastic ways to accomplish God's purpose, not David's or Saul's but God's purpose. While you're thinking on these things you might want to review the story of Joseph in the book of Genesis. Joseph had a tough road to follow to arrive at God's destination, just as David did. Both glorified God in the end!

1 Samuel 19

And Jonathan spake good of David unto Saul his father, and said unto him, "Let not the king sin against his servant, against David; because he hath not sinned against thee, and because his works have been to thee-ward very good. For he did put his life in his hand and slew the Philistine, and the Lord wrought a great salvation for all Israel: thou sawest it, and didst rejoice: wherefore then wilt thou sin against innocent blood, to slay David without a cause?" And Saul harkened unto the voice of Jonathan: and Saul sware, as the Lord liveth, he shall not be slain. (1 Samuel 19:4-6)

His own son confronts Saul's hypocrisy. The sad part is that Saul's word is worthless. Saul will try several more times to kill David. David will have two opportunities to kill Saul, finally Saul will give up his quest. There is almost a word of prophecy in Saul's words, "As the Lord lives, he shall not be killed." It's true David won't be killed but not because Saul didn't try.

It wasn't long ago that your word was as good as your hand shake. Today it is determined by how many lawyers you have. It's so easy today to say whatever suits the occasion, whether it's true or not. Many times, when the truth is known there is no remorse, no regret, just excuses. We have lost that quality in our culture. I believe the ninth Commandment deals with lying.

"Thou shalt not bear false witness against your neighbor."
(Exodus 20:16) (NKJV)

It's interesting that this same Commandment follows murder and stealing.

Did you notice Jonathan's argument? He reminded Saul of all the things that David had done FOR HIM. That David walks uprightly while it is his father, Saul, who is the sinner. I'm sure that Jonathan didn't realize that this was salt in Saul's wounds. Saul hated David for this very thing. David had accomplished what Saul couldn't. David had God on his side and God had departed Saul, and Saul knew it.

Somewhere along the line Saul had taken a separate path than God. Saul had lost the fellowship with the Lord. You can see it, can't you? I think the tell-tale sign was when Saul became impatient and offered the sacrifice instead of Samuel. (1 Samuel 13:8-9). He had taken it into his hands to do God's work. Shortly after, he disobeyed Samuel by not killing the king of the Amalekites.

(1 Samuel 15). Here is a great verse, that speaks to Saul's disobedience,

> So, Samuel said, "Has the Lord as great delight in burnt offerings and sacrifices, as in obeying the voice of the Lord? Behold, to obey is better than sacrifice, and to heed than the fat of rams." (1 Samuel 15:22) (NKJV)

You can see in Saul the defiance and disobedience, and also the results of that disobedience, God removed His hand from Saul.

There are so many Commandments broken today. So much disobedience. It's no wonder so many are struggling, much like Saul did. So long as we remain rebellious, God will continue to deal with us. As you continue to read these chapters of David and his struggle with Saul think about how long God put up with Saul's disobedience. Twice David had the opportunity to kill Saul, but he spared him. God's grace is amazing. His grace toward you is amazing. How long will God wait for you to return to following Him?

Think for a minute and put yourself in each of these three characters shoes. How would you respond if you were Saul? You knew David was walking with God and you hated that. The shoes of Jonathan, stuck between his father and his "kindred-Spirit", David. Trying to resolve the conflict. And finally, David, simply trying to be faithful to God and yet constantly hunted by Saul and threatened. Think about each one, how would you respond?

Saul also sent messengers unto David's house, to watch him, and to slay him in the morning: and Michal David's wife told him, saying, If thou save not thy life tonight, tomorrow thou shalt be slain. So Michal let David down through a window: and he went, and fled, and escaped. And Michal took an image, and laid it in the bed, and put a pillow of goats' hair for his bolster, and covered it with a cloth. And when Saul sent messengers to take David, she said, He is sick. (1 Samuel 19:11-14)

Take a minute and think back. See how many people you can remember who passed through your life. If you remember them they had an impact on your life. They may have taught you something, led you down a certain path, good or bad, encouraged you, or discouraged you. They had an impact or you would not remember them. It is amazing how the people that pass through our lives contribute to who we are. That was Michal.

Saul will still try to kill David regardless of any promises he made to Jonathan. Later, after David twice refuses to kill Saul, Saul says he will cease from his attempts. What would you do if there was a person determined to kill you?

God puts certain people in our lives for a reason. If we are walking with God, we will take heed to those "teachers" in our path. We will ask God what He is trying to teach us. Why are we traveling together at this point in our lives?

David escapes that night thanks to Michal. What a great co-incidence! Really? People pass through our lives, events are put in our path that change the course of our lives, good and bad, and we chalk it up to co-incidence. What a strange name for God, co-incidence. Nothing happens in our lives that God has not planned or allowed. Take a minute and read the first couple chapters of Job.

David was anointed for a reason. Samuel was led to David and chose him out of the family of Jesse for a reason. David was spared that night to fulfill the purpose God intended for him. I would like you to think about something. God's holy Spirit is the author of His Word. Now ask yourself, Why, would God think this episode was so important that He would make sure it is included in His Holy Word? There is a lesson here!

Saul's pick for a wife, Merab (18:17) didn't work. Michal was in love with David so Saul thought he could use her. God used her in a far greater way than Saul could have thought. God used Michal, the right place, the right time, to make sure David fulfilled his mission. The mission that God had planned from the beginning.

Do you wonder why certain people are put into your life? When I began teaching there was a friend in my class, John, who would ask the strangest questions. I would get so frustrated. He challenged me. As a teacher, I should be prepared in what I was teaching. He really irritated me. Later, as I look back God put him there to teach me a valuable lesson. If I was going to teach I must know what I am teaching. God bless you John!

It is usually the people that irritate us that have a lesson for us to learn. We need to open our minds, pray and ask God, what am I to learn from this person God has put in my life? If God is going to use us, we must be willing to learn and grow in the grace and knowledge of God the Father!

Michal shows up later in David's life. David has several other wives, each with a lesson for David to learn. What better teacher than a spouse. Pray and ask God, "what are You trying to teach me, Lord?"

So David fled, and escaped, and came to Samuel to Ramah, and told him all that Saul had done to him. And he and Samuel went and dwelt in Naioth. (1 Samuel 19:18)

I can hear David's question to Samuel, "Why me? Why is Saul treating me this way? After all the battle's I have fought and won for him. Why does he threaten to kill me every time I get near him? His son likes me, his daughter loves me, why is this happening." How would you answer David?

I want you to notice where David went. It's important! David went to the one "person" who might talk to God for him. Who was led by God to anoint him. David knew Samuel had a relationship with God. So, where do you go when the circumstances in your life don't make sense? Just a note here. Where did Saul go to get answers? Look at 1 Samuel 28:7. Saul sought the advice of a witch.

Let me offer you three sources to consider when you question what God is doing in your life. First, of course, is the Word of God. I'm not talking about closing your eyes, opening the book and pointing to a verse. I'm talking about a daily reading, getting to know God through His word. The more you read Old Testament and New Testament you get a closer relationship with a God who loves you. Look at one of my favorite verses:

For I know the thoughts (plans) that I think toward you, says the Lord, thoughts of peace and not of evil, to give you a future and a hope. (Jeremiah 29:11). (NKJV)

God has always had a plan for your life! Get in His word and learn about God's love for you. Just a note as you read, listen to the thoughts that creep into your mind. God may be trying to get your attention.

Next, pray! God thought prayer was so important, that even His Son made it a priority! He took time to teach His disciples to pray and His desire is that we have a regular, daily "quiet time" with God in prayer. Here again, listen to that voice that's speaking to you while you pray. I used to get so frustrated that my mind would wander when I prayed. God was trying to get my attention about something. When I began to listen, I found that God was guiding me, through His Holy Spirit. I learned to listen.

Third, find some godly friends to hang with. You don't need to share all your inner-most feelings and concerns. Just fellowshipping with godly friends can help you. You will be surprised how God will use them to guide you.

The very morning that I went forward in church and made my profession of faith God sent a godly couple to invite Mary and I to lunch at their house. Later, many others in our church nurtured and guided and supported me as I grew in my walk with the Lord. Look at Hebrews:

For though by this time you ought to be teachers, you need someone to teach you again the first principles of the oracles of God; and you have come to need milk and not solid food. For everyone who partakes only of milk is unskilled in the word of righteousness, for he is a babe. But solid food belongs to those who are of full age, that is, those who by reason of use have their senses exercised to discern both good and evil. (Hebrews 5:12-14) (NKJV)

David knew where to go for godly counsel. He went to a man who had demonstrated a relationship with God. Samuel also demonstrated a willingness to be obedient to God. If you look back to just prior to Samuel anointing David, Samuel was taking his life in his hands just seeking out David. But Samuel was willing to be obedient to God no matter the cost.

Where do you go for "counsel"? Is it a godly source, the word of God, prayer, godly friends? I hope you will think about what David did, a man after God's own heart!

Now it was told Saul, saying, Behold, David is at Naioth in Ramah. Then went he also to Ramah, and came to a great well that is in Sechu: and he asked and said, Where are Samuel and David? And one said, Behold, they be at Naioth in Ramah. And he went thither to Naioth in Ramah: and the Spirit of God was upon him also, and he went on, and prophesied, until he came to Naioth in Ramah. And he stripped off his clothes and prophesied before Samuel in like manner, and lay down naked all that day and all that night. Wherefore they say, Is Saul also among the prophets? (1 Samuel 19:19, 22-24)

The power of the Spirit of God! This also shows the work of the Holy Spirit in the Old Testament verses the New Testament. As Christians, once we have received Christ as our Savior we receive the Holy Spirit who takes up permanent residence in our heart. In the Old Testament, the Spirit would come and go in a person that God chooses. Samson is another good example.

Saul, as we have seen, was so determined to kill David he traveled wherever he heard that David was staying. Determined to kill him. Saul finds David and Samuel in Ramah. So, what happens? The Holy Spirit comes upon him and totally distracts him from his mission. So much so, that the nearby observers think that Saul in preaching. Such is the power of the Holy Spirit.

Just a note about God's Spirit. Look at Genesis,

> *The earth was without form, and void; and darkness was on the face of the deep. And the Spirit of God was hovering over the face of the waters. (Genesis 1:2)* (NKJV)

Someone once described it this way. God, the Contractor, determined what was to be done. Jesus, the architect, drew up the plans. The Holy Spirit was the force that completed the project. Interesting theory. The fact is that God created the heavens and the earth.

The verses above illustrate another, very important, work of the Holy Spirit. He changes lives. God had already rejected Saul for many reasons.

Here He simply used the Holy Spirit to distract him from his mission to kill David. Today, God's Holy Spirit can literally change lives. I have heard countless stories of individuals who totally reject the message of the gospel then one day, God's Spirit speaks to their heart and changes their life!

My favorite is Josh McDowell. A college student that got so tired of hearing his classmates talk about the power of God and Jesus that he set out to disprove their faith. Josh has written several books. Not about disproving God but confirming who Jesus was. One is entitled, "Evidence That Demands a Verdict". I have heard of countless other testimonies that confirm the power of the holy Spirit to change lives.

In John's gospel, we can see the reason Jesus sent the Holy Spirit:

> "Nevertheless, I tell you the truth. It is to your advantage that I go away; for if I do not go away, the Helper will not come to you; but if I depart, I will send Him to you. And when He has come, He will convict the world of sin, and of righteousness, and of judgment: of sin, because they do not believe in Me; of righteousness, because I go to My Father and you see Me no more; of judgment, because the ruler of this world is judged. (John 16:7-11) (NKJV)

You see, no one comes to the saving knowledge of Jesus Christ except the Holy Spirit draw him, convict him of his need of a Savior. Then God's Spirit speaks to his heart and he begins to seek answers, then God puts someone in their path to share the Gospel with them and lead them to Christ. It must begin with the Holy Spirit.

Never underestimate the power of God's Spirit. Here is a great example in Saul. As determined as Saul was to kill David, now he had the opportunity, God's Spirit changed his focus and determination, although briefly. Is God's Spirit speaking to you right now?

1 Samuel 20

Therefore, thou shalt deal kindly with thy servant; for thou hast brought thy servant into a covenant of the Lord with thee: notwithstanding, if there be in me any iniquity, slay me thyself; for why shouldest thou bring me to thy father? And Jonathan said, Far be it from thee: for if I knew certainly that evil were determined by my father to come upon thee, then would not I tell thee? (1 Samuel 20:8-9)

Have you noticed how this word has vanished from our vocabulary? Sure, we don't use the word "covenant" today, how about "promise?" I talked about this before. That's what makes the covenant between David and Jonathan unique! They made a promise to each other, despite their trying circumstances. What about Jonathan's loyalty to his father? Why would David be drawn to his sworn enemy's son? God's Spirit has such awesome power.

In the front of this book I have listed over 40 men, who have influenced my walk with God. 40+ men who helped me, in seeking God's direction for my life. Much as Jonathan had for David.

We noted earlier how David just didn't understand why God was allowing this threat on his very life to occur. What had he done wrong? We have all asked that question at one time or another, especially me. When God begins to use someone, Satan must take a hand and do what he can to discourage, or disrupt God's working. From the time David left the shepherd's field to begin to follow God's leading Satan has put every road-block he could muster to try to stop him. Even having several spears thrown at him from across the room.

This covenant with Jonathan will last all of David's life. We will see this covenant play out later. How about your word? When I was first saved I made a commitment to God that I would be in His house whenever I possibly could, regardless if my family went with me or not. I have done my best, after over thirty years, to keep that covenant. I believe God has blessed that covenant. I can't begin to count the number of times I made a special effort to go to church and God has blessed me in the service. Either a kind word from someone there, an insight in the message the pastor preached, even an answer to a problem I was dealing with.

Did you catch that in the verses above? I just noticed it. *"into a covenant of the Lord with you."* Maybe if we realized that when we give our word, especially as Christians, we have God's testimony at stake. People know if we claim to be a Christian, therefore, our word has the testimony of God behind it. Think about it.

Are you in the middle? I spoke about this earlier. Jonathan is in a tough spot. His father hates his best friend. What is he to do? There is another element in this we can't ignore. God's influence in both lives. It seems Jonathan has a connection with God that is sorely lacking in Saul. Jonathan senses it in David. How much Jonathan sensed of God's purpose for David we can only guess. Surely Jonathan knew that if David became king, his inheritance, the throne, would be null and void.

This treatise is supposed to be about David's walk with God. In our walk, we will encounter individuals who will affect our lives along the way. Some will try to discourage, some will encourage, some will draw us away from God some will point us to God. Jonathan, as we will see later, was one who helped David seek God's purpose for his life. Jonathan was a vital part of God's maturing David to later become king. I hope you have people in your life that will point you to God, and not lead you astray. The holy Spirit is key, listen to God's prompting!

And thou shalt not only while yet I live shew me the kindness of the Lord, that I die not: but also thou shalt not cut off thy kindness from my house for ever: no, not when the Lord hath cut off the enemies of David every one from the face of the earth. (1 Samuel 20:14-15)

It's important that we understand the culture of the day. When a king assumes the throne his first duty is to kill all existing family members of the previous king. By doing this he assures himself that no one will seek his throne. This was weighing on Jonathan's mind in the passage above. Not only that, this was Saul's greatest fear. Why Saul did not understand why Jonathan would be so close to David.

What's interesting to me, both Saul and Jonathan knew David was to be the next king. Whether through Samuel, the working of God's Spirit, who knows how they knew. Saul was deathly afraid of David. Jonathan loved him even though he knew that David would take his place on the throne.

Did you catch the word that Jonathan uses? Kindness. Not just kindness but *kindness of the Lord.*

Do you remember when God sent Israel, finally, into the Promised Land? What was God's mandate? The Israelites were to kill every living soul that occupied the Promised Land. Israel was to purify the land and to bring God's justice on the pagan inhabitants. The same would apply to the family of a deposed king. They were to be eliminated. That's what Jonathan is talking about here.

Look at the following verses:

> So, Jonathan made a covenant with the house of David, saying "Let the Lord require it at the hand of David's enemies." Now Jonathan again caused David to vow, because he loved him as he loved his own soul. (1 Samuel 20:16-17) (NKJV)

This must have been a rough time to live. The customs we cannot imagine. The sad part is that David would have every right to slay Saul's family as the new king. That was the custom of the day. We cannot imagine. Jonathan's fear was real. Yet, Jonathan also knew the bond he had with David. I believe Jonathan also knew David's heart.

We have spent a lot of time on this relationship between Jonathan and David. Our goal, of course, is to understand why David was a man after God's own heart. We need to examine how David's relationship with Jonathan can be reflected in our own relations, both horizontal and vertical. God's love for us is just as strong as Jonathan's and David's. Can we have that kind of relationship with God? Of course, through a personal relationship with Jesus Christ.

As far as the horizontal that is Jesus' command to us.

Love one another as I have loved you! (John 13:34).
(NKJV)

This may very well be the reason God has seen fit to include this episode of David's life for us to study. Just what does it mean to "love one another"? This was not just between David and Jonathan but Jonathan's household (family) throughout David's life. We will see this later on in one of my favorite stories about David.

Is there someone you can show kindness to? Someone who needs a word of encouragement, a helping hand? Pray about it. Ask God to put someone in your path that you can bless, you can pray for, and give them a boost in a time when they need it the most. That's what we are here for, is it not? Sharing, caring, encouraging, and blessing those we have opportunity to bless.

"For as long as the son of Jesse liveth upon the ground, thou shalt not be established, nor thy kingdom. Wherefore now send and fetch him unto me, for he shall surely die". And Jonathan answered Saul his father, and said unto him, "Wherefore shall he be slain? What hath he done? And Saul cast a javelin at him to smite him: whereby Jonathan knew that it was determined of his father to slay David. (1 Samuel 20:31-33)

Bitterness, resentment, jealousy can destroy a family. Even to the point of trying to kill his own son. Where is God in all this? He is nowhere to be found. Saul has totally lost sight of God. If this treatise is about David why are we talking about Saul and Jonathan?

Did you catch the phrase above? "Why should he be killed, what has he done?" Gee, I believe those same words were said by Pilate to the people concerning Jesus. If we are looking for reason and justice it is nowhere to be found. Man does not deal in reason and justice and mercy, only God.

It's important to examine this relationship between Saul and David with Jonathan in the middle. By looking at these three individuals we might see some of ourselves in them. Look at Saul: blinded by ambition and totally losing focus on God. In the beginning, he was hopeless and helpless. God gave him some victories and now he is superman. Then along comes David and steals his thunder. Instead of talking with God, seeking His counsel, he determines to kill the usurper. God has left the scene and Saul's heart.

Jonathan, we mentioned before, saw God working in David's life. Jonathan was drawn to David for many reasons, I'm sure the primary reason being he saw a relationship with God that Jonathan wanted. How about those around you? Do they see God in your life and conduct? Are you drawing people to you, and thus to God? Your testimony should point people to God!

And David. David is not in this scene but he is the focal point. Saul recognized David's influence on Jonathan and thought to destroy it by killing his son. Why was Saul so jealous? Did he fear that Jonathan would not receive his rightful place as king? I think not. Saul was not concerned for his son but for his power and authority. As long as David was alive, Saul was threatened. The story is so familiar, then as it is today, take your focus off God and you miss life itself!

O.K. Let's move on. That's easy to say. If David was so significant in this tale why are we spending so much time on Saul and Jonathan? Well, it was important to God. Remember that God chose these words. God, through His Spirit, spoke to Samuel to relate this story. It was important to God to tell us about these relationships. Take some time and meditate on these three relationships. Their individual relationships and each one's relationship with God. That's where we are at.

I'm a "people watcher"! When my wife is shopping, and I am unfortunate enough to be along, I love to watch people. I will set in my car in the parking lot, I can't do all that walking, and observe the people going in and coming out of the store. It is quite an education. After a while, you learn to notice certain mannerisms and actions that stand out. I can't go into specifics but just try it sometime.

That is what we are doing here, with the limited information we have. We are observing their actions and looking for God in each situation.

1 SAMUEL 21

So the priest gave him hallowed bread: for there was no bread there but the shewbread, that was taken from before the Lord, to put hot bread in the day when it was taken. And David said unto Ahimelech, And is there not here under thine hand spear or sword? For I have niether brought my sword nor my weapons with me, because the king's business required haste. And the priest said, The sword of Goliath the Philistine, whom thou slewest in the valley of Elah, behold, it is wrapped in a cloth behind the ephod: if thou wilt take that, take it: for there is no other save that here. And David said, There is none like that; give it me. (1 Samuel 21:6,8-9)

David, after saying goodbye to Jonathan, fled from Saul. He lied to the priest but asked for food, and later a weapon. David told the priest that he was on a mission for the king. He was hungry and needed food. The only food there was the showbread in the temple. For the origin of the showbread read Exodus 25:23-30.

This episode is also mentioned by Jesus in Mark chapter two. (2:25-28). Jesus uses this episode with David to make the point about the Sabbath,

> And He said to them, "The Sabbath was made for man, and not man for the Sabbath. Therefore, the Son of Man is also Lord of the Sabbath." (Mark 2:27-28) (NKJV).

We need to be careful what things we make holy and what things are idols. The Pharisees, as the spiritual leaders, made a lot of "rules" that had nothing to do with God. We can do the same thing. We can set up personal rules and think that these are from God. We should ALWAYS filter our conduct through the Word of God. What does God require, not our own inclinations?

David is on the run. What do you know? He happens upon a temple! He finds food and much needed weapons. I think it's interesting that he "happens" on the sword of Goliath. Remember, there are no accidents concerning God. The priest knew he was breaking the rule that says the showbread was for the priest' consumption only. Here was a man in need. The same can be said for the church today. We find spiritual food and the weapon to fight the world's lies in the Word of God.

I think it is interesting that the hardest Sunday school class to maintain is the Young Adult class. That time between graduating high school and creating a family. Why is that? Maybe we have the mistaken idea that we are in control of our destiny. That's sad. Once we begin creating a family we realized that we didn't know as much as we thought we did.

The first step, or should be, is to find a church. Much as David did here. David begins his journey toward being the king of Israel. Oh, he's been anointed sure, but there is a journey to that end. David begins in the only place he can begin, the house of God. It's no accident that he happened to find exactly what he needed here. God is always ready to supply our needs when we recognize His leadership and guidance. Nothing happens in the Bible by accident.

David may be on the run, but God has a plan. Much as God did when He led Israel out of bondage from Egypt, and a roundabout way to the Red Sea. God knows what is needed every step of our journey toward serving Him. When we want to go our own way, we think we know better than God, that's when we get into trouble. Just like when Israel refused to enter the Promised Land.

I wonder how many times David reflected on his days in the field with the sheep? I wonder if David ever asked God what lies ahead, why is Saul intent on killing him? And most important, I wonder if David looked forward to the future and marveled at what God was going to do in his life?

And David arose, and fled that day for fear of Saul, and went to Achish the king of Gath. And the servants of Achish said unto him, Is not this David the king of the land? Did they not sing one to another of him in dances, saying, Saul hath slain his thousands, and David his ten thousands? And David laid up these words in his heart, and was sore afraid of Achish king of Gath. (1 Samuel 21:10-12)

This doesn't make sense! Why would David run from Saul, who desperately wants to kill him, into the land and the king of the Philistines? Just after David had killed their greatest weapon, Goliath. This just doesn't make sense. I don't suppose you have ever asked God why?

Of all the places David could have escaped to, why Gath? Could it be that it is where God led him? Do you need to be reminded of Joseph? If anyone in the Bible had the right to ask why, it was Joseph. Yet, he trusted God, made the best of each situation, and kept God in focus!

I'd like you to finish reading this scene. Verses 13-15. David acts the fool in front of the king to remain in the land. I love what the king says in verse 15:

> "*Have I need of madmen, that you have brought this fellow to play the madman in my presence?*" (1 Samuel 21:15) (NKJV)

The king essentially says, don't I have enough madmen around me already?" I just wonder how much of this whole scene was God's idea? David, playing a lunatic, enabled him to take up residence in Gath, the last place Saul would look for him. We will see later the unfolding of God's perfect plan.

But, what about us? Has God ever led you somewhere that just didn't make sense to you at the time? That is why "reflection" is so important in the Christian's life. We need to stop and reflect why and how we have arrived where we are. First, we must determine whether God led us here are our own foolishness. Are we walking close enough to God that we can't make a wrong turn? David was walking with God!

After we have determined that God has brought us to this point, then we need to ask, why am I here? Is there a reason God has brought me to this point? Again, remember Joseph, God had a plan for Joseph, the moment he left his father's house at seventeen and thirteen years later became second in command of Egypt. Because we have the narrative in front of us makes it easy, Joseph didn't. The lesson for us is "trust God."

The whole reason for this study, is to see if we can discern why God called David, "a man after God's own heart." We need to ask ourselves, as we make this journey, what characteristics of David's life can we incorporate into our own relationship with God. I believe this is a critical one: trusting

God's leadership. But remember, it must be God's leadership and not our own desires. I can speak from experience! Don't be fooled. You must stay close to God to discern His will.

Has David escaped? It's like that saying, "out of the frying pan, into the fire." David must be scratching his head. Yet, I can't point this out enough, he made the best of the situation. I can look back and see how some insignificant event led to another turn and another and then I realize I am right where God wanted me all along. We just need to open our heart and minds to God's leadership. One of my favorite verses, I will quote often:

> For I know the thoughts (plans) that I have for you, says the Lord, thoughts (plans) of peace and not of evil, to give you a future and a hope. Then you will call upon Me and go and pray to Me, and I will listen to you. And you will seek Me and find Me, when you search for Me with all your heart. (Jeremiah 29:11-13) (NKJV)

Don't overlook the last part of these verses. "when you search for Me with all your heart." That was David. Because David is walking with God, he accepts God's leadership and guidance.

1 SAMUEL 22

David therefore departed thence, and escaped to the cave Adullam: and when his brethren and all his father's house heard it, they went down hither to him. And every one that was in distress, and every one that was in debt, and every one that was discontented, gathered themselves unto him; and he became a captain over them: and there were with him about four hundred men. And David went thence to Mizpeh of Moab: and he said unto the king of Moab, Let my father and my mother, I pray thee, come forth, and be with you, till I know what God will do for me. (1 Samuel 22:1-3)

Does the name Mizpah sound familiar? First in Genesis 31 it was the sight of a covenant between Jacob and Laban. More recently, Samuel gathered Israel there to pray for them. In 1 Samuel 7 we read:

> *So, the children of Israel put away the Baals and the Ashtoreths, and served the Lord only. And Samuel said, "Gather all Israel to Mizpah, and I will pray to the Lord for you." (1 Samuel 7:4) (NKJV)*

Mizpah was where they felt the presence of the Lord. It symbolized God's presence.

David sought the wisdom and guidance of the Lord where he knew God had shown Himself before. You know how I feel about the local church. It has been my refuge from the day I was saved. When I can't seem to communicate with the Lord I head to church. The quiet before the service, the quiet times in the service, fellowship with Christian friends, etc. So many time's in church God has opened His heart and will to me, it amazes me!

Why didn't David just find a quiet spot in the corner of his cave? I'm sure God would have met him there. So, why did he take his father and mother and travel to Mizpah, to secure their safety? He wasn't sure about the cave but he was sure about Mizpah. When you have met God in a certain place you want to return there, where you know He dwells.

As a novice Christian, I felt so strongly one year that I needed to be in church on New Year's Eve. My car had some valves knocking and it was several miles (30+) to the church. I almost talked myself out of going. I eventually did. That night they showed a film about a martyr named Hess. About half-way through the movie I had to get up and go and get a drink of water. God was so real that night. I could literally feel His presence. Not long after that I gave my life to the ministry. That was where God got a hold of my life.

Don't miss the end of verse 3. What did David say? *"Till I know what God will do for me."* Here is a classic example of why David was close to God's heart. There are several events throughout the Bible where the option to ask God's advice is there. Some have sought it, some have not. I think of the Gideon's in Joshua (Chapter 9) when they deceived Joshua and he made a treaty with them, big mistake. Take note of these throughout the Bible. David isn't perfect. He surely should have sought God's guidance with Bathsheba, but he didn't.

Where do you go to talk with God? Do you talk with God? Let me ask you this, "Has God met you there"? You want to go someplace where God has met you. You can have your quiet place, etc. I'm sure God has met you there, maybe. There is a reason Jesus established His church on this earth. He even promised that the gates of Hades would not prevail against it. (Matthew 16:18). It was His call, His will, His church. He established it for a reason!

David has drawn over four hundred followers. He has begun to form an army. Did you notice who were drawn to David? Much as those who were drawn to Jesus. Those in need, those whom the world has cast out. That is the God we serve. A God who is always ready to comfort, encourage, and by the power of His Spirit give a new life. You must follow Him first. You must be a part of His family to partake of the grace He offers freely. Have you joined this band?

Then the king said unto the footmen that stood about him, Turn and slay the priests of the Lord; because their hand also is with David, and because they knew when he fled, and did not shew it to me. But the servants of the king would not put forth their hand to fall upon the priests of the Lord. And the king said to Doeg, Turn thou, and fall upon the priests, and Doeg the Edomite turned, and fell upon the priests, and slew on that day four score and five persons that did wear a linen ephod. (1 Samuel 22:17-18)

I pray this is my last reference to King Saul. It is an important example and lesson to learn here. Saul has reached the bottom of his hatred of David. I think it's interesting that Saul never raised his hand, but instructed those under him to do it. How typical!

When Christmas comes around I look forward to watching the Christmas movies on Hallmark channel. I have noticed in a large percentage of movies, a recurring theme. Someone in the movie doesn't celebrate Christmas anymore because of a tragedy that occurred earlier in their life around Christmas time. So, they blame Christmas, and refuse to celebrate the holiday. Never mind what the holiday represents or celebrates. Of course, later they are brought back to "Christmas".

In the same manner how many people blame God for misfortunes in their life? Too many I'm sad to say. It's so easy! God can't defend Himself, it's easier to blame ANYTHING other than providence or their own mistakes in choices. We must blame someone or something, surely not us.

That is what Saul is doing here. He is so frustrated that he can't get his hands-on David, he takes it out on these priests. Never mind his own rejection of God, and God's blessing on his life. Remember that God chose him to reign. He had the opportunity to obey God and walk in His ways and will. But he chose to go his own merry way. Remember, he even stepped in for Samuel the prophet and tried to perform the office of priest (1 Samuel 13:8-10).

Hate is a powerful emotion. It can destroy a person's life and testimony in no time. It is also a cancer that can eat away to paralyze anyone from any kind of relationship with God.

Have you noticed Saul's slow journey downhill from God? It begins with disobedience and, as we have seen here, complete rebellion.

Don't misunderstand here. David traveled the same road with Uriah and Bathsheba. So, what is the difference between David and Saul. If you notice Saul's sin was driven by hatred and he never repented of his hatred for David. David's sin was driven by fear. David would be exposed. His sin would be open. He tried to remedy the situation by his own logic, it didn't work. So, what was David's response? "I have sinned against the Lord." (2 Samuel 12:13). David acknowledged his sin and confessed to God. Saul never did!

Why is it so hard to say, "I'm guilty", I made a mistake, I'm sorry, speaking of blame, do you remember the episode in the Garden of Eden? What happened, when God confronted Adam about his disobedience? First, notice who God came to first! Adam's response:

> "*The woman whom You gave me, she gave me of the tree, and I ate." (Genesis 3:12).* (NKJV)

In a way Adam was blaming God, surely not. Do we not do the same thing? Think about it.

To be honest I am tired of looking at Saul. This treatise is about David. There are a lot of lessons to learn as we observe the life of David. Many of the lessons have to do with the contrast between David and those around him. Saul is a great example. We can learn just as much from negative examples as well as positive ones. The point is that God included these examples in His word for our learning. Don't just skip over these examples they are for our learning!

1 Samuel

Then David enquired of the Lord yet again. And the Lord answered him and said, "Arise, go down to Keilah; for I will deliver the Philistines into thine hand. (1 Samuel 23:4)

Do you see the contrast? God's hand was on David, not Saul. Why is that? David sought the will of God, Saul was determined to do his own will. The verse above says, "once again" If you have read this chapter you see that David sought God's will right off, but his followers were afraid. David sought God's will a second time. How determined are you to be in God's will? Does God have His hand on you?

God promised David a victory at Keilah. There was a victory.

As a child of God, we have the same resource as David. How many times do we use it? We make so many life changing decisions in our life yet how many do we even consider seeking God's guidance?

God wants to accomplish so much in your life. God has a plan (Jeremiah 29:11) for your life. This plan will bring glory to Him and blessings to you. How many times have you attempted to accomplish something without a plan? Men are notorious for looking at the instructions as a last resort. The Bible fits into that category as well. We want instructions for life, we search and search, read all kinds of "self-help" books. The answers are right in front of us. . . the Word of God. Why not consult the one who created us?

Now there is one other important component to God's leading and God's plan. You must be a child of God. If you're not, you do not have the Holy Spirit living within you. That Spirit is God's very presence living with us. He will give you a peace about a decision you need to make, a path to follow. But you must listen first!

So, how do I get this connection to God? How do I become a child of God?

"If you confess with your mouth the Lord Jesus and believe in your heart that God has raised Him from the dead, you will be saved. For with the heart one believes unto righteousness, and with the mouth confession is made unto salvation." (Romans 10:9-10) (NKJV)

Let me give a few other verses to read with these: Romans 3:23, 5:8, 6:23. This is known as the Romans road. One more, my favorite, Revelation 3:20. Check out these verses and if you're not a child of God, pray and ask God to come into your heart.

David learned at a very young age to trust God. In the fields, watching the sheep, he had to trust God for the strength and courage to fight off the bear and lion to protect his sheep (1 Samuel 17:34-35). He also saw that God was faithful to bring him victory against Goliath. The more we trust God and lean on His strength and guidance (His hand on us) the more God will work in our lives. God must know first if He can rely on us, if we will walk in His path.

Look what it says in Psalms 31:15a, "My times are in Your hand". I remember a quote I was given as a young Christian. I think it was D.L. Moody or it was said to him, it goes, "the world is yet to see what God can do with a life fully committed to Him." That has always been a challenge in my life. Many time's I have been tempted to do something out of God's will. Each time I would think, "I don't want God to take His hand off of my life." That is so critical in our relationship with Him.

David is a great example of someone whom God had a hand on. Once, when he was not where he should have been, did David stumble. Yet God was there, after acknowledging his sin, God picked him up and continued to use him. Does God have His hand on your life?

And it came to pass, when Abiathar the son of Ahimelech fled to David to Keilah, that he came down with an ephod in his hand. And David knew that Saul secretly practised mischief against him; and he said to Abiathar the priest, "Bring hither the ephod." (1 Samuel 23:6,9)

The ephod first appears in Exodus 28. I think it is interesting that God gives instructions for the construction of the tabernacle THEN the priest garments. In chapter 28 verses 6 through 14 we are given specific instructions for the creation of this priest apparel. It was to be worn as a chest protector in front of the priest. You can read the details in chapter 28. There was also created a robe to go with the ephod in verses 31-36 of the same chapter. The point being this was part of the priests' garment that was worn into the Holy of Holies.

I think, to David, this represented the presence of God. Personally, I think of my Bible in the same way. It contains God's holy word, my instructions. Much as David was seeking God's direction from the priest with the ephod.

What do you use to connect with God? Is it material, as this ephod? Our connection with God today is through His Holy Spirit that lives within us. When we accepted Christ as our Savior God put within us the third part of the Trinity, the Holy Spirit. That is our "ephod" if you will. Remember in the Old Testament the Holy Spirit would come and go as God determined His purpose. Today He indwells every believer.

When we began this journey, looking at David's life to try to determine what made him a "man after God's own heart" we can see here a key principle. Granted David didn't always use it, neither do we. David sought God's direction and will for his life. Whenever he ran into a situation, a problem, an unanswered question, he sought God's direction. Note this principle!

Where do you turn for direction? How do you solve problems that confront you? Sometimes we don't have "time" to pray to seek God's guidance. That's where the Holy Spirit comes in. Trust Him. That is assuming you are open to His direction and guidance. Sometimes He will warn us, or convict us, or just not give us a peace about something, but we do it anyway. Of course, we know better than God what is best for us, right?

Many times, we do have the time to pray about things. Then we want to argue with God, again, we know better. I want you to think about something. Can you see the future? Of course not. God can, and God knows the right path, the right decision to make based on His knowledge of what is ahead. We don't!

Did you notice that it was the priest that had the ephod? When was the last time you asked your pastor to pray with you about something? It always amazed me, when I was a pastor, that people would ask my presence, at the hospital, the bedside of someone ill, or different events. What is it about the "presence" of a man of God? I think subconsciously we feel that because a man of God is present that God is present. There is a great comfort in knowing that someone representing God is there.

Here is a trivia question for you. Where did the first "priest" appear? The Bible goes into great detail in Exodus about his garments and procedures. Look at Genesis 14.

> *Then Melchizedek king of Salem brought out bread and wine; he was the priest of God Most High. (Genesis 14:18) (NKJV)*

Did you notice that he was a king AND a priest? The first priest appears shortly after God called Abraham to become the father of the nation of Israel.

David sought the direction of God! Whether through a priest, an ephod, but he was always seeking God's direction. How about you?

Then David and his men, which were about six hundred, arose and departed out of Keilah, and went whithersoever they could go. And it was told Saul that David escaped from Keilah; and he forebare to go forth. And David abode in the wilderness in strong holds, and remained in a mountain in the wilderness of Siph. And Saul sought him every day, but God delivered him not into his hand. (1 Samuel 23:13-14)

When would you have given up? Saul thought that David was trapped in Keilah, but he got away. Saul will continue to pursue David for many years. Take note of these verses. There is no time period given. We can read them in a couple of minutes but we may be talking months if not years. Would you consider that God drove David into the wilderness? God is in total control of all that is transpiring, believe it. Look at the end of verse 14.

I hope you remember that our Lord, right after His baptism was led into the wilderness (Matthew 4). Have you had a "wilderness" experience? When you might have thought that God was nowhere to be found. What was your response? Remember, Jesus didn't eat for forty days. It can feel like that in the wilderness.

I recently heard a sermon from Dr. Charles Stanley about the 23rd Psalm. Every time I hear "Thy rod and Thy staff" I am reminded of something I learned when our Sunday school class studied this same passage. Thy rod is for "correction" and Thy staff is for "direction" both characteristics and responsibilities of a shepherd. Today our rod and staff is the Word of God, and our Shepherd.

I wonder, during this frustrating time in David's life, how many times he prayed and asked God? He knew he had to avoid Saul, it was his life at stake. But why didn't he just turn and fight Saul. You notice David had an army of six hundred men. Why not fight, we would. Because David knew God had a plan. David "respected" the fact that God called Saul to be king and his time had not come. He knew that God, in His time, would put him on the throne—in God's time!

Ever want to second guess God? Maybe you think you have figured out God's plan and God wasn't acting fast enough so you would help Him out. That is dangerous. Never get ahead of God, it can only end badly. David was led into the wilderness to regroup and, I think, to reconnect with God's plan.

God had spared him in Keilah by keeping him ahead of Saul. God had led David to this wilderness camp. It was up to David to determine GOD'S next step, not David's. When you seem to be in this valley that David mentions in the 23rd Psalm what is your response? Talk about perspective. Before I was saved I used to think that there were two valleys for every mountain top experience. After I was saved I realized that it took two mountains to make one valley. It all depends on your perspective.

Sometimes, when we get too wrapped up in the cares of this world God needs to bring us to the wilderness experience to get our attention, to bring our focus back to Him. To rely on God once again instead of our own devices, our own strength and wisdom. Sometimes it's to humble us to remind us that God is still in control, not us!

David is on a journey, running from Saul, but in the process David has some lessons to learn. In the process God is going to test David's commitment to Him. Much as He used Jesus in the wilderness, not as a test, but an illustration of who has control, who makes the decisions, who determines' the will of God. Satan thought he was in charge, Jesus demonstrated otherwise!

Go, I pray you, prepare yet, and know and see his place where his haunt is, and who hath seen him there: for it is told me that he dealeth very subtilly. See therefore, and take knowledge of all the lurking places where he hideth himself, and come ye again to me with the certainty, and I will go with you; and it shall come to pass, if he be in the land, that I will search him out throughout all the thousands of Judah. (1 Samuel 23:22-23)

It has always, since I learned the ways of God, that there is a certain principle that God uses pertaining to our walk with Him. The principle: There are things we are supposed to do, then there are things God does. Where we get into trouble is trying to do the things of God and neglecting our duties.

I wonder how many times David asked himself, "Why am I always running from Saul, what have I done to deserve this peril?" It's God's plan, David! It's God's timing, David! Be patient, wait on God and He will bring it to pass. That is so hard!

When I realized that God had called me to the ministry I didn't know what to do next. I had first thought of quitting U.P.S., where I was working, and going to seminary or something like that. Then God revealed that I was to stay with U.P.S. and retire with 25 years of service. Then I could use that retirement to supplement the salary from a small church that could not afford a "full-time" pastor. I retired, then my pastor said I needed to write a resume and turn it in to the Association. I hate resumes!

I kept putting it off. Then this principle was revealed. God will not lead me to a church until I write a resume. Something I needed to do before God took over. I, with the help of my daughter, finally wrote my resume and God led me to a church in Freeman, Missouri. Several years later I learned another lesson: You can't force doors open that God does not want open. That's a long story but a tough lesson.

Just a reminder, remember the story of Joseph? For thirteen years he went through very tough times including prison and slavery just to be where God wanted him when He wanted him there.

It's easy for us because we know that David will eventually be king. David doesn't know that at this point. The thing about David is that he isn't trying to force God's will. He was patient enough to wait on God and God's timing. Part of being a man after God's own heart.

Is there something you want to do but God seems to be blocking the way? Are you trying to knock down doors that God seems to be keeping closed? Wait on God! God will open the right door at the right time, to a blessing you could not believe. You can force those doors, of course, but the consequences are too horrible to think about. The greatest grief from forcing a door open is being out of God's will. That will hurt more than anything.

The rest of this chapter deals with David staying one step ahead of Saul. Look at verse 17:

> *And he said to him, "Do not fear, for the hand of Saul my father shall not find you. You shall be king over Israel, and I shall be next to you. Even my father Saul knows that." (1 Samuel 23:17) (NKJV)*

David, with another visit from Jonathan, was encouraged to stay the course. It is hard sometimes, but necessary! Another thing about these verses, we don't know the time involved. It could have been months of running and hiding.

Is God telling you to "wait" when you want to charge ahead? Don't do it. Think about David, just wait for God to open the doors! You won't be sorry.

1 SAMUEL 24

And it came to pass, when Saul was returned from following the Philistines, that it was told him, saying, "Behold, David is in the wilderness of En-Gedi. Then Saul took three thousand chosen men out of all Israel, and went to seek David and his men upon the rocks of the wild goats. (1 Samuel 24:1-2)

Do you remember how many men David had? Look at chapter 23, verse 13. David had six hundred men. Three thousand against six hundred, AND God! Who do you think will win? Also, remember earlier that Saul was at the threshold of killing David and God raised up the Philistines to distract him. God is always at work concerning His children.

I think we need to be reminded that events in our life are not accidents. Many time's they are God's way of directing our footsteps, leading us in the direction He wants us to go. The events can have many purposes. Teach us a lesson in obedience. Put us in the right place for a blessing. Put us where we can be a blessing to others. Put us in the place to affect the life of someone else. We need to be open to God's direction. This En Gedi experience will benefit David, Saul and David's army in several ways, as we will see.

Anytime we see the wilderness used we need to think about Jesus' experience in the wilderness and how we can use our wilderness experiences to grow in our relationship with God. The hardest part of these wilderness experiences is the length of time we are there. We are so impatient many times we miss God's lesson or blessing. Pray, meditate, look around you, can you see a reason that this might be happening? Ask God to open your eyes.

Don't forget the message Jesus gives us in His wilderness experience. What was His weapon against the wiles of the devil? The Word of God. How familiar are you with your weapon? Can you use it properly? Its effectiveness is only determined by your willingness to use it! Jesus put His trust in the Father's words! Can you?

We have the tremendous benefit of hindsight. David didn't know what was going to happen. David's faith was in the promise of God. What promise? Remember when Samuel anointed him when David came out of the shepherd's field? David recognized then that God had a plan for his life. As children of God we must also recognize that God has a specific plan for our life. God will work in our life until that plan is fulfilled! We need to always seek God's will and not our own.

I think it is interesting that Saul's total focus is seeking David's demise. Threatened to the point of losing all contact or connection with God. We can be that distracted. Maybe there is a person or event in our life that so distracts us from God's working in our life that we miss God's prompting. God is trying to get our attention, we miss out on God's blessing by focusing on someone or something we can't see God working in our life. That is so sad!

This is an interesting chapter in David's life. Take your time through these verses. Notice how David has his focus on God and not on Saul. We are so easily distracted, David had a core set of principles that should guide us in every situation. Values that should come from the Word of God, or godly people in our life that have experienced a unique relationship with God the Father.

Just a reminder. Do you think David is in the Wilderness of En Gedi by accident? Do you think it was an accident that Saul is now free to pursue David here? There is a great lesson to learn in these verses, pray that God will open your eyes to God's message for you.

And the men of David said unto him, Behold the day of which the Lord said unto thee, Behold I will deliver thine enemy into thine hand, that thou mayest do to him as it shall seem good unto thee. Then David arose, and cut off the skirt of Saul's robe privily. And it came to pass afterward, that David's heart smote him, because he had cut off Saul's skirt. And he said unto his men, The Lord forbid that I should do this thing unto my master, the Lord's anointed, to stretch forth mine hand against him, seeing he is the anointed of the Lord. (1 Samuel 24:4-6)

Can you see David's heart here? His own men told him, "Now is your chance to get revenge and relief from this guy who wants to kill you." The people around him encouraged him to do "the right thing". Does that make it right? Only David's relationship with God stayed his hand. David knew it was not God's timing or God's way of dealing with Saul.

Don't overlook the circumstances here. They are in a cave. David's men are all around him. Saul is alone, relieving himself. No one would know, only the men who supported this act. A perfect time to get revenge and spare any more running and risking his life from Saul. The door was wide open. Because David was walking with God he knew it was not right. Even with all those around him, encouraging him. How about you? Are you walking close enough to God that the world has no influence on your walk?

How many "opportunities" do you see where you might do the right thing in the world's eyes but totally contrary to God's will and purpose in your life? It is so easy to be swayed by the world's logic, isn't it? A lot depends on the foundation you have laid between you and the Lord.

Remember, you have, as a Christian, the Holy Spirit of God living within you. The problem is most of us are not listening, the world drowns Him out. We mentioned earlier about praying before making decisions, that's part of listening to God's direction.

Look at John 16:

> "However, when He, the Spirit of truth, has come, He will guide you into all truth; for He will not speak on His own authority, but whatever He hears He will speak; and He will tell you of things to come. He will glorify Me, for He will take of what is Mine and declare it to you." (John 16:13-14) (NKJV)

Did you catch something in this verse? "He will guide you into things to come." God knows the future, He will prevent you from making tragic mistakes, if you will listen. That's what happened with David. God takes care of Saul later in His own way and time. It was not David's call!

Sometimes we think the door is wide open to do something we think God wants to do. Pray before crossing that threshold. Make sure what you are doing is God's will not your own.

As far as listening to the world, look what Jesus said in John,

"These things I have spoken to you, that in Me you may have peace. In the world, you will have tribulation; but be of good cheer, I have overcome the world." (John 16:33) (NKJV)

The world has one set of standards and God has another. Which are you listening to? Don't overlook that his men "justified" David killing Saul. They have their reasoning, but God is so much more knowledgeable. Listen to the One who knows the end from the beginning. Pray and ask God to give you clear guidance in the decision you need to make. The closer you are walking with God the easier it will be to make the right move.

Just remind yourself of all that David endured from Saul, javelins cast at him, many attempts at his life. Giving him one of Saul's daughters to spy on him, etc. Saul was a "pain" here was a great opportunity to escape, yet David sought God's heart and not his own. Think about it!

The Lord judge between me and thee, and the Lord avenge me of thee: but mine hand shall not be upon thee. As saith the proverb of the ancients, Wickedness proceedeth from the wicked: but mine hand shall not be upon thee. After whom is the king of Israel come out? After whom dost thou pursue? After a dead dog, after a flea? The Lord therefore be judge, and judge between me and thee, and see, and plead my cause, and deliver me out of thine hand. (1 Samuel 24:12-15)

This is such an important characteristic of David's that we need to learn! Do you see what he is doing? It would have been SO easy to take things in his own hand. Look at verse 11. David, as we talked about earlier, could have easily ended his misery. He could have taken righteous revenge against his tormenter. What did he do?

How about you? How are you dealing with the thorns in your flesh? Those acquaintances who drive you to distraction. Those who daily torment you. Do you come back with a witty retort? Do you try to under mind them at work? Do you take every opportunity to let them know you don't like them? Really? Where is God in all this? Have you turned it over to God? Probably not. He is too slow, He can't possibly understand what you are going through. Take a minute and reflect on what Jesus went through.

Jesus did nothing but good. He healed all those who came to Him.

It was a major task for Him to get away for some quiet time for prayer and meditation. The people were always wanting something from Him. The scribes and Pharisees were constantly trying to entrap Him. His own disciple betrayed Him to the authorities. Yes, Jesus knows what you are going through. And what would He have you do? Trust Him!

I like what Dr. Charles Stanley says, "Obey God, leave all the consequences to Him." What sound advice. But, like all good advice it is so hard to follow. We must do something. God just doesn't know what I'm going through.

I would like you to listen to someone who has learned this lesson the hard way. First, God can do a much better job than you can. He can deal with those circumstances better because He knows much more than you do. Second, there is such a peace when you turn it over to God. You no longer have this cancer eating away at you, distracting you from the great things God is trying to do in your life. Give it to God! Trust Him to do what needs to be done. Oh, the third thing? God may deal with YOUR heart as well. There may be something you don't know about that will influence the way you see things.

How many times have you judged a circumstance only to find out later you were totally wrong? That is not good.

Do you think David knew what God was going to do? Not hardly. God is not in the habit of sharing His plans with us. He simply wants us to do the right thing and trust Him. It's not easy, believe me. This can be a very large barometer on measuring our faith. How much are you willing to trust God to do the right thing? Enough to turn your irritants over to God? Don't do it half way. Give it to God, step back, and watch God deal with the situation.

I have spent a lot of time in this chapter but there are some great truths here that we can learn from David's response to this situation that God has allowed to occur. It was God who put David and Saul together in this cave, make no mistake about that. We have a record of this episode for our benefit, for our learning to examine and try to learn how God expects us to respond to the "enemies" in our life. Of course, we can read ahead and see the ending. Today we can't do that in our own struggles, we can only trust God to make things right. David did!

And it came to pass, when David had made an end of speaking these words unto Saul, that Saul said, Is this thy voice, my son David? And Saul lifted up his voice, and wept. And he said to David, Thou art more righteous than I: for thou hast rewarded me good, whereas I have rewarded thee evil. And thou hast shewed this day how that thou hast dealt well with me: forasmuch as when the Lord had delivered me into thine hand, thou killest me not. (1 Samuel 24:16-18)

How do you define "righteous"? To me, it makes me think of the word "faith." Either one can't be measured, can they? Think about it. The Bible has a lot to say about righteousness. Look at 1 John,

> "Little Children, let no one deceive you. He who practices righteousness is righteous, just as He is righteous. (John 3:7) (NKJV)

I could quote so many verses. What is righteousness in your eyes? What is righteousness in God's eyes? I heard this definition of righteousness once, "RIGHT-LIVING" Can you see righteousness in David's life?

David has confronted Saul about the opportunity he had to kill Saul. Saul recognized that David simply spared his life. It was David's for the taking and David refused to take it. Maybe we could include this in the definition: Rewarding evil with good. Basically, doing the "right thing" when you have the means to do otherwise. One more thought on "righteousness" how about "a right relationship with God."?

Let's reflect on some of the characteristics of David we have learned so far. First, his heart was right with God. Remember when Samuel sought David God said he had examined his heart. God knows the heart (1 Samuel 16:7). Next, David trusted in God's strength (1 Samuel 17:37). Next, David sought God's direction (1 Samuel 23:2). Finally, David trusted in God's justice (1 Samuel 24:6). This is the reason we are walking with David through these scriptures. To try and determine these important characteristics and incorporate them into our own lives. God put this marvelous life in word so we can better understand God's will for our lives. How we might learn the righteousness of David, and thus God.

I also think that is why He also gave us the story of Saul. To learn what NOT to do, how to remove God's hand from our own lives. What disappoints and hurts our relationship with God. God eventually turned His back on Saul. That is not what we want in our life. We want God's blessing, guidance, protection, and peace in our lives. Things Saul threw away with his disobedience.

As we finish this chapter David makes a promise to Saul that he would not destroy Saul's family once he becomes king. Saul has accepted the fact that David will one day become king. We want to think that this was on Jonathan's behalf but I think not. Saul was still thinking of himself. Here is a characteristic we will visit later. David is a man of his word. Another characteristic of "righteousness".

Now, as we finish this section, I don't want you to think that this "righteousness" will get you into heaven, God forbid. Righteousness is works, works will never get you into heaven! Only a relationship with God through His Son Jesus Christ is the only key to heaven. It is very simple. Look at Romans:

> "If you confess with your mouth the Lord Jesus and believe in your heart that God has raised Him from the dead, you will be saved." (Romans 10:9) (NKJV)

It sounds simple, doesn't it? It is! Christ reconciled us to God on the cross of Calvary. He paid for our sins to give us access into His holy presence. Only by the blood of Christ do we have the right to be called children of God. Have you asked Jesus into your heart?

1 SAMUEL 25

And there was a man in Moan, whose possessions were in Carmel; and the man was very great, and he had three thousand sheep, and a thousand goats: and he was shearing his sheep in Carmel. Now the name of the man was Nabal; and the name of his wife was Abigail: and she was a woman of good understanding, and of a beautiful countenance: but the man was churlish and evil in his doings; and he was of the house of Caleb. (1 Samuel 25:2-3)

Have you ever thought this: what do those two people see in each other? I love to people watch. I can set outside Walmart or Price Chopper for a long time just watching people and their reactions. It is so interesting. Here is one of those questions I frequently ask. I'm sure some people have said the same thing about my wife and me.

Abigail is one of my favorite Old Testament characters. She is in the same mold, to me, as Leah, Jacobs first wife. They don't "impact" the narrative much but God saw fit to include them in the story for a reason. Each contributes to the ultimate storyline. God's grace!

I think the one thing that could be said of Abigail, much like we have said of David, she did the right thing. I tried to see if she had any impact later, I couldn't find anything. Of course, she was David's wife when he chased after Bathsheba. As far as I can tell Abigail had one child by David, Chileab. He is only mentioned in 2 Samuel 3:3 as the son of Abigail the widow of Nabal the Carmelite. That is the only reference I could find.

I have often wondered what Nabal might have said to her when she returned from taking food to David. God evidently didn't think it was worth sharing. What is significant to me is how God worked this all out. Remember the opportunity David had to slay Saul. David could have taken care of this guy as well. In fact, he was on his way to do just that when

Abigail intercepted him. She averted, what could have been a disaster, and kept David from getting ahead of God's plan.

We have talked about this before. You know as well as I how hard it is to wait. Give it to God. Trust Him to do what needs to be done. But we know so much more than God, don't we? Did you notice that David doesn't bother praying about his response to Nabal? We tend to assign certain things to prayer and then there are things that we don't need to pray about, right? Then when they don't work out we are sorry we didn't take a minute or two to pray about it.

I like Abigail's spirit. She didn't discuss it with Nabal, who in that culture, would not have paid much attention to his wife anyway. She simply did what was right. She also knew that David would not take kindly to this slight. Again, protecting her family by doing what was right. How do you deal with people who are not walking with God? Do you try to correct them? Encourage them to pray about it? You know they are making a mistake but won't listen. What do you do? Sometimes we can't respond the way Abigail did. We can only pray for them, that God will open their eyes.

How hard is it sometimes just to do the right thing? Wait a minute, the right thing according to who? Sometimes we can get in the way of God's working in a situation. Abigail simply averted a situation. Did you notice, as you read this story, that God had a greater end in mind. Be careful when you get involved. Is it God leading you or something else?

In the beginning of this chapter Samuel the prophet has passed away. Saul has lost any connection with God, if he even considered it at this point. Samuel quietly passes from the scene. Samuel has done what God had called him to do. He made a difference in Israel's history. He transitioned from "The Judges" to a king. It has always been an interesting thought that, when I get to heaven, the people my life had touched and I didn't even know it.

And when David's young men came, they spake to Nabal according to all those words in the name of David, and ceased. And Nabal answered David's servants, and said, Who is David? And who is the son of Jesse? There be many servants that break away every man from his master. (1 Samuel 25:9-10)

David had given his men instructions to go to Nabal's camp and ask for some provisions for his men. They brought the request to Nabal. Nabal claims to not know who David is. I think that's funny because Abigail knew who he was. I think it's interesting that, it seems, the more we have the less likely we are to share. Remember the Lord's parable about the fella who had to build more barns? (Luke 12:16-20)

Here is another character that enters David life. How many people like Nabal do you encounter in your life. At least one I'm sure. How do you respond to them? Of course, we can read ahead and see the end of the story, we know how it ends but David didn't. How do you deal with individuals like this? What does God say? We respond with love. I'm sorry but that's the way. We talked about this with Saul. Our responsibility is to leave them with God. God will deal with them. It's amazing how much peace that gives us.

It doesn't happen here but it has happened in my own life. Sometimes these individuals are a test in our life. If we burn this bridge here we may find later that we will need to apologize later. That scoundrel now can become your best friend later. We never know, God does. We should treat everyone in our path with kindness and respect! We never know when we will cross paths again.

That's another thing. Other than marrying Abigail later, this is a snapshot in David's life that God saw fit to include in His narrative. Why? There is a lesson here. As with everything that God chooses to include in His word. Pay attention. What was David's response to Nabal's insults. We will see. How would you respond? Remember we don't know what will happen next.

David's men provided protection for the shepherds and flocks in that region. I don't know if Nabal knew that, I tend to think he did. That was the custom in that culture. I'm sure David's exploits had been revealed throughout the land. Remember, David had won several victories before Saul had run him off. I would think the story of Goliath would have been spread far and wide. Nabal just didn't want to part with his goods.

We are always going to be tested by people and events in our life. God wants to see if our relationship with Him is superficial or real. Has it penetrated to our hearts or just exists in our minds. Our thoughts can trick us. Not our hearts. If God has taken up residence in our heart our response to evil will be good. We will respond the way Jesus did, with kindness and the Word of God. Don't let this glimpse of David's life slip by. There is a great lesson to learn here.

David had just escaped an encounter with Saul in a cave. David did the right thing. He passed the test. Then he goes right into another test. Why does God continually put these tests in our path?

> "My brethren, count it all joy when you fall into various trials, knowing that the testing of your faith produces patience. But let patience have its perfect work, that you may be perfect and complete, lacking nothing". (James 1:2-4) (NKJV)

I was told long ago to never pray for patience. God doesn't give it, He teaches it. How do you deal with the trials in your life? Keep this verse close to your heart. It's God's word!

Now therefore, my lord, as the Lord liveth, and as thy soul liveth, seeing the Lord hath withholden thee from coming to shed blood, and from avenging thyself with thine own hand, now let thine enemies, and they that seek evil to my lord, be as Nabal. And now this blessing which thine handmaid hath brought unto my lord, let it even be given unto the young men that follow my lord. I pray thee, Forgive the trespass of thine handmaid: for the Lord will certainly make my lord a sure house; because my lord fighteth the battles of the Lord, and evil hath not been found in thee all thy days. (1 Samuel 25:26-28)

No wonder David took Abigail to wife after Nabal's death. I'm getting ahead of myself. We will discuss Nabal's death later. Did you notice how she recognized God's hand on David? I sense a relationship between Abigail and God. God can open our eyes to His working around us in a lot of different ways.

I want to get your attention on the two different uses of the word lord. Capitalized is in reference to God. The other is the cultural reference to those in power at the time. In many Bible's the word LORD is in all caps to signify God. It's worth noticing, so not to be confused.

Did you notice that Abigail recognized God's hand in saving Nabal's life? After the slight from Nabal that we talked about previous, David was on his way to discuss the matter. Abigail intercepted them and gave them the food they requested. She knew where they were headed. She also recognizes God hand and plan for David.

Did you catch this reference, "*because my lord fighteth the battles of the Lord.*"? (25:28) Abigail knew who David was. That's why it's unlikely Nabal didn't.

Have you ever wondered why certain things work out the way they do? Your headed on a task. In your mind, it must be done. Then you get sidetracked. Why? God is trying to head you in another direction, the right direction. I have shared this many times, I love it. Do you know how to make God laugh? Tell Him your plans. When you get up in the morning do you pretty much have the day planned out? Of course, you do. There are certain "things" you want to accomplish today and you set out to get them done. Then something happens and you are thrown off track. Why?

I like the way the NIV words this verse, "*I know the PLANS I have for you*" (Jeremiah 29:11) In the KJV it says "thoughts". The point being that God has this perfect plan to bring us to a better end. When we are determined to have it "our way" we get into trouble. God may make an effort to change your course but if you fight hard enough He will let you continue. At the end of the day you will wish you had listened. Always keep your life in neutral and allow God to direct. You can have plans but remember they are always "subject to change".

Abigail is one of those instruments that God used to change David's plans. He had every right to "speak" to Nabal. Abigail not only changed his direction but reminded him of God's calling in his life. He was to be king. He was to follow God's leading, not the emotions of the minute. Do you remember that old saying, "count to ten"? There is wisdom in those words. Instead of counting to ten you might want to offer a simply prayer. Nothing is too small not to pray about it. Did you read anywhere where David prayed before going after Nabal?

I think that is the greatest challenge for a child of God! Seeking and obeying God's direction in our life. It seems against our nature to ask for help or direction. When we can learn to seek God's guidance and then TRUST it, we will be much better off!

And Abigail came to Nabal; and, behold, he held a feast in his house, like the feast of a king; and Nabal's heart was merry within him, for he was very drunken: wherefore she told him nothing, less or more, until the morning light. But it came to pass in the morning, when the wine was gone out of Nabal, and his wife told him these things, that his heart died within him, and he became as stone. And it came to pass about ten days after, that the Lord smote Nabal, that he died. (1 Samuel 25:36-38)

Life and death, as much as we try we still have no control over it. Our life "expectancy" keeps going up. Modern medicine and a cleaner lifestyle, but we can never accept that it is God who determines the time. We grieve at the loss of a child who died too young. We grieve when an older person goes home to meet the Lord, because we will miss them. Death is so cruel. How many unfortunate individuals "blame" God when a loved one is taken? How many stopped to thank God that they are in a better place and free of pain? It all depends on our perspective of death.

How about life? Have you ever noticed that we have no control over a natural birth? Oh, they can induce labor but it is still God who determines the "time" of birth. We can predict and read all kinds of tables and charts and still miss it by weeks. Again, God is in control. God determines life and death. Just like the life of Nabal. If God was going to take Nabal why didn't he just let David do it? How do you suppose that would have affected Abigail?

I can get into a lot of trouble here but let me just make this one statement: Conception is totally in God's hands! Think about that. The timing and ability are all in God's hands.

I was privileged to witness God's timing one day. I had been called, by the family, to be at the bedside of a family who were going to remove life support to their loved one. When I arrived, different family members were in a contentious mood. There was bickering and disharmony.

The doctors removed the life support and everyone's attention was drawn to the monitor with that wavy line that said he was still around. We waited and waited and waited but he just wouldn't "leave". Soon the family began reminiscing and thinking about good times they had as children. When everyone had calmed down and made amends—he left. He just didn't want to leave with them bickering. It's God's call, and God can use death to impact our lives, in many different ways.

One of the greatest opportunities to witness for the Lord is at a funeral. Those attending are confronted with that final day. That day when we all will give account for the life we've lived. It is right there before you, that final day. It brings that decision time to your attention. I have even heard of pastor's who give an invitation at a funeral. For sure there ought to be the gospel message given. The sad part is that once you have departed this world it is too late to make that decision. When you stand before God and say "now" I believe, it's too late. That decision must be made while you still have that option.

Think about the peace that David had knowing that God had taken care of something he thought he should have. David trusted God, left it up to God and God did what He wanted not what David wanted. The same is true with Saul. God's time God's plan.

How do you deal with death? Do you ignore it, refuse to talk about it? It must be dealt with in THIS LIFE not the next. Are you ready to meet God? My wife and I have purchased our grave sites. Do you think we could get our kids to check it out? Not in your life. That is simply where our mortal bodies will rest, our souls will be with our Lord. Can you say that? Why not?

1 Samuel 26

David therefore sent out spies, and understood that Saul was come in very deed. And David arose, and came to the place where Saul had pitched: and David beheld the place where Saul lay, and Abner the son of Ner, the captain of his host: and Saul lay in the trench, and the people pitched around about him. (1 Samuel 26:4-5)

Do you remember when Jesus fed the 5,000 (Matthew 14)? Did you know He also fed 4,000 (Matthew 15)? So why does God see fit to repeat these examples? Anytime God repeats a truth it is to "underline" the significance. To get our attention. To say you need to pay attention to this lesson.

I hope you haven't forgotten what Saul said back in 1 Samuel 24:17-22. Saul was caught red-handed. I just read that passage again. You will notice that Saul admitted his mistake, asked David not to destroy his family but didn't say he would stop pursuing him. Interesting. Saul has one objective in mind. Destroy David!

Where is your focus today? Of course, it is something in the future. Usually something you have no control over. Does it consume you? I hope not. Let's try this. Put your finger in front of your face. Now focus on your finger. What do you see behind your finger? It's blurry, out of focus. Now focus on something past your finger. Is your finger blurry? Of course, it is. It is so important what we are "focused" on because that is what we see clearly. If you are focused on something in the future you will miss the blessing of today!

Look what Jesus said in Matthew:

> *"But seek first the kingdom of God and His righteousness,*
> *and all these things shall be added to you. Therefore, do*

*not worry about tomorrow, for tomorrow will worry about
its own things. Sufficient for the day is its own trouble".
(Matthew 6:33-34). (NKJV)*

Jesus gives us the priority right here. Focus on the things of God right now. God has already taken care of tomorrow. Besides, we have no guarantee of tomorrow anyway.

One last thing about David here. I asked my youth class once if they could name ONE conviction they had. One thing, that no matter what, they would not compromise. This seems to be the one thing David will not compromise on. Remember in the last episode, David was alone with Saul in this cave (with his men). He could have very easily have taken Saul's life and none would be the wiser (except David's men). Still he refused to kill Saul.

Someone once said that integrity was what you did when no one was looking. David knew it was wrong to kill Saul. Even with all that Saul had done to him, Saul was still God's anointed king. I don't know if God was testing David for the second time here. Of course, I think, God knew how David would respond. The important thing was David's testimony before his men. David was God's example before his army.

God can use us, so many different ways, being a testimony to Him is a great one. Most people know you're a Christian, or should. They know it by the way you act. They also are watching you to see if you will trip up and dishonor your God. That can also be the case with a back-slidden Christian. If they don't get their act together God may just take them home rather than for them to dishonor His name. Our testimony is very important to God. This could be a key ingredient in why David is said to be, "a man after God's own heart."

Did you notice the setting? Saul is in range of David. This time Saul is "surrounded" by his army, three thousand strong. Saul's going get him this time. He thinks his victory is at hand. Saul never recognizes that God is so much greater than he. A lesson we need to learn!

So David and Abishai came to the people by night: and behold, Saul lay sleeping within the trench, and his spear stuck in the ground at his bolster: but Abner and the people lay around about him. Then said Abishai to David, God hath delivered thine enemy into thine hand this day: now therefore let me smite him, I pray thee, with the spear even to the earth at once, and I will not smite him the second time. (1 Samuel 26:7-8)

Saul and his army of three thousand men were encamped near David's stronghold. Three thousand men! David asks for volunteers to go with him into the camp to confront Saul. Abishai went with him. Get this picture! David and Abishai walk into this camp and stand beside Saul and are ready to kill him. And the rest of the army? Asleep!

When was the last time you used the phrase, "Too good to be true"? Abishai offers to kill Saul on the spot. Here was an opportunity to end this endless pursuit by Saul. The endless running and hiding by David. I have often wondered how did they think the rest of the army would respond when they killed Saul?

We are presented daily with "opportunities". How we respond can tell a lot about our character and our relationship with God. The more the Holy Spirit is in control of our lives the greater the chance we will respond the way God wants us to. Have you ever left a situation and said to yourself, "I should have said _____, or I could have done _____? Hindsight is 20/20. Why didn't you respond at the moment? Check your walk with God. Is God in control of your life?

David had already established his mindset in the previous encounter. He had a conviction that he would not lift a hand against God's king. Remember, I talked earlier about convictions. David had set a course, established a precedent and was sticking with it. Maybe he knew God had a plan or not but he was determined to leave it in God's hand. Can you do that?

How did you respond when your plans didn't go the way you wanted? Did you pout, blame God, determine to make it work your way? Did you think to ask God why it didn't work out. It is amazing to me how we can have a peace about something that goes against our plans. God gives us that peace through His Holy Spirit that He is in charge and we should wait on Him.

Did you notice the confidence that David had to walk right in the midst of this three-thousand-man army? He stood right at Saul's head. You know he had to be in the middle of this army. That is confidence in God's power. I want you to remember the name Abner. He will appear later in David's army. Remember the name Abner. Why would David even try this? He is tempting fate. No, he is trusting God to give Saul one more opportunity to do the right thing. We have looked at David's opportunity, how about Saul's?

We are given opportunity after opportunity to turn our lives over to God. To accept His Son as our Savior, to turn our lives over to God. How many times have you refused? Once is too many! Maybe you've done this in the past but have never really committed your life to God. You are missing one of the greatest blessings in life. An intimate relationship with God the Father will change your life. There is a peace and assurance about the future you have never experienced before.

David had that peace. The peace to walk into the midst of this army to confront Saul. I want you to note what David does next. Of course, he doesn't kill Saul but he makes sure that he leaves a message for Saul. The message God leaves for us. It's time to make a decision about our priorities! Time to take the opportunity to give our life over to God and have that right relationship that God wants with us!

And David said to Abishai, Destroy him not: for who can stretch forth his hand against the Lord's anointed, and be guiltless? David said furthermore, As the Lord liveth, the Lord shall smite him; or his day shall come to die; or he shall descend into battle, ad perish. The Lord forbid that I should stretch forth mine hand against the Lord's anointed: but, I pray thee, take thou now the spear that is at his bolster, and the cruse of water, and let us go. (1 Samuel 26:9-11)

It's important that you get this picture. David and Abishai are standing at Saul's head. In the midst of three thousand soldiers! Really! Do you think God had anything to do with David's safety? I should hope so. I think David knew it too. It is scary how many such things God does around us daily and we never see God's hand at work around us.

Here is a verse that would be important for you to note!

"My times are in your hands; Deliver me from the hand of my enemies, and from those who persecute me." (Psalm 31:15) (NKJV)

I wonder when David wrote that song? How far are you willing to trust God? Look at the verse prior to 15,

> *"But as for me, I trust in You, O Lord; I say, 'You are my God.'" (Psalm 31:14) (NKJV)*

One of the key characteristics for a man to be after God's own heart is to trust in God's providence.

In the verse above David didn't know how God was going to deal with Saul, he just knew He would. That takes faith! That takes trusting God to solve a problem, not you! Just think of the peace that can give you when you put it in God's hands! That's a key ingredient too. God will not solve the problem as long as you have your hands on it or in it. Until you turn it over to God He will not do anything.

Can you imagine the story Abishai has to tell his friends when they get back to camp? David stood right there, and yet refused to kill Saul. David is walking with God.

Remember, this is the second opportunity David has had to kill Saul. Remember also, the numerous opportunities Saul had to kill David. The many times Saul cast a spear at David. The many battles that Saul sent David to fight, hoping they would kill him. Once in order to marry one of Saul's daughters, Michal, David was to kill 100 Philistines. (1 Samuel 18:25-28). Saul was constantly trying to get rid of David after his victory over Goliath and the people praised David over Saul.

Do we seem to be nit-picking the events in David's life prior to his being king? We are studying David's life in search of some characteristics that we can incorporate into our own life to have that close, intimate relationship with God that David had.

I was thinking about David the other night and realized something. I remarked that when David was anointed as a shepherd right out of Jesse's family that Samuel didn't specify that the anointing was to be king. The more I thought about that, I wonder if that anointing wasn't of the Holy Spirit. We noted earlier that the Holy Spirit had a different ministry in the Old Testament than He does in the New Testament. Just as in the ministry of Samson. It seemed the Holy Spirit would come and go depending on Samson's need. In the New Testament, once a person becomes a child of God through accepting Jesus as his Savior, the Holy Spirit becomes a PERMANENT occupant of the believer.

I think that day when Samuel came and anointed David it was to empower him with the Holy Spirit to carry out God's purpose for David. And just like us, when David ignored the prompting of God's Spirit he got into trouble. The more we are aware of God's prompting us, through His Spirit, the closer our walk with God and the more God will guide us to make the right decisions in our life. Listen to God's voice through His Spirit!

And David said to Abner, Art not thou a valiant man? And who is like to thee in Israel? Wherefore then hast thou not kept thy lord the king? For there came one of the people in to destroy the king thy lord. This thing is not good that thou hast done. As the Lord liveth, ye are worthy to die, because ye have not kept your master, the Lord's anointed. And now see where the king's spear is, and the cruse of water that was at his bolster. (1 Samuel 26:15-16)

After David had snuck into Saul's camp of three thousand men, he escaped with Saul's spear and water jug. After the camp awoke David confronted Abner, the general in charge of Israel's army. How could you let this happen? You should die for your incompetence. I asked you to remember Abner's name. Another that God will deal with later.

Who are you accountable to? I remember as a child, especially a teenager, how I couldn't wait to leave home and all the rules and my parents who were over me. I wanted to be in charge, I wanted to make the decisions! When I left home, on my way to basic training, it hit me. I can't expect anyone to provide for me any longer. If I wanted something I had to ask or get it myself. I was on my own. From that day forward I was accountable for my needs AND my actions!

Later I also realized something—there is ALWAYS someone over you to whom you are accountable. We all will answer for our actions in this life.

"For why do you judge your brother? Or why do you show contempt for your brother? For we shall all stand before the judgment seat of Christ." For it is written, "As I live, says the Lord, every knee shall bow to Me. And every

tongue shall confess to God." So, then each of us shall give an account of himself to God. (Romans 14:10-12). (NKJV)

I think that is David's thinking toward Saul as well. We are not the judge, as much as we would like to be. God is the judge and the jury. God will determine our life. Wait a minute, there is something we can do now to prepare us for that judgment. Once you become a child of God, we have an advocate (lawyer) to stand before the Judge on our behalf. Jesus Christ, the Son of God, our Judge, will speak to the Judge on our behalf. I think He has some sway with the Judge.

I think it's a good thing to have someone we are accountable to. Look what Hebrews 13 says,

"Obey those who rule over you, and be submissive, for they watch over your souls, as those who must give account. (Hebrews 13:17a) (NKJV)

We are told in the Bible that those in leadership will be held accountable for those we have authority over. That's a promise from God. Whether fathers over their family, teachers over their class, bosses over their employees. Anytime we have authority over others we will be held accountable. That is what David is saying to Abner!

No one is free to do as they please. David will find this out later.

One last thought as we move on. I wonder how many people think that when they stand before God and witness the fact that everything God said in His Word is true, now they can accept it as fact and accept Christ as Savior and they will gain entrance into heaven? It doesn't work that way. That is not faith. Faith is believing God's Word today, accepting Christ as your Savior and becoming a child of God in THIS life, not the next! Here is a verse to underline!

"And Thomas answered and said to Him, "My Lord and my God!" Jesus said to him, "Thomas, because you have seen Me, you have believed. Blessed are those who have not seen and yet have believed." (John 20:28-29) (NKJV)

I have always had this fantasy thought: The rapture has taken place and as I am going up to heaven to be with the Lord I look back and say, "See I told you!" Maybe not biblical or compassionate but we will be held accountable for the decision we made here!

Then said Saul, I have sinned: return, my son David: for I will no more do thee harm, because my soul was precious in thine eyes this day: behold, I have played the fool, and have erred exceedingly. And David answered and said, Behold the king's spear! And let one of the young men come over and fetch it. The Lord render to every man his righteousness and his faitfulness: for the Lord delivered thee into my hand to day, but I would not stretch forth mine hand against the Lord's anointed. (1 Samuel 26:21-23)

Is it over? Yes. Saul's search for David anyway. I'd like you to look at three "repentance" statements, compare the three. The first is Saul's the first time he confronted David:

> *"Then he said to David: "You are more righteous than I; for you have rewarded me with good, whereas I have rewarded you with evil. And you have shown this day how you have dealt well with me; for when the Lord delivered me into your hand, you did not kill me. For if a man finds his enemy, will he let him get away safely? Therefore, may the Lord reward you with good for what you have done to me this day." (1 Samuel 24:17-19) (NKJV)*

Did you read any repentance? He was sorry he got caught!
Now take another look at the verse above? Repentance?
Now look at one more.

> *So, David said to Nathan, "I have sinned against the Lord."*
> *(2 Samuel 12:13). (NKJV)*

Simple. David acknowledged his sin and God stated the consequences. That is the first step to repentance. We must acknowledge that we have sinned against God. We accept God's judgment and move on.

In the verse above Saul has finally admitted that he will no longer pursue David. Why? David won. Look again at Saul's first response, "*You are more righteous than I.*" Saul recognized then that David was in the right. Why was this instance different than the first? You don't suppose it was because this one was public? The first time Saul was in a cave, alone. This time his whole army witnessed David's righteousness!

There is such a difference in true repentance and just admitting that you got caught. Remember a lesson we learned early on about God? God knows the heart. We may fool those around us but God knows what's true. Repentance is described as an "about-face", a complete 180 degrees away from our sin. We can't sugar coat it, or deny it. We face it and turn from our wicked ways. Can we do it alone? Of course not. Only by the power of the Holy Spirit can we repent.

Have you ever tried to witness to someone and they tell you, "I'm not worthy yet! Let me get my act together then I'll come to the Lord." Friends that will never happen. We, by our standards, will never be righteous enough to come to God. First, we ask Jesus to save us, then He will begin the process of cleaning up our act. Then we have the power of God working within us to complete the repentance.

Look at this verse:

> *Therefore, if anyone is in Christ, he is a new creation; old things have passed away; behold all things have become new. (2 Corinthians 5:17). (NKJV)*

Mark that down. When we are saved our old life is history and our future is a mystery, wondrously new each day as God begins to clean up our life and put us on another path. An intimate relationship with God the Father who wants only the best for us. A relationship sealed with the presence of God's Holy Spirit working within us to guide us to the path God would have us walk. Oh, don't forget your new title! Child of God. We are now God's children and our heavenly Father wants only the best for us as a testimony to His grace and love for us!

1 Samuel 27

And David said in his heart, I shall now perish one day by the hand of Saul: there is nothing better for me than that I should speedily escape into the land of the Philistines; and Saul shall despair of me, to seek me any more in any coast of Israel: so shall I escape out of his hand. And David arose, and he passed over with six hundred men that were with him unto Achish, the son of Maoch, king of Gath. (1 Samuel 27:1-2)

These are tough verses. Why did God choose to share them with us? Let's look at Saul's last remarks to David:

> Then Saul said to David, "May you be blessed, my son David! You shall both do great things and also still prevail." So, David went on his way, and Saul returned to his place. (1 Samuel 26:25) (NKJV)

Earlier Saul had admitted to David his sin (26:21). The chase was over Saul has given up his pursuit of David. You would think David would be celebrating.

I think there is an interesting thought here. David was never in this hunt. Twice David had opportunity to end it. He could have killed Saul privately in a cave, or openly in these last verses. He chose not to lift a hand against God's king. There is more to this relationship than foe and enemy. I think David cared about Saul. Saul was his king, anointed by Samuel to be king. David had respect for Saul.

I think, also, that David grieved for what he thought might be the condition of Saul's soul. I wonder if David recognized, in Saul's tone, that Saul had given up. That Saul recognized the inevitable. David would be king. We saw earlier that Saul pleaded to David for Jonathan's life. David would not follow the custom of the time and destroy the previous king's family. I think David heard in Saul's voice the emptiness Saul felt because God had removed His hand from Saul.

How about you? Is there someone in your life that you have tried to share God's love with? Have they repeatedly rejected you? How did you feel when you felt you had done everything in your power to bring them to God but they refused? It hurts, doesn't it. That's what I see in David's words.

I was in my twenties I think. I was constantly in pain with my back, and just felt hopeless. I told my dad that I didn't think I would see forty. I was so depressed. At thirty-five I came to know the Lord as my Savior. My whole outlook on life changed. Today I'm approaching 72. We go through those valleys of despair, just as David is going through. So, what do you do?

If you're a child of God you think back to that day that Jesus came into your heart. You remember that God has a very special plan for your life (Jeremiah 29:11-13). You trust God for each day that He gives you to serve Him and worship Him. You will be surprised what a difference that can make. Next you pray! "Lord, what would You have me to do?" He may not answer right then, but suddenly doors will start opening. A path will appear, you will need faith and trust in God to take that path. Then hold on and watch God work.

There are several times in David's life when he might have written the 23rd Psalm. This might be one of them. I think it's interesting that, after making this statement, he goes home. He gathers his six hundred men and they return to the land they had settled in after escaping Saul the first time. That is an interesting thought. When we start having our "pitty-party" we need to stop and return to the time when God first came into our life. We need to remember our "Goliath's" that God defeated and how He has been with us through those valleys.

We have all been "down" it's what we do when we get there that will make the difference in the end. God is right beside you, trust him and walk with Him!

Then Achish gave him Ziklag that day: wherefore Ziklag pertaineth unto the kings of Judah unto this day. (1 Samuel 27:6)

Do you see what's happening? After David leaves his last encounter with Saul he goes back to Achish. He talks Achish into giving him a city called Ziklag. From there he raids three other nations around Achish. All enemies of Israel (Judah). It's like the enemy is housing you while you strike at them. David always seems to be in the right place at the right time. Except for later.

I guess David got over his "pitty-party" (27:1) and is back to focusing on God's plan for his life. David may not know it right now but God is still using him to fulfill his plan for David. It is so easy to get distracted from God's plan when we take our eyes off of God and focus on "self".

It is the same tactic Satan used in the Garden of Eden. Instead of Adam and Eve focused on what God has provided for them, the task God set before them (till the garden) Satan comes in and changes their focus to the fruit on the forbidden tree. Get your mind off the things of God and focus on the desires of the flesh, whatever that may be.

Satan does the same thing to us. We make a covenant with God to be faithful to His will and right away Satan will put distractions to detour our commitment to God. Most of the time it doesn't take much. An emergency, a change in schedule or priority, etc. Anything to draw us away from the commitment we made to God.

It doesn't say in the text whether David prayed and asked God for direction but somehow God got David back on track. He got his focus off of Saul and back to the defense of his country and fighting those enemies. The funny thing is that Achish had no idea David was fighting from Achishs' own land.

Are you distracted from what God has called you to do? Don't misunderstand me. Being focused can get you into trouble. I'm not talking about tunnel vision. I'm talking about what God wants to do in your life. Are you focused on God's will or yours? God may change your direction and circumstances but He always has a purpose in mind to use you. Don't be so heavenly minded that your no earthly good.

God is going to use this change of direction later to put David right where he needs to be. God is training him and his men in warfare and with the countries around them. God, many times, will put challenges in our life to train us for a battle we may face later in life. We need to learn from every situation God puts us in.

Did you notice the time frame mentioned? One year and four months. We read over that in a second and fail to realize that span of time. Over a year and no running from Saul. No hiding and being focused on saving your life. One year and four months can be a very long time. It can be a very short time when you're focused on God and what He is doing in your life. I can imagine the peace David has right now. He has been freed from Saul and now is doing what God called him to do "lead his army in battle." I'm sure the time flew by. David is being prepared for many battles yet to be fought. God is preparing you today for something God wants accomplished. Are you trusting Him, getting prepared, watching for that direction from God?

And Achish said, Whither have ye made a road to day? And David said, Against the south of Judah, and against the south of the Jerahmeelites, and against the south of the Kenites. And David saved neither man nor woman alive alive, to bring tidings to Gath, saying, lest they should tell on us, saying, So did David, and so will be his manner all the while he dwelleth in the country of the Philistines. And Achish believed David, saying, He hath made his people Israel utterly to abhor him; therefore he shall be my servant for ever. (1 Samuel 27:10-12)

David was busy alright. He was fighting the enemies of Israel while Achish thought he was fighting his own people. Remember our timeline, 16 months since his last encounter with Saul. David didn't just hide out, he didn't just sit around waiting for the next encounter. David got busy doing what he could for his people.

That is so important today. There is always work to be done on behalf of God's people. His children should have a task, use their spiritual gift to further God's purpose in this world. When my wife and I were saved we had no idea what that meant, what our spiritual gifts were or that we even had any. We began by signing up to clean the church on Saturdays. It was voluntary. We filled in whatever blanks were left when the quarterly sign-up sheet came to us. We started serving.

One time, as Sunday School Director I had a class of first and second graders. Their teacher was discouraged because the kids would not be still and listen to the lesson, they ran her ragged. One of men, Brother Don, offered to sit in the class. He wasn't a teacher. Don simply sat each Sunday in the class, his presence brought calm out of chaos. Later, he would read the story for the teacher. Don could have chosen not to get involved, but he saw a need, and offered. That class grew from 6-8 to 10-12 in attendance.

When you become a child of God, received Jesus Christ as your Savior, you will receive a spiritual gift that comes with the seal of the Holy Spirit. This spiritual gift is a God-given ability to serve in His church, and thus others. Some people never find their spiritual gift because they don't seek to know. I learned early on, my gift was teaching. Since then I have served as teacher, and Sunday School Director for over thirty years.

I used to get upset when, after the service was over, my wife would mingle and talk with others while I wanted to go to lunch. Then one day I realized she was using her spiritual gift of hospitality. Now I simply wait for her. Do you know what your gift is? You might begin with 1 Corinthians 12 or Romans 12. Seek to find it. Start using it. God will bless you far more than you can imagine.

At the time, I'm sure David had no idea why he was conducting these raids, why he was lying to Achish. It may become clear later. But he had 16 months that he could have just sat around or he could be doing something for his people. That is the choice you have today. It doesn't matter your age. Brother Don was in his fifties when he sat in a Sunday School class to bring order. There is something for you to do. I am in my 70's and God has given me these books to write.

Through the years I have seen so many gifted people serving the Lord. If you were to ask them, they would tell you, first, they had no idea God would call them to this particular ministry, second, God has blessed them so much since they began serving. I see it a lot in the Sunday School ministry. People who have said, "I'm not a teacher", later will fight to keep their class.

Teaching is not the only gift, again, read 1 Corinthians 12 and Romans 12. There are several surveys you can take that will help. Just get busy, God will show you where to serve, and will bless you in the process.

1 Samuel 28

And Samuel said to Saul, Why hast thou disquieted me, to bring me up? And Saul answered, I am sore distressed; for the Philistines make war against me, and God has departed from me, and answereth me no more, neither by prophets, nor by dreams: therefore I have called thee, that thou mayest make known unto me what I shall do. Then said Samuel, Wherefore then dost thou ask me, seeing the Lord is departed from thee, and is become thine enemy? (1 Samuel 28:15-16)

Wait a minute! I thought Samuel was dead? There is a lot of controversy about this chapter. I chose these two verses to cover this whole chapter. Saul, as you see, has lost all connection with God. God has turned His back on Saul. In desperation Saul searches out a medium, many refer to her as "the witch of Endor". Saul has come to the point of doing everything he can to determine God's will.

I was hoping to avoid any more references to Saul, after all this narrative is about David. But there is an important contrast to note here. Shortly after God chose Saul to be king, Saul became jealous and fearful of David. Saul also began making decisions on his own, not thinking to consult God. Even to the point of total disobedience to God's directives from Samuel (Amalekites) (1 Samuel 15). When you ignore divine guidance, it becomes less and less available.

David on the other hand sought God's direction and will on several occasions. There is the difference. What about you? How do you make critical decisions? What is the basis for your decisions? A lot is determined by the foundation that is laid by our parents. Then there is the influence of our peers, we will see this later in Solomon's life. Some may be determined by our education. To me, the most critical input we can have in making decisions is the word of God. How much of God's wisdom is there ingrained in our decision-making process?

Notice the plea in Saul's voice in the verses above: *"God has departed from me and does not answer me anymore."* What a devastating feeling that must be. I wonder if Saul ever recognized exactly where his power came from? Do you? Or, are you one of those who think you have done it all?

One of my favorite scenes is in the movie "Shenandoah" with James Stewart. He is about to bless the food before eating and says something like, "Lord, we plowed the fields, we planted the seed, it wouldn't be here if we hadn't done it all ourselves, but we thank You anyway. Amen." That seems to be the attitude of Saul, until he is headed to battle.

Many times, the source we trust the most for making decisions is a "proven" source. One that we had tried before and proved trustworthy. If you receive bad advice you tend not to return to that well. Have you ever been disappointed in the advice from God's Word? Of course, that depends on two things: One, did you follow it to the letter and two, was it from God? Many times, we think we know God's will but fail to really consult the Bible or God's Spirit if we are a Christian.

Just stop a minute and ponder Saul's position. He refused to obey God (1 Samuel 15), he attempted to offer a sacrifice against God's plan (1 Samuel 13). His jealousy, over David being proclaimed greater than he, many things mounted up for God to turn his back on Saul. Then when Saul needs direction, God is not there. I pray God has not turned His back on you. If you are a child of God, He is ready to guide you but you must be obedient! If you are not a child of God you need to pray and ask Jesus to come into your heart right now, and through His Holy Spirit He will guide your steps along God's plan for your life.

1 Samuel 29

Then said the princes of the Philistines, What do these Hebrews here? And Achish said unto the princes of the Philistines, Is not this David, the servant of Saul the king of Israel, which hath been with me these day, or these years, and I have found no fault in him since he fell unto me unto this day. (1 Samuel 29:3)

The Philistines and the Jews are about to go to war. This will be Saul's last battle. We saw earlier that David was living in the Philistine land (Ziklag). Now Achish has invited David to join him to fight Israel. Achish thinks David would be an ally in the battle but his fellow generals think otherwise. They think David will betray them.

To be honest I don't know why David is here. Maybe to continue to deceive Achish, maybe he doesn't realize what is about to happen. The generals are suspicious since David is a Jew. I think it's interesting that David has a reputation with Achish who says, "*I find no fault in him.*" Even though David has been attacking the Philistine villages up north. Evidently Achish has not found out.

I am reminded of a phrase that would be the greatest sound to any Christian when they arrive in heaven:

> *"His lord said to him, 'Well done, good and faithful servant; you have been faithful over a few things, I will make you ruler over many things. Enter into the joy of your lord. (Matthew 25:23). (NKJV)*

"You have been faithful over a few things" that is awesome to me. God doesn't ask for miracles, just be faithful. He simply asked that we be obedient. To hear Jesus tell us, *"Well done good and faithful servant"* will be the greatest reward we could possibly ask.

David was so faithful to God that he would not lift his hand against a king God had anointed. When David was confronted with seeking direction he sought God's guidance. I don't want you to forget where David came from. He didn't come from seminary, he wasn't a church deacon or pastor, he didn't even teach Sunday School, he was a shepherd boy. God plucked him from the field and made him, eventually, the king of Israel.

God wants to use you as well. How and why are His domain. He simply asks that you to be willing and obedient—much like David. Oh, David made mistakes, we know that, but he always turned to God for forgiveness and repentance and always gave God the glory for his successes!

Achish asks David to return to Ziklag (29:7). Isn't it interesting how God can take, what might prove, a tragic situation and change the course of events. Read this 29th chapter. Do you see God's hand in the events? Because of David's faithfulness to God, God prevents a tragic confrontation. David would not fight his people, and God prevented that.

God is at work in your life right now. If you are a child of God. God has a perfect plan for your life. (Jeremiah 29:11). You just have to trust Him. Ask for His guidance. The neat thing about following after God is that He knows the future. He knows this upcoming battle will be Saul and Jonathan's last. He doesn't want David anywhere near what is about to happen. God will watch over us IF WE LET HIM!

David has come a long way from being a shepherd boy to the next in line for the throne. I still wonder what might have gone through David's head that day that Samuel came to his house, called him out of the pasture and anointed him. It doesn't say in the text if Samuel gave a reason. Then David defeats Goliath, marries, fights many victorious battles. Saul tries to kill him, etc. When you think of the life that he has led to this point you have to see how God's hand was on David. God can work in your life as well. Just look to Him for guidance and strength!

And Achish answered and said to David, I know that thou art good in my sight, as an angel of God: notwithstanding the princes of the Philistines have said, He shall not go up with us to battle.' Wherefore now rise up early in the morning with thy master's servants that are come with thee: and as soon as ye be up early in the morning, and have light, depart. So David and his men rose early to depart in the morning, to return into the land of the Philistines. And the Philistines went up to Jezreel. (1 Samuel 29:9-11)

I almost skipped this passage. There is a great truth here I want to chew on. First, one of my favorite movies is "The Inn of the Sixth Happiness." It's about a missionary to China, a woman with no experience only a calling. In the end, her testimony, converted the leadership of a small village to a saving knowledge of Christ. Just by her actions.

In John it says,

"If you were of the world, the world would love its own.
Yet because you are not of the world, but I chose you out
of the world, therefore the world hates you. (John 15:19)
(NKJV)

Also, one more verse,

And do not be conformed to this world, but be transformed
by the renewing of your mind, that you may prove what is
that good and acceptable and perfect will of God. (Romans
12:2) (NKJV)

Maybe you can see where I'm going with this.

David, while running from Saul sought refuge in Gath which is the land of the Philistines. Basically, hiding in enemy territory. Saul, at this minute, is heading to Jezreel to battle the Philistines. That's why they didn't want David with Achish. Anyway, David was not in his world (Israel) David was in enemy territory. Much like us today.

We are living in enemy territory! This is Satan's world, for a time. We are much like David. What did David do? He made raids against the Philistines, right under Achishs' nose. We have opportunities every day to make a difference while in enemy territory. We have a chance to tell someone about Jesus and how much God loves them. Do you see it?

Later David will become king of Hebron and eventually king of Israel. David doesn't know that yet. Right now, he is doing the best he can with the conditions he is in. What about you? I mentioned a while back about being too earthly minded that we are no heavenly good. We can also be too heavenly minded that we are no earthly good. Our focus should be on what God wants to do with us right here, right now. Also, when we are doing what God wants us to, we can be amazed at what God will do around us.

There is a reason God led David to be in Ziklag at this time. God never does anything by accident. David has a purpose to fulfill. You have a purpose for where you are and what you are doing right now. Have you asked God to reveal what purpose you are to serve? He may not tell you right now, later at some point if you stay focused on God He will reveal His plan. Keep praying, if it serves God's purpose He will show you.

I went through a very trying period in my life. I questioned God every day, "Why is this happening?" A year later on the way to work God revealed it to me. He said, "I wanted to see if you would be faithful." I cried all the way to work. It is sad, today too many people want to blame God right away, and turn their back on Him. God wants people who will be faithful, just as He is faithful. It has always been a practice, since then, when I'm going through a trial, to ask God, "What is the lesson to learn in this storm?" That should be our focus. We will soon see why God put David in the land of the Philistines at this time. Later David will defeat the Philistines in battle.

We are not of this world, we are simply passing through!

1 Samuel 30

And it came to pass, when David and his men were come to Ziklag on the third day, that the Amalekites had invaded the south, and Ziklag, and smitten Ziklag, and burned it with fire; and had taken the women captives, that were therein: they slew not any, either great or small, but carried them away, and went on their way. So David and his men came to the city, and, behold, it was burned with fire; and their wives, and their sons, and their daughters, were taken captives. (1 Samuel 30:1-3)

At this point you start making your list. I defeated Goliath, I won several battles, I married the king's daughter, I spared the king's life twice, I have served You and trusted You. Why is this happening to me? Have you ever done this? You are going through a trial you don't understand and you stark complaining to God, you compare lists. That will never work! God only has one thing on His list, I gave My Son for you! Don't go there!

I wonder if David did that? He has, as I listed, been faithful to God. If you notice in that list I deliberately began each one with "I". We do NOTHING on our own. Any victories we enjoy are simply by God's grace!

I like the way Dr. Charles Stanley explained it: Because God is "All-knowing" He knows where we are at in the storm. Because God is "All-present" He is with us in the storm. And, because He is "All-powerful" He will bring us through the storm. I saw this plaque in Branson once that summarizes that statement: "If God brings you to it, He will bring you through it."

I know because I've been there! The one lesson I've learned from the trials I've experienced is to ask one question of God: "What is the lesson I'm to learn from this test?" As children of God we are expected to grow up as His children. Take a minute and think of all the things you had to learn before even leaving home. I remember when my dad taught me how to hold a knife and fork to eat a piece of meat on my plate, etc. From Kindergarten through College we are constantly learning. It's the same way as a Christian. God has so many lessons to teach us. The biggest, of course, is to wait on His will and plan.

Imagine what might have gone through David's mind when he arrived home. Despair, questioning, etc. Does it say he questioned God? Here is another trait we can add to our list of why David is a man after God's own heart.

I think it's interesting that both here and when Abraham's family (Genesis 14) was kidnapped that they never killed the family members but took them captive. Even in the trial God is still in charge. How do you deal with circumstances you don't understand? Do you rationalize them, do you justify them (it's because I sinned), do you trust that God will reveal the next step? It all depends on your relationship with God. If you have a close relationship, parent to child, type relationship you realize that God only wants the best for you and is trying to teach you something. Have you ever responded to your parent when they spanked you with, "I hate you!" Have you ever responded to God that way? I hope not!

Many times, our response to God's chastisement will determine our relationship with Him. Look at this verse:

> *"And you have forgotten the exhortation which speaks to you as sons: My son, do not despise the chastening of the Lord, nor be discouraged when you are rebuked by Him; for whom the Lord loves He chastens, and scourges every son whom He receives. If you endure chastening, God deals with you as with sons; for what son is there whom a father does not chasten? (Hebrews 12:5-7) (NKJV)*

Do you have that kind of relationship with God? Think about it!

Then David and the people who were with him lifted up their voices and wept, until they had no more power to weep. And David's two wives, Ahinoam the Jezreelitess, and Abigail the widow of Nabal the Carmelite, had been taken captive. Now David was greatly distressed, for the people spoke of stoning him, because the soul of all the people was grieved, every man for his sons and his daughters. But David strengthened himself in the Lord his God. (1 Samuel 30:4-6)

Always ask yourself what would you do. One of the sad results of grief, many times, is that we feel we have to blame someone. I guess it makes the pain easier. It never really helps anything, does it? What a terrible time for David's people. 600 men, David's soldiers, his army, out doing battle against the Philistines only to return home to find their families gone. Want to give up?

Do you have a pencil or pen? Underline these words, *"But David strengthened himself in the Lord his God."* Another trait that makes David a man after God's own heart. David, instead of grieving, took his strength from God. I think this is a great indication of David's relationship with God. The focus is God, the strength comes from God, the comfort comes from God!

I had a relative call me once, struggling with a trial in her life. Almost immediately these verses came to my mind:

> *Blessed be the God and Father of our Lord Jesus Christ, the Father of mercies and God of all comfort, who comforts us in all tribulation, that we may be able to comfort those who are in any trouble, with the comfort with which we ourselves are comforted by God. (2 Corinthians 1:3-4) (NKJV)*

There are two ways to approach these verses in Corinthians. When I first found these, I had thought that the comfort we could give was because we had endured the same trial, thereby we could relate to the one suffering and thus give comfort. Then I backed up and took another look. The comfort we offer is the comfort we have received from Christ. That same peace, comfort and assurance that God has blessed us with through our trials we are able to share that comfort with someone who also is suffering. The point? The comfort comes from God, just as David sought in this passage.

So, think about it. There are two responses: Blame God or trust God! Which do you invoke? There are people that I have run into that will never darken the door of a church again because God disappointed them. Maybe the death of a loved-one. The loss of a job or a child, etc. In every case it is something that happened to them and they blamed God. Of course, more than likely they never prayed and asked God why. Not that God was obligated to answer, sometimes He does sometimes He won't.

The people are ready to stone David, they had to blame someone. David sought comfort in God. I wonder if God, at that time, gave him directions to retrieve their loved ones? At any rate, the key I want to stress is this basic principle of grief. Seek God's comfort and peace and direction. He may not explain why it happened, sometimes we need to just trust God and move on. I know that is hard to accept in the heat of the moment. Meditate on this verse and 2 Corinthians. Ask God for the kind of relationship where, when these tragic events occur, we turn to Him. The One who craves that kind of relationship it talks about in 2 Corinthians. *"The God of all comfort."* Remember that He knows our heart, He created our heart, He does not want it broken! Who better to lean on than the One who gave up His Son for our salvation. Who can explain that much love for His children?

And David said to Abiathar the priest, Ahimelech's son, I pray thee bring me hither the ephod". And Abiathar brought thither the ephod to David. And David enquired at the Lord, saying, Shall I pursue after this troop? Shall I overtake them? And he answered him, Pursue: for thou shalt overtake them, and without fail recover all. (1 Samuel 30:7-8)

Do you have an ephod? This isn't the first time David used an ephod to inquire of the Lord, look at chapter 23:1-6. The creation of the ephod is described in Exodus 28:6-14. It is part of the priests' apparel. This seems to be David's way of determining God's will. How do you determine what God wants you to do?

One thing I noticed about this passage. What would be the "common sense" response to their families being kidnapped and taken away? You would jump on your horse and go after them, right? Of course, you would, it just makes sense. Here David stops and inquires of the Lord. It is very interesting to me. What would normally make common sense David seeks God's will. Why?

God had worked miracles in David's life before, remember Goliath? David had this unique relationship with God. David's life was totally in

God's hands. You can read that in many of his psalms. David trusted God to do the right thing in his life. So naturally he would turn to God for wisdom. Many times, God will do things in our life that may not make sense at the time but later you can see what God was doing—if you're looking!

Again, how do you determine God's will for your life? First you need to be in God's word daily. If for no other reason than to have the mind of God. By getting in His word daily you learn how God thinks, what His priorities are, you learn to "walk with God". Second, you need to be familiar with prayer. I don't mean just asking God's blessing on this or that. I'm talking about seeking God's direction daily.

> "Ask, and it will be given to you, seek, and you will find; knock, and it will be opened to you. For everyone who asks receives, and he who seeks finds, and to him who knocks it will be opened." (Matthew 7:7-8) (NKJV)

We must seek and ask God, to receive direction. To determine God's will.

Thirdly, we must listen. As a child of God (Christian) we have been given the Holy Spirit who dwells within us at conversion. The Holy Spirit will give us direction if we listen. Have you ever heard someone say, "I don't have a peace about that."? They are simply saying that God's Holy Spirit is trying to warn them not to go there. Too many times we have learned to ignore His prompting, His guidance to the point that we are on our own. That doesn't mean He is not there, we have just locked Him in a closet and only take Him out on Sunday, maybe!

David was always, almost, seeking God's will. There are a couple of times when he strayed and it cost him dearly. We should always be open to God's will for our life, His direction. The hardest part, for me anyway, is the waiting. Suppose you have a desire to do something but God's Spirit says no. You argue and debate and give all kinds of reasons why you need to do it now. So, you ignore God, go ahead with your wishes, and disaster happens. You paid a price for getting ahead of God. You see, God might very well have wanted to give you your desires but not at this time. When you get ahead of God you're in for a tragic result!

Just because something seems like plain common sense, you need to pray. It may be God's will but not right now. The closer you walk with God the more peace you will have about every situation, trusting in God's timing is one of the hardest lessons to learn as a Christian. It's important to keep a journal and look back and see how God has worked in your life!

Another thing, did you notice how David got access to the ephod? In both instances, he called for Abiathar, the priest. The priest was given possession of the ephod in Exodus. It was part of his wardrobe. The fourth way we might determine God's will is by attending church, listening to the Word of God and being around God's people.

I can't list how many times I had been struggling with a problem. I go to Sunday morning worship, Sunday School class, even Wednesday night prayer service. I'll be setting there waiting for the service to start, and suddenly, the answer comes. It has happened more times than I can count. Even an idea for my newsletter, Sunday School lesson, a sermon, anything I have been struggling with or even a new idea that I can't wait to get home to research. God has a funny habit of speaking to us in His house! Try it!

Just another note about "common sense". Do you remember Joshua going into the Promised Land? What did Common Sense have to do with the way Joshua defeated Jericho? Think about it. March around the city each day for seven days. On the seventh day march around it seven times and then blow the trumpets. Really? Is that how you defeat a city? There is nothing Common Sense about it. God doesn't deal in Common Sense, God deals in Faith!

And David said to him, Canst thou bring me down to this company? And he said, Swear unto me by God, that thou wilt neither kill me, nor deliver me into the hands of my master, and I will bring thee down to this company. And when he had brought him down, behold, they were spread abroad upon all the earth, eating and drinking, and dancing, because they had taken out of the land of the Philistines, and out of the land of Judah. And David smote them from the twilight even unto the evening of the next day: and there escaped not a man of them, save four hundred young men, which rode upon camels, and fled. (1 Samuel 30:15-17)

Let's set the scene. David had arrived back in Ziklag to find his village had been raided and all the women and children had been taken. The men were so devastated that they blamed David. David rounded up his army to pursue the Amalekites who raided their village. Along the way they found this Egyptian slave. He had escaped his captors. David asked him if he could lead them to the Amalekites. He said he would if they promised not to harm him. Because of this chance encounter with this slave David could find their women and children and free them.

Do you believe in accidents? I mean the "chance" encounter with the people that pass through our lives. In the opening of this book I listed about 40+ men who had passed through my life and left their mark. Take a minute, and make a list of your own. Get a piece of paper and think back to all the different people that had an impact on your life up till now. Do you think they crossed your path by accident? This slave just didn't "happen" to be in David's path. Remember, before David left he asked God if he should go after them. God was in this from the beginning.

The people who pass through our lives serve a purpose. Of course, we must be discerning about their intentions. Satan will also put people in our path to try and lead us away from God. We must be discerning and aware. Those who help in our walk with God, help us to grow in God's word, those who encourage us in the Lord, those we want to listen to.

Do you remember this passage in Hebrews?

> "Let brotherly love continue. Do not forget to entertain strangers, for by doing some have unwittingly entertained angels." (Hebrews 13:1). (NKJV)

You never know if that person who crosses your path, impacts your life, if they were sent from God. Just like this Egyptian slave "just happened" to be found by David's army. Just when he needed him.

I have such fond memories, as a baby Christian, going on youth ministry trips. There would gather, with our pastor, two or three pastors and our youth leaders around the kitchen table with plenty of coffee, talking. I absorbed it all. I listen as a hungry baby wanted to learn as much as I could from those who had walked the walk far longer than I. These are fond memories that contributed to me eventually becoming a pastor for a while, and a lifetime of Sunday School ministry. A young couple who invited us to their home for lunch, shortly after joining the church, to make us feel welcome. The encouragement we received regularly as we grew in the Lord.

Think about this passage when you encounter a stranger. When a visitor comes into your church. If no one else offers, you need to welcome them, encourage them and welcome them into the fellowship. If you read the founding of the early church this is a big part of the growth. Love one

Just a hint. Remember how this began in verse 8, *"So David inquired of the Lord saying, 'Shall I pursue this troop?'"* God gave them the okay, and David later met an escaped Egyptian slave. Interesting!

And David came to the two hundred men, which were so faint that they could not follow David, whom they had made also to abide at the brook Besor: and they went forth to meet David, and to meet the people that were with him: and when David came near to the people, he saluted them. Then answered all the wicked men and men of Belial, of those that went with David, and said, Because they went not with us, we will not give them ought of the spoil that we have recovered, save to every man his wife and his children, that they may lead them away, and depart. (1 Samuel 30:21-22)

After leaving Ziklag, some of David's army of six hundred men, two hundred, became weary. David told them to wait there and rest and the four hundred went on to battle the Amalekites. After the battle David returned to pick them up. Those of the four hundred refused to share the bounty with those who stayed behind. They did not share in the fighting, so they would not share in the bounty.

Maybe it's not the same but I have always marveled at those who work behind the scenes. Those who don't get any recognition, they are not "up front" but without them the work would not get done. For example, the pianist and organist in the church service. Many times, they seem to blend into the overall service. Yet, they are so important for the worship experience.

The trucks that bring the produce to the stores so we can go in and pick up whatever our daily needs might be. The millions of people who work every day behind the scenes to see that our communication system works, we really take them for granted! It's like the fella that remarked that the pastor only works three or four hours a week. They need to walk in his shoes for a week.

These six hundred men of David's had been through many battles prior to this trip back home. Who knows the hardships they endured? Everyone is different. To condemn them for not being able to go on is heartless. From what I read it was David's idea for them to stay behind. I would think if they had been forced to go they might well have endangered the venture or been killed themselves. This shows David's heart.

I think it is interesting that they are referred to as "wicked and worthless". These same fighting men that followed David through the years of running from Saul. How quickly we forget. Why do you suppose God put this episode in His Word? Is there a lesson here for us? I think back to the time Samuel was looking for a king to replace Saul. He came to Jesse's home. Samuel began choosing by the stature of the sons. Then God had to remind Samuel,

> But the Lord said to Samuel, "Do not look at his appearance or at his physical stature, because I have refused him. For the Lord does not see as man sees; for man looks at the outward appearance, but the Lord looks at the heart." (1 Samuel 16:7). (NKJV)

We can see the heart of these four hundred. Granted it probably wasn't the sentiment of all four hundred. Just a few loud mouths that seemed to speak for the rest. That is usually the case. Anyway, it was evident the condition of their heart.

How would you have responded? It isn't "fair" that those who didn't fight should share in the bounty. Really? We have many decisions to make in this life. Some will not be <u>fair!</u> Let me try this: A young man is saved at age 18. He goes on to serve the faithfully for decades. There is an old man around seventy lying on his death bed. He asks Jesus into his heart. He dies shortly after yet both go to the same heaven. Is that fair? It is not for us to say. God deals with each of us differently. You might want to read the words of Jesus in Matthew 20. We need to be careful what we call "fair" and what God calls fair.

Then said David, Ye shall not do so, my brethren, with that which the Lord hath given us, who hath preserved us, and delivered the company that came against us into our hand. For who will harken unto you this matter? But as his part is that goeth down to the battle, so shall his part be that tarrieth by the stuff: they shall part alike. And it was so from that day forward, that he made it a statute and an ordinance for Israel unto this day. (1 Samuel 30:23-25)

The purpose of this study is to find out why David was called, "A man after God's own heart." So, just exactly what is the heart of God? What does that mean? Before we can seek something, we must know what our goal is. So how do you define God's heart?

A good place to start might be:

> *"For God so **loved** the world that He gave His only begotten Son, that whosoever believes in Him should not perish but have everlasting life." (John 3:16) (NKJV)*

So, if God loves us that much, so much that He would offer His Son to establish a personal relationship with us. I think we can assume that God's heart is love towards His creation.

In the verses above do you see that kind of love? Notice something else about those verses. Who does David give the credit for his success? Not his mighty army but to God. I think this is another factor in understanding God's heart. Like it or not God wants the glory! When God does a work in our life, He blesses us, performs great things in our life, God wants the glory. It's that simple. The day we begin to think that we are "special" that's the beginning of our end. Granted we can take pride in our accomplishments, only to the extent that God chose to work through us.

Do you remember David's thought when he went out to retrieve their loved ones? Look here,

> *So David inquired of the Lord, "Shall I pursue this troop?" (1 Samuel 30:8) (NKJV)*

I mean, really? We talked about this earlier. It would be common sense to go after their family but David "inquired of the Lord." God wants to be a part of everything that happens in our life.

> *Behold what manner of love the Father has bestowed on us, that we should be called children of God! Therefore, the world does not know us, because it did not know Him. (1 John 3:1) (NKJV)*

I love that description of us, "the children of God". And our Father wants only the best for us!

There you go, the definition of the heart of God. The relationship of father to child. What a picture of God's heart. There is a relationship there that transcends daily ups and downs, mistakes we might make as a child. There is a word that we hear today that describes that: Unconditional love! That is God's heart! That is the relationship God has with us and we should have with Him.

Our Sunday School class is beginning a study in 2 Samuel. Just today there is that phrase again:

> It happened after this that David inquired of the Lord, saying, "Shall I go up to any of the cities of Judah?" And the Lord said to him, "Go up." David said, "Where shall I go up?" And He said, "To Hebron." (2 Samuel 2:1) (NKJV)

It would be interesting to note just how many times it says, "And David inquired of the Lord." How often do you seek God's guidance?

I hope this investigation into David's life will help us understand better the relationship God wants with us. To seek His guidance, His input into everyday decisions we make. To just automatically know and do God's will in our life. The closer we walk with God the easier it is to discern God's will and purpose for us. When was the last time you turned off ALL distractions and just sat and listened to God? It takes some practice because our minds are wired today for instant actions. We must do it now. Our minds will wander through a huge list of "to dos". We must learn to put those aside and LISTEN for God's direction!

1 SAMUEL 31

Now the Philistines fought against Israel: and the men of Israel fled from before the Philistines, and fell down slain in mount Gilboa. And the Philistines followed hard upon Saul and upon his sons; and the Philistines slew Jonathan, and Abinadab, and Melchi-shua, Saul's sons. And the battle went sore against Saul, and the archers hit him; and he was sore wounded of the archers. Then said Saul to his armourbearer, "Draw thy sword, and thrust me through therewith; lest these uncircumcised come and thrust me through, and abuse me. But his armourbearer would not; for he was sore afraid. Therefore Saul took a sword and fell upon it. (1 Samuel 31:1-4)

What a tragic loss. Here a man who God chose to lead his people now dies in defeat. Not only him but his sons as well. His big concern was his son following him on the throne and now he follows him in death on the battlefield. You can ask one question in Saul's life, "Where was God?" Oh, God was there but not in Saul's life. Saul never sought God's direction like we have noted in David's life. Saul's faith was in himself not in God. Such a huge lesson to learn today!

We left David with his men having victory over the Amalekites who invaded his home.

This is the battle that Achish, king of the Philistines, wanted David to fight in. Isn't it interesting that David was spared this trial? I think it is telling how Saul died. He couldn't even get his armorbearer to perform a noble act because he feared Saul. The fruit of his reign, possibly?

Over these past fifteen chapters which we have read quickly, there are years that have passed. We can miss the concept of time in our reading. For a perspective, remember where we first met David? Here again, we have already had a knowledge of David. If you've never read the Bible you still have heard of David, King of Israel. David was chosen, he didn't volunteer, by God to be the next king of Israel. Look at 1 Samuel 16 again. There is no mention of the reason David was anointed. Was it just understood? David didn't respond as the next king, David went back to the fields. It wasn't until his father, Jesse, sent him with lunch for his older brothers, that David became involved. Later he became Saul's general. When David won some victories and the people began praising David instead of Saul that the conflict between the two emerged.

We don't know the time span. I'm sure it was years. Keep that in mind. To me it seemed that David basically played it by ear. Always seeking God's direction, God's next step. If he knew he would be king he didn't act like it. He trusted God for the time and circumstances.

How about you? We all have dreams, desires, plans, etc. Have you asked God? Has He said, "Wait!"? Can you do that? Maybe you want to help God out and try and move the plan along. DON'T DO IT! God has a plan, God has a time table, God has a purpose for everything that He does. When you begin meddling in God's plans you change the whole over all, objective. You see, God knows what's going to happen ten years from now. If you begin messing with the conditions you can destroy the blessing God had planned! Believe me, I know!

So. Saul is dead, now David can move into Jerusalem and take over. It will help us to watch what David does. How David responds to this tragic ending to Israel's king. That's an interesting question. How would you respond to a great blessing from God? Have you ever heard people say, "If I win the lottery I'm giving God ten percent"? Wow, ten percent when it all came from God in the first place. Like we can buy God off with ten percent. Seriously!

You don't bargain with God. His blessings are for His obedient children. Those who look to Him for guidance and direction. How many great stories have you heard of those who won the lottery? They have a TV series about how the lottery ruined their life. Of course, that wouldn't happen to you, right? Where is your faith? In the lottery or God's provision?

PART TWO: 2 SAMUEL

It is my understanding, in the original Hebrew the books of 1st and 2nd Samuel, 1st and 2nd Kings and 1st and 2nd Chronicles were three books. I believe they were separated in 1611 under King James.

We are beginning, as it were, the second half of King David's life.

David, if you remember, was minding his own business in the field tending his father's sheep. Samuel comes to Jesse looking for someone. It is interesting to me that Samuel never tells Jesse or David why he is looking for someone. Is it implied? Nevertheless, after looking at Jesse's sons, Samuel asks, "Are there any other sons?" They call David from the field. At this point Samuel anoints David.

Not long after that David is sent by his father, from the field, to take a lunch to his bothers. David hears the boasting of Goliath. He asks, "Why doesn't someone fight him?" David takes up the challenge and kills Goliath with a stone right in the forehead. After this David becomes a commander in Saul's army. David receives greater praise from the people than Saul. Saul becomes jealous and attempts, on several occasions, to kill David.

David becomes friends with Jonathan, Saul's son. David is pursued relentlessly by Saul. On two separate occasions David has opportunity to kill Saul. Once, in the cave and later among Saul's own army. Both times David refuses to kill Saul. Eventually David runs to Gath and king Achish gives David the city of Ziklag.

From Ziklag David raids the nearby towns, all in Philistine territory. while keeping this from Achish. When it comes time for Achish and the Philistines to battle Israel, the commanders of the Philistines don't want David anywhere near the battle for fear he would turn on them and fight for Israel. Achish sends him back Ziklag.

When David's 600 men arrive in Ziklag they find that their families and livestock have been kidnapped by the Amalekites. After seeking God's direction David pursues the Amalekites and retrieves their families and belongings.

While this is happening, the Philistines go to war with Saul and the Israelite army. In the battle Saul and his sons are killed. Saul is no longer king of Israel. Israel is without a king. Saul's body is mutilated and his army is disarray.

We pick up the second half of David's story with David receiving word of Saul and Jonathan's death by the Philistine army.

Remember the purpose of this search. We want to find in these writings, why David was called, "A man after God's own heart." One thing we have noticed is that on at least two occasions, before going to battle, David sought God's direction. Before you make a critical decision, what is your source of direction? Your own wisdom? How about the Bible? How about prayer? How do you determine your next step?

Next, thing we notice about David is his reverence for God's anointed. After being threatened twice and then later he has two chances to kill Saul yet he refuses. Logically he has every right. Yet Saul was anointed by God to be king. David refused to lift a hand against Saul.

2 Samuel 1

Now it came to pass after the death of Saul, when David was returned from the slaughter of the Amalekites, and David had abode two days in Ziklag; It came even to pass on the third day, that, behold, a man came out of the camp from Saul with his clothes rent, and earth upon his head: and so it was, when he came to David, that he fell to the earth, and did obeisance. And David said unto him, From whence comest thou? And he said unto him, Out of the camp of Israel am I escaped. (2 Samuel 1:1-3)

When was the last time you received bad news? Depending on the news, we may act in many different ways. You have a loved one, they have been ill for many months, you receive word that they have passed away. How do you react? It could depend on what you know about that person. Do they know the Lord? That can make a huge difference in how you react. Your sorry for the loss but at peace about where they are.

You receive news that your bank account has been hacked and all your money is gone. Besides that, your identity has been stolen. How do you react? Total despair? Maybe not so much when you have your faith in the God who owns everything. That was HIS money that was taken. You still have your identity in Christ. It can make a huge difference in how you look at the situation.

My first call, as a new pastor, was to go to the hospital to a couple who had just lost their baby to S.I.D.S. I'm thinking all the way to the hospital, "What could I possibly tell them?" There wasn't a lot I could say then. I made several visits with them afterward. Encouraging them, praying with them. When I left the church, I had news that were going to have another baby. How do you respond to bad news?

David has just come from a great victory over the Amalekites! All his family and possessions were restored. His army was celebrating. Here comes a messenger with bad news. Doesn't that always seem to be the case? It seems God will not let us be happy very long. Friends, remember where we are. A world without God very seldom has good news to share. Unless, that news is about the love of Jesus!

As Christians, we can respond to bad news in a way that the world doesn't understand. We can respond with peace. Because we know who is in charge. That doesn't mean we don't mourn, that doesn't mean we celebrate a loss. It means we have a peace within us that tells us there is another day.

Recently, I watched a movie called, "90 Minutes in Heaven." The thing that intrigued me the most was the time he spent just greeting those he knew from his past. Continually walking through crowds of people he knew in this life. Greeting them, smiling, laughing, rejoicing that he got to see them again. That's what heavens is. Reuniting with our loved ones who have long since departed this world.

David is about to receive some bad news. The idea I want you to think about is, how do you respond to bad news? Where is your faith? Are you focused on this world at this time? Or, do you have such a relationship with God that you can look passed tragedy and see God's hand in the circumstance? From what I know of David, so far, David will respond with that special relationship that comes from an intimate walk with God.

And David said unto him, How went the matter? I pray thee tell me. And he answered, That the people are fled from the battle, and many of the people also are fallen and dead; and Saul and Jonathan his son are dead also And David said unto the young man that told him, How knowest thou that Saul and Jonathan his son are dead? And the young man that told him said, As I happened by chance upon mount Gilboa, behold, Saul leaned upon his spear; and, lo, the chariots and horsemen followed hard after him. . (2 Samuel 1:4-6).

Do you remember this man being mentioned in the previous text? Me neither.

David knew there was to be a battle. Remember, he was to be a part of it until Achishes generals told him otherwise (1 Samuel 29). David went back to Ziklag only to find his village was raided by the Amalekites. He has returned to Ziklag and now this messenger comes from the battle and David wants to know what happened.

Don't miss his reference to "by chance". Understand that nothing happens by "chance". I think it is interesting today just how many people "happen" to have their cell-phones handy to record an incident. Nothing happens by chance!

As far as witnesses go. I'm sure you have asked yourself why are their four gospels? Before I answer that, let me remind you that First and Second Chronicles cover pretty much the same material that is in First and Second Samuel. In the gospel's we have four testimonies of the same event. All four gospels were written years after Jesus ascended into heaven. All of them over 50 years after Jesus left. Thank God for the Holy Spirit that brought these events to the apostle's mind. There are just a few events that are mentioned in all four gospels. Why is that? Matthew was written to the Jews. Mark to the Greeks, Luke to Romans and John to the Gentiles. Each with a different theme and focus. Most of the parables are in Luke. Matthew is constantly referring to their past history, "As it is written". Matthew keeps pointing to the prophecy fulfillment.

So, what is the greatest message we have as Christians to share our faith? Simple! What God has done in our life. We can know the Roman's Road, and a bunch of other Scriptures but when we share what God has done in our life, they can't dispute it! It's actual living proof of how God can change a life! That has the greatest impact on a lost person! And the prompting of the Holy Spirit of course!

That is what is supposed to give authority to the message this guy brings. He was there. He saw it happen. David takes him at his word. Wait till you see what happens, because of his testimony.

Just as an aside. Notice the concern in David's voice. He wants to know the outcome. I wonder what went through his mind. Here is Saul, the one who has chased him, hounded him, and tried to kill him. In the same battle is David's closest friend, Jonathan. This may be another insight into why David was called, "A man after God's own heart." How he responds to Saul's death. His arch-enemy, dead!

How do you process that which you hear? Someone once said, "Believe none of what you hear, and half of what you see." Skeptic? That is even more true today. What about what you read? The only true source of truth today is what is written in the word of God. Chew on it, meditate on it, absorb it. It can be a foundation to filter all other messages through. The more we know the word of God the harder it is for us to be fooled by the messages of this world. Get grounded in God's word and then trust God's Holy Spirit to reveal His truth to you!

And when he looked behind him, he saw me, and called unto me. And I answered, here am I. And he said unto me, Stand, I pray thee, upon me, and slay me: for anguish is come upon me, because my life is yet whole in me. So I stood upon him, and slew him, because I was sure that he could not live after that he was fallen: and I took the crown that was upon his head, and the bracelet that was on his arm, and have brought them hither unto my lord. (2 Samuel 1:7-10)

Have you ever run across someone like this? They know the Christian lingo, they talk a good talk but the Spirit is not there! The devil is constantly trying to deceive us. He knows the words, but they are not of God. As a young Christian, we can be tricked into thinking someone knows the Lord but our Spirit does not bear witness with them. Their words are hollow.

This messenger brought, what he thought, was the message David wanted to hear. He knew that Saul had chased after David for years. He knew that Saul wanted David dead. He thought he was bringing the message that David wanted to hear. But, it didn't stop there. He thought that if he was the one who brought it to pass that David would reward him. Those who "speak" the language of God and expect that God's people will be impressed, I'm sorry. Words are cheap. It's the life that is measured, and God does the measuring!

I met a guy once in a Christian camp that went out of his way to tell me that he led over three-thousand souls to Christ. My thought was, were they discipled? He was looking for a notch on his belt. I'm sorry! That may seem cruel, there is far more to the Christian witness than just leading people to the Lord.

This messenger, I think it's interesting that he is an Amalekite, sought to please David. He didn't know David. This can be amplified in what we see on TV. The "evangelist" tells us what we want to hear. Not what the Bible says. Think about what happened in the Garden of Eden. Satan knew just what to tell Eve to get her focused on that fruit instead of what God told them. This Amalekite was David's enemy. He thought that by telling him that Saul was dead it would save his life.

You remember how Saul died? He fell on his own sword. This messenger was taking glory for himself, so he thought. This is a great principle we need to learn. All truth is the Word of God. Truth is what we are about. When was the last time you heard someone warn us about the decision we need to make about eternity? Most don't want to be confronted about life after death. We shy away from grave yards. We don't want this discussed at funerals. The truth! We will all stand before the judgment seat of Christ one day.

Beware of the preacher who brings the message we want to hear instead of the message we NEED to hear. I heard someone say recently, "If the pastor doesn't step on my toes, he is not doing his work!" I love that. I wonder what David's response would have been, had this soldier told David the truth. It never hurts to tell the truth.

I see a messenger who couldn't wait to bring this news to David. Maybe thinking a reward. It's almost like people who live a "good" life and think that message will get them into heaven. The truth is, it's our relationship with God's Son, and only that relationship that will get us into heaven. When we have asked Jesus into our heart and accepted Him as our Savior, God sees the truth and will open the gates of heaven for us. If God does not see that relationship we will be as this soldier, bearing a lye hoping to win God's favor. The only thing God wants to see in us is the blood of His Son Jesus!

And David said unto the young man that told him, Whence art thou? And he answered, I am the son of a stranger, an Amalekite. And David said unto him, How wast thou not afraid to stretch forth thine hand to destroy the Lord's anointed? And David called one of the young men, and said, Go near, and fall upon him. And he smote him that he died. And David said unto him, Thy blood be upon thy head; for thy mouth hath testified against thee, saying, I have slain the Lord's anointed. (2 Samuel 1:13-16)

Is there something in your life, no matter what, you will not do? Remember, God gave David two opportunities to kill Saul. Both times

David said, "I will not lift a hand against God's anointed." (1 Samuel 24:6, 26:11). From the very beginning David had made a covenant in his heart that he would not lift a hand against Saul, even though Saul had tried to kill him many times and relentlessly chased him.

I had the funniest thought with this entry. I wonder if we could put the "church" in the place of Saul? Saul is far from perfect, much like the church. But, Saul was anointed by God to be king of Israel. Jesus established the church to do His work in this lost world. How many times have we turned our back on "the Lord's anointed" because we were wronged, misunderstood, offended, etc. David recognized that Saul, as imperfect as he was, was God's chosen king for the time being. The church is God's chosen vessel, for the time being, to bring His message to this world. Is it a stretch? I don't know.

Too many times we are so quick to judge and turn our backs on the things of God. Maybe it's our way of blaming God for our mistakes. The church gets blamed for a lot of things, it's true. It is still God's chosen vessel to accomplish evangelism, mission work, community service, etc. in this world. Don't turn your back on God's anointed!

I think it is interesting that this guy was an Amalekite. Remember, David had just returned from killing a bunch of Amalekites for raiding his town. I don't think it really mattered. He could have been a Jew and David would have had him killed. This was a principle David lived by, and stood on!

Again, how about you? Are there standards in your life that you refuse to relinquish? Standards that you simply will not compromise? Can you list them? One more thing, beware, by taking a stand on these principles that is the one area Satan will attack over and over. If he can get you to compromise on one of these he has you by the neck.

Do you think David had the opportunity to say, "well in this case it's okay.?" It can be so easy sometimes to justify breaking your conviction "just this once". Really? If that's the case it is not a conviction but a suggestion. Compromise is the devil's tactic. Either you have a standard or you don't.

Great! Saul is dead, now David can go to Jerusalem and take his rightful place on the throne, right? One of the hardest lessons I ever had to learn was to not get ahead of God. It's God's time, God's place, God's will. When you go around knocking down the doors that God has not opened you are looking for trouble! David knows this. Another reason David was a man after God's own heart was that David knew how to wait on God. You can see that principle all through the Psalms. To wait on God, you must trust His timing and His leadership and to do that you must be walking in God's footsteps, following close behind and allowing God to open the doors at the right time and the right place.

PSALM OF DAVID

And David lamented with this lamentation over Saul and over Jonathan his son: (Also he bade them teach the children of Judah the use of the bow; behold, it is written in the book of Jasher.) The beauty of Israel is slain upon thy high places: how are the mighty fallen! Tell it not in Gath, publish it not in the streets of Askelon; lest the daughters of the Philistines rejoice, lest the daughters of the uncircumcised triumph. (2 Samuel 1:17-20)

Joshua also quotes from the Book of Jasher:

> *Then Joshua spoke to the Lord in the day when the Lord delivered up the Amorites before the children of Israel, and he said in the sight of Israel, "Sun, stand still over Gibeon; and Moon, in the Valley of Aijalon." So, the sun stood still, and the moon stopped, till the people had revenge upon their enemies. Is this not written in the Book of Jasher? So, the sun stood still in the midst of heaven, and did not hasten to go down for about a whole day. (Joshua 10:12-13). (NKJV)*

God literally stopped the sun for a whole twenty-four hours to allow Israel to have a victory.

Did you catch the last part of verse 20? *Lest the daughters of the Philistines rejoice."* Do you remember what the Philistines did when they found Saul's body in the field? They took his head to Gath and celebrated his death. David will soon avenge God's people. It has always fascinated me; the attitude David has for Saul.

I have struggled with an assumption made in 1 Samuel 16. Samuel was told by God that he was to search out another king for Israel because He has taken His hand off Saul. When Samuel goes to the house of Jesse, he eventually finds David and anoints him. Nowhere in this text does it say that Samuel told David he was anointed king. God told Samuel, but did Samuel tell David. Later Saul knew about David.

The reason I bring this up is the attitude of David. Suppose he was told by Samuel he was being anointed king. Did you notice where David went after being anointed? He went back to being a shepherd. He didn't raise an army and go after Saul. Maybe, David had so much faith in God's plan, God's will, that he simply said, "Okay, I will wait until God opens the door, for the proper time for me to become king." Isn't that amazing?

Another thought, David, when he was anointed knew that God had set him apart for something but God didn't reveal that purpose until later, maybe when he fought Goliath. We can't know what took place that day in Jesse's house. We can only marvel at how God worked in David's life up to this point.

David had such a reverence for King Saul, God's anointed, that David would not lift a hand against him, no matter the circumstances. We've covered this before. Here is another trait we can mark down in our search, why David was called a man after God's own heart. The trait? Faith in God's timing and God's plan. Don't forget how many times, when David had a decision to make, it was said, "And David inquired of the Lord." That needs to be an act of our daily living and meditation.

To walk with God, you must allow Him to lead. When we start making decisions on our own, not seeking God's guidance, we are influenced by so many other factors that we can get out of God's will. Unless we have a daily relationship, we are so easily distracted and led astray. When it comes time, you might want to remember David's principle: "Inquire of the Lord." Pray, ask God to show you the right path to take. Don't be in a hurry to make a decision. If you make the wrong one, the results will be far costlier than if you waited for God's guidance! Believe me, this is from experience!

Ye mountains of Gilboa, let there be no dew, neither let there be rain, upon you, nor fields of offerings: for there the shield of the mighty is vilely cast away, the shield of Saul, as though he had not been anointed with oil. From the blood of the slain, from the fat of the mighty, the bow of Jonathan turned not back, and the sword of Saul returned not empty. (2 Samuel 1:21-22)

We continue in David's lament for the death of Saul and Jonathan. I have talked with some pastors and I also agree, the hardest funeral to do is for a lost person. Of course, we can never be sure of their spiritual condition. We can only try to judge by their life testimony. Only God knows their heart. If such is the case, there is no hope for that lost loved one. There is no rejoicing. Still, a funeral is a fantastic place to present the gospel message of salvation by faith in Jesus Christ. People are confronted with their own mortality, death is a certainty!

When I came across this psalm I noticed something, and I underlined it. Three times David says, *"How the mighty have fallen."* (v. 19,25,27). To me this makes Saul's death even more tragic. I'm sure you've thought at some point, "what might have been?" If things had turned out different, etc. You can surely say that of Saul. I talked about this earlier, maybe David had the same thought. If Saul had just kept his eyes on God and not turned them on his own pride and arrogance. Of course, this is the lesson we must learn as well. The minute we begin to think we are something God has a way of bringing us back to earth.

Yet, we see in this psalm David's reverence for the relationship Saul once held. The office that God called Saul to. You might say that David honored the "office" far more than the man. Three times David mentions Jonathan in this tribute. Recognizing Jonathan's expertise with the bow. We know from our reading how close David was to Jonathan. It was with the bow that Jonathan signaled David to flee Saul.

I want you to note another term used here, "high places" this was where the Israelites made a place to worship outside of Jerusalem. This was also the place where they kept their idols. When you read through Kings you will notice this term used a lot. The king's relationship with God is determined, many times, by what they did with the "high places."

In a sense, you could read that David honored their bravery, their valiant fight, their willingness to fight for Israel. David kept his focus on his country's loss, and not on Saul's spiritual condition. He honored Saul for his authority not his relationship with God. It's a shame we must distinguish between the two. Our testimony should be God first, then country, then family. It has ever been so in the early days of the founding of our country.

There is a phrase that might speak a bit to what I just said. *"The shield of Saul, not anointed with oil."* (21b). We talked earlier about the anointing of David in Jesse's house. If the picture of "anointing" is that God has His hand on that anointed. What is David saying here? That God removed His blessing on Saul's sword. I thought it was funny. In the movie, "The Longest Day" one of soldiers asked if God was behind their invasion of France at Normandy (because of the bad weather). It was reported that during the Civil War both sides thought that God was on their side. Interesting thought, considering David's description of Saul's sword.

There is something else we need to note here about David. He never mentions anything about who will reign in Israel now. You think he would gather his men and head to Jerusalem. He doesn't. I won't spoil our search. But it also gives us an insight into David's heart. His king has fallen, his best friend has fallen, his focus is on acknowledging their country's loss. His heart is broken over Jonathan and grieves for his country!

First, I want us to think back a moment. Look at these two verses:

> Then Samuel took the horn of oil and anointed him in the midst of his brothers; **and the Spirit of the Lord came upon David from that day forward**. So, Samuel arose and went to Ramah. (1 Samuel 16:13). (NKJV)

Now look at this verse:

> **But the Spirit of the Lord departed from Saul,** and a distressing spirit from the Lord troubled him. (1 Samuel 16:14). (NKJV)

I have been troubled about whether David was aware that he was anointed king of Israel. One more verse:

> Now the Lord said to Samuel, "How long will you mourn for Saul, seeing I have rejected him from reigning over Israel? Fill your horn with oil, and go, I am sending you to Jesse the Bethlehemite. For I have provided Myself a king among his sons." (1 Samuel 16:1). (NKJV)

Maybe Samuel told David he was the new king. I think not. God's Spirit is not in the habit of revealing God's plans in advance. Maybe on very rare occasions, but not now. I think David simply trusted God to lead one day at a time. Why else would David, after being anointed, head back to the shepherd's field? The few times that David turned a deaf ear to the promptings of God's Spirit, he got in trouble!

Saul and Jonathan were lovely and pleasant in their lives, and in their death they were not divided: they were swifter than eagles, they were stronger than lions. Ye daughters of Israel, weep over Saul, who clothed you in scarlet, with other delights, who put on ornaments of gold upon your apparel. (2 Samuel 1:23-24)

What kind of spirit would it require of David to "sing" this psalm for Saul and Jonathan? It just amazes me. Until I remembered a principle that Jesus taught in the Gospels. In the Sermon on the Mount Jesus said:

> "But I say to you, love your enemies, bless those who curse you, do good to those who hate you and pray for those who spitefully use you and persecute you. (Matthew 5:44). (NKJV)

Isn't it interesting that this biblical principle, taught by Jesus, would be demonstrated in the life of David? Not so amazing, God's principles are consistent throughout the Bible. What is taught in the New Testament is demonstrated in the Old Testament.

Have you ever heard a rabbi or Jewish person "sing" a psalm? It is awesome. The feeling and passion and expression is amazing. Close your eyes and imagine David singing this psalm for the people who have lost their king in battle. The sorrow in David's heart for his kindred-spirit, Jonathan. David is not thinking about what comes next, he is mourning the loss of his king.

David makes a note that the two died together, *"and in their death, they were not divided."* Father and son. David knew the conflict between the two, because of him. That doesn't make it any easier, does it? Jonathan loved David, Saul hated him. Those feelings are lost in this mourning process. I think it is interesting how our loved ones, after they have departed, can still have a profound effect on our lives. The feelings we have toward them seem to carry over in our lives. Though they have long sense gone to be with the

Lord, or not. They still effect our lives. Either we want to make them proud, or we want to carry on their names, etc.

Many times, our relationship with someone who has left, can hurt our relationship with God. How many times have you attended a funeral in a church, only to find out later that family members will not return to that church, because that was the last place they saw their loved one. That's sad really. Are your memories sad ones? Yes, they have departed, the great thing is that one day you will be with them forever. Why do you take out your grief on the Lord's house? I will get off my soapbox. I only share this because I have seen it too many times, as a pastor, and a church member. Maybe I chose to think of it positively. When I go back to that place I am reminded of what they meant in my life and look forward to seeing them again!

How are the mighty fallen in the midst of the battle! O Jonathan, thou wast slain in thine high places. I am distressed for thee, my brother Jonathan: very pleasant hast thou been unto me: thy love to me as wonderful, passing the love of women. (2 Samuel 1:25-26)

As we come to an end of David psalm on the passing of King Saul and Jonathan I'd like to take a different tack. It's known that God will use neighboring countries to work His will on Israel. The Philistines are His favorite.

Remember how and when David entered the picture? He was tending his sheep, after Samuel anointed him, and his father asked him to take a lunch to his sons on the battlefield with Saul. Who was Israel fighting? The Philistines, who had this tremendous soldier named Goliath. David defeated him and became famous as a warrior for Saul. This made Saul jealous of David. Saul tried to kill him several times.

David runs from Saul. Where does he go? He goes to Achish, the king of the Philistines. Achish allows David to hide in a city called Ziklag. There David conducts raids on Philistine cities. Kills everyone so that Achish doesn't find out what he is doing. Later, Achish invites David to fight with him in a battle. Who are the Philistines fighting? Israel! The generals object to David being there and David is sent back to Ziklag. There he has a confrontation with the Amalekites.

While David is fighting the Amalekites, Israel is being defeated badly by the Philistines. In the battle Saul and Jonathan are killed. It's interesting that David had two opportunities to kill Saul but it was not God's plan. God used the Philistines to accomplish His plan of removing Saul and setting up David as eventual king of Israel. So, what does this have to do with me?

Think about it. Is there a Philistine in your life? That person that just irritates you like crazy. Are their forces around you, that seem to be working against your every desire? You know what you want to accomplish but it just can't seem to come together. Have you asked God?

When we won't listen to God, like Saul, God must use other means to get our attention. If that still doesn't work, then He will use others, and other circumstances to accomplish God's purpose. Our first response, of course, must be to pray. "God what is it You are trying to tell me?" When we are in God's will there is a certain peace that helps us know we are on the right track. I'm sure David experienced this peace when he refused to kill Saul. Killing Saul was the "logical" thing to do. Here, were two perfect opportunities, but David refused, it was not the time.

We need to be aware of God working in the people He brings into our lives. Remember that passage in Hebrews:

> *Do not forget to entertain strangers, for by doing some*
> *have unwittingly entertained angels. (Hebrews 13:2)*
> *(NKJV)*

Angels are God's messengers. They are sent into our lives to get out attention, change our direction, get us to look to God. God used the Philistine army to get Israel's attention. To begin the process of installing David as their king. David will later defeat the Philistines in a great battle.

I think that is one of the great lessons from the Old Testament. That is how God will sometimes use enemies, to get us to return to God. To look up, to pray for God's guidance. What does it take to get your attention? To get you to ask God, "What's going on in my life?" If we will not listen to God's Spirit within us He must use other means to bring us where He can use us. We must be yielded for God to begin a great work in us. In *Experiencing God* by Dr. Henry Blackabye, he tells us to find out where God is at work and join Him there. God has to get us to turn around and see where God is working, to do that He uses the Philistines!

COFFEE BREAK

Take a trip with me. Let's go on an imaginary trip back in time. I'd like you to picture in your mind a meeting in heaven. Try to imagine what might take place when the psalmist David has the opportunity to meet Miss Fanny Crosby. Of course, Miss Crosby has her eyesight at this time. Just imagine the conversation that might have taken place.

Now let's imagine an earlier meeting. Try to picture the first time Miss Crosby meets her Savior. The writer of such hymns as: "All the Way My Savior Leads Me", "Tell Me the Story of Jesus", "Jesus Keep Me Near the Cross", "I Am Thine O Lord", "Pass Me Not O Gentle Savior", "Jesus Is Tenderly Calling", "Blessed Assurance, Jesus Is Mine", "Redeemed"!

Can you imagine that meeting?

Okay, let's imagine one more meeting. You guessed it. Imagine when David, the writer of the 23rd Psalm and so many others, gets to meet his Shepherd face to face. That would be something to see, wouldn't it?

There is one more meeting we need to try to imagine. The Bible tells us there will be no tears in heaven. I must disagree. Think about that time when YOU, first meet Jesus face to face. For me, my eyes will be filled with tears of joy. Just the thought of that first meeting with the Savior who gave His life on a cruel cross just so I might have the honor of meeting Him face to face, and to spend eternity in heaven with Him. I wonder if it would be proper to hug Jesus?

I don't care for the flavored coffees. I have been drinking Folgers since I was ten years old. Just give me a hot, black, coffee with no sugar, no milk, perfect!

I don't know what your feelings are about the church. I was saved when I was thirty-five. I believe in the work of the church with all my heart! Jesus did!

The morning worship service on a Sunday morning is the perfect way to start a new week. In the Bible, it's called the "first day of the week." It's the beginning of a new work week. A week full of promise of what God can and will do in your life. It's exciting! Hymns of praise. Great Bible teaching in the message from our pastor. Great Bible teaching in our Sunday School class! Great fellowship with fellow believers. Oh, the power of prayer throughout the service! It's just a great time to begin a week.

Now here's what's weird! The evening worship service!

To me the evening worship service has the feeling of putting a period at the end of a sentence. It is a celebration of a week concluded, where God worked His miracle of life throughout the past week. God has concluded a week of blessing, just watching and reflecting on what God has done this past week. It just seems to be a perfect conclusion to a week that God was present. There are the hymns, the Bible study and the fellowship. There is also a sense of completion. God has done His thing in the past week. He has brought me to this time of reflection and meditation in His house. I can only respond with "Thank you Jesus" for being with me over this past week. Thank you for making your presence known and for the prayers you answered, and those You have yet to answer.

I know this seems backward but it's how God has laid this important day of the week on my heart. I hope you are a regular church attender. Leave the politics at home, and the fellowship with God!

2 Samuel 2

And it came to pass after this, that David enquired of the Lord, saying, Shall I go up into any of the cities of Judah? And the Lord said unto him, Go up. And David said, Whither shall I go up? And he said, Unto Hebron. So David went up thither, and his two wives also, Ahinoam the Jezreelitess, and Abigail Nabal's wife the Carmelite. And his men that were with him did David bring up, every man with his household: and they dwelt in the cities of Hebron. (2 Samuel 2:1-3)

I don't think I need to point out the beginning of these verses. *"And David inquired of the Lord."* Think about what just happened. The king is dead. The "logical" move would be to go to Jerusalem and take over, right? David sought God's direction AND timing! That is so important. We all know how this ended. David didn't! David wanted to do it God's way in God's time!

Remember where we left David? He and his army had just returned from defeating the Amalekites and rescuing their family members and possessions. They are in Ziklag. David had just buried Saul and Jonathan. So now what? "Inquire of the Lord!"

Judah and Benjamin will eventually become what was known as "The Southern Tribes" or Judah or Jerusalem. The "Northern Tribes" consisted of the remaining ten tribes of Israel. They were known as Samaria, or Israel. At this time, there is another divide, Judah or Hebron verses the north. God tells David to go to Hebron, the capitol if you will of the south. It seems Israel is always divided. Even in Israel today.

David's two wives, at this time, are always noted the same way. I think it's interesting that Abigail is always called, "the widow of Nabal". The picture is EVERYBODY is now headed back to Israel and the province of Hebron. All by God's direction. I wonder what David's men were thinking here? From the beginning, they wanted to kill Saul and take over. Saul's dead why are we not going to Jerusalem?

Hebron, is about thirty miles south of Jerusalem. Hebron and Judah are essentially the same designation. If you have read much of the Old Testament, especially in this time period, you will notice that they may have several different names for the same territory. It isn't until after Solomon's reign that a clear split is registered. The northern ten tribes and southern two, Judah and Benjamin.

This also reminds me, at that time God will use Assyria to punish the northern tribes and Babylon to punish the southern two tribes. Like I mentioned before.

I have been a Christian for over thirty years. This lesson has been difficult for me to learn. The lesson of "asking God for direction." Too many times I thought or wanted to go a certain direction only to find out that I left God at the crossroad. Not long after leaving God do I realize I am without a rudder!

Do you think this might be a critical reason David was called "a man after God's own heart?" David sought God's direction. But, of course, we know better than God what's best for us. We are able to see way into the future and know just the right moves to make. Sorry, I couldn't resist. We don't know what's going to happen in the next hour, let alone weeks from now.

I love the parable Jesus teaches in Luke 12:

> So, he said, "I will do this: I will pull down my barns and build greater, and there I will store all my crops and my goods. And I will say to my soul, 'Soul, you have many goods laid up for many years; take your ease; eat, drink, and be merry.'" But God said to him, "Fool! This night your soul will be required of you." (Luke 12:18-20) (NKJV)

And the men of Judah came, and there they anointed David king over the house of Judah. And they told David, saying, That the men of Jabesh-gilead were they that buried Saul. And David sent messengers unto the men of Jabesh-gilead, and said unto them, Blessed be ye of the Lord, that ye have shewed this kindness unto your lord, even unto Saul, and have buried him. And now the Lord shew kindness and truth unto you: and I also will require you this kindness, because you have done this thing. Therefore now let your hands be strengthened, and be ye valiant: for your master Saul is dead, and also the house of Judah have anointed me king over them. (2 Samuel 2:4-7)

Do you have a definition for the word "kindness"? My definition is: doing something for someone, not expecting any reward or recognition. It's an interesting word. David recognized the kindness of Jabesh Gilead for seeing to the burial of Saul. You might want to read the end of 1 Samuel 31. The way the Philistines treated the body of Saul when they found him in the field of battle.

In the margin of my Bible I wrote these three references: 1 Samuel 16:13; 2 Samuel 2:7; and 2 Samuel 5:3. These three references refer to the three times David was anointed. First, by Samuel in Jesse's house. Here in 2 Samuel as the king of Judah or Hebron. Thirdly as king of Israel in the fifth chapter. That is amazing to me.

Did you catch David's reference in the verses above, *"You are blessed of the Lord for you have shown kindness to your lord (Saul).* Do you think God takes note of the kindness we show? David thought so. I think so. We may not experience it right away but God recognizes that character in our hearts. It's really not something you consciously think of. I think your heart has to be right with God. When you have the right heart, the kindness comes automatically.

Does that mean that only Christians can be kind? Of course not. Kindness is taught not caught. When you are raised around kindness it becomes part of your thought process. One of my favorite country songs is by Clay Walker, it's called "Chain of Love". I don't expect it did very well on the charts. It talks about passing on a kindness to the next person you meet. The neat thing about the song is that the kindness comes full circle. Accident? I think not!

Here is another trait that is, sadly, disappearing in our culture. Look at these words: *So, David sent messengers to the men of Jabesh Gilead, and said to them, "You are blessed of the Lord."* The point is that David basically thanked them for their kindness. "Thank you" is disappearing from our culture, that's sad. If you think not, just pay attention to those around you in public places. Courtesy to each other is getting scarce. Just observe those in the super-market, etc. It's sad.

Now David has been anointed the king of the south, the southern tribe (Judah). He still hasn't achieved the destination that God has planned for him. So, he takes his army and goes to Jerusalem and takes the throne? No. Again, David is honored that the men of Judah have called him as their king. Now he continues to wait on God to bring to pass God's plan for his life.

You might be getting annoyed with me stressing this point. It is so important. We can really mess things up by getting out ahead of God. We think if we don't act right now we are going to miss something. Nothing is further from the truth! It must be in God's time and above all in God's way. He is working behind the scenes to bring you to the right place at the right time to perform His perfect will!

But Abner the son of Ner, captain of Saul's host, took Ishbosheth the son of Saul, and brought him over to Mahanail; and made him king over Gilead, and over the Ashurites, and over Jezreel, and over Ephraim, and over Benjamin, and over all Israel. Ishbosheth Saul's son was forty years old when he began to reign over Israel, and reigned two years. But the house of Judah followed David. And the time that David was king in Hebron over the house of Judah was seven years and six months. (2 Samuel 2:8-11)

Just a brief history lesson. This isn't the first time Abner appears.

> *And David called out to the people and to Abner the son of Ner, saying, "Do you not answer, Abner?" Then Abner answered and said, "Who are you, calling out to the king?" So, David said to Abner, "Are you not a man? Why then have you not guarded your lord the King? For one of the people came in to destroy your lord the king. This thing that you have done is not good. As the Lord lives, you deserve to die, because you have not guarded your master, the Lord's anointed." (1 Samuel 26:14-16a). (NKJV)*

This is the second opportunity that David had to kill Saul. David and Abishai had crept into Saul's camp and stole Saul's spear and jug of water that lay at Saul's head and left. Here, David is confronting Abner who was supposed to be guarding Saul. Oh, Saul was surrounded by three-thousand soldiers. David was furious that Abner had allowed *"the Lord's anointed"* to be vulnerable this way. Abner was commander of Saul's army.

Abner wasted no time in installing HIS man as king. Did you notice that Abner didn't "inquire of the Lord?" Of course, since Jonathan was also killed in the battle the line of the king would continue to the next-of-kin, that being Ishbosheth.

I'd like you to note the language used in these three verses. This will continue through the books of First and Second Kings. Even at this point, as I said earlier, there is a divide in Israel. The northern tribes, and here, Judah. Another name for the northern tribes is Ephraim. I had always thought the division between the north and south began with the son of Solomon, Rehoboam. It began long before that. Even in David's reign. David united the kingdoms for a short time.

I mentioned earlier to keep an eye out for Abner. He is like the guy behind the throne that manipulates and maneuvers his way to success. David will deal with him later. Did you catch the first part of verse 9? "and he (Abner) made him king." We need to always ask "where is God in this process?" I guess Abner had the same problem Saul had. He thought he didn't need God's input. Abner had no authority to install anyone as king. Of course, Ishbosheth was the next in line, the "logical" successor. God never operates in logic!

In my Bible, I underlined the end of verse 11, "seven years and six months." It is important to note time periods when they are given. We can read the passage quickly and forget sometimes the time involved! Notice that Ishbosheth was only king for two years. Here is another part to watch in Kings. The overlapping of kings, it can be confusing at times. It was the way they measured time then.

Here, we can see a transition period. The death of Saul. David, following God's time table, then becomes king of Judah, one of the twelve tribes of Israel. Notice how David became their king? He was called by the people. This has always been a principle I have lived by since God called me to ministry. I have never "asked" for an opportunity to speak. I have always felt that If God wanted me to speak, He would lay it on the heart of someone to ask me. God must always lead in every work of ministry!

And Abner said to Joab, Let the young men now arise, and play before us. And Joab said, Let them arise. And Joab returned from following Abner: and when he had gathered all the people together, there lacked of David's servants nineteen men and Asahel. But the servants of David had smitten of Benjamin and of Abner's men, so that three hundred and threescore men died. (2 Samuel 2:14,30-31)

The rest of chapter 2 details the battle between Abner and Joab. This isn't over, as we will see later. Also, in this chapter you will notice the lopsided defeat of Abner. I am still amazed at how early this divide shows up. David will also need to deal with this conflict after he is made king of Israel.

There is an over-arching battle also taking place here. The remnants of Saul, verses, the army of David which began back in 1 Samuel. The battle continues even though the names have changed. The battle of God's people verses those who know not God. This battle will continue till our Lord returns for the final battle in the book of Revelation. This battle continues today.

Have you noticed the spiritual battle today? Slowly those forces against God are systematically trying to remove God from our culture. I first started to say "marketplace" but it's really more serious than that. God has left our marketplace back when He was removed from our schools. Today you must be careful when you speak of God. The sad part to me is how prevalent the words GD are used in the movies of the day. I think this is proof of God being ridiculed and maligned in our culture. It makes me sick!

So why did God bother to include this battle in His narrative? It's important to get the context of the battles David faced all through his reign. David never had an easy ride. From the day, he was anointed by Samuel, fresh out of the shepherd's field, to the day he passes the baton to Solomon. It's almost like the struggles the Apostle Paul suffered for Christ. Walking the Christian walk is not easy, wasn't meant to be in this world. But we need to remember two things: One, God is with us, fighting with us, and He will win. Two, we may win some battles here, but God will eventually win the war!

So, if David was a man after God's own heart, why is this struggle so difficult? We are in the enemies' camp (this world). Just as Paul spoke of the battle between the flesh and the Spirit within him, we will battle the forces of evil in this world.

This concludes the second chapter of second Samuel.

We are walking with David through this process to becoming king of Israel. Of course, becoming king doesn't negate his problems. David has many, many lessons to learn as he travels the path that God has set out for him. Much as we have many pitfalls in our path toward a closer relationship with God. It is a journey not a destination. We will only arrive when we stand before our Lord in glory. We can read these passages, we can know what's coming, and we can know how it will turn out.

We need to remember that David doesn't know what's up ahead. There is a key saying here that we should take from David's walk. *"And David inquired of the Lord."* that is so important in our walk. When we can get in the habit of "inquiring of the Lord" we will have a much easier walk. It won't be easy, or simple, but if we would ask God's direction instead of relying on our own wisdom, we will be much further ahead. Begin your day, each day with this prayer: "Lord, guide my steps, help me to glorify you in all that I say and do!"

2 Samuel 3

Now there was a long war between the house of Saul and the house of David: but David waxed stronger and stronger, and the house of Saul waxed weaker and weaker. And unto David were sons born in Hebron: and his firstborn was Amnon, of Ahinoam the Jezreelitess; And his second, Chileab, of Abigail the wife of Nabal the Carmelite; and the third, Absalom the son of Maacah the daughter of Talmai king of Geshur; and the fourth, Adonijah the son of Haggith; and the fifth, Shephatiah the son of Abital; and the sixth, Ithream, by Eglah David's wife. These were born to David in Hebron. (2 Samuel 3:1-5)

Just a couple of names to keep in mind. Adonijah and Absalom. Both of these sons will figure prominently in the years ahead. It is interesting to follow the "Scarlet Thread" through the Bible. We begin with Adam of course, then through his son Seth, we travel to Noah in Genesis 5:6-32. From Noah, and his three sons, Shem, Ham and Japheth, we continue through his son, Shem, in Genesis 11:10-27. From Shem to Abraham. Many, many generations from Adam to Abraham. A shorter version is in 1 Chronicles 1:24-28. Much of the genealogy picture is also in 1 Chronicles.

We get a closer look at the Patriarchs from Abraham, Isaac, Jacob whose name was changed to Israel. You would think that the line would continue through Joseph, it doesn't. The line continues through Jacob's fourth son, Judah. In Genesis 38 we see an interesting chapter, dropped into the narrative of Joseph. In Genesis 38 Judah is tricked into having twins, Perez and Zerah (38:29-30). Then the story returns to Joseph. Why was this inserted? Turn to the fourth chapter of Ruth.

The book of Ruth is inserted between the time of the Judges and 1 Samuel when David is called to be king. God needs to make the connection between the 38th chapter of Genesis and David. In the fourth chapter of Ruth we see that connection (4:18-22). In 1 Chronicles 2:3-15 it brings the line to David. We will see David's line through Solomon and then Rehoboam. It is a fascinating study. Of course, there are two genealogies listed in the Gospels. Matthew traces the line from Abraham (father of the Jews) to Jesus. Luke takes the line from Adam to Jesus.

Why is this important? The Jews believed, through prophecy, that the Messiah would come through the line of Abraham, David, etc. Jesus had the pedigree to prove his authority as the Messiah. From the Jewish point of view. This was very important to God as well. That is why He took such pains to give us this narrative!

There is one more aspect of this "genealogy" thing I want you to consider! We, as Christians, are in that line. Really?

> *For as many as are led by the Spirit of God, these are sons of God. For you did not receive the spirit of bondage again to fear, but you received the Spirit of adoption by whom we cry out, "Abba, Father." The Spirit Himself bears witness with our spirit that we are children of God, and if children, then heirs—heirs of God and joint heirs with Christ, if indeed we suffer with Him, that we may also be glorified together. (Romans 8:14-17) (NKJV)*

Let those words sink in a minute. We are included in the "genealogy" of Christ. We are children of God. When you get a minute read First John. If God's children ever really grasped our relationship to God, He could and will change your life!

And he said, Well; I will make a league with thee: but one thing I require of thee, that is, thou shalt not see my face, except thou first bring Michal Saul's daughter, when thou comest to see my face. (2 Samuel 3:13)

Abner was insulted by Ishboseth. He threatened to leave the house of Saul and went to David. When he talked to David he made a covenant in which David welcomed him provided he bring Michal, whom Saul had given him for a wife. Let's be reminded of some verses:

Saul tries to use Michal to get David killed:

Then Saul said, "Thus you shall say to David: 'The king does not desire any dowry but one hundred foreskins of the Philistines. to take vengeance on the king's enemies.'" But Saul sought to make David fall by the hand of the Philistines. So, when his servants told David these words, it pleased David well to become the king's son-in-law. (1 Samuel 18:25-26) (NKJV)

So, David acquired the foreskins and Saul gave Michal to David to wed. When this didn't get David killed Saul tried to use Michal to kill David in another way.

Saul also sent messengers to David's house to watch him and to kill him in the morning. And Michal, David's wife, told him, saying, "If you do not save your life tonight, tomorrow you will be killed." So, Michal let David down through a window. And he went and fled and escaped. (1 Samuel 19:11-12). (NKJV)

Michal loved David. At the risk of her own life by her father Saul, Michal saved David's life.

Now, with Saul dead, and Abner is now the head guy in Ishbosheth's army. Abner then defected to David's side, is asked by David to get Michal back. By this time Michal had been given in marriage to another guy, Paltiel. That didn't seem to matter in those days. Abner gets Michal and takes her to David.

We need to keep an eye on this guy Abner. I just never trusted him.

I'm not sure David trusts him either. In order for Abner to desert Ishbosheth, David told him to retrieve his first wife, Michal. Abner does so. I think that David loved Michal more than the text suggests. We know that Michal loved David. At first, Saul gave a daughter named Merab to David. David went to battle and Saul gave her to someone else. This is getting weird. In 1 Samuel, it says:

Now Michal, Saul's daughter, loved David. And they told Saul and the thing pleased him. (1 Samuel 18:20) (NKJV)

And we saw earlier that Saul used her, to try to kill David.

Get used to this family "drama". David will be dealing with this his whole life. Part by his own making and part by God's judgment for his disobedience.

Did I give you the impression that David was something special? David is no different than you or me. He makes mistakes, he is disobedient to God, he has his failings. Don't let me put him on a pedestal! So why are we looking so closely at his life? The Bible says, "A man after Goes own heart." (Acts 13:22, 1 Samuel 13:14). That must be our goal in our walk with God. We can learn several lessons from David, both what to do, AND what not to do!

Are you willing to think about your relationship with God? Is there any improvement that can be made? Have you seen anything in David's life that can be changed in your own life? Think about it, pray about it. God put this man's story in the Bible for a reason. There is more about David's life than any other individual in the Bible, except Jesus of course. It would be well for us to see how God works in David's life and learn the lessons David learned and be challenged to put some of those "truths" into our own walk with God.

The one thing that has my attention to this point is the phrase, "David inquired of the Lord." David sought God's guidance whenever he had a decision to make! How about you?

And Abner had communication with the elders of Israel, saying, Ye sought for David in times past to be king over you: now then do it: for the Lord hath spoken of David, saying, By the hand of my servant David I will save my people Israel out of the hand of the Philistines, and out of the hand of all their enemies. And Abner also spake in the ears of Benjamin: and Abner went also to speak in the ears of David in Hebron all that seemed good to the while house of Benjamin. (2 Samuel 3:17-19)

Let's do a little exercise. Let's replace a few words in the verses above. Try this, "By the hand of My Son Jesus, I will save My children from the hand of Satan." Close? The same principle! God chose David to free Israel from bondage to the Philistines, and other nations around them. God sent His Son Jesus to free us from the bondage of sin, every sin, that plagues us!

Look at this verse:

"Stand fast therefore in the liberty by which Christ has made us free, and do not be entangled again with a yoke of bondage. (Galatians 5:1). (NKJV)

It was Jesus' death on the cross that gives us victory over the sin of the flesh that we battle every day. Paul talked about the battle between the flesh and the Spirit of God within us. The old nature vs the new nature. Paul struggled with it as do we. (Romans 7:15)

Do you ever think of the influence of those around you? How they can lead you in directions you really don't want to go. I can see Abner doing this. He has defected from the army of Saul, from the authority of Ishbosheth and went to follow David. His words above are commendable, yes, but what is his motive? We will watch and see.

Something else to note, concerning history. I mentioned before that after the death of Solomon and through the leadership of his son, Rehoboam, the nation of Israel split into two kingdoms. The Northern Kingdom, consisting of the ten tribes. The Southern Kingdom consisting of Judah and Benjamin. I can see that alliance beginning here. A glimpse into history we need to remember. Divide and conquer. That is the tactic the devil is using today with families, churches, and even nations!

God uses different people at different times to accomplish His will. I just got through watching a documentary on Billy Graham. What an awesome man of God. A man who consistently preached the simple Word of God. We are all sinners, we need a Savior, Jesus died on the cross to be our Savior, to pay for our sins that we would be children of God. I recently read "A History of the Church" Throughout history God has always had a man or woman who carried His message through history. There are so many throughout the scriptures that we could study.

Someone once told me that, besides Jesus, there are only two men, in the Bible, that nothing negative is said of them. Can you guess the two? Joseph and Daniel. Now think about all the men who are mentioned in the Bible. Only two? That means all the rest were flawed! Does that give you hope that God might be able to use you?

Take a few minutes, right now, think about your life to this point. Has God been working in your life? Can you sense a relationship with Him?

Why not? First, have you asked Jesus into your heart? That's the first step. Next, have you asked God, in prayer, to give you direction? Are you afraid He will send you to China as a missionary? Not likely. Maybe after years of trusting Him He might lead you into something like that. But that takes years of demonstrating your willingness to obey His leadership. God wants a willing heart! A surrendered heart! The more you learn to trust God, the more God will use you. It's a growing process. Much like we do with our own children. The more they obey us, the more we trust them! Right?

So Abner came to David to Hebron, and twenty men with him. And David made Abner and the men that were with him a feast. And Abner said unto David, I will arise and go, and will gather all Israel unto my lord the king, that they may make a league with thee, and that thou mayest reign over all that thine heart desireth. And David sent Abner away; and he went in peace. (2 Samuel 3:20-21)

I'm sorry, maybe I'm nit-picking but I don't see God in Abner's statement. I see someone pandering to the ruler of Hebron. I keep remembering where Abner came from. Is this a verse from a song? When you're not with the one you love, you love the one you're with. It just seems weird to me.

From the beginning, it was God's plan that David was to be king. Not Abner's, not even David's. David was a shepherd boy. It was God's plan. I get the feeling that Abner thinks it's his idea. That Abner will make it happen. That is a very hard lesson that I learned the hard way. It must be in God's time and God's way. Saul is a great example.

David had two opportunities to do "God's will". David could help God out by eliminating Saul in that cave. Assuming David knew God's plan. David chose to wait on God's plan and God's time. Let's suppose David had gone ahead and killed Saul. Saul's blood would forever be on David's hands. By letting God's plan in God's time David gave a lesson to his troops and those who followed him. God's plan in God's time.

That is what screams at me from these verses. Abner thinks he is going to go out and rally Israel behind David and by Abner's sheer will David will become king. Let me ask you, who gets the glory? Abner of course. Is that God's plan. You might want to ask, what does Abner get out of this? You know of course.

I used to walk the halls of my "home church" and imagine being the pastor. Everyone in the church loved me, and I was in a leadership position and just "knew" that God would call there if He had the chance. I accepted a call to a smaller church as a sort of "training" for when my home church would call me.

Two years passed, I saw an opening to make it happen. I went through the "process" of meeting with the people I had grown up with as a Christian. I interviewed, etc. Then I waited. It didn't happen. No need for details. The door was closed. Instead of focusing on the church I had been called to, I began thinking of ways to "make it happen". I am so sorry! I resigned from the church I was pastor and began attending my home church. God would have none of it. The door was shut, period! I tried to make it happen in my own strength, leaving God out. It failed!

I can't begin to imagine Abner's motive. I have my suspicions, but only God knows his heart. I can only judge by his actions. We will see soon enough how God deals with Abner.

It is so hard sometimes to sort out our desires from those of God. I still believe that God was planning on me going to my home church. But, because I got ahead of God He shut the door to that dream in a hurry. It is one thing to know God's will but it is entirely another to wait for God's timing. That was a tough lesson to learn. You won't believe how patient I am today, waiting on God!

That is the hard part of this study about David. We know the end from the beginning. David didn't. Here is another trait we can learn from David. Waiting on God. David simply took each day as it came and trusted God for the results. God's plan, in God's time, for God's glory!

Then Joab came to the king, and said, What hast thou done? Behold, Abner came unto thee; why is it that thou hast sent him away, and he is quite gone? Thou knowest Abner the son of Ner, that he came to deceive thee, and to know thy going out and thy coming in, and to know all that thou doest. (2 Samuel 3:24-25)

Take a minute here. Get a pad and pencil and set for a minute. Begin searching your memory and make a list of all the people who have passed through your life. Chances are if they impacted your life you will remember them. Is it a big list? Depends on your years I suspect. Now, depending on your age, how many new people do you suspect will pass through your life? You don't know, do you? Of course not.

Now here is another list: Samuel, Jonathan, Saul, Joab, Jesse, Michal, Nabal, Abigail, Achish, just to name a few that come to my mind. There are many others that are not named. People pass through our lives all the time. The impact they have on our future we can never know till years later. If you remember their names, they had an impact. In the beginning of this book I tried to list those men who passed through my life, and who made an impact. It's a worthy exercise!

I listed a few of those who passed through David's life. Do you think they passed by accident? Certainly not. An all-knowing God brought these people through David's life for a reason. Some, to teach him, some to hinder him, some to encourage, and some to bless. The same is true in your life. Those whom God has chosen to send into your life have a purpose. It is up to you to discern their mission. There were several others I could have included in my list, they did not contribute to my life in a good way, other than to teach me a lesson.

We first saw David in the shepherd's field. Think about all the people who passed through David's life to this point. How have they contributed to David's walk with God? That is the question we need to ask of everyone who passes through our lives: "How have they contributed to my walk with God?"

Think about this as the story of Abner and Joab continues through David's life. Abner, once a general in Saul's army. Joab is a general in David's army. At this point we might want to give him the benefit of a doubt. That is the advantage we have with David. We can look ahead or have read this story and know the outcome.

In our own lives' we don't have that luxury. There is a source we can rely on to critic those who pass through our lives. As children of God we have the Holy Spirit to warn us of those people that we may need to avoid in our lives. There is a certain uneasiness that we feel when we meet someone who doesn't have our best interest at heart. Listen the Spirit. Satan also sends people into our lives to draw us away from God, and to head us down a path we do not wish to go. Be discerning!

Many times, we can be too quick to judge those who pass through our lives. If the Spirit doesn't warn us, we need to allow them to build a relationship. If you have that warning, watch out!

Have you ever met someone whom you have been warned of in advance? You hear their "reputation" from someone. So, before you meet them you have already determined that you will not like them. Be careful. God may have sent them into your life for a reason. By pre-judging them you may block someone who God wishes to use in your life to teach you something. It's not up to you or your friends to close that door. Listen to God's Spirit, allow God to use them in your life. They could be a blessing sent from God!

And when Abner was returned to Hebron, Joab took him aside in the gate to speak with him quietly, and smote him there under the fifth rib, that he died, for the blood of Asahel his brother. So Joab and Abishai his brother slew Abner, because he has slain their brother Asahel at Gibeaon in the battle. (2 Samuel 3:27,30)

When I had a Sunday School class of high school students, I challenged them to memorize:

> "Whoever sheds man's blood, by man shall his blood be shed; for in the image of God He made man." (Genesis 9:6) (NKJV)

For me, this is my stand, on capital punishment.

> However, he refused to turn aside. Therefore, Abner struck him in the stomach with the blunt end of the spear, so that the spear came out of his back; and he fell down there and died on the spot. So, it was that as many as came to the place where Asahel fell down and died, stood still. (2 Samuel 2:23) (NKJV)

There are things in the Bible that we would just as soon not include. There are things that God would rather not write. Such as this tale. So, what is the lesson? We need to constantly remind ourselves that God included this episode for a reason. There are far too many things that God wants us to know to waste space on insignificant details. I think Genesis 9:6 is illustrated here.

Later, toward the end of David's life he will caution Solomon about Joab. You have seen so much already, of the drama David endured in his life. Here, again, another illustration of David's relationship with God. We tend to think that no family has more "drama" in their family than they do. Watch David. God has brought these events into his life for a purpose. Just as the events in your life have a purpose. Sometimes it's just to get us to back away and think about God and what He is trying to teach us. Usually it's patience. God never gives patience, He teaches it. The less patient we are the more God will send trials to get us looking up!

Here is something else to think about in this scenario. How long had Joab carried this "hatred, and revenge" around inside him? It's a cancer that can eat you alive. Until you learn how to give those feelings to God you will never have true peace. Joab was hoping to catch Abner at David's place when he returned. He wasn't, so Joab sent for him. Just to kill him, to get his revenge. This did not go well with David.

Revenge, hatred, prejudice, jealousy, envy, all tools the devil uses to ruin our lives. It's is only through a relationship with God through His Son Jesus can you be rid of these terrible emotions. God can change your heart! Look at this verse in 2 Corinthians,

> "Therefore, if anyone is in Christ, he is a new creation; old things have passed away; behold, all things have become new. (2 Corinthians 5:17). (NKJV)

Someone once said, God changes our "want-tos". He gives us a new focus, a new purpose, a new relationship and above all a new heart! Look at this verse in Jeremiah,

> "Then I will give them a heart to know Me, that I am the Lord; and they shall be My people, and I will be their God, for they shall return to Me with their whole heart. (Jeremiah 24:7) (NKJV)

The day we ask the Lord Jesus into our heart He begins changing us, working on those things I listed above and cleaning up that mess and filling our heart with new feelings, like it says in Galatians:

But the fruit of the Spirit is love, joy, peace, longsuffering (patience), kindness, goodness, faithfulness, gentleness, self-control, against such there is no law. (Galatians 5:22-23). (NKJV)

God will change your heart. Not the bitterness and revenge that Joab felt but a willingness to leave those things in God's hands!

So they buried Abner in Hebron: and the king lifted up his voice, and wept at the grave of Abner; and all the people wept. And the king lamented over Abner, and said, Died Abner as a fool dieth? Thy hands were not bound, nor thy feet put into fetters: as a man falleth before wicked men, so fellest thou. And all the people wept again over him. (2 Samuel 3:32-34)

A stark difference between this funeral and that of Saul. Funerals are tough. Especially when the person who died, died "before his time." That might be David's complaint and the violent way he died. We are not in control of the time or the means of our death (for the most part). Suicide is another matter.

The doctors told my mother-in-law she had less than a year to live, she lived another 8 years. I'm sure you've heard similar stories. By natural causes we have no control over the time. Of course, if we don't take care of our bodies the time is shortened, but we still can't predict. It's in God's hands!

I did a funeral once and used this text:

Jesus Christ is the same yesterday, today, and forever. (Hebrews 13:8) (NKJV)

Thinking there are three time periods represented at a funeral. Yesterday: At a funeral, we love to be reminded of the memories of the one who has past. Things we did with them, funny stories, etc. Many funerals today allow those attending to offer remarks about their memories of the deceased. Today: Today, is a time of grieving. We can only think of how much we will miss the departed. It is also a time of comforting each other with family and friends. Forever: It is a time to think of eternity. Funerals are a great opportunity to remind people that we are mortal. That one day we will all stand before God and give an account. The key to these three time periods, of course, is Jesus Christ. He is with us in the past, in the present and we will stand before Him in the future.

You can tell David is upset at Abner's funeral. It should not have been. David will deal with Joab later. But notice, David did not take it upon himself to avenge his death. David has a characteristic that we should all consider in our lives. David was willing to wait for God's timing! That is so hard in the culture of today. Yet, waiting is one of the key themes throughout the Bible. Look at this verse in Galatians:

> But, when the fulness of time had come, God sent forth
> His Son, born of a woman, born under the law, to redeem
> those who were under the law, that we might receive the
> adoption of sons. (Galatians 4:4-5). (NKJV)

God has His timetable, the sad part is we have ours, and they often conflict. If you get the chance spend some time in Psalm 37. David talks about waiting on the Lord. And, especially, my favorite verse:

> But those who wait on the Lord shall renew their strength;
> they shall mount up with wings like eagles, they shall run
> and be weary, they shall walk and not wait. (Isaiah 40:31)
> (NKJV)

If you spend any time in the Bible you will notice this principle of waiting on God.

Twice, with King Saul, and now here with Joab. David could very easily have gotten ahead of God, or gotten out of His will totally. We have so many opportunities in our life to do things "in our own time" that is not God's way! When God does it, in His time, it's done right, and God gets the glory and we remain on God's timetable, not ours. Got any "plans" for the future. Have you asked God about it? Have you left those plans in God's hands? That's the wise thing to do!

I wonder why this death hit David so hard? It seems harder than even Jonathan's. I gave Abner a bum rap earlier. I missjudged him. He left a bad king and wanted to help David. Maybe David saw that in him. He really took his death hard. Funerals are so hard sometimes!

And all the people took notice of it, and it pleased them: as whatsoever the king did pleased all the people. For all the people and all Israel understood that day that it was not of the king to slay Abner the son of Ner. And the king said unto his servants, Know ye not that there is a prince and a great man fallen this day in Israel? And I am this day weak, though anointed king; and these men the sons of Zeruiah be too hard for me: the Lord shall reward the doer of evil according to his wickedness. (2 Samuel 3:36-39)

That takes too long! We want action now! Have you ever felt that way? God just doesn't act fast enough for me. I want action now. Can you do a better job than God? And what of the consequences if you act now instead of waiting for God? David was grieving! "It isn't fair!" Of course not.

Tell me something. What have you been able to accomplish in your life apart from God's province? You don't really know do you? As far as you are concerned you have accomplished it all, right? Not hardly. Take a minute and think back over your life. Tell me you don't see sometimes when you couldn't explain certain things that happened, good or bad. I speak from experience!

Look at David's life to this point. Do you see God's hand in David's life that has protected him to this point? Of course, you do. Wait a minute, we're talking King David here. Of course, God is going to bless him. Oh, you think David was "special" that God would bless him and not you. You haven't done anything to "earn" God's favor. Really? Where did God call David from? David was standing in line, waiting for God to tap him on the shoulder and say, "follow Me". God called David the same way He calls us.

Have you ever heard someone say, "I went looking for God, and I found Him."? God is the one doing the looking. He is always looking for those who will trust in His Son Jesus, then look out. God will work miracles in your life that you won't believe. Only, when you have that relationship with the Son of God.

When a pastor dropped by our house that night and lead my wife and I to the Lord. I never dreamed that I would one day be a pastor for two and a half years. Serve as a Sunday School Director for over thirty years, then write a couple of books. If you had told me then what God was going to do, I would have laughed so hard!

David has the faith, and that's what it takes, to trust God to make things right. The faith to do the right thing at the right time, His time! That is a faith worth seeking. I think it is so interesting that in the gospels Jesus is always condemning His disciples for their lack of faith and yet marveling at the faith of some Gentiles! Check it out!

Of course, God worked some amazing things in David's life, early on. Let's get back to that list I asked you to make earlier. You know, that list of "unexplained" events in your past that you don't understand why or how they happened. As an example, how did you meet your husband? Was that an accident? Teenager, how about those "near-misses" when you first started driving? How about that fantastic job that you worked so hard for? Think back. I know for a fact there are unexplained events in your life that you think "just happened". Nothing "just happens" God has a plan and He is working in your life right now. If you're not a Christian you have no idea what I'm talking about. If you are a Christian God will bring these events to your memory and all we can do is "Praise the Lord!"

You are on a path. You need to find out who you are following. Who's in charge!

2 SAMUEL 4

And Jonathan, Saul's son, had a son that was lame of his feet. He was five years old when the tidings came of Saul and Jonathan out of Jezreel, and his nurse took him up, and fled: and it came to pass, as she made haste to flee, that he fell, and became lame. And his name was Mephibosheth. (2 Samuel 4:4)

Here we are introduced to someone, a brief introduction, to someone who will appear later. David made a promise to Jonathan. He will fulfill it with Mephibosheth.

For when they came into the house, he lay on his bed in his bedchamber, and they smote him, and slew him, and beheaded him, and took his head, and gat them away through the plain all night. And David answered Rechab and Baanah his brother, the sons of Rimmon the Beerothite, and said unto them, As the Lord liveth, who hath redeemed my soul out of all adversity, When one told me, saying, Behold, Saul is dead, thinking to have brought good tidings, I took hold of him, and slew him in Ziklag, who thought that I would have given him a reward for his tidings: how much more, when wicked men have slain a righteous person in his own house upon his bed? Shall I not therefore now require his blood of your hand, and take you away from the earth? (2 Samuel 4: 7,9-11)

Does this story sound familiar? David mentions the one who came with the news that he had killed Saul, thinking a reward. David had him executed. Just these two will be executed. This is a gruesome passage! What do we see about David?

There are always those who seek the favor of men. Have you noticed that? Each trying to impress David with what they "thought" would please

David. The one who claimed he killed Saul, didn't really, but wanted credit. Look what God says in Proverbs:

"When a man's ways please the Lord, he makes even his enemies to be at peace with him." (Proverbs 16:7) (NKJV)

Our aim in life must be to please God, not man. Of course, we see the results here, but it is a truth worth thinking about.

David didn't always please God, of course, he is no better than we. The key is what do we do when we have strayed from His path? We repent and ask forgiveness and get back on track. David was far from perfect, we will see that. David always came back to God on his knees, seeking forgiveness. Can we do any less?

Again, there is an important lesson here. What do you do to please man? Our peers, our, co-workers, even our family. Do we skirt the will of God? Do we try to bend the rules to gain favor with those around us? To what lengths do we go to please man? The answer to these questions will reveal our walk with God, our relationship with God. God is the one we should seek to please. Read Proverbs 16:7 again. Let those words sink in. It's the Word of God.

How might our ways please the Lord? You can learn a lot about that by spending time in His word. Attending church, fellowshipping with fellow believers. Listen to their trials and triumphs. Above all we must pray for God's direction in our walk. Remember what David did several times, *"David inquired of the Lord."* there is a start!

2 Samuel 5

Then came all the tribes of Israel to David unto Hebron, and spake, saying, Behold, we are thy bone and thy flesh. Also in time past, when Saul was king over us, thou wast he that leddest out and broughtest in Israel: and the Lord said to thee, Thou shalt feed my people Israel, and thou shalt be a captain over Israel. So all the elders of Israel came to the king to Hebron: and king David made a league with them in Hebron before the Lord: and they anointed David king over Israel. David was thirty years old when he began to reign, and he reigned forty years. (2 Samuel 5:1-4)

David is now king over all of Israel. I mentioned before that this is his third anointing. 1 Samuel 16:13, 2 Samuel 2:7, and 2 Samuel 5:3. David is thirty years old now. As a shepherd boy, we are not told his age at the time. He was not in the army, as his brothers, he could very well have been a teenager. Much like the story of Joseph in Genesis. Many years have passed that we have read about in just a few minutes. Keep that concept in mind!

Did you catch that part about David? *"and the Lord said to you, 'You shall shepherd My people Israel.'"* I wonder where the people got that. Notice that they also recognized who led them in battle. Can you recognize when a leader is God's choice or not? What characteristics might you look for? It's a challenge we face today! It is getting harder and harder to tell. It is politically incorrect to demonstrate "godly" characteristics!

Remember this one very important trait of David's. David waited for God, just as Joseph. I'm sure there were many times when David wondered what God was up to. I'm sure Joseph believed God had abandoned him. Do you feel that way sometimes? How about Job? If your walking with God, trusting Him, you can trust Him for the next step, and the next, and the next. That is all He will reveal, you must trust Him!

One of my favorite verses, when I struggle with the daily "waiting":

"Trust in the Lord with all your heart, and lean not on your own understanding; in all your ways acknowledge Him, and He will direct your path." (Proverbs 3:5-6) (NKJV)

You need to memorize that! Four lines, four truths, four basic principles to trusting God and allowing Him to guide your life down the path He has chosen. Joseph did! David did! What about you?

Did you notice that David didn't go, at Saul's death, from general to king? He went to Hebron, a province or city of Judah. Judah was in the south, next to Benjamin. In the northern part of Judah was a city called Jerusalem. Jerusalem will figure prominently in David's life, as we shall see. It was David's courage, resourcefulness, his army, and his genius, that brought him to be anointed king. Really? I hope you don't fall for that. That's the world's lies. We did it all on our own. You can see clearly the hand of God in David's life, his walk from the shepherd's field to the throne. It's only when David forgets this fact that he gets into trouble.

The same is true in your walk. When you start getting puffed up about what "you" have accomplished, God may need to let some air out of your pride. The day we recognize from whence comes our strength and blessing that day we will improve our walk with God immensely. Did you notice that David reigns for forty years? A generation. A testament to his relationship with God.

And the king and his men went to Jerusalem unto the Jebusites, the inhabitants of the land: which spake unto David, saying, Except thou take away the blind and the lame, thou shalt not come in hither: thinking, David cannot come in hither. Nevertheless David took the stronghold of Zion: the same is the city of David. And David said on that day, Whosoever getteth up to the gutter, and smiteth the Jebusites, and the lame and the blind, that are hated of David's soul, he shall be chief and captain. Wherefore they said, The blind and the lame shall not come into the house. So David dwelt in the fort, and called it the city of David, and David built around about from Millo and inward. (2 Samuel 5:6-9)

Here is a trivia question for you. Is there any other city called, "The City of David?"

> *"Joseph also went up from Galilee, out of the city of Nazareth, into Judea, to the city of David, which is called Bethlehem, because he was of the house and lineage of David." (Luke 2:4) (NKJV)*

My guess is that since it was near Jerusalem, in the province of Judah it was also referred to as "the City of David."

Here is another little "tiny-tidbit-of-trivial-information" Jerusalem consists of nine letters. Look at the "middle" three letters. Make of it what you will.

David is now King of Israel. He has established Jerusalem as his capitol. Since the time of David Jerusalem has always been the capital of Israel. I am blessed to have lived in a time when our President, against many critics, has chosen to move our embassy to Jerusalem! Prophecy or not it was awesome to see!

Do you know what the verses above are talking about? Jerusalem was thought to be invincible to any army. The walls so high, etc. So was Jericho, but that's another story. There are no walls God cannot defeat. There was a stream that ran under the wall into the city. The inhabitants were so sure of their protection that they said, *"but the blind and the lame will repel you."* Notice what David said, *"Whoever climbs up by way of the water shaft"* that was how they entered the city and thus defeated it. When God's will is at stake, nothing will stop it from being fulfilled!

So, how does this apply to me? I used two principles when I taught Sunday School. (1) The Historical Perspective. What takes place in this passage from a historical perspective. How does this fit in history? What is the historical context. (2) What is the Personal Application to be made here? God doesn't put anything in His word that doesn't give us some insight into His will and purpose for our lives. This event was not by accident.

How many times have you made these great plans, only to have them totally go astray? Can you count the times? God is still in charge. We can see all through the Bible where kings, and mighty men have thought they could thwart the will of God. God will have His way. Jericho, Jerusalem,

Satan himself must give way to God's plan and purpose. Look at the first few chapters of Job. Satan could do nothing except God "allowed" it!

Always make your plans subject to God's will. It's safer that way. If the plans change just ask, "Okay Lord, where do we go from here?"

We can look back from our perspective and say, "Of course Jerusalem is David's capitol" not so in David's time. Did God lead David to choose Jerusalem, I think so. David learned early on to listen to God. How about you? How many busted plans does it take before you check with God first? I learned the hard way to just take your hands off the wheel, put it in neutral, and enjoy the ride.

And Hiram king of Tyre sent messengers to David, and cedar trees, and carpenters, and masons: and they built David an house. And David perceived that the Lord had established him king over Israel, and that he had exalted his kingdom for his people Israel's sake. (2 Samuel 5:11-12)

Hiram had resources, God had a need. Funny how that seems to find each other. Does God need people like Hiram? Of course not! God can do anything He chooses, He chooses to use people with resources to accomplish His will. Has God used you lately? Maybe we could ask ourselves, who claims possession of those resources? Do they belong to God or do you think you have worked hard to achieve this position and you have control over what is yours? That can be dangerous!

Are you looking for opportunities to give? Or, are you focused on how much you have accumulated? Checking your bank balance, or noticing a need in your church?

I think it's interesting that God chose to build David a house before laying on David's heart to build a church. Which was the opposite in the books of Ezra and Nehemiah. God sent first to build the temple, then they built the wall. Why do you suppose God provided David a house then they worked on the Temple? God knew David's heart. God knew His servant's heart to serve Him.

When our priorities and focus is on God, God will provide needed resources to accomplish His will and purpose. I love the illustration I saw on Dr. Stanley's show. When our hands are open, we can both give as much as God will provide. And then, our hands are open to receive from God the blessings He provides.

When our men's ministry began looking for a name, and a ministry.

We decided to be called the "Rivermen". The idea being that we are to be rivers of God's blessings, not a lake. We pass the blessings of God through our hands to those who are in need. A lake simply holds the blessings. They become stagnant, stale, and useless. The blessings of God are meant to shared not held on to.

Did you notice in our text that Hiram was not asked by David to provide these resources? God laid it on his heart. Maybe he had been watching the conflict between Saul and David. Maybe God said, "Wait". We don't know. It's interesting that as soon as David was anointed king, Hiram sent the materials. He didn't ask David if he had a need, he just sent them. Is your relationship with God in such a manner that you recognize needs around you and have those "open hands"? Maybe your focus is within instead of without. Think about it.

Do you remember this episode, just before Jesus makes His triumphal entry into Jerusalem? Look,

> "Go into the village opposite you, and immediately you will find a donkey tied, and a colt with her. Loose them and bring them to Me. And if anyone says anything to you, you shall say, 'The Lord has need of them,' and immediately he will send them. (Matthew 21:2-3). (NKJV)

Has the Lord said to you, "I have need of it?" What would be your response?

Because of David's walk with God, his relationship, God provided for David's need. Of course, we have our "want" list. Don't mistake the two. When we can trust God to provide, wait for God's timing, God's plan, the blessing will be all that much sweeter. We noticed that David didn't ask Hiram for the resources. Imagine the look on David's face when this stuff arrives. I can see David now raising his hands and eyes to heaven and saying, "Praise God for this blessing!

And David took him more concubines and wives out of Jerusalem, after he was come from Hebron: and there were yet sons and daughters born to David. And these be the names of those that were born unto him in Jerusalem: Shammuah, and Shobab, and Nathan, and Solomon, Ibhar also, and Elishua, and Nepheg, and Japhia, and Elishama, and Eliada, and Eliphalet. (2 Samuel 5:13-16)

Someone remarked in our Sunday School class, "Why can't they have names like, John, George or Steve? Good question. Maybe the Hebrew language had something to do with it.

This is a good place to have a short Bible study.

Of course, you remember back in Genesis that God created man in His own image. Remember this?

> *And the Lord God said, "It is not good that man should be alone; I will make him a helper comparable to him." (2:18 NKJV). And the Lord God caused a deep sleep to fall on Adam, and he slept; and He took one of his ribs, and closed up the flesh in its place. Then the rib which the Lord God had taken from the man He made into a woman, and He brought her to the man. (Genesis 2:21-22). (NKJV)*

I wonder why God didn't make two wives, there are plenty of ribs to choose from. At least two would make his rib count even on each side. Sorry, couldn't resist! Another thing, why didn't God just create her like He created Adam? There is a very important picture to learn here. Many pastors have preached countless sermons on the "first wedding" using this passage. I don't need to cover that. The point to make is that it was God's plan to have one woman for one man.

Let's jump ahead to the first person to have multiple wives. Can you guess who that was?

> *Then Lamech took for himself two wives; the name of the one was Adah, and the name of the second was Zillah. (Genesis 4:19) (NKJV)*

Lamech was a descendant of Cain.

Now we move on to Noah. How many wives did Noah have? One! Even his three sons had one wife:

> *So, Noah, with his sons, his wife, and his son's wives, went into the ark because of the waters of the flood (Genesis 7:7) (NKJV)*

Of course, his sons may have had multiple wives but, imagine spending a year on the ark with someone having more than one wife. Anyway, I'm sure the sons followed the leading of their father.

Next, we have Abraham. We know that Abraham ended up with two wives, Sarah and Hagar. Look at this verse:

> So, Sarai said to Abram, "See now, the Lord has restrained me from bearing children. Please, go in to my maid, perhaps I shall obtain children by her." And Abram heeded the voice of Sarai. (Genesis 16:2). (NKJV)

First note where Abram received his instructions, Sarai. God had already promised him offspring (15:5). I won't go into detail here but it didn't turn out well for Abram. Read Genesis 16-18.

The next in line was Isaac (Genesis 21). Isaac had one wife Rebekah. Great story of how Isaac came to marry Rebekah (Genesis 24). Rebekah had two sons, Esau and Jacob. In Genesis 29 and 30 we can read how Jacob ended up with four wives, Leah, Rachel, Bilhah, and Zilpah. Through these four wives Jacob ended up with twelve sons and a daughter. Was Jacob's life tranquil, serene; not a chance. The wives competed for his attention. Constant strife and conflict.

Now I want to bring your attention to a warning from God. Look at these verses:

> "When you come to the land which the Lord your God is giving you, and possess it and dwell in it, and say, 'I will set a king over me like all the nations that are around me' You shall surely set a king over you, who is not your brother. But he shall not multiply horses for himself, nor cause the people to return to Egypt to multiply horses, for the Lord has said to you, 'you shall not return that way again.' Neither shall he multiply wives for himself lest his heart be torn away; nor shall he greatly multiply silver and gold for himself. (Deuteronomy 17:14-17) (NKJV)

Did you catch all that? In the book of Deuteronomy, long before the Promised Land, Joshua and claiming the Promised Land. Long before Judges etc. Notice that God already knew there would be a king in Israel.

He cautioned that this king should not multiply: Horses, wives, gold and silver. You can read the story of Solomon in 1st Kings. Solomon had all three! For our study, we note that David had several wives as well.

I just think, if we follow God's story in the Old Testament, through these men that God used to accomplish His will, they weren't perfect, of course! They made a lot of mistakes. Have you heard the argument that since it's in the Bible it's okay? Of course not! It's included, under God's leading, to teach us a lesson. Have any of these men been blessed by having more than one wife?

Just look at Jacob in Genesis 29. Jacob was tricked into marrying Leah. Leah had six sons. The fourth son was named Judah. It was through the line of Judah that the lineage continues to Christ. If Jacob had confined himself to one wife the purpose of God would have been fulfilled! It's no accident.

I was tempted to skip the verses above (2 Samuel 5:13-16). There is cause for looking back and reflecting on how God teaches, leads, and His will is brought to pass. Again, I remind you that the passage on Israel's king was written by Moses in the book of Deuteronomy. We can learn so much to apply to our own lives if we study how God works through His people.

But when the Philistines heard that they had anointed David king over Israel, all the Philistines came up to seek David; and David heard of it, and went down to the hold. The Philistines also came and spread themselves in the valley of Rephaim. And David inquired of the Lord, saying, Shall I go up to the Philistines? Will thou deliver them into mine hand? And the Lord said to David, Go up: for I will dountless deliver the Philistines into thine hand. (2 Samuel 5:17-19)

The Philistines? I thought these guys were defeated. Remember David and Goliath? Wait a minute, do you remember who killed King Saul and Jonathan? Yes, the Philistines. These guys, this nation, seems to continually attack, annoy, and pester the Israelites. Why is that? Do you think God could have prevented it? Of course, He could. Then why?

Let me ask you this, "Is there a sin, or a habit, that just continually pesters you?" You try everything in your own strength to defeat this "thorn" but you just can't seem to get a victory. Have you "inquired of the Lord?" I thought not.

The reason I used the word "thorn" is because I was reminded of the apostle Paul's struggles with his "thorn" (2 Corinthians 12). Something that God had afflicted him with. God will use everything and anything to bring us to Him. So many times, God has used neighboring countries to get Israel's attention. Especially in the book of Judges this is very evident! So, God will use things in our life to get us to focus on Him. What will it take for you to turn to God?

Now you would think, with David's reputation, that the Philistines would have nothing to do with David. They had just killed Saul and his son Jonathan (1 Samuel 31). They figured this was a good time to take David out. Of course, the enemy never figures on God. I think it's interesting here. David is "specific" *"will you deliver them into my hand?"* And God is also "specific" in His response. Have you asked God "specifically" to remove this thorn?

David has a score to settle with the Philistines anyway. So, if David knew it was the right thing to do why didn't he just go do it? Have you ever started out to do something you "knew" was right but then, half-way through it, you realized you made a mistake? It seemed like the right thing at the time. Did you "inquire of the Lord?" Of course not. It just seemed right. It never hurts to check with God!

I teased my brother years ago. He had just made a profession of faith in our church. Later that week I had seen him at work. He had a gash on his forehead. I asked what happened. He told me he had run into a beam by accident. I kind of grinned. He looked at me funny. I explained, it was the devil trying to distract you from what God had just done in David's life. It is almost a given that when we begin walking with God, the devil will try everything he can to trip up our walk. If he can get us early in our walk he can pull us away from God.

David had just been anointed as king of Israel. Here come the Philistines. Where does David turn? To his army, to his own prowess, to his wives (sorry). No, he turns to God. Where do we turn when the enemy attacks? Our wisdom, our experience, our standing in the community, we need to turn to God, "inquire of the Lord."

Who is attacking you today? I like what Dr. Stanley says, "You are either headed into a storm, coming out of a storm, or in a storm." There is always reason to "inquire of the Lord." Are you facing a storm, a major decision, or is something just driving you to distraction? What are you doing about it? One more hint, "leave it with God." Don't hang on to it, covet that thorn. Sometimes we inquire of God then continue to cling to it. Leave it with God!

And David came to Baal-perazim, and David smote them there, and said, The Lord hath broken forth upon mine enemies before me, and the breach of waters. Therefore he called the name of that place Baal-perazim. And there they left their images, and David and his men burned them. And the Philistines came up again, and spread themselves in the valley of Rephaim. And when David enquired of the Lord, he said, Thou shalt not go up; but fetch a compass behind them, and come upon them over against the mulberry trees. And let it be, when thou hearest the sound of a going in the tops of the mulberry trees, that then thou shalt bestir thyself: for then shall the Lord go out before thee, to smite the host of the Philistines. (2 Samuel 5:20-24)

And the Lord gave David the victory! There is an interesting lesson here! Have you read through the Gospels? Did you notice that when Jesus healed someone He never did it the same way twice? That's interesting to me. Why do you suppose that is? Maybe He didn't want people to think it was the method not the miracle.

God does the same thing here. Just a note. God did the same thing with Joshua and Jericho. Did God ever tell Joshua to circle a city again? No.

Just suppose, you have been praying for something in a certain chair at a certain time of day, with certain things in your hand (crucifix). Now God answers your prayer. Would you not be inclined to "repeat" the circumstances again, to get another prayer answered? Of course, you would. You think the power is in the "picture" and not in God. The same can be said for praying on your knees, for holding your Bible, for saying certain words, (except saying, "In Jesus name." that is a must!). The point is, you need to watch where you think the power is. It is not in what we do, it's in God alone. I think that's why He told David to do it this way.

Remember, God had already given him a victory just prior to this. Now God changes the format, why? To give God the glory!

I hate to keep harping on this, it is important! "Inquired of the Lord!"

This is so important that Samuel makes it a point to repeat it several times concerning David. When David sought guidance from God, God blessed him! When he didn't (as in a census) we will see the results later. It is a critical lesson for us.

Notice also, in the first victory, who David gave the credit to. When we forget where our victories come from God is hurt. God does things in such a way as to remove all doubt where the victory comes from. When you begin to think that anything you accomplish is all do to your own efforts, you begin so sink in a hole called "pride". It is a very deep hole and tough to get out of. Think about it. When you are in a hole what is your first response? You look up don't you. That is the only way out.

David will make a lot of mistakes from here on out. David never fails to look up when he has fallen or dug himself in a hole. That is a tough lesson to learn as a Christian. Look at this verse:

> "I can do all thing through Christ who strengthens me."
> (Philippians 4:13). (NKJV)

Notice we can do anything, but it's God who gets the glory! Never forget that. I love it so much on Wednesday's prayer meetings to hear "praises".

When I did the bulletin in a couple of churches I included a column for "Praises". We need to be reminded when God answers our prayers. The sick we have been praying for, to get well. The trials that needed our prayer are solved. God answers prayers. If there were no praises how long would we continue to pray? Interesting question!

2 SAMUEL 6

Again, David gathered together all the chosen men of Israel, thirty thousand. And David arose, and went with all the people that were with him from Baale of Judah, to bring up from thence the ark of God, whose name is called by the name of the Lord of hosts that dwelleth between the cherubims. And they set the ark of God upon a new cart, and brought it out of the house of Abinadab that was in Gibeah: and Ussah and Ahio, the sons of Abinadab, drave the new cart. And they brought it out of the house of Abinadad which was at Gibeah, accompanying the ark of God: and Ahio went before the ark. (2 Samuel 6:1-4)

First Samuel says,

> "Then the men of Jirjath Jearim came and took the ark of the Lord, and brought it into the house of Abinadab on the hill, and consecrated Eleazar his son to keep the ark of the Lord. So, it was that the ark remained a long time; it was there twenty years. And all the house of Israel lamented after the Lord. (1 Samuel 7:1-2) (NKJV)

If you read earlier the ark was taken captive by the Philistines. The men of Jirjath Jearim, retrieved it and took it to Abinadab.

David has defeated the Philistines and now he wants to move the ark into Jerusalem. Do you remember where the ark came from? Exodus 25. After God had given Israel the Ten Commandments He instructed Moses to build an ark to keep them in. The first thing that was constructed after Moses returned from the mountain. Following that God gave instructions for the first house of God, the Tabernacle.

The reason the Philistines had possession of the ark was because they thought it was a "good luck" charm. Look in 1st Samuel 4:19-22, *And she* said, "*The glory has departed from Israel, for the ark of God has been captured.*" (v. 22). Israel had thought that if they carried the ark of God into battle they would naturally have victory. The things of God are not "good luck charms". Have you ever thought that carrying your Bible would bring you luck? Be careful!

I wonder if David ever attended a Sunday School class? Ever had instruction from Jesse about the Laws of God? How much did David know about the law, about transporting the ark? Look here,

> *You shall put poles into the rings on the sides of the ark, that the ark may be carried by them. (Exodus 25:14) (NKJV)*

Also mentioned in Exodus 37:1-5. Finally look at this,

> *Therefore, all the men of Israel assembled with the king at the feasts, which was in the eleventh month. So, all the elders of Israel came, and the Levites took up the ark. Then they brought the ark, the tabernacle of meeting, and all the holy furnishings that were in the tabernacle. The priests and the Levites brought them up. (2 Chronicles 5:3-4) (NKJV)*

You see Solomon, maybe learned from his father's mistake, knew how to transport the ark.

God will not wink at our ignorance. I think that was one of the key reasons that Jesus established His church. I love the word Charles Swindoll uses to describe the functions of the church: W.I.F.E. Worship, Instruction, Fellowship, Evangelism. What better way to describe the "bride of Christ" than with the word wife!

We will see soon the impact of David's ignorance. Maybe he knew but felt it wasn't important. You see, David was doing the right thing. Everyone can agree on that. But sometimes when we attempt to do the right thing, we may need to "inquire of the Lord." Especially pertaining to the things of God. It's always best to do the things of God, God's way!

And when they came to Nachon's threshingfloor, Uzzah put forth his hand to the ark of God, and took hold of it; for the oxen shook it. And the anger of the Lord was kindled against Uzzah; and God smote him there for his error; and there he died by the ark of God. And David was displeased, because the Lord had made a breach upon Uzzah: and he called the name of the place Perez uzzah to this day. (2 Samuel 6:6-8)

Have you ever been mad at God? What were the circumstances? Was it something you did that didn't turn out the way you wanted? Did God neglect to act the way you thought He would. Remember, David's intentions were to honor God by bringing the ark into Jerusalem. Isn't it interesting that it doesn't say, "David inquired of the Lord?" Did you notice that?

God will not wink at our ignorance of His word, His laws, His statutes, etc. God went go to great pains to provide us with His letter to us, to instruct us in what He requires of us. What He expects of us. How we can have a personal relationship with Him. He even went so far, as to send His Son, to emphasize the importance of that relationship. So much so that His Son died on a cruel cross to demonstrate His desire for that relationship. We cannot have a relationship with a holy God unless the barrier of sin is removed. God took it on Himself to remedy that problem. Christ died on that cross so that we could have that relationship with a sinless God.

It is understandable that David would be upset. But as we will see, that act of God made David research the "right" way to accomplish what he wanted to accomplish. When God does something in our life that we don't understand, the first thing we need to ask Him is, "why?" God won't be offended, He will be blessed that you want to make things right. Next, we need to examine the situation, with the attitude, is there something that I have done contrary to God's plan, or will for my life. Just like David.

Excuse me a minute, but this points out the need to attend church. Church is the school where we learn what God wants to do in our life. What are God's "dos and don'ts" Just like David, if he had known the book of Exodus he may have known the "proper" way to transport the ark. Instead, and I repeat, he did not inquire of the Lord. Let me use this illustration: Suppose you want to start a church, a noble desire of course! Did you pray about it? Did you ask God about it? We all know that is a proper desire, but is it God's timing, God's place, God's will? That must be known first!

Some lessons come with terrific consequences. Most of the time it's because we don't seek God's guidance and direction. If something tragic happens, stop and ask God, "What are you telling me? What am I to do that I am not doing, etc.?" Good intentions do not impress God. His will and purpose are of the highest priority!

Uzzah was an innocent bystander. He was in the wrong place at the wrong time. That happens far too often today.

As far as the ark goes let me encourage you to read a very interesting story in 1 Samuel 5 and 6. This happens before David comes on the scene. It involves the Philistine's god called Dagon. This is when the Philistines had possession of the ark. It's interesting how the Philistines solved the problem. Check it out. One of my favorite stories concerning the ark.

Let me remind you also, how do you or, for that matter, the Jews look at the ark? Granted at one point, it was the place where God made Himself present. Exodus 40. They completed construction of the tabernacle and God's glory filled the tabernacle. You might want to put yourself in Israel's place. What did they think of the ark?

And David was afraid of the Lord that day, and said, "How shall the ark of the Lord come to me?" So David would not remove the ark of the Lord unto him into the city of David: but David carried it aside into the house of Obed-edom the Gittite. And the ark of the Lord continued in the house of Obed-edom the Gittite three months: and the Lord blessed Obed-edom, and all his household. (2 Samuel 6:9-11)

So, how did the ark get into Obed-Edom's home? God simply needed to make a point to David. The things of God are handled by the people of God. He didn't need to kill everyone who touched it. Is God trying to make a point in your life? How has He chosen to do that? Many times, God will simple act, unexplained experiences that try to get your attention. If that doesn't work He will progress to "louder" methods. One day you will ask, "Okay, God what are you trying to tell me?"

Notice that it took David three months, going to Sunday School and listening to the preacher preach until he realized that God had specific instructions for moving His ark! Have you spent any "consistent" time under the word of God? Have you learned anything? A fellow once told his pastor that he needed to move on. He can't remember what the pastor preached on, so he thought he ought to look for another church. The pastor asked him, "Do you remember what you had for dinner last Sunday?" The fellow replied, "No". "You received nourishment, didn't you?" Said the pastor.

We may not remember all that the pastor "feeds" us each Sunday. But, believe me, it will add to our knowledge and relationship with God. BUT, it must be on a consistent basis. What happens when you skip a meal? You get weak! By skipping, or a piece-meal approach to learning about God will not nourish you. It takes a consistent weekly diet!

Wouldn't it be nice if we could go back and list all the things we have learned through the years? Reminds me of a teenager who thought his parents were pretty dumb. He couldn't wait to leave home. After serving in the military for four years he came home. He was amazed at how much his parents had learned! Learning God's word is a daily, methodical, practice that takes years to grasp God's desire for you and His plan for your life.

Walking with God, like David, is a growing, continuous process. It's like keeping a journal. At first you don't see the benefit, but later, after a few weeks you can look back and see the benefit of starting it. But, at the time you couldn't see the benefit! David has come a long way since his time in the field with his father's sheep. It has all been a growing process. Has God taught you anything lately? Why not!

We saw earlier in 1 Samuel 6, how the Philistines captured the ark. God cursed the Philistines until they set the ark on a cart and sent it away. It came to the people of Kirjath Jearim and eventually ended up in the house of Abinadab. God will bless those who serve Him! David has some theological lessons to learn about the things of God. He will pass those on to his son Solomon. Solomon will have many lessons to learn himself. When he constructs the Temple, he will need to know these lessons. David, through his walk with God, will pass these lessons on to his son. As it should be.

David's anger with God was short-lived. His desire to bring the ark into Jerusalem will be achieved. But first David must find the right people and learn the proper way to accomplish God's will. We must also, pray and ask God what He wants to accomplish in our life, and ask for the proper method to achieve God's will for us! That's important!

Now it was told king David, saying, the Lord hath blessed the house of Obed-edom, and all that pertaineth unto him, because of the ark of God.

So David went and brought up the ark of God into the city of David with gladness. And it was so, that when they that bare the ark of the Lord had gone six paces, he sacrificed oxen and fatlings. And David danced before the Lord with all his might; and David was girded with a linen ephod. (2 Samuel 6:12-14)

Do you have a study Bible? You may wonder what happened. Did David just go and try the same thing twice, expecting God to wink this time? Look at these verses:

> Then David said, "No one may carry the ark of God but the Levites, for the Lord has chosen them to carry the ark of God and to minister before Him forever." And David gathered al Israel together at Jerusalem, to bring up the ark of the Lord to its place, which had been prepared for it. (1 Chronicles 15:2-3) (NKJV)

It's just like the Gospel accounts. Four stories, four authors, telling the same story. My Bible says the author of Chronicles is unknown. It is another version of David's story. It helps to fill in the blanks.

David checked with his pastor to find out the "proper" way to move the ark. Just as we can consult the word of God to discover the proper way to serve, worship, and have a relationship with the God of the universe!

I think it is interesting that Samuel says, "God is blessing Obed-Edom, so we need to get the ark in Jerusalem" (paraphrased). Notice also in Chronicles that it says they had "prepared a place." My guess is that he had constructed the tabernacle to house the ark. God was very particular where and how it was housed. Except for the two homes it rested in temporarily. The latter part of Exodus gives us the details.

This is interesting to me. Notice toward the end of the verses quoted, David offered a sacrifice every six paces. I hope they didn't have to go far. The point is, it is almost like saying, "I'm sorry" every step of the journey. Of course, believing in those days that God smiled on a sacrifice. God smiles at obedience, not sacrifice. David had come to do it the way God intended, that is what God has always wanted!

How do you please God? The greatest way we can please God is by obeying his commands. It's just that simple. The trick is, just like David, we need to know what God expects of us. The sad part is that most of us, just don't take the time to read His instruction book. The Bible is an awesome book. Full of instructions and praise! If you just spent a few minutes a day in the Psalms you would be taken into the presence of God. Fantastic pictures and words of praise for our God.

The Old Testament is a book of illustrations. Through the life of Abraham, Jacob, Noah, Isaac, etc. we have stories of how God works in our life. Just the story of Abraham and Isaac, how God tested Abraham's faith. Later how Isaac found his wife through the hand of God. If we would read the Old Testament we would get such an understanding of how God works in our lives. Then of course there is the apostle Paul. Nothing but trials in his life, yet God used him in a mighty way.

David learned a lesson with Uzzah. Learn God's way of doing things. It is interesting that when David thought to move the ark, he did not "inquire of the Lord". We must always seek God's way not our way. Even though it may seem like a great, godly, idea we must still seek God's plan and direction first!

So David and all the house of Israel brought up the ark of the Lord with shouting, and with the sound of the trumpet. And as the ark of the Lord came into the city of David, Michal Saul's daughter looked through a window, and saw king David leaping and dancing before the Lord; and she despised him in her heart. And they brought in the ark of the Lord, and set it in his place, in the midst of the tabernacle that David had pitched for it: and David offered burnt offerings and peace offerings before the Lord. (2 Samuel 6:15-17)

Why did God choose to tell us this story? David had accomplished his desire to bring the ark of God into Jerusalem. Why would He include these details? Let's look.

Look at David's enthusiasm! First let me clarify something. Some think David was naked here. If David did some research, as he probably did because of Uzzah, he would know that it was forbidden in Leviticus to "expose yourself". That's my take anyway. Have you ever been so excited that you wanted to dance? Not with a partner, but just to show your excitement.

What do you do at a baseball or basketball game when your side scores, you stand and cheer! You just can't just sit there.

David had scored a great victory. How many years has the ark of God been tossed around, between the Philistines and others. The ark has arrived again back into the tabernacle. That's interesting as well. It says that David had built the tabernacle. That is contrary to Exodus. That task as well was reserved for the Levites. I'm sure David checked their ID's before allowing them to build the tabernacle.

Notice also that David offered burnt offerings and peace offerings, straight out of Leviticus. I think David took a crash course on the books of Moses during those three months before transporting the ark. As we should. I have already covered that.

It's funny that God kind of slips in that comment about Michal. I'm surprised really. Michal loved David, saved his life. Notice that it says, *"Despised him in her heart."* Do you think there are people around you that envy your relationship with the Lord? I think so. Of course, we don't flaunt it. They can tell when you're walking with God. Why would they despise that? I think deep down everyone wants to know God. Most are embarrassed to approach God. They don't know how to go about creating a close relationship with the God of the universe.

Let me give you a hint. Just ask Jesus to come into your heart. Tell God your sorry for your past sins. A relationship with God begins with accepting Jesus, the Son of God, as your Savior. After that God will come into your heart through the person of the Holy Spirit. He will begin cleaning house. He will work slowly removing those things that offend God, and begin bringing your spirit in line with God's and begin establishing that intimate relationship with God.

Michal was offended. People knew she was David's wife. It's interesting that of all of David's wives she was the only one offended. Maybe the others didn't see, who knows. Again, why would God point this out. Are you "offended" by expressions of worship? There are a few in our church who will raise their hands during certain hymns. Praise can be expressed in many different ways, that's between them and God. Michal, maybe, was not used to praising God. Remember she was Saul's daughter.

We should all praise God in our own way. David chose to dance. Personally, I love to sing the hymns in our hymn book. They are full of praise. I can't sing out loud anymore, I start coughing. That doesn't keep me from mouthing the words. I must express, somehow, my love for the Lord, in praise!

And as soon as David had made an end of offering burnt offerings and peace offerings, he blessed the people in the name of the Lord of hosts. And he dealt among all the people, even among the whole multitude of Israel, as well to the women as men, to every one a cake of bread, and a good piece of flesh, and a flagon of wine. So all the people departed every one to his house. (2 Samuel 6:18-19)

You know, when God blesses us our natural response is to bless others. I hope that is how it is with you. I think I mentioned this before, but God never intended us to be lakes. Where all the blessings simply sit and stagnate. God meant up to be rivers, where God's blessings simply FLOW through us to others. What a fantastic way to live.

Did you notice David's priority? Do God's will first, then God will intern bless you. The priority must always be God first. I know that might sound cruel, or weird, but the blessings come from God in the first place. He blesses us to bless others! I think it is interesting that David provided, bread, meat and dessert, wow!

This, for some reason makes me think of when Jesus fed the 5,000. To me, it seems, God has this plan, provide for the physical needs of His people, so they will be open to hear God's message. So many missionary efforts begin with food and clothing, etc. After their physical needs are taken care of they tell them the good news that God loves them.

What better way to celebrate the accomplishment of a task than to praise God.

When you receive your paycheck, do you praise God that you have a job? When you get up in the morning do you praise God that He has given you another day? We take so many things for granted. These verses in David's life can so easily be overlooked. Ho hum. There is a great message here. What is our response to the blessings of God. David provided a great feast after God had blessed him. Who provided the meat and bread? Not David, God did!

David recognized the power that provided this great celebration. Notice

David's blessing, *"he blessed the people in the name of the Lord of hosts."* David knew, and acknowledged the author of this deed.

So, what makes David, "a man after God's own heart?" We can add this to our list. David recognized where his blessings, authority, and power comes from. We will see other examples of David's recognition of his relationship with God. When we begin to realize that nothing we have belongs to us. We simply are the stewards of God's blessing and will be held accountable for what we do with those blessings of God. Then the sooner we will have that special relationship that David enjoyed.

All that we have is because God blessed us with it. God expects us to use it wisely. Look for a minute at the parable Jesus tells in Matthew 25. "The Parable of the talents." It is repeated in Luke 19. Look at the servant who buried the blessings of God,

> *"Then he who had received one talent came and said, 'Lord, I knew you to be a hard man, reaping where you have not sown, and gathering where you have not scattered seed. And I was afraid, and went and hid your talent in the ground. Look, there you have what is yours.'"* (Matthew 25:24-25) (NKJV)

I beg to differ with the cruel master picture. God had "given" him that one talent. The thought is, "what did you do with what you were given?" The servant just buried it. The servant was admonished that he could have at least put it in the bank, and earned interest. Check out the parable. We are accountable for what God sees fit to bless us with! David was blessed to become king, to bring the ark of God to Jerusalem, etc. David returns that blessing by feeding the people!

And David said unto Michal, it was before the Lord, which chose me before thy father, and before his house, to appoint me ruler over the people of the Lord, over Israel: therefore will I play before the Lord. And I will yet be more vile than thus, and will be base in mine own sight: and of the maidservants which thou hast spoken of, of them shall I be had in honour. Therefore Michal the daughter of Saul had no child unto the day of her death. (2 Samuel 6: 21-23)

There are many who think David was naked from the comments of Michal. The definition of naked today, I believe, is not the same as then. Knowing the Law of Moses, I just can't believe David would shame himself in today's definition of naked. Maybe I'm wrong. I just choose not to think that David would do that, while honoring God in front of the ark.

That would of course explain Michal's comment. But David brings up another thought. See what he says, *"It was before the Lord, who chose me instead of your father and all his house, to appoint me ruler over the people of Israel."* When Michal was given to David as a wife, then taken away and given to another, then later David asked for her back, you must wonder about her loyalties. Was she bitter that it was David who was returning the ark to Jerusalem under his kingship?

Bitterness can ruin a life. It will eat away like a cancer. The sad part is that 99% of the time the one you are bitter against has no idea you feel this way. It may be a departed loved one, a long gone boss, or supervisor, etc. The point is that bitterness never accomplishes anything worthwhile. But, it can very well destroy your life. It will tear at your attitude, your health, your disposition, etc. It never cures anything!

How do you deal with bitterness? Give it to God. If there is something to be done, God will take care of it. Think of the relief that will come when you have given it to someone who can remedy the bitterness. It is amazing! Trust me, give it to God.

Did you catch the chronology of David? First, he accomplished the task God sent him to do. Then he praised God with offerings and sacrifices, then he blessed his people with food, and finally arrived home to bless his family. Take that for what it's worth. I think Jesus said something similar.

> *"He who loves father or mother more than Me is not worthy of Me. And he who loves son or daughter more than Me is not worthy of Me. (Matthew 10:37). (NKJV)*

Jesus challenges us to consider our priorities! Of course, we love our father and mother. The fifth Commandment says HONOR your father and mother. Jesus says we must love Him above all, including our own life.

We know David loved Michal, that's why he asked her to be returned to him. David loved God more. Her bitterness cost her the one thing the women, in those days, held paramount, children. By David depriving her of children he sentenced her to a life of shame. Much like she accused David of bringing on her. Interesting.

Remember this story. You must watch your tongue, your judging, your criticism, etc. God always has things in control. God took care of Uzzah, do you think if David shamed God He would have done something? Of course, He would. God will not allow His name to be dishonored! God was honored, David was blessed, the ark had been brought home.

2 Samuel 7

And it came to pass, when the king sat in his house, and the Lord had given him rest round about from all his enemies; That the king said unto Nathan the prophet, See now, I dwell in an house of cedar, but the ark of God dwelleth within curtains. And Nathan said to the king Go, do all that is in thine heart; for the Lord is with thee. (2 Samuel 7:1-3)

See! Again, we think because something is "logical" it must be God's will. I'm disappointed in David. Maybe it's not his fault, we are the same way. When do you think of God? Sunday, really? We are "suppose" to think of God on Sunday. What about during the week? Maybe God has blessed you by saving you from an accident, an injury, etc. Do you remember to thank Him? A prayer need, during the week. Okay, I'll share it on Wednesday Night Prayer Meeting. Why not pray now? My point is, when do you "think" of God?

David has been anointed king. He has defeated the Philistines. He has brought the ark of God into Jerusalem and returned it to the tabernacle, he has had help from Hiram and now has built a grand home. Now he thinks of God. Guilt? I don't know. I don't want to presume, maybe he had to be led by God's Spirit. I just think it's interesting.

I think, again, it's interesting that Nathan doesn't say, "Let's inquire of the Lord." David didn't ask either. There is a great lesson we need to learn here. Don't let it slip away. You see a beggar on the street, you want to help him out. Do you stop and ask God? Of course not. The guy needs help we shouldn't have to ask God. Maybe God is dealing with this guy to draw him to Himself. You will really go against God's plan for them. Maybe a poor example, but you get the point. We should never presume to know God's will. If there is a decision to be made, offer a little prayer.

Let me draw your attention to Nehemiah chapter 2.

Then the king said to me, "What do you request?"
So, I prayed to the God of heaven. *And I said to the*
king. . .(Nehemiah 2:4-5a) (NKJV)

Did you catch that? The king just asked what he wanted. Nehemiah
wanted permission and supplies to go to Jerusalem and rebuild the walls
of Jerusalem. He knew what he needed, he asked God for the words to say.
Have you ever just asked God for the words to speak? It's a simple prayer.

I think the key message here, I hate being redundant, but we should
never take God's will for granted! The greatest way is to be walking so close
to God that you sense God's will. That's tough to do. To be sure, just ask!
"Lord, what would you have me do?"

I get in trouble sometimes from my wife for picking up hitchhikers. I
have a system. First, I drive by them, I noticed them, too late. I will go to the
next overpass, cross over and go back to the next overpass and then by the
hitchhiker again. If he is still there I might pick him up. This gives me time
for two things, (1) someone else to pick them up. (2) For God to give me a
warning to pass them by. Maybe, again, a simple illustration but I hope by
now you get my point. There is nothing so urgent that a minute or two in
prayer, seeking conformation from God, couldn't hurt.

We all want God's best, God's will in our life. Most of the time He will
not put "warning signs". Just like Nathan here. We must get in the habit of
bringing every decision to God's wisdom and direction.

And it came to pass that night, that the word of the Lord came to Nathan,
saying, Go and tell my servant David, Thus saith the Lord, shalt thou build
me an house for me to dwell in? Whereas I have not dwelt in any house since
the time that I brought up the children of Israel out of Egypt, even to this
day, but have walked in a tent and in a tabernacle. In all the places wherein
I have walked with all the children of Israel spake I a word with any of the
tribes of Israel, whom I commanded to feed my people Israel, saying, why
build ye not me an house of cedar? (2 Samuel 7:4-7)

Nathan is to take a message to David. The sad part is that we need
desperately to hear this message as well. We work so hard at putting God
in a box, it must be frustrating to God. Is that what David is trying to do?
I hope not. It is a good lesson for us. God doesn't belong in a box, or in a

house. God is all around us, and IN us! The person of the Holy Spirit, the third person of the Trinity dwells within us!

By putting God in a box, we have the idea that God is "limited" in what He can do. If we can't conceive of it God can't do it. I wonder if Moses ever conceived that God could part the Red Sea. I wonder if Abraham ever thought that God would produce an offspring when he was near 100 years old. If we can't conceive of it God can't do it! We put God in a box. We restrict the power of God by our LIMITED imagination. All throughout the Old Testament we see example after example of God doing the unimaginable! That's a great word, that's a perfect illustration of what we think God can do.

Our pastor this morning made a big point about the followers of Jesus. Look at this verse in the Gospel of John,

> "Then a great multitude followed Him, because they saw His signs which He performed on those who were diseased. (John 6:2). (NKJV)

Jesus was so frustrated and disappointed that so many people followed Him because of the miracles and not His message. Are you that way?

You're a believer because you hope God will work a miracle in your life. He will, of course, through His Holy Spirit God will change your life. Is that the miracle you're looking for? I think not. You're looking for God to turn lead into Gold, water into wine, etc. You want the miracle without the message: You're a sinner saved by grace! Don't miss the message!

God is getting on Nathan and David's case here. You might want to look toward the end of 1 Kings 8,

> And it came to pass, when the priests came out of the holy place, that the cloud filled the house of the Lord, so that the priests could not continue ministering because of the cloud; for the glory of the Lord filled the house of the Lord. (1 Kings 8:10-11). (NKJV)

Isn't this an awesome picture! God filled the temple that Solomon built for God. Did God just take up residence? No! The temple was destroyed. Was God left homeless? Come on!

God, like the point that He is making to David, does not dwell in a house made with hands, He dwells in our hearts! The temple to David was an expression that was passed down through several generations. From Mt. Sinai when Moses received the directions for the Tabernacle. It was always meant to be temporary. God would later, in the New Testament, take up residence in our hearts!

The temple became the same as the ark of God. It became a symbol of God's presence and protection. A material thing cannot represent God. We begin to put our faith in the "thing" instead God Himself! Take note as we travel through David's life. David learns to trust God not material things.

Let's think about this a minute. Where is the first place God makes an appearance?

> *And they heard the sound of the Lord God walking in the garden in the cool of the day. (Genesis 3:8)* (NKJV)

Man had fellowship with God. God likes to spend time with His children! Next, we see God in a box. Look at this verse,

> *Then the Lord said to Noah, "Come into the ark, you and all your household, because I have seen that you are righteous before Me in this generation. (Genesis 7:1)* (NKJV)

God was in Noah's ark. Just a couple of "pictures".
For New Testament believer's, here is one of my favorites!

> *Do you not know that you are the temple of God and that the Spirit of God dwells within you? (1 Corinthians 3:16).* (NKJV)

Is that not an awesome concept if we could truly grasp its significance! God, in the person of His Holy Spirit dwells within us.

I know I'm repeating myself. This is so important. In the Old Testament, we have this picture of a God who is impersonal, housed in a temple. So, holy that He is unreachable. The sad part is that Israel, many times, worshipped the "thing" instead of God. The ark of God, the temple, etc. God, if you notice, dwells where His obedient children dwell. God walks among us. His Holy Spirit is as close as our next prayer.

The point, again, is that we tend, as Israel did, to put God in a box. He is confined to what we think He can do. God will only be as strong in our life as we will let him. One of my favorite verses in the New Testament is in Matthew,

> *Then He touched their eyes, saying, "According to your faith let it be to you."(Matthew 9:29).* (NKJV)

You see, this all-powerful God is "limited" by the amount of faith we have in Him. The more we learn to trust Him, put those problems and difficulties in His hands, the more God will make Himself known in our lives! Trust Him!

I will close with this. God wants to work miracles in your life. You must believe that He can!

Now therefore so shalt thou say unto my servant David, Thus saith the Lord of hosts, I took thee from the sheepcote, from following the sheep, to be ruler over my people, over Israel: And I was with thee whithersoever thou wentest, and have cut off all thine enemies out of thy sight, and have made thee a great name, like unto the name of the great men that are in the earth. Moreover I will appoint a place for my people Israel, and will plant them, that they may dwell in a place of their own, and move no more; neither shall the children of wickedness afflict them any more, as beforetime. (2 Samuel 7:8-10)

Interesting that God reminds David where he came from. Was David getting a little ahead of God? God uses Nathan here to build a case for David not to build the temple. We will see more of this later. I want to make a great point about this later.

I'd like you to take a close look at verse 10 in light of today's news. In the margin of my Bible I have written "Iran". I don't think the Koran mentions this fact. God has promised Israel a place. In 1948, what was then Palestine became recognized as the nation of Israel. There was a huge uproar at the time. There still is today. I am privileged in my lifetime to see our embassy moved from Tel Aviv to Jerusalem. Do you remember the uproar at just that historic moment?

Let me also remind you of the promise God made to Abraham in Genesis 12,

> "I will make you a great nation, I will bless you and make your name great; and you shall be a blessing. I will bless those who bless you, and I will curse him who curses you; and in you all the families of the earth shall be blessed." (Genesis 12: 2-3). (NKJV)

God has built His hedge around His chosen people. Other nations beware!

Why would God go to such lengths to remind David, through the prophet Nathan, of all that God has done for him? We need that reminder as well. How quickly we forget what God has done in our lives. A journal is a great reminder. To look back over the past year and be reminded of what God has done. Maybe this was God's way of letting David down gently.

Notice the beginning of verse 9, "And I have been with you wherever you have gone." That was Saul's weakness. God had departed Saul after his disobedience. One of the many things I ask myself is, "Will this change my relationship with God? Will God take His hand off of my life?" It never hurts to ask that question. God had His hand on David, even after the Uzzah event. David made a mistake, which he quickly corrected and brought the ark of God into Jerusalem.

Do you think God would ever take the time to explain to you why He did something? Have you asked? Many years ago, I thought I knew what God wanted. It was just my pride and arrogance. After God had closed the door, I was so hurt and disappointed. I kept asking God, why? a few months later He explained that I had gotten ahead of His plan. That because of that, this ministry was closed to me. A tough lesson, but God knows best. He will answer you if you trust Him and WAIT for His answer.

I mentioned this in the beginning of this book. All through the books of Kings, God used David as the measuring rod for each king that followed Solomon. Look at this verse:

> "And he did what was right in the sight of the Lord, yet not like his father David; he did everything as his father Joash had done. (2 Kings 14:3). (NKJV)

Notice, even though his biological father was Joash, David was referred to as his father as well. You will see this all through Kings. Each king, for the most part, is compared to David. David is the measure of a good king. What a legacy to leave behind for future kings of Israel. "A man after God's own heart!"

And as since the time that I commanded judges to be over my people Israel, and have caused thee to rest from all thine enemies. Also the Lord telleth thee that he will make thee an house. And when thy days be fulfilled, and thou shalt sleep with thy fathers, I will set up thy seed after thee, which shall proceed out of thy bowels, and I will establish his kingdom. He shall build an house for my name, and I will stablish the throne of his kingdom for ever. (2 Samuel 7:11-13)

Did you notice something about this passage? I see that all that has taken place is solely under God's command. The judges, etc. He is telling David, through His prophet Nathan, all that David wishes will come to pass, but not by David, but by his offspring.

We had an interesting discussion about this passage in our Sunday School class. Many want to see Christ in this passage. You could make that argument, but! Be careful reading into a passage what might not be there. We could read Christ into several passages, doesn't mean He is there. Always remember this rule of interpretation: Always consider the context. Nathan is telling David about a future temple to be built.

Notice these words, *"Also the Lord tells you that He will make you a house."* (v. 11) God is talking about David, and then Solomon, etc. The Temple will be built, but by Solomon, his seed. If you want to "read into" anything, think about the fact that our bodies are the temple of God, the Holy Spirit! You could read that into this passage. It is best to stick to the context.

In a sense God is affirming David's desire to build God a house. God is just saying, "not now!" God is also promising David that his descendants will be the ones to build it. Some want to take this to Jesus. Remember what Jesus said about the temple?

Jesus answered and said to them, destroy this temple, and in three days I will raise it up." (John 2:19) (NKJV)

Of course, we know that Jesus was talking about His body. We also know that about 70 years later the Temple was destroyed.

I think, maybe, what we are missing here, is God's promise to David. I made note of that earlier, how each king after Solomon was "measured" by David. That David was the standard used to measure each king. David is also mentioned in the book of Acts. Paul writes in chapter 13,

> "And when He had removed him, He raised up for them David as king, to whom He also gave testimony and said, 'I have found David the son of Jesse, a man after My own heart, who will do all My will.'" (Acts 13:22) (NKJV)

Of course, God was caught off guard when David had his affair with Bathsheba. Really? God knew what He was getting with David. Yet God knew David's heart. David knew God's heart. It is a great example of what God can do with us, as imperfect as we are, God can still use us. God has a way of bringing out His best in us, when we try to walk with Him.

God knew in David's heart that he simply wanted to honor God with a temple. God also explained to David that his family would always have strife, contention, maybe not without the kingdom, but within. David would be distracted by a temple. David needed to focus on his own family first. Sometimes we can be so heavenly minded that we are no earthly good. God will not work in chaos! One of my favorite verses is in 1 Corinthians, mark this down!

> Let all things be done decently and in order. (1 Corinthians 14:40) (NKJV)

Look at verse 33 same chapter,

> For God is not the author of confusion but of peace, as in all the churches of the saints. (1 Corinthians 14:33) (NKJV)

Is your life a mess? Confusion, the term today is "drama" that is not of God. God knew what was coming in David's life. He encouraged David to trust in God's plan and to wait on Him!

I will be his father, and he shall be my son. If he commit iniquity, I will chasten him with the rod of men, and with the stripes of the children of men: But my mercy shall not depart away from him, as I took it from Saul, whom I put away before thee. And thine house and thy kingdom shall be established for ever before thee: thy throne shall be established for ever. According to all these words, and according to all this vision, so did Nathan speak to David. (2 Samuel 7:14-17)

Here is another verse where we try to read "Jesus" into it. Be careful. What I get from these verses is God's commitment to David. Notice, also, *"If he commits iniquity, I will chasten him with the rod of men and with the blows of the sons of men."* And especially the next part, *But My mercy shall not depart from him, as I took it from Saul.* Comparing God's compassion and mercy for David verses Saul. Interesting. What did Saul do that David did not? Saul "willfully" disobeyed God. Saul took on the office of priest, etc.

We can be like David when we are disobedient, God will chasten us, but will not remove His mercy, why? The blood of Jesus Christ! As a child of God, we have a special relationship with God that Saul did not!

If God makes you a promise you can take it to the bank. *"Your throne shall be established forever"* That is a promise from God. I mentioned earlier about how much David is mentioned in reference to the kings that followed Solomon. Check it out.

I think the first few words might lead you to think that this is about Jesus. What is our relationship to God the Father in the New Testament?

> *For you did not receive the spirit of bondage again to fear, but you received the Spirit of adoption by whom we cry out, "Abba, Father" The Spirit Himself bears witness with our spirit that we are children of God. (Romans 8:15-16) (NKJV)*

It would do you well to underline these verses. In the word of God, God says we are His children. Think about that for a minute. That is what God is telling David here!

Do you have doubts about who God is, what He wants with you, what His plan for your life is? Ask Him! God will not lay out the blueprint of your life, He will give you a peace that He is in control and your only concern is trust Him every day for direction and instruction. Can you do that?

I love the picture of God as our heavenly Father. There are so many parallels to our earthly father and our heavenly Father. God loves us more than our earthly father, He created us. Just as our earthly father corrects us, to help us grow better, so our heavenly Father corrects us to get us back on the right track, to get our attention before something bad happens. Embrace the correction and thank God for caring enough to set us straight!

Nathan's final words here to David, God will give David a legacy far beyond just building a temple. David's legacy will be everlasting, established as long as there is a Word of God. How many preachers and evangelist have preached about David's exploits. Either about David and Goliath or David and Bathsheba. There is so much more about his life than those two episodes.

As we continue our journey, walking with David through these scriptures and trying to discover why David is called "a man after God's own heart" we will learn many things. Something else we might learn, God's heart. If David is close to God's heart, by studying David we can learn what is in God's heart. What it is that God loved about David to make him this promise. *"And your house and your kingdom will be established forever before you. Your throne shall be established forever"* (v. 16). (NKJV)

Stick with me, as we walk with David and learn about God!

Second Samuel Seven

Then went king David in, and sat before the Lord, and he said, Who am I, O Lord God? And what is my house, that thou hast brought me hitherto? And this was yet a small thing in thy sight, O Lord God; but thou hast spoken also of thy **servant's** house for a great while to come. And is this the manner of man, O Lord God? And what can David say more unto thee? For thou, Lord God, knowest thy **servant.** (2 Samuel 7:18-20)

We are going to spend some time here. The title is my way of remembering where this passage is. Why? Here, I think, is one of the biggest reasons David is a man after God's own heart. David has a servant's heart. A servant of God! Look what Jesus, God's own Son said,

> *"And whoever desires to be first among you, let him be your slave—just as the Son of Man did not come to be served, but to serve, and to give His life a ransom for many." (Matthew 20:27-28) (NKJV)*

A servant's attitude, I'm sure you have heard this once or twice. Also, remember this verse? In the Sermon on the Mount Jesus says,

> *"No man can serve two masters; for either he will hate the one and love the other, or else he will be loyal to the one and despise the other. You cannot serve God and mammon. (Matthew 6:24). (NKJV)*

Did you notice David's awe at what God had said? David couldn't believe that God would even consider his house. That God would take note of David. That is the attitude we should have. All our blessings from God are totally undeserved! Only by the grace of God do we achieve anything in this world. In Matthew 6:24 God challenges us to consider our priorities! What do we place first in our life?

In my Bible, I have underlined the word "sat" in verse 18. Is this an act of irreverence? I think not. David had such a relationship with God that his attitude was, let's talk this out. Let's have an intimate conversation, maybe it was "we are going to be here awhile." I just think it's interesting.

Of course, don't overlook David's attitude, "*Who am I, O Lord?*" David recognized where his blessings were from. He knew that he would not be king, living in a house of cedar, blessed beyond his imagination if it were not for God's hand on his life. The minute we begin to think that we have achieved anything apart from God we begin a downward spiral. Just like in Matthew, "*No man can serve two masters.*" Sometimes we think we are on the throne. God is the only occupant of that place. Be it in heaven or in our hearts!

Just so you know, there are eleven references to "servant" in the conclusion of this chapter. I think the thing that jumped out to me was, just who was calling himself "servant". Here is the King of Israel, the mighty warrior, the one who defeated the Philistines, etc. David knew his place. When we can have that "servant's" heart it will go a long way to strengthening our relationship with God. God is looking for hands and feet, that will accomplish His will here on earth. They begin with a willing heart and faith to trust God and be obedient to His will!

Look out now! Every time I start bragging on David I have to caution myself and remind myself that David is human, David will make mistakes, just like us. It's not being perfect that God is looking for. It's an open desire to have a relationship with the God of the Universe. To seek His will for our lives. To be used of God. We are human, we will make mistakes, it's our response after those mistakes that God is looking at. Do you turn to God or do you make excuses? That will determine your relationship. This morning I was reading through Psalm 51. Is that not the attitude we should have when we slip up? Of course, it is. Do you have a "servant's" heart? Pray about it. Ask God to "search your heart".

For thy word's sake, and according to thine own heart, hast thou done all these great things, to make thy **servant** know them. Wherefore thou art great, O Lord God: for there is none like thee, neither is there any God beside thee, according to all that we have heard with our ears. And what one nation in the earth is like thy people, even like Israel, whom God went to redeem for a people to himself, and to make him a name, and to do for you great things and terrible, for thy land, before thy people, which thou redeemest to thee from Egypt, from the nations and their gods? (2 Samuel 7:21-23)

Does David seem a little humble here? Of course, he does. We would be too if God worked in our life as He did in David's. The funny thing is that God does work in our lives. Until David mentions Egypt, I thought he was talking about me as a Christian. Think about it. Doesn't it sound like he was describing our relationship with God as a Christian? That's what I got.

Did you catch those words? *"For Your word's sake."* What are you holding in your hand? The Word of God. That must be the greatest revelation to a young, believer that has ever happened. When we realize that the VERY word of God is within our reach it will change our lives. We can know the mind AND the heart of God. Just in this study of David we can see how God responds to David's actions. How God feels about certain events in David's life is how God will respond to events in our life. Some He will bless, some He will need to correct us in.

Here is a scary thought. As a child of God, we reflect God in our daily testimony as we walk with God. Are we an example of God working in our life, or are we an example of God's grace? Think about that a minute.

Notice that David turns from God's blessing on him to God's blessing on His people. If we want to see God working today we can look at the nation of Israel. Many say that God has turned His back on Israel, per say. I don't think so. God will not forsake His chosen people. They have their problems, sure. But you let another nation think that God will allow their destruction and you will see God take a hand. God is letting them find their way right now, it's up to the Lord, when he will step in.

Look at these words, *"the one nation on the earth whom God went to redeem for Himself a people, to make Himself a name."* Does that not sound like what Christ has done for us. God started with a man, Adam, then He moved to a family, Abraham, then a nation Israel. Today, through His Son He has embraced the world. He gives us the option to become a child of God simply by asking Jesus to come into our hearts and save us.

Look at this, *"to make Your servant know them"* David is a witness to what God has done in his life. He is a witness to what God has done in the life of his country. How about you? Can you give testimony of what God has done in your life? Can you tell others how God has blessed you? Why not? Maybe you're not one of God's children. You think that everything that happens "just happens". I pray that's not the case. Take a minute and turn to Jeremiah 29:11-13. Read these verses a couple of times. Pray and ask God what they mean to you. Don't overlook the word "seek" in these verses!

David only mentions the word "servant" once in these three verses. He is humbled by what God is doing through his nation, Israel. There is a great example to follow through this story. God not only deals with David individually, but all through the Old Testament we can see how God deals with Israel. When they "inquire of the Lord" God directs them, guides them, empowers them to great things. When Israel "goes it alone" God does just that, leaves them to their own devices, which never turns out good.

Do you have the attitude of David? I hope so. Oh, one more thing, are you a child of God? Pray about your relationship with your heavenly Father.

For thou hast confirmed to thyself thy people Israel to be a people unto thee for ever: and thou, Lord, art become their God. And now, O Lord God, the word that thou hast spoken concerning thy **servant**, and concerning his house, establish it for ever, and do as thou hast said. And let thy name be magnified for ever, saying, The Lord of hosts is the God over Israel: and let the house of thy **servant** David be established before thee. (2 Samuel 7:24-26)

What is it about a house? Look how many times in the verses above that David is concerned about a house. This all began with David wanting to provide a "house" for the ark of God. What is it? It's permanent. It has the feeling, the context, the effect of permanency. Isn't that the American dream, to own your own house? Not so much today, I think. We have become a transient society. Nothing is permanent anymore. That was the heart of David here. The idea that the ark of God would have a "permanent" place.

That is the gift that God gives us when we become a child of God. When God's Holy Spirit comes to dwell in our hearts it is permanent. God, not like the Old Testament, takes up residence in our heart as a believer and never leaves. Just like God always had His hand on Israel. Yes, Israel made a lot of mistakes, at Mount Sinai God was ready to destroy them and start over, but Moses talked Him out of it. In Exodus 32, when Moses came down from the mountain, Israel had made a golden calf, God was ready to destroy the lot of them, Moses interceded for them.

God has taken up a "permanent" residence within the heart of every believer. He will not leave because we may have sinned and turned our back on God. If our conversion was real, God will not leave us. God wishes to use us, perfect us, give us a far greater life than we could even imagine. If we let Him! It's our choice.

When I was little my dad had this huge work bench. On the back board, he had mounted so many tools I would stare and stare and try to figure out what each tool was. Later I bought this device to flange copper tubing. I thought it was so cool because I knew how to use it. That is the key! You can have every tool devised by man, but until you actually use it, it is simply a decoration. That is how it is with God's Holy Spirit. Until you actually use Him and listen to Him and obey Him He is simply there.

These eleven verses in 2 Samuel 7 are redundant I'm sure. They can be. But read them a couple of times. Try to put yourself in David's place. He is having this conversation with the God of the Universe. He is setting down, speaking to God as a friend. We do that today because of the presence of God's Spirit within us. We can be on a boat in the middle of a lake, and have this conversation with God. In fact, that's a good place, no distractions!

We see here very clearly David's relationship with God. Why David is referred to as "A man after God's own heart." Because David has that special relationship, intimate relationship that can only come from talking and listening to God. I must remind you, David is no different than we are. We can have that kind of relationship. The problem is we are too busy, to sit down and have that conversation with God. We have this "to do" list that must be addressed and runs through our minds constantly and takes real effort to put it away and talk with God.

Let me share this. Every morning I get up, check my blood sugar, turn on the coffee pot, set in my chair in the living room and have my talk with God. As usual I do most of the talking. Every so often, God will interrupt my prayers by bringing things to my mind that need to be addressed. I have learned to listen. I used to get annoyed that these thoughts kept interrupting my prayers. Then one day I realized that God was trying to get a word in. I started listening closer. I love my time with the Lord. It has been such a blessing. You need a time and place to meet God.

For thou, O Lord of hosts, God of Israel, hast revealed to thy **servant**, saying I will build thee an house: therefore hath thy **servant** found in his heart to pray this prayer unto thee. And now, O Lord God, thou art that God, and thy words be true, and thou hast promised this goodness unto thy **servant**: Therefore now let it please thee to bless the house of thy **servant**, that it may continue for ever before thee: for thou, O Lord God, hast spoken it: and with thy blessing let the house of thy **servant** be blessed for ever. (2 Samuel 7:27-29)

As we conclude this prayer of David's, don't miss the context! In verse 18 we read, *Then King David went in and sat before the Lord.* The temple has not been built. The priests were the only ones allowed to enter the Holy of Holies, etc. I'm wondering where David went to talk with God. Does it matter? For years I used to drive over-the-road for United Parcel Service. Those hours between Kansas City and St. Louis were my prayer time. The music tapes got old quickly. I was a new Christian and I had a lot of questions for God. We had some interesting conversations. Where do you pray?

There is another point to make about David's prayer. How much time do you spend in prayer just "praising" God for who He is? Just recognizing His hand on your life. What He has done, where He has brought you to, etc. Just thanking God for His blessings. One of my main points in prayer is praying for my family. Lifting them up, their needs, even for their salvation. It never hurts to lift them up for salvation. I always pray, "Lord, if they don't know Your Son as their Savior, put someone in their path to share with them the gospel of Jesus Christ." Sometimes that's all we can pray. God's Holy Spirit will do the rest.

It never hurts to reflect, on where you have come. To be reminded of God's grace and how He has changed your life. David is always mindful of what God is doing in his life. You can see that in his prayer. David is overwhelmed at how much God has blessed him. That should be our attitude. We don't need a list. Just the fact that we have access to the throne of God is reason enough to be blessed!

One of my favorite techniques in praying is to remember this scene from The Robe with Richard Burton and Jean Simmons. It's the end of the movie. The king is giving them one last chance to renounce their faith. They both refuse, even though it would mean their death. The picture is this huge throne room with marble columns and this huge throne at the end of the hall. I like to imagine I'm walking down this hall into the presence of God. Kneeling, offering my sacrifice of praise. It helps me remember to whom I'm praying.

Then I have another image. I'm in heaven sitting on a park bench in a quiet, peaceful park. Jesus is setting next to me and I'm pouring out my heart through my tears, just to have the opportunity to be in His presence. The funny thing is, they are both the same God. The Almighty God sitting on His throne and Jesus sitting with me on a park bench. Isn't that awesome? That is what is meant by an intimate relationship with God.

David had that relationship with God. We can see that in these eleven verses. The ability to come into God's presence and sit and chat, and still recognizing that He is the Creator of the Universe and ruler of His people Israel. That He should bless His servant with the blessings he has received is amazing!

David will have his struggles. Dr. Charles Stanley talks about mountaintops and valleys. We will all go through our valleys. We should never forget those mountaintop experiences. When God was as close as a park bench and talking with us. We should always treasure those moments when God's grace allows us to set down and have a conversation with our heavenly Father and talk things out. And trust God to bring everything into His perspective!

2 SAMUEL 8

And David reigned over all Israel; and David executed judgment and justice unto his people. And Joab the son of Zeruiah was over the host; and Jehoshaphat the son of Ahilud was recorder; and Zadok the son of Ahitub, and Ahimelech the son of Abiathar, were the priests; and Seraiah was the scribe. And Benaiah the son of Jehoiada was over both the Cherethites and the Pelethites; and David's sons were chief rulers. (2 Samuel 8:15-18)

We will skip the details of this chapter. It mainly consists of the battles and victories that David achieved after his conversation with God about building a temple. I do want to note a verse in chapter seven:

> *"And your house and your kingdom shall be established forever before you. Your throne shall be established forever. (2 Samuel 7:16). (NKJV)*

Before God will allow a temple to be built God must establish Israel and peace. That is what chapter 8 is about. He begins with the Philistines and the list goes on to describe the surrounding nations. It was God's purpose for the warrior king to bring peace to Israel and security before He would allow His temple to be built.

God must bring order into your life before He can begin to work miracles in your life. Those miracles being, peace, security, love, companionship, and an intimate relationship with God the Father. You must, with the help of God of course, get your house in order. God must change your heart. He brings in a whole new view of the world around you. He brings in a totally new perspective on your friends and relatives. He opens your eyes to the actions of God all around you. You begin to pay attention to the promptings of the Holy Spirit. Your faith begins to grow as God increases His work in you.

David needed to get the surrounding nations under God's province. He couldn't very well construct a temple while he was away fighting these nations. His attention would be divided and God can't work with a divided heart! If your life is conflicted between, family, work, priorities other than God, God can't use you effectively. There is no concentrated power. Your life is in conflict, your heart is divided, your focus is everywhere but on God. When God begins to get you focused on Him you will be amazed at what God can accomplish through you!

I think I missed that chapter where David argues with God about wanting to build the temple himself. He didn't want to wait for his offspring. He wanted the glory of building a temple to his God. It wasn't fair after all he had done for God to let someone else have the honor of building the temple. I missed that chapter because it isn't there! That was not David. David was committed to God's will and plan for his life. It was God's way or not at all. David had the attitude we need to learn for ourselves. He trusts God, he wants what God wants, etc. No jealousy here!

What goes through your mind when someone under you is promoted over you? Think about that. Next what do you think when you see God bless someone else in the church that you thought you should receive. You know what I mean. Are you jealous, envious, mad at God for neglecting you? I hope not. You can take your complaints to God, but remember you are debating with the Creator of the Universe! Do you have it in you to praise God for blessing another person? For thanking God that He has blessed someone else? Think about it. Where is your focus? David's total focus was on God and His work in him. There is a greater lesson coming up. Pay attention!

2 Samuel 9

And David said, Is there yet any that is left of the house of Saul, that I may shew kindness for Jonathan's sake? And there was of the house of Saul a servant whose name was Ziba. And when they had called him unto David, the king said unto him, art thou Ziba? And he said, Thy servant is he. And the king said, Is there not any of the house of Saul, that I may shew the kindness of God unto him? And Ziba said unto the king, Jonathan hath a yet a son, which is lame on his feet. (2 Samuel 9:1-3)

Look at this verse from 1 Samuel:

> *"And you shall not only show me the kindness of the Lord while I still live, that I may not die; but you shall not cut off your kindness from my house forever, no, not when the Lord has cut off every one of the enemies of David from the face of the earth. So, Jonathan made a covenant with the house of David, saying, "Let the Lord require it at the hand of David's enemies. (1 Samuel 20:14-16). (NKJV)*

This occurs long before David begins his flight from King Saul. Jonathan knew what God's plan was. David would one day become king.

The custom in those days when a new king took over that he would destroy all kin from the previous king's family. Assuring no claims to his throne from the previous king. Jonathan knew that and wanted assurances from David that he would not continue the custom.

I think it is interesting in the passage in 1 Samuel it says, *"when the Lord has cut off every one of the enemies of David."* Did you notice that? That has been completed at the end of the last chapter (8). There is peace. As soon as that occurs David seeks any offspring of Saul's family.

In 2 Samuel 4 we read,

> "Jonathan, Saul's son, had a son who was lame in his feet. He was five years old when the news about Saul and Jonathan came from Jezreel; and his nurse took him up and fled. And it happened, as she made haste to flee, that he fell and became lame. His name was Mephibosheth. (2 Samuel 4:4). (NKJV)

This is a great example of paying attention to what you read. This description occurred in chapter 4 while David's seeking for a relative is in chapter 9. This has happened to me many times. I hear the name then I think, "where have I heard that name before?"

Have you ever been watching a movie and the camera happens to pick up something that seems at the time, unrelated to the plot? Make a note, because it will be useful later. The same is true with the word of God. God doesn't waste time putting things in His word that have no meaning. Just like the covenant with Jonathan. It is ALL important. Thank God for a concordance!

Why do you suppose, at this particular time, God brought Mephibosheth to David's mind? Not by name, but a commitment he had made to Jonathan years earlier? Why do you say years? Look at chapter 8. Do you think all those victories, battles, etc. came over night? I'm sure it took David years to finally bring peace to Israel. When that task was completed, God brought Jonathan's son to David's attention. God does not forget promises He has made to us. It must be in His time according to His plan.

This is another great chapter. Digest it with me and let's see if there is another trait we learn to incorporate in our walk with God. We have seen David's compassion already with Abigail, and not killing Saul, and his relationship with Jonathan. There is much more to learn!

And the king said unto him, Where is he? And Ziba said unto the king, Behold, he is in the house of Machir, the son of Ammiel, in Lo-dedar. Then king David sent, and fetched him out of the house of Machir, the son of Ammiel, from Lo-debar. Now when Mephibosheth, the son of Jonathan, the son of Saul, was come unto David, he fell on his face, and did reverence. And David said, Mephibosheth. And he answered, Behold thy servant! (2 Samuel 9:4-6)

I had heard somewhere that Lo Debar was like the wilderness. Mephibosheth was hiding from David. I shared earlier the custom of the day. He feared for his life. I guess he didn't know the relationship David had with Jonathan. Maybe he did know how Saul felt about him. Anyway, I mentioned that years probably have gone by. Why would David, all of a sudden, think to find offspring of Jonathan or Saul for that matter?

David made a commitment years earlier to Jonathan. He also had respect for Saul, at least his office. I think it was God who brought this to David's memory. God works that way. I can't count the number of times God has brought old friends or circumstances to my mind to remind me of something. It is amazing! I'm sure He has done the same for you.

Can you imagine what went through Mephibosheth's mind when Ziba came and said, "King David wants to see you?" Fear, probably. Notice when he arrives at David's house he prostrates himself on the floor. He says, *"Here is your servant."* He probably thinks he will not rise from the floor.

Has God brought people from your past to your mind? If He hasn't said or given you reason, you might want to pray for them. I don't know how many testimonies I have heard of God working in someone's life later to find that a friend, thousands of miles away, was praying at that time for them. When God brings someone to your mind, pray, ask God why, if anything just lift them in prayer! There is a reason God brought them to your mind. Of course, if you don't know God, have not asked Jesus into your heart, have no relationship with God, you needn't worry. It was not the Spirit of God who brought them to your memory.

Most of the time, when I reflect on the past, it is on the church at Freeman where I ministered for two plus years. I will always regret the way I left there. It was not pretty on my part. I had some of the most amazing experiences there. God worked in me through those godly people.

I have so many fond memories of my "ministry" days. The years of taking a youth group to Camp Joy. Freeman, of course, many, many years working in the Sunday School ministry. Memories. Just like David. I think when David saw Mephibosheth he remembered the days he spent with Jonathan. Memories can be a blessing or a curse. David decided to fulfill a commitment he had made to Jonathan. Again, I believe the time was right for God to bring his promise to Jonathan to his mind, it was time to fulfill that promise!

I pray you have no "unfinished memories" to reconcile. Pray, ask God to search your heart, reveal anything that was left "undone". A misunderstanding that may need corrected. A promise, as yet, unfulfilled, etc.

This chapter is about a little boy, the son of Jonathan that will help David heal an old wound. We never know why God brings certain people into our lives, if just for a minute. Remember, God never does anything by "accident," there is always a plan, a reason.

And David said unto him, Fear not: for I will surely shew thee kindness for Jonathan thy father's sake, and will restore thee all the land of Saul thy father; and thou shalt eat bread at my table continually. And he bowed himself, and said, What is thy servant, that thou shouldest look upon such a dead dog as I am? Then the king called to Ziba, Saul's servant, and said unto him, I have given unto thy master's son all that pertained to Saul and to all his house. (2 Samuel 9:7-9)

Do you know what comes to my mind when I read this passage? To start, I heard a sermon on this passage by Dr. Jack Hyles years ago as a very young Christian. A very memorable sermon! Dr. Hyles stressed the idea of eating at the "King's" table. As we will one day in heaven. Look at this passage:

> "Let us be glad and rejoice and give Him glory, for the marriage of the Lamb has come, and His wife has made herself ready." Then he said to me, "Write: Blessed are those who are called to the marriage supper of the Lamb!" And he said to me, "These are the true sayings of God." (Revelation 19:7,9) (NKJV)

So, who is the bride of Christ? The best reference I could find is Ephesians 5:22-28, check it out. It clearly pictures the church as Christ's bride. Next, we see "The Lamb". How do we know that is Christ? First look at this:

> The next day John saw Jesus coming toward him, and said, "Behold! The Lamb of God who takes away the sin of the world!" (John 1:29) (NKJV)

So, what significance the lamb? One of the greatest revelations to me was when I asked myself, "Why did Jesus have to die?" Until I read Exodus 12 I had no idea. Have you asked yourself that? Read Exodus 12, John 1:29, I hope the picture will be clear.

We like to joke in the Baptist Church that when you go to church on Sunday you should bring a Bible and a bowl. We like to eat. Don't laugh! Check out Acts:

> *And they continued steadfastly in the apostles' doctrine and fellowship, in the breaking of bread, and in prayers. (Acts 2:42) (NKJV)*

Around the dinner table there is "fellowship" consummated! I can't begin to list the number of conversions that have occurred at a church "dinner," or social gathering, we like to call it "pot luck". There is something that binds the fellowship around food.

Look how David words it: *and you shall eat bread at my table continually.* Your part of my family now. Your safe, secure, "no worries". This is the grandson of the king who pursued him to kill him. Who threw javelins at him several times. Who sent him out, hoping he would be killed, etc. A picture of forgiveness? You decide!

Do you remember the feeling when something you have wanted to happen for years had finally come to pass? Wasn't that a glorious feeling. Here David finally gets to demonstrate his great love and commitment to his friend, Jonathan. It's like he has come full circle and now the loop can be closed. He has kept his word to Jonathan. Stop for a minute and think about how that must have felt.

I mentioned that I think Lo Debar was considered a wilderness. That was the picture I was given. Here, Mephibosheth was pluck from that meager existence and placed at the king's table with anything his heart desired. The neat thing about this is, that is us! That was the picture Dr. Hyles painted. As children of God, no matter our status in this life, one day we will be seated at that banquet table presented with anything our heart desires. As a child of God, we will have access to the marriage supper of the Lamb.

I think it is interesting that God put this forgotten pledge on David's mind at this time. All the fighting, the warring country's around him had been defeated. There was peace in Israel. Now David can do something that would bless God, and reward David for his faithfulness. I'm sure David's heart was full just to be able to repay Jonathan in this simple gesture.

Thou therefore, and thy sons, and thy servants, shall till the land for him, and thou shalt bring in the fruits, that thy master's son may have food to eat: but Mephibosheth thy master's son shall eat bread always at my table. Now Ziba had fifteen sons and twenty servants. Then said Ziba unto the king, According to all my lord the king hath commanded his servant, so shall thy servant do. As for Mephibosheth, said the king, he shall eat at my table, as one of the king's sons. And Mephibosheth had a young son, whose name was Micha. And all that dwelt in the house of Ziba were servants unto Mephibosheth. So Mephibosheth dwelt in Jerusalem: for he did eat continually at the king's table; and was lame on both feet. (2 Samuel 9:10-13)

As we conclude this chapter about Mephibosheth, we need to ask, why did God think it important enough to include this episode in David's life? Of course, my first thought is "compassion". A very important trait in David's life. His heart is the heart of God. Paul talked about it a lot in the New Testament. In the gospels Jesus demonstrated it over and over. This is a trait that we will definitely need to incorporate into our own lives. When we fail to exhibit compassion, there is something dead within us.

I can't overlook this reference to eating at the king's table. As Dr. Hyles pointed out, it is a great illustration of our welcome into heaven. An unending feast! One of my favorite passages is in Luke 24:13-32. Here is my verse,

> Now, it came to pass, as He sat at the table with them, that He took bread, blessed and broke it, and gave it to them. Then their eyes were opened and they knew Him; and He vanished from their sight. And they said to one another, "Did not our heart burn within us while He talked with us on the road, and while He opened the Scriptures to us!" (Luke 24:30-32). (NKJV)

I love this story. Jesus was walking with them all the time until they arrived at the restaurant. When they began to eat, Jesus blessed the meal, then their eyes were opened. I wonder. Do you bless your food out in the public? How about at home? I just wonder if the act of blessing the food invites the presence of the Lord? Just a thought.

According to my Bible the name Mephibosheth means "destroying shame". Interesting. When you see a crippled person, or someone less blessed than you, what is your response. David had no idea who, if anyone, would turn up when he made his request. If there were any offspring of Saul or Jonathan? David's response is our response. Don't you think so? Maybe that is why Mephibosheth was hiding in Lo Debar. For fear and maybe shame. David brought him to the king's table!

David not only set him at his table, but instructed his servants to work his land and provide for his future. Look at it again. David instructed Ziba to work the land of Mephibosheth and provide for his well-being. If my memory serves Mr. Ziba will appear again later.

Again, I must ask myself, "Why did God think it important enough to include this scenario in His Holy Word? I am sure there is an important lesson here for us. Maybe it's just to give us a picture of our future in heaven. To have the ability to sit at the King's table. My own personal joke is that they would serve ham at the marriage supper. Think about it. It might shine some light on how much you know about the Bible.

You don't suppose this episode contributed to David's relationship with God? Remember what Jesus said,

> "Then He will answer them, saying, assuredly, I say to you, inasmuch as you did not do it to one of the least of these, you did not do it to Me." (Matthew 25:45) (NKJV)

You need to read the whole passage (25:34-46). If your familiar with the New Testament your familiar with this passage. You could almost put this passage in Matthew, right after this story of Mephibosheth. David illustrates the message of Jesus. God takes note of how we treat others, we might think it isn't important, but from what I read in the Bible it is very important to God. One last thing, don't overlook Matthew 25:46, think about it!

2 SAMUEL 10

And it came to pass after this, that the king of the children of Ammon died, and Hanun his son reigned in his stead. Then said David, I will shew kindness unto Hanun the son of Nahash, as his father shewed kindness unto me. And David sent to comfort him by the hand of his servants for his father. And David's servants came into the land of the children of Ammon. And the princes of the children of Ammon said unto Hanun their lord, Thinkest thou that David doth honour thy father, that he hath sent comforters unto thee? Hath not David rather sent his servants unto thee, to search the city, and to spy it out, and to overthrow it? (2 Samuel 10:1-3)

Has this ever happened to you? You prejudge someone's motives based on input from others. This is so pervasive today with "social media" isn't it? By the time you have reached a conclusion you have fifteen people telling what you should think. I'm glad the Lord included this vignette. Remember, we talked about this earlier. Everything in the Bible God has put here for a reason!

Let me clarify something if you haven't figured it out yet. In the beginning, it says Ammon was the father of Hanun. Later it says Nahash was his father. If you read through the book of Kings you will notice that even after several generations some of the kings have referred to David as their father. Of course, he wasn't. He was there great-great-grandfather, etc. This is the culture of the time. Don't get confused. I think they referred to Nahash as his father because at one point David had dealings with Nahash, not Ammon.

This reminds me so much of the counsel Solomon received when Israel became divided. First, he asked the elders. The elders cautioned restraint. His peers told him to threaten them with harsher treatment. How many decisions do you make based on the counseling of others? How many decisions do you make based on the wisdom of the Word of God? Think about it.

Sometimes we don't have time to ask "counsel" do we? We need to make a snap decision. That is when it is so important to have digested as much of the Word of God as you can. Probably beginning with the book of Proverbs. Daily wisdom from God. The more that is implanted into our thought processes the more we will act instinctively in God's will. Spend some time in Proverbs. It's hard to read! Each verse is a chapter in itself! There is a plan that if you read one chapter a day you will read the whole book in a month. If you do that, take the time to digest each verse. Chew on it a while, ask God to show you His wisdom from each verse. The interesting part is that, that book is so appropriate for TODAY!

David, not long after his encounter with Mephibosheth, desires to show kindness to a friend's family after a death. Well intentioned, condolences, etc. His emissaries are greeted with suspicion. Do you do that? What is the term today, "Beware of Greeks bearing gifts" or something like that? A gift automatically comes with catches. I hope you will spend a minute in this chapter and ask yourself, "am I that way?" Do we greet everyone with suspicion? It is my habit, when I can, to talk to someone, face to face. I will drive a good distance, rather than phone them, just to speak face to face. It is important to me. It can save a lot of problems later. The written word is even riskier. You can't put emotion into the written word very well. It is easy to be misunderstood, very easy! Don't jump to conclusions, hear them out, make sure you understand where they are coming from. Hanun didn't!

Wherefore Hanun took David's servants, and shaved off the one half of their beards, and cut off their garments in the middle, even to their buttocks, and sent them away. When they told it unto David, he sent to meet them, because the men were greatly ashamed: and the king said, Tarry at Jericho until your beards be grown, and then return. And when the children of Ammon saw that they stank before David, the children of Ammon sent and hired the Syrians of Beth-rehob, and the Syrians of Zoba, twenty thousand footmen, and of king Maacah a thousand men, and of Ish-tob twelve thousand men. (2 Samuel 10:4-6)

Have you ever done something rash and regretted what you had done? Of course, you have. What was your response? 33,000 men were recruited by Hanun to fight David. This may give us an indication of David's army. The question I want to ask, "Why does God think this episode is important enough to include in His Holy Word? In our minds, this isn't really important enough to include in David's narrative. Why did God think it was?

First let's look at the context. This scenario occurs right after David shows compassion to Mephibosheth, Jonathan's son. Now we have this story. Of course, David is also showing compassion to a family who lost their father, the king. The theme of compassion runs through David's life. I think of Abigail, Jonathan, even Saul when David had two opportunities to kill him and didn't. That is a key component in David's heart, and God's as well. Without God's compassion, there would not have been a cross at Calvary!

Why are people so cruel? Those who know Jesus can ask that question. Others may not think it a big deal. Cruelty seems to be a part of man's sin nature. It seems, we go out of our way to think of significant ways to improve on cruelty. The cross is a great example. In David's time, it was unheard of. In Roman days, someone devised this method of cruelty. If you have seen any stories of the Holocaust you must wonder, what is the extent of man's cruelty to man?

What is so cruel about cutting off someone's beard. Again, we need to understand the culture and customs of the day. I can't think of an equivalent for today. These servants were so embarrassed that they could not return to their people. I just think it demonstrates just plain cruelty.

Weird thought. I wonder how many times this scenario was played out in the winning of the west from the native Indians. Offers of peace were misinterpreted with dire consequences. Of course, you have never falsely jumped to conclusions, right? Maybe there is something to thinking about why God included this vignette in David's story.

This also points out why we are making this journey with David. Observing how he responds, how God responds, etc. As impartial observers, with the whole story before us, we can analyze and learn key lessons from the illustrations God chose to include in His Word. So many today want to ignore the Old Testament and focus on the New. The principles taught in the New Testament are demonstrated for us in the Old Testament. It also shows that attitudes and mistreatment were just as prevalent in the days of Moses as they are today!

So, what is your response when you make a bad mistake? Do you raise an army of 33,000 men? Today our response is to "justify" our mistake. Maybe we can blame someone else, like Adam and Eve in the Garden. That didn't work out very well. Anything but take responsibility for our actions. I wonder what David would have done if Hanun had gone to David and apologized for his mistake and asked forgiveness? What do you think. We never think of that today, do we?

Don't pass over these lessons in David's life. They are so useful in our lives today. Learn from them. Think about your "first response" to perceived threats. I think Hanun used an old Western response, "Shoot first and ask questions later" interesting. Is that how you respond to strangers?

And he said, If the Syrians be too strong for me, then thou shalt help me: but if the children of Ammon be too strong for thee, then I will come and help thee. Be of good courage, and let us play the men of our people, and for the cities of our God: and the Lord do that which seemeth him good. And Joab drew nigh, and the people that were with him, unto the battle against the Syrians: and they fled before him. And when the children of Ammon saw that the Syrians were fled, they fled also before Abishai, and entered into the city. So Joab returned from the children of Ammon, and came to Jerusalem. (2 Samuel 10:11-14)

Can you pray the prayer Joab did? *"And may the Lord do what is good in His sight."* That is an awesome prayer. Have you ever come to the point where you just need to take your hands off the wheel and leave it in God's hands? It is a tough lesson to learn. I won't bore you with all these verses on faith. Plenty of time for that.

One of my favorite verses is in Daniel, it concerns Shadrach, Meshach, and Abed-Nego. Daniel chapter 3. The three have refused to bow down to Nebuchadnezzar's statue. The penalty was to cast into a huge furnace. They refused. Look at this verse,

> "If that is the case, our God whom we serve is able to deliver us from the burning fiery furnace, and He will deliver us from your hand, O king. **But** if not, let it be

known to you O king, that we do not serve your gods, nor
will we worship the gold image you have set up." (Daniel
3:17-18). (NKJV)

They trusted in God, BUT if it wasn't God's will to spare them, they were ready to die than bow down to the image. That is the picture I get here with Joab and Abishai. They prepared for battle but they trusted God for the victory. It reminds me of the story about two farmers who were praying for rain. One farmer was on his knees, praying. The other farmer was plowing his field getting ready for the rain. Which had more faith?

Daniel's three friends trusted God for the outcome, whatever God's will. The same with Joab and Abishai. Do you.

Have you given God instructions on how He can answer your prayer? You pray, and pray, and maybe God has answered your prayer. It wasn't the way you wanted it answered. Did God answer? Of course! According to His will, not yours!

Joab and Abishai had their strategy but they trusted God to give them the victory. Just like with Joshua. God would give Joshua the victory over Jericho, but it had to be on God's terms, for God's glory. That is the key to our prayers. It's not like God doesn't know what you're struggling with. God already has a plan to answer your prayers, He's working on it before you even pray. Don't try to tell God how to answer your prayer. Just stand back and see who gets the glory!

It doesn't say, *"they inquired of the Lord."* That is evident in the prayer that was recorded. They asked God's assistance then went into battle. How about you? Once you have prayed and put it in God's hands, do you try to help God out? I did that once, I learned a very hard lesson. God's time, God's way, for God's glory! Learn that now!

This whole major battle was started because the leaders of Ammon mistook David's efforts to show compassion for the friend who had died. So many, many times a simple misunderstanding can blow up into war between friends. It must be dealt with right away. Apologies given where warranted, forgiveness as quick as possible. Begin healing the wounds as quickly as possible. The problem is never solved by silence. Just ignore it, it will go away. Not likely. An open wound must be dealt with quickly!

And when it was told David, he gathered all Israel together, and passed over Jordan, and came to Helam. And the Syrians set themselves in array against David, and fought with him. And the Syrians fled before Israel; and David slew the men of seven hundred chariots of the Syrians, and forty thousand horsemen, and smote Shobach the captain of their host, who died there. And when all the kings that were servants to Hadarezer saw that they were smitten before Israel, they made peace with Israel, and served them. So the Syrians feared to help the children of Ammon any more. (2 Samuel 10: 17-19)

Finally, peace for Israel. Not hardly. Now you understand why God didn't want David to build their temple. The men were constantly fighting. God wanted focused, committed servants to work on His temple. Is your mind divided? Are you trying to fit the world into your relationship with God? It won't work. You can function in this world without being a part of it. Look what the apostle John wrote,

> "Do not love the world or the things in the world. If anyone loves the world, the love of the Father is not in him. (1 John 2:15). (NKJV)

David's life was divided. God wants focused servants!

These battles served a purpose. They would eventually bring peace to Israel. THEN God would work through Solomon, David's son, to build His temple. The same is true in your life. If you are dealing with strife, desires, plans of your own, God will not derail YOUR plans. He will simply wait patiently by, waiting for you to discover that your plans will turn to ashes. His plan is perfect. The neat thing is that God's plan will bring you far greater blessings than your plans ever could. You must focus on Him and not the world.

I think it is interesting in the passage above that it says, *"David killed seven hundred charioteers and forty thousand horsemen."* I'm sure David didn't do it all by himself. Ask any pastor worth his salt, and he will tell you that nothing gets done in the church, except for the help and support of the men and women in the church. The deacons, the support staff, the Sunday School teachers, the pianist and organist, etc. Of course, the pastor gets the lion's share of the credit, but if it were not for the power of the Holy Spirit working in the support staff, if would fail!

This, in a sense, brings to close these area battles with neighboring countries. The battles now will turn inward. With family and his own personal relationships, even with God. This is a dividing point in David's life. The mighty warrior, who led Israel to many, many victories will have to deal with family matters. Beginning with him and Bathsheba. In all of David's struggles we need to note how often he turns to God. You can read that all through the psalms that David wrote. Not only his struggles with his enemies, but with his relationship with God. He was always asking God's intervention, His forgiveness, restoration in his relationship with God.

In this transition, it's a good time to pause in our walk and take a personal inventory. Examine OUR relationship with God. How much time do we spend in prayer? Do we believe in prayer? If you didn't believe that God would answer your prayers you wouldn't bother, would you? If you didn't think that reading your Bible would be of any benefit, you wouldn't do it, would you? These are all symptoms of our relationship with God. Oh, let me include one more, if I may. How often do you worship God, in His house?

This is so close to my heart. I cannot think of any other place I would rather be on The Lord's Day than in God's house! Jesus made a point of creating His church to worship Him. Not just worship, Bible study and fellowship, spend time in the early chapters of Acts. See what was important to the early church. This is one of my dearest times when I get to set with God's people and listen to the hymns, talk with "family" members. I am closer to my church family than I am most of my own family. A kindred-Spirit type of relationship. We all have the same Father, Amen!

2 Samuel 11

And it came to pass, after the year was expired, at the time when kings go forth to battle, that David sent Joab, and his servants with him, and all Israel; and they destroyed the children of Ammon, and besieged Rabbah. But David tarried still at Jerusalem. And it came to pass in an eveningtide, that David arose from off his bed, and walked upon the roof of the king's house: and from the roof he saw a woman washing herself; and the woman was very beautiful to look upon. And David sent and enquired after the woman. And one said, Is not this Bathsheba, the daughter of Eliam, the wife of Uriah the Hittite? (2 Samuel 11-1-3)

How many times have we noticed that David, "Inquired of the Lord?" Tonight, he inquires of those around him, "who is this woman?" A question he had no business asking. He knows why he is asking.

Where was the Holy Spirit at this point? You want to scream, "WATCH OUT". Because we know what is coming. David didn't know, and neither do we. Do you think God's Spirit was attempting to get his attention? Of course, but it is so easy to "ignore". The warning signs can be all around us, but we know better, don't we?

We notice, of course, right off that David was not where he was supposed to be. He should have been with Joab. Why he stayed home, we don't know. That is the first question we need to ask ourselves, and God. Where am I supposed to be? Then we might want to ask, "What am I supposed to be doing?" We have talked so much in the past about "walking with God". If we are walking with God we will be where we are supposed to be. Pray about it!

To me, this is one of the saddest sections in the whole Old Testament. David has had a great testimony up till now. Here is where we realize that David is human. Up till now he has been almost "Super-Christian". Following God, trusting God, seeking God's direction. It is a warning to us! Satan is constantly looking for a "crack" where he can slip in and destroy a Christian testimony.

Let's see how did Peter describe the devil?

> "Be sober, be vigilant, because your adversary the devil walks about like a roaring lion, seeking whom he may devour. (1 Peter 5:8). (NKJV)

Did you notice the word Peter uses? Peter didn't say hurt, or attack, he used the word "devour". Meaning completely consume his enemy. Satan is out to "destroy" God's people. His greatest weapon is to destroy their testimony in this lost world.

That's why it is important for us to observe David here. We are going to make mistakes, it is what we do in response to those mistakes. God knew we would fall. That's why He loved us so much that He sent His Son to pay for those sins on the cross of Calvary. That we would have a means to restore that relationship with our Heavenly Father. Without that blood payment, we would all still be lost in our sin.

Remember, we talked about Saul's sin of pride? Here is another of those three deadly sins John talks about it here:

> For all that is in the world—the lust of the flesh, the lust of the eyes, and the pride of life—is not of the Father but is of the world. And the world is passing away, and the lust of it; but he who does the will of God abides forever. (1 John 2:16-17) (NKJV)

Ponder these verses a minute, is Satan attacking you?

And David sent messengers, and took her; and she came in unto him, and he lay with her; for she was purified from her uncleanness: and she returned unto her house. And the woman conceived, and sent and told David, and said, "I am with child." (2 Samuel 11:4-5)

How many lives have been turned upside down because of these four words, "I am with child?" Then again how many married couples are so excited, and blessed because of these same four words? It all depends on the circumstances, doesn't it? Why is it, we never seem to consider the word, "consequences?" Every deed we do, every action we take has consequences. We never stop to think how this will affect, friends, relatives, those in the circle around us. Oh, we can try to hide it sometimes, but it's funny how the truth comes out.

David is the king! David can do whatever he pleases! Really? Did that relieve David of the consequences?

How do you respond to consequences? You can deny it, you can dispute it, you can ignore it, etc. Does any of these responses eliminate it? You notice I didn't include "accept" it? That is the last resort. Today we can always have a doctor take care of the evidence, but not the consequences in our soul. Why do we never think of that before the act occurs?

Do you remember how many wives David has? I can think of four, I'm sure there are more by now. His son Solomon had four-hundred. I think that may dilute the relationship with a wife. The culture in those days, of course, is different than today. If it was "acceptable" why did David try to cover it up? We will look at that shortly.

Do you think God's Spirit might have said something to David when he asked his servants to go get the girl? I think so. I'm sure of it. So why didn't he listen? Why do you not listen when God convicts you of that little lie you told your co-worker the other day? The words you used when that guy cut you off in traffic? How about your rudeness to the salesperson who gave you a hard time at the store? Where was the Holy Spirit then? You were just not listening!

Just a thought. How did Bathsheba know it was David's baby? Her husband was with the army, serving under Joab in battle. Where David should have been. There is an interesting story in Genesis 38. Take a minute and read it. The interesting thing to me is that God pauses in the middle of Joseph's story to tell us this "unrelated" story, why? It is a link in a chain.

I was not looking forward to this chapter. To me, it is one of the saddest in the Old Testament. We tend to put our heroes on pedestal's, don't we? What happens when they make a mistake? They fall from that pedestal. We never consider that "for the grace of God" we could succumb to the same temptation, the same disobedience of God's will. It's easy. So, how do we fight this?

I am a firm believer that it begins with our foundation. Of course, that didn't help David. I think he had a foundation, maybe the crack was his many wives. If we disrespect women we will act accordingly. Anyway, many times it can be traced back to the principles our parents taught us. The foundation is laid, that doesn't mean it is fool proof, but it is a start. Next, we need to consider our relationship with God, through Jesus Christ. David was NOT where he should have been. You could say the same for his walk with God. Sometimes, God will bless us, and walk with us, we tend to "take it for granted". We can just think that God will just bless anything we do because He was there before.

We should never ignore God's standards. They are NOT flexible. When Moses went up on Mount Sinai, God didn't write them in pencil and give him an eraser. They were carved in stone no less. They were not suggestions, they are Commandments! When we break those Commandments there are consequences, make no mistake.

And David sent to Joab, saying, send me Uriah the Hittite. And Joab sent Uriah to David. And when Uriah was come unto him, David demanded of him how Joab did, and how the people did, and how the war prospered. And David said to Uriah, Go down to thy house, and wash thy feet. And Uriah departed out of the king's house, and there followed him a mess of meat from the king. But Uriah slept at the door of the king's house with all the servants of his lord, and went not down to his house. (2 Samuel 11:6-9)

We have noted so many times how much God used David in the past. How God blessed him in battle and his relationship with Jonathan and protecting him from Saul. God had His hand on David. Why in heaven's name did he throw that all away. Have you ever asked that question? We do the same thing. God has blessed us with wonderful children, a loving wife, a great job, etc. We go out and make a stupid mistake that destroys this whole scene. We just make stupid mistakes, don't we?

In the verses above we see David's feeble attempt to cover up his mistake. To what extremes have you gone to try and cover your mistakes? Did it work? Probably not. Sin has a way of being discovered. If anything, God will arrange it to be uncovered.

From this point on David's relationship with God changes. Part of God's judgment against David is disharmony throughout his family life.

We will see that later. I talked earlier about consequences. No need to go there again.

Let me make something clear here. We all make mistakes, granted. Does the blood of Christ cover those mistakes? Yes. If we have asked Jesus to become our Savior we have a promise from God that we will spend eternity in heaven with Him. Will this affect our time spent here on earth, YES! Like I said, there are consequences. Are we forgiven? Yes. That is a great lesson to learn from David. David's son will still build God's temple.

Think about this a minute. Look at the chronology. When did God tell David that his son would build the temple? Long before Bathsheba showed up. It was God's plan from the beginning that Solomon would build the temple. This was not part of God's consequences for Bathsheba. This is not David's last mistake either. There are several lessons to learn from this episode. The main thing is, though God punished David He did not turn His back on him. We are usually the one's to turn our back on God.

I can hear our plea now, "Why did You put her in my life?" Really? That sounds like the Garden of Eden. We want to blame everyone but ourselves, beginning with God! That's what Adam did,

> Then the man said, "The woman whom You gave to be with me, she gave me of the tree, and I ate." (Genesis 3:12). (NKJV)

I wonder how that flies with God? Not well I would think. God gave us the ability to choose. What we do with it is up to us!

Have you seen God in any of David's response? I thought not. God is nowhere to be found. David didn't "inquire of the Lord." When you're out of God's will He is the last one you want to talk to. That's why it is so important to maintain that fellowship with God.

I can't find it right now, but I seem to remember an Old Testament prophet that chastised Israel, because God had blessed them so, and yet they got so lazy in the things of God. Basically, they had taken God's blessings for granted. That, I think, is where David is at. Because God's hand has been on your life don't think that God will wink at a sin. No, God will quickly take His hand from your life and turn it into misery. Repentance? Sure, God will accept your repentance, there can still be consequences, never forget that. We are held accountable for the freedom that God gives us. We have the freedom of choice, but that freedom comes with a responsibility to follow God's leadership and His will for our lives. Never take that for granted!

And when they had told David, saying, Uriah went not down unto his house, David said unto Uriah, Camest thou not from thy journey? Why then didst thou not go down unto thine house? And Uriah said to David, The ark, and Israel, and Judah, abide in tents; and my lord Joab, and the servants of my lord, are encamped in the open fields; shall I then go into mine house, to eat and to drink, and to lie with my wife? As thou livest, and as thy soul liveth, I will not do this thing. (2 Samuel 11:10-11)

Isn't it interesting that the harder we try to cover or deny a wrong doing it just gets deeper and deeper. What is our first response to doing something wrong? First, we try to deny it. I think it is interesting that, according to the Bible, David didn't demy it was his baby. That is usually the first response, isn't it? Next, we try to figure ways out of it. That was David's scheme here. It is so frustrating when you run across someone more righteous than you!

Does anyone want to shout? "Not fair!"? Of course, we do. Uriah did nothing to deserve this. Don't miss the fact that God recognized that fact and David is dealt with accordingly! Uriah is blameless, such is life. Sometimes we never realize the number of people we hurt when we break God's laws. The old remedy for sin? Cover-up! It never works. It is amazing how eventually the sin will find you out.

Let's suppose Uriah had spent the night with his wife. The baby is born and David thinks he got away with something. What do you suppose David's response would be? You see, when we get away with sin we can't help but do it again, and keep doing it until we get caught! David wouldn't have wiped his brow and swore never to do it again. He would have thought God winked at it and found some other sin. Have you ever known a bank robber, after robbing a couple of banks say, "I've got enough, I think I'll quite?" Not a chance.

God cannot wink at this. The rule is, there are consequences to sin. I hate to keep beating this. If reminding you can discourage just one person from doing something they will regret the rest of their lives, then I have succeeded. David had a good plan....if it had worked. So. This plan didn't work we move on to plan "B".

Think back a bit. When David became king what was one of the first things he did? (3:14-15) He instructed Joab to bring Michal to him. Michal had already married someone else. Sound familiar? David didn't have to kill Uriah. It was to save face, no other reason. I wonder if he really thought he would get away with it. Of course, we do the same thing. We think we can fool everybody and get away with our sin. The problem is, God knows!

Do you see David digging? The hole gets deeper and deeper. A sin becomes doubled, and doubled, and finally it comes full circle and you're at the end of the rope.

It doesn't have to be adultery. There are plenty of other sins we commit. We are all human. We make mistakes. What is the right response? Of course, repent, confess, bring it to God and say, "What would You have me do.?" Who do you make things right with? God will give you instructions. God will also chastise, or punish you, if you are a child of God you will get a spanking! If you are lost, your penalty is already set. God chastises His own because He loves us enough not to let us get away with sin.

I know it sounds crazy but because David was a man after God's own heart, probably prevented him from being killed on the spot. Oh, David will pay a price for his sin. Here is a critical principle when one of God's children fail Him. You will lose the fellowship with God but never the relationship. You will always be a child of God. Just as David was. God will use David's own family to punish him. BUT! God is also a merciful God. Even this story has a happy ending. It is to me anyway. I think it is a great picture of God's grace. As a child of God, He must correct us, but He will always love us!

And David said to Uriah, Tarry here to day also, and tomorrow I will let thee depart. So Uriah abode in Jerusalem that day and the morrow. And when David had called him, he did eat and drink before him; and he made him drunk: and at even he went out to lie on his bed with the servants of his lord, but went not down to his house. And it came to pass in the morning, that David wrote a letter to Joab, and sent it by the hand of Uriah. And he wrote in the letter, saying, Set ye Uriah in the forefront of the hottest battle, and retire ye from him, that he may be smitten, and die. (2 Samuel 11:12-15)

What started out as adultery ended in murder. It is a road far too many people travel. Not this specifically but what may begin as a "little white lie" soon becomes deceit, betrayal, and much worse. That is a road far too many of us travel. At first it seems insignificant. Then we need to lie again to cover the last and down and down we go. Till it can't be stopped and comes to a tragic result. How many divorces begin and end with one mistake?

Look at the innocent ones in this story. I include Bathsheba in this. We don't know the culture of those days. What may be unacceptable today may have been necessary in those days. It all comes down to David sending his servants to bring Bathsheba to him! She could have refused? Really, again it's the culture, you DON'T refuse the king's request. It was all David's doing from the beginning to the end. Our King David whom we have come to admire and respect. I cautioned earlier about putting "people" on a pedestal. God is the only one who belongs on a pedestal. That could very well be why God chose to share this episode in David's life.

So, what can we learn from this sordid tale? I guess number one would be: Be where you're supposed to be. If you are required to be at work, go to work. Idleness begets mischief. If you have authority over others, guard your testimony carefully. Satan has many tools at his disposal, he is bent on destroying the family at every opportunity, guard your home! Lying is another tool he uses. One lie leads to another to cover that lie. lying led to Uriah's death.

I think it is interesting that David tried everything he could think of to cover his adultery. It finally resulted in murder. I think it is interesting that David says specifically, *"that he may be struck down and die."* There was no doubt in Joab's mind what David wanted. A clear case of murder. Notice also that Joab is now part of this wrong-doing. Joab knows better. His excuse would be that he had to obey his king. I wonder if that would work in God's eyes? I doubt it.

It is sad to see David, "A man after God's own heart" fall this way. It is a warning to all of us. When we begin to think that we are walking so close to God that nothing can happen, beware, Satan takes that as a challenge. Remember, in the Garden of Eden, Adam and Eve had a "perfect world" they wanted for NOTHING. In comes the serpent and plants rebellion in their hearts. God gave them everything but they wanted more. Is that not a description of David. He had at least four wives, it's not like he didn't know what it was about. He wanted what he could not have.

That is our world today. We are never satisfied with the blessings God gives us, we want more. Notice this verse in one of my favorite Psalms:

Delight yourself also in the Lord, and he shall give you the desires of your heart. (Psalm 37:4). (NKJV)

I hope to look at this Psalm following our study of David. It is my favorite Psalm! Did you catch the catch? First, you must delight yourself in the Lord. Trust His priorities, His will and plan for your life. God will bless you far greater than you could possibly imagine if you begin with God's plan, not yours.

David lost sight of God, when he was not where he should have been. Indulge me a minute. Are you attending church regularly? I wonder if that would fall under "not being where you should be"? But that is my only day to rest. I can think of no better way to begin your rest day than to be in God's house on the Lord's day. Think about it.

And it came to pass, when Joab observed the city, that he assigned Uriah unto a place where he knew that valiant men were. And the men of the city went out, and fought with Joab: and there fell some of the people of the servants of David; and Uriah the Hittite died also. Then Joab sent and told David all the things concerning the war; And charged the messenger, saying, When thou hast made an end of telling the matters of the war unto the king, And if so be that the king's wrath arise, and he say unto thee, Wherefore approached ye so nigh unto the city when ye did fight? Knew ye not that they would shoot from the wall? And the shooters shot from off the wall upon thy servants; and some of the king's servants be dead, and thy servant Uriah the Hittite is dead also. (2 Samuel 11:16-20,24)

The deed is done. The sad part is that Joab is in on this as well. In our efforts to conceal our wrongdoing we involve others. We may never know the extent of the effect of our misdeeds. We may think no one is hurt but us. Not true. The consequences can be far reaching and devastating!

I want you to think seriously about something. There are ALWAYS two options, two forks in the road of life. It is your choice which fork you take.

When David stood on that balcony and saw Bathsheba, he had two options. Send for Bathsheba or go back to his other wives. When David received the word that Bathsheba was pregnant, he had two options: try to conceal what had happened, or confess to Uriah and ask forgiveness, or at least take her as his wife like he did Michal. When Uriah would not cooperate, and go to his house, he could have confessed, or any other option. The point is there are always options. Forks in this road. It is your choice how you deal with a situation. Most of us think no further than the hour or the present day. We never seem to consider the "long-term" consequences.

I skipped the details of the battle. Not important. The deed is done. I wonder if David thinks God is busy somewhere else and doesn't see what happened. Maybe he thinks because God made him king that gives him license to do whatever he thinks he wants to. Do you ever take God for granted? Think maybe He might wink at your transgression because you're a "good Christian"? God doesn't work that way. Think how that cheapens what Jesus did on the cross!

Our relationship with God should be precious to us. We should make every effort to safeguard it and take nothing for granted. It is sad how often we go our separate path and expect God to just go along. That's not a relationship. Not one that God would honor.

As we will see God has His way of letting David confront his sin. God works the same way with us. We may think we have gotten away with something. God will deal with us eventually. Maybe, as soon as we think we are in the clear, that God was busy doing something else, we sigh with relief, then God lowers the boom! Nothing escapes God's notice.

This is not a great episode in David's life. Why would God bother to tell us? It is a great lesson in our relationship with God. Remember in the book of Acts 13:22 David is still referred to as "a man after God's own heart." We may break fellowship with God, as David has done, but as Christians in the New Testament we cannot break our relationship as children of God. We can lose our fellowship, not our relationship. It's the fellowship that should be precious to us. We want to know that God has not taken his hand off us.

It is a sad day when we realize, that because of our sin, we have lost

God's fellowship. It's what we do then that reflects our faith in God. Do we come to God in repentance, seeking His forgiveness, or do we think we can cover it up, like David? Foolish Christian if you think God will wink at your sin. He would never cheapen the cost of our salvation by winking at our sin! Think about it!

Then David said unto the messenger, Thus shalt thou say unto Joab, Let not this thing displease thee, for the sword devoureth one as well as another: make thy battle more strong against the city, and overthrow it: and encourage thou him. And when the wife of Uriah heard that Uriah her husband was dead, she mourned for her husband. And when the mourning was past, David sent and fetched her to his house, and she became his wife, and bare him a son. But the thing that David had done displeased the Lord. (2 Samuel 11:25-27)

We can't understand this situation. It goes totally against our culture, well, maybe. We don't understand Bathsheba's response. In that culture and time women had no say. They couldn't refuse, reject the advances, etc. Today they would be yelling "rape!" There would be law enforcement all over the place, etc. Women in those days were basically servants. Even the wives.

Bathsheba didn't ask for this. She really was powerless. Except in God's eyes. He will take a hand in the next chapter. He is the only advocate a woman had in those days. Let's think about today. Today we have contraceptives, and other methods to avoid pregnancy. Sadly, there is even abortion. There are "remedies" for unwanted children. That does not erase the fact that a child is born. One of my favorite verses talks about our "creation" Psalm 139 says:

> "For You formed my inward parts; You covered me in my mother's womb. I will praise you, for I am fearfully and wonderfully made. (Psalm 139:13-14). (NKJV)

Today we are in the courts trying to determine when life begins. Read that Psalm again. A birth is NOT an accident. God must be in the creation! I truly believe that every child was created by God from it's very inception. From that moment on God has a very specific plan for that life. God also gives us the ability to choose between our course and God's course.

I don't think it is insignificant that this child is a male. Can you imagine, when David heard it was a boy what he must have thought. It is interesting what we think we can get away with between us and God.

This is a critical phase in David's life. We must always keep his life in context, as well as our own. We must also, always remember that God is sovereign. Nothing escapes God's will and purpose in our life. You would be amazed how this one fact can influence your walk with God.

Well, David messed up, I will just leave him, like I left Saul, and find another king. You would think that might be the case. But David had something in him that God was not going to give up so easily. What do you think that was? Think about Saul. What was his response to disobeying God? He doubled-down. He continued to forget God, and do things his way. Where David, would almost always seek God's guidance. I said almost because of this episode.

God is a forgiving God, but He will only forgive so long. If there is no repentance, no remorse, no turning back to God, He will move on to someone who wants to walk with God. Remember in 1 Samuel 16,

> *But the Lord said to Samuel, "Do not look at his appearance or at his physical stature, because I have refused him (Eliab). For the Lord does not see as man sees; for man looks at the outward appearance, but the Lord looks at the heart." (1 Samuel 16:7) (NKJV)*

God saw something in David's heart He did not see in Saul's.

If you have ever taken the Lord's Supper in church there is a verse that is often quoted:

> *But let a man examine himself, and so let him eat of the bread and drink of the cup. (Galatians 6:28). (NKJV)*

I don't think it is used that much. The Apostle Paul exhorts us, before we partake of the bread and cup, to "examine" ourselves. Is there something between us and God that needs to be resolved before celebrating the communion with God. Just imagine if God looked at David's heart vs Saul's heart. What a contrast. I believe that's why God was willing to work with David along his walk with God.

2 SAMUEL 12

And the Lord sent Nathan unto David, and he came unto him, and said unto him, There were two men in one city; the one rich, and the other poor. The rich man had exceeding many flocks and herds. But the poor man had nothing, save one little ewe lamb, which he had bought and nourished up: and it grew up together with him, and with his children; it did eat of his own meat, and drank of his own cup, and lay in his bosom, and was unto him as a daughter. And there came a traveller unto the rich man, and he spared to take of his own flock of his own herd, to dress for the wayfaring man that was come unto him; but took the poor man's lamb, and dressed it for the man that was come to him. (2 Samuel 12:1-4)

I wrestled with whether to include Nathan's illustration. Of course, David didn't know it was an illustration. God uses so many ways to get His point across. One of Jesus best teaching tools was His parables. Short stories but with so much meat. That method also helps make it unforgettable! We learn so much from stories about real life. Someone who made great use of this method was Aesop. Ever hear of Aesop's Fables? Here is another who used rhyme to illustrate a truth, Mother Goose. It makes it easy to remember by challenging our minds to figure it out.

God had a special message for David. I want you to notice how clearly Nathan describes the relationship between the poor man and his lamb. It tugs at your heart, doesn't it? That is the point. I think God wanted David to know how much, what he did, hurt God! It was so effective that David was outraged, as we will see. That is the point. God said it was totally unacceptable!

Did you know that Nathan has a counterpart in the New Testament? The Holy Spirit! That's how the Holy Spirit works in our heart. It won't take Him long before we know God is not pleased with something we did.

He will even go so far as to try to warn us before we do it. If we are listening. I wish I knew what went through David's mind when he inquired about the lady he saw. Then after he found out she was Uriah's wife. We will never know.

There is so much to learn from this episode in David's life. I hope I can do it justice. I am simply sharing what God has laid on my heart. What my impressions are of David's walk with God. We may not have a "Bathsheba" experience but I'm sure we have struggled with sin and situations in our life that we wish we could go back and change. We can't! So, what do we do.

Let's watch David and see how he deals with this, and how God deals with David. That is the lesson to learn here. Maybe by watching how God responds it might give us some insight into how God will respond to our sin. That's why God has chosen to include this story in His Word. It is a lesson to pay attention and learn from. Study, take notes even, lest we forget. I'm sure a lot of people, even the lost, know the story of David and Bathsheba. There was even a movie made of it. Not sure how accurate it was. The point is, watch closely and note how God responds. Put yourself in David's place. Maybe even think about how Bathsheba felt.

That is why God chose to give us His Holy Word. To study, to learn, to incorporate God's principles into our daily living. By observing how God responds to David we will understand why God responds to us in our daily struggles. We will make mistakes, we will fall. Some will have life-changing consequences. We must learn to listen to God's Holy Spirit that may stop us from making that one mistake that will cost us our fellowship with God. That broken fellowship that only repentance will restore.

And David's anger was greatly kindled against the man; and he said to Nathan, As the Lord liveth, the man that hath done this thing shall surely die: And he shall restore the lamb fourfold, because he did this thing, and because he had no pity. And Nathan said to David, "Thou art the man". Thus saith the Lord God of Israel, I anointed thee king over Israel, and I delivered thee out of the hand of Saul; (2 Samuel 12:5-7)

I would love to have seen David's face at this point. I like the King James version, "Thou art the man!" I would be willing to bet that David thought he had gotten away with it. Look at this verse,

*And when her mourning was over, David sent and brought
her to his house, and she became his wife and bore him
a son. But the thing that David had done displeased the
Lord. (2 Samuel 11:27) (NKJV)*

It has been at least nine months since David had Uriah killed. I'm sure
he thought he had gotten away with something. That is always the case
with God. Just the time we think we are free, we missed Gods wrath, God
shows up!

Notice something else: Look at verse 5 of chapter 11: *And the woman
conceived; so, she sent and told David, "I am with child."* Four words. Here's
another four words: *You are the man!* (v. 12:7). I may be crazy but this makes
me think of the words we might hear when we stand before God one day.

*And then I will declare to them; I never knew you depart
from Me, you who practice lawlessness. (Matthew 7:23).
(NKJV)*

Or will our Lord say,

*His lord said, "Well done, good and faithful servant; you
have been faithful over a few things, I will make you ruler
over many things. Enter into the joy of your lord. (Matthew
25:23). (NKJV)*

The four words, in either case, were not the words David wished to
hear. It has always been my belief that the reason a lot of people don't spend
a lot of time in God's word is that it convicts! It touches their heart in ways
they don't wish to be touched! Between the Word of God and the work of
the Holy Spirit we just try to avoid remembering God's working in our life.

Remember what you felt, when you read about this poor shepherd,
his one ewe lamb, a part of his household. How you felt when, for no real
reason, it was taken and killed for a stranger. That emotion is exactly what
Nathan was getting in David. He wanted David furious, upset, vengeful.
That was the emotion God was bringing to the table. Here was God's
champion, God's anointed King of Israel, to do something like this, even to
the point of murder, how it must have hurt God.

Sometimes we can get "detached" from God. God will not force Himself into our life. It is strictly on a voluntary basis. He wants us to come to Him. Seek His guidance, His wisdom, even His peace in our life. We go to Him because we want to. We seek His face. When He is ignored He will just set back and wait. He knows the battle that goes on in our flesh. He knows we are unable to win apart from Him. Without His power, we are helpless to fight the wiles of the devil. He is there whenever we get tired of fighting and surrender and let God back into our circle.

The sad part about this episode in David's life is that his fellowship with God has been permanently damaged. God will set in motion events that will totally distract David, and frustrate his fellowship with God. There are things we do that breaks that fellowship with God. We "grieve the Holy Spirit". We can also "quench God's Spirit. By our ignoring the presence of His Holy Spirit and going our own way, we grieve the heart of God. God so wants to be an intimate part of our lives, but we turn our back on Him and treat him shamefully.

Take a minute here a do a check-up on your fellowship with God. Remember, if you're a Christian your relationship is sealed through His Holy Spirit. But, your fellowship may be in danger!

And I gave thee thy master's house, and thy master's wives into thy bosom, and gave thee the house of Israel and of Judah; and if that had been too little, I would moreover have given unto thee such and such things. Wherefore hast thou despised the commandment of the Lord, to do evil in his sight? Thou hast killed Uriah the Hittite with the sword, and hast taken his wife to be thy wife, and hast slain him with the sword of the children of Ammon. Now therefore the sword shall never depart from thine house; because thou hast despised me, and hast taken the wife of Uriah the Hittite to be thy wife. (2 Samuel 12:8-10)

What about you? Can God make a list for you? How long would that list be? How many transgressions, of what sort might they be? Imagine how much this pains God to bring this list to David, "a man after God's own heart." You cannot imagine how much it grieves the Lord when we disobey Him! Here, ponder, this verse a minute:

> "If you love Me, keep My commandments." (John 14:15)
> (NKJV)

It is simple. Yet it seems so hard to do, isn't it?

Does God wink at our disobedience? Not hardly. When your children disobey you, and you ignore them, what happens? They quit, right? Not hardly. They will continue until you get their attention, correct them. God is no different. If you think you can disobey God and God will ignore you, think again. God has a very special way of getting our attention, believe me!

I think it is interesting that God totally blames David for the death of Uriah. David didn't "pull the trigger" but he is just as guilty. We think because we didn't commit the act that we are guiltless. In Jesus' Sermon on the Mount, chapter five of Matthew's gospel, Jesus makes it very clear that if we "think" to do harm to someone we have already committed the act. There are no grey areas.

Notice what God says above, "*I also would have given you much more.*" David already had five or more wives. Interesting, this reminds us of the Garden of Eden, doesn't it? Adam and Eve had everything they could possibly want, food, shelter, anything they wanted God would provide. They HAD to have that forbidden fruit. It cost them, just as this will cost David.

Remember why God refused to let David build the temple? Because of the conflict with the nations around Israel. Now David is faced with perpetual conflict in his own family. An interesting judgment, isn't it. God is so creative in His method of judgment. Make no mistake, God's justice is divinely inspired! Would you have thought of this? God knew just what would affect David the most, as we will see.

That "man after God's own heart" has broken God's heart. The same way we do when we disobey God. Turn our back on God, blame Him for our own decisions and mistakes.

We have something that David didn't have. A license to sin? God forbid, as Paul would say (Romans 6). No, we have a Savior, who gave His life on a cruel cross so we can come to God, in repentance and seek His forgiveness.

Does this mean that God has forsaken David? No. Does it mean that God will no longer bless David? No. Does this mean that David has missed out on God's best? Yes! God will and has forgiven David. The matter is closed. The punishment will continue the rest of his life. Again, there are consequences for our actions. Sometimes those consequences will last a lifetime. Let me repeat what I have said earlier, it's important! We live in the

New Testament era. God has sent His Son to die on the cross of Calvary for our sins, past, present, and future.

Today, though, we can break that fellowship with God, just as David has done here. But, we can never break our relationship with God. Look at Romans 8:

> For as many as are led by the Spirit of God, these are sons of God. For you did not receive the spirit of bondage again to fear, but you received the Spirit of adoption by whom we cry out, "Abba, Father." The Spirit Himself bears witness with our spirit that we are children of God. (Romans 8:14-16) (NKJV)

Thus saith the Lord, Behold, I will raise up evil against thee out of thine own house, and I will take thy wives before thine eyes, and give them unto thy neighbour, and he shall lie with thy wives in the sight of the sun. And David said unto Nathan, I have sinned against the Lord. And Nathan said unto David, The Lord also hath put away thy sin; thou shalt not die. Howbeit, because by this deed thou hast given great occasion to the enemies of the Lord to blaspheme, the child also that is born unto thee shall surely die. (2 Samuel 12:11-14)

Wow! This is such a critical passage. God goes to great detail to tell David what His sentence is. There are consequences to sin. Let me make something clear. God never acts the same way twice. Watch when Jesus heals someone, it's always different. We cannot use this passage to say, the same will happen to me. That's not the point.

I have quoted Acts, where Luke reminds us that David was "A man after God's own heart." (Acts 13:22). Even centuries later. But there is another time when God said,

> "But now your (Saul) kingdom shall not continue. The Lord has sought for Himself a man after His own heart, and the Lord has commanded him to be commander over His people, because you have not kept what the Lord commanded you." (1 Samuel 13:14). (NKJV)

Something to note about this verse. It was before Samuel called David.

Let me remind you of one more verse:

> *But the Lord said to Samuel, "Do not look at his appearance or his physical stature, because I have refused him (Eliab). For the Lord does not see as man sees; for man looks at the outward appearance, **but the Lord looks at the heart.**" (1 Samuel 16:7). (NKJV)*

Don't miss this! We all will sin. It's what is in our hearts that God judges us by. Of course, He is disappointed, as we should be. We cannot fool God. Our words are meaningless, it's what is in our heart that God examines!

Something about this too. Do you remember Adam's response in the Garden when God confronted him in his sin? Look:

> *Then the man said, "The woman whom you gave to be with me, she gave me of the tree, and I ate." (Genesis 3:12). (NKJV)*

Now look at David's response when Nathan confronted him: *"I have sinned against the Lord."* That shows us David's heart. This also demonstrates to us what God is looking for when we make mistakes. Not, excuses! Did you notice that Adam blamed God? Of course, we wouldn't do that, really?

The deed is done. The sentence is passed. Also note this phrase:

> *"The Lord also has put away your sin; you shall not die."*
> *(2 Samuel 12:13b). (NKJV)*

That was an option. God could have taken him home right there. That is His choice. The same is true with us. God can take us home at His desire. God also has the option to forgive us. Maybe God knows there are some deeds worth keeping us around for. We can only hope. Did David suffer greatly in the years to follow, of course! Will we suffer for our sin, of course! Is it worth it, certainly not! But we are human. I think it all boils down to our relationship with God. Take a minute and examine your relationship!

One last thing. I know you noticed at the end that God said the child would die. There are consequences to sin. I can't stress that enough. Maybe, just one time, if that crosses our mind and keeps us from a mistake, it will be worth it. We seem to forget that so easily! God will even turn that into a "teachable moment."

I hope that is what you have gotten out of this chapter. "A teachable moment". That phrase could best describe the purpose of the Old Testament. As we continue our walk with David, and see how David responds and how God responds to David, we need to remember that this is "The Word of God." God has assembled these lessons for our great benefit. Stories and truths that will help us better understand what God wants from us, and what He wants to give us. I don't have the room here, but refresh your memory on Jeremiah 29:11-13. Check it out!

And Nathan departed unto his house. And the Lord struck the child that Uriah's wife bare unto David, and it was very sick. David therefore besought God for the child; and David fasted, and went in, and lay all night upon the earth. And the elders of his house arose, and went to him, to raise him up from the earth: but he would not, neither did he eat bread with them. And it came to pass on the seventh day, that the child died. And the servants feared to tell him that the child was dead: for they said, Behold, while the child was yet alive, we spake unto him, and he would not hearken unto our voice: how will he then vex himself, if we tell him that the child is dead? (2 Samuel 12:15-18)

It is tough to leave our story here. Especially if you know what happens. There is a lesson here for us. I have already covered the consequences of sin. God's sovereignty, etc. We have established that God is in control. God has already told David that the child would die, hasn't he? So why would David go through this praying process? David believed in prayer. At this point it was all he had left. As David says later,

> "Who can tell whether the Lord will be gracious to me." (2 Samuel 12:22). (NKJV)

There is always hope in prayer!

Have you ever "prayed through" something? David is "praying through" his child's illness. Praying until God gives you an answer. Persistent prayer. Has God ever answered and said, "No"? Can you accept that answer? No! We want to argue with God, we want to dispute His judgment, don't we?

Does it work? Can you change God's Mind? God has a sovereign will. It will be accomplished. The more we try to fight God, the further away from Him we get.

There is a certain peace when we leave those decisions in God's hands. I like to think that God knows what is going to happen next month, next year, etc. If He thinks it's best to not answer my prayer, He has a reason that will only benefit us.

God is so cruel! We all have a special feeling for children. Do you think God doesn't? I have to keep reminding you, and myself, that it wasn't God who brought this about. This is the result of David's sin. When we can come to grips with that fact. When we can get past blaming God for our sin, we have come a long way in our walk with God. I have already quoted the bible in the New Testament where we are called, "children of God." (Romans 8:15) Do you think he loves us any less than David loved his new-born son?

Do you see what is going on here? In this Old Testament story of David, it is demonstrated that A life was paid for the sin of David. Look at the New Testament. A life was paid for the sin of the world. God's Son gave His life on the cross of Calvary to pay for our sin. Like I have said so many times before. The principle that is taught in the New Testament is demonstrated in the Old Testament. God can do no less. We saw it further illustrated in Exodus 12,

> "Now the blood shall be a sign for you on the houses where you are. And when I see the blood, I will pass over you; and the plague shall not be on you to destroy you when I strike the land of Egypt. (Exodus12:13). (NKJV)

When we eventually stand before God He will be looking for one thing. Not our status in life, not what we have "accomplished" nothing on this earth will matter except are we covered by the blood of Jesus Christ. That is ALL that will count. So, how do you get this blood? You simply, ask! "Jesus, I am a sinner, I want to become a child of God. Jesus, I ask you to come into my life and change me. I ask the Holy Spirit to begin working on me, just as He did with Your servant David. I want to be 'born again'!"

The principle has been established from the very beginning in Genesis 3:21. The payment for sin is blood. I am so grateful that Christ died on the cross, shed His blood for my sin, that I might become a child of God. It is demonstrated again, here, in the life of David's child. Don't mourn for the child. Mourn for David. His sin cost a huge price. So, what does David do now? Look and see.

But when David saw that his servants whispered, David perceived that the child was dead: therefore David said unto his servants, Is the child dead? And they said, He is dead. Then David arose from the earth, and washed, and anointed himself, and changed his apparel, and came into the house of the Lord, and worshipped: then he came into his own house; and when he required, they set bread before him, and he did eat. Then said his servants unto him, What thing is this that thou hast done? Thou didst fast and weep for the child, while it was alive; but when the child was dead, thou didst arise and eat bread. And he said, While the child was yet alive, I fasted and wept: for I said, Who can tell whether God will be gracious to me, that the child may live? But now he is dead, wherefore should I fast? Can I bring him back again? I shall go to him, but he shall not return to me. (2 Samuel 12:19-23)

I have that last verse (23) underlined in my Bible. Did you catch this awesome promise from God? Children, when they die will go to be with God. Mark that down. The death of a child is a horrible thing. One of the worst things that we can imagine, to happen. But this promise from God is very dear to me. We need to remember it, and take solace in it.

Did you notice that David had a confidence that he would join his child in heaven? How does he have that confidence? There was no cross. There was no Savior, to pay for his sins. Remember when David was called from the field tending his sheep? Look:

> Then Samuel took the horn of oil and anointed him in the midst of his brothers; and the Spirit of the Lord came upon David from that day forward. So, Samuel arose and went to Ramah. (1 Samuel 16:13). (NKJV)

God's Holy Spirit assured David of his relationship with God. Just as His Spirit assures us today!

I want you to notice something else here. What was the first thing David did when he realized the child was gone and he cleaned up?

And he went into the house of the Lord and worshipped.
(2 Samuel 12:20b). (NKJV)

It was made clear to David that the life of this child would belong to God. I want you to pay close attention to what I'm saying. Too many times we want to blame God for our own mistakes. We think if we stay out of God's house, somehow this will punish God. Really? We are the ones suffering! David recognized God's grace. God could very well have taken him out. He spared David.

I am not a fan of funerals in the church. I have heard too many of God's people say they can't go anymore because it brings that memory back. The memory of the celebration of a godly life that has gone to be with the Lord? Is that a BAD memory? I would think you would want to be reminded of that special relationship you had with that loved one. One day you will be reunited in heaven. That was David's solace. He knew one day they would be reunited, and they are!

I have struggled with this passage. It's not a pretty story. But, at the same time there is a great promise here. Not only of God's righteousness but of His grace. Look at this. Sin has a price. The price has been paid. It is forgotten in God's eyes. David asked forgiveness. David suffered the loss of the child. The debt was paid. It is time to move on. I think there is another truth here. Like I said, God could have taken David, but, God still has work for David, a purpose to fulfill.

There is another subtle lesson here. When there is hope, we must continue to pray. There is a line I caught in the first episode of "The Hunger Games." You must see the movie to know what I'm talking about. They have these games where twenty-four people fight to the death for one lone survivor. The winner lives and is treated handsomely. The president of the games asks this guy, "Why do we have a winner?" "I don't know" replied the other guy. "To give them hope!" replied the president. Without hope we have nothing friends. David had hope that God might change His mind about the child. Prayer is our expression of hope in this world. God is still on the throne, God can accomplish whatever He wishes, we must pray daily!

And David comforted Bathsheba his wife, and went in unto her, and lay with her: and she bare a son, and he called his name Solomon: and the Lord loved him. And he sent by the hand of Nathan the prophet; and he called his name Jedidiah, because of the Lord. (2 Samuel 12:24-25)

"Forgive and forget," how many times have you heard those words? We hear that so often, but do we really forget? We can't help it. We can't help remembering those wrongs that were done to us. Those misunderstandings, those slights, we remember those. Can we forgive? That is our choice, no one else's.

I love these verses. I don't know of any other demonstration of God's grace, other than the cross, that is contained in these verses. As much as God was hurt by David's actions, God could forgive David enough to give him another son. This may, if you will, show God does not blame Bathsheba.

Don't pass over these verses. Chew on them a bit. Think back to that night David stood on his balcony and saw this woman. Then the conspiracy to have her husband killed. God's words through Nathan, "You are the man!" Caught in sin, and punished! Now, God has forgiven and forgotten and it's time to move on. You mean God will never hold us accountable for our sin? Did I say that? Was David held accountable for his sin? Of course, he was, and it's not over. But the sentence was pronounced, it's time to move on!

No. We must hold on to it ourselves. We must keep bringing it up, either with the guilty party or with God. We can't let this thing rest, even though God has! We must keep digging up our past mistakes. We must remind God how awful we are. God doesn't need reminding, God has cast it into the sea.

Look at these verses:

As far as the east is from the west, so far has He removed our transgression from us. (Psalm 103:12) (NKJV)

I want you to think about this one. If you begin traveling straight north what will happen when you reach the top? You begin going south. There is a "limit" to traveling north or south. Now use the same technique. You begin traveling east. When do you start traveling west? You don't! There is no END to traveling east. You see my point? God knew what He was saying. There is no point that you reach your transgressions!

One more:

He will again have compassion on us, and will again subdue our iniquities. You will cast all your sins into the depths of the sea. (Micah 7:19). (NKJV)

Do you know that with all our modern technologies today there are still depths of the sea that man has not explored! Notice who does the casting! God!

Again, I go back to this passage. There is so much grief, and hurt here. Both on David's part and God's. Not to mention the grief of Bathsheba, who lost her child. God is the great healer, if we want to be healed. No, we want to hold on to those sins. Forgiveness is out of the question. We must keep score. Maybe you're like I was before I was saved. "I don't get mad, I get even." Was that, or is that your motto? I pray you will take it to God. Leave those hurts, that unforgiveness at the cross, where it belongs. That burden is too heavy to continue to carry through your life. Give it to God.

What a beautiful way to bring to a close this chapter in David's life. I dreaded dealing with this chapter. It's not something we want to remember David for. I asked earlier what comes to mind when you think of David? Either Goliath or Bathsheba, victory or defeat. God took that defeat and turned it into something good. One more verse, you know where I'm going:

*And we know that all things work together for good to those **who love God**, to those who are the called according to His purpose. (Romans 8:28) (NKJV)*

If you're not familiar with that verse, mark it down!

2 SAMUEL 13

And it came to pass after this, that Absalom the son of David had a fair sister, whose name was Tamar; and Amnon the son of David loved her. And Amnon was so vexed, that he fell sick for his sister Tamar; for she was a virgin; and Amnon thought it hard for him to do any thing to her. But Amnon had a friend whose name was Jonadab, the son of Shimeah David's brother: and Jonadab was a very subtil man. And he said unto him, Why art thou, being the king's son, lean from day to day? Wilt thou not tell me? And Amnon said unto him, I love Tamar, my brother Absalom's sister. (2 Samuel 13:1-4)

God told David, because of his sin with Bathsheba. Remember?

> "Now therefore, the sword shall never depart from your house." (2 Samuel 12:10) (NKJV)

This is part of that sword. If anyone thinks that the Bible is just full of God's love, hasn't read it! There are stories I would love to just skip over. But, if we skip them we will miss the lesson God has included for us. This is one of those stories!

We had talked earlier about having more than one wife. Here is another reason: Amnon is the son of Ahinoami, one of David's wives. Absalom is the son of Maacah, another of David's wives. And on it goes. It was never meant to be! When you disobey God's laws you reap what you sow! This is just one example!

I remember growing up having a crush on my cousin. I think we all might have some of those feelings. They are quickly squashed. We know what is right and what is wrong. We can't help those feelings. It's how we respond and deal with them that affects our relationship with God.

Amnon knew it was wrong. He was weak. Instead of going to David and telling him, and getting his counsel, he didn't deal with it. Along comes Satan with a plan. Satan is always there to help us accomplish anything that hinders God's testimony. A lot of our strength can come from a close relationship with God. Especially if we have the Holy Spirit living within us. He will convict us and can turn us in the right direction. if we are willing to listen and obey. Amnon was not!

Again, we must ask, why did God see fit to include this sordid tale? For one, it reminds us that God keeps His promises. This was part of God's chastisement for David, part of His "sword" in David's family. As we saw at the end of chapter 12, David and Joab had another victory on the battlefield. God's dealings with David are in his family. As the sin was committed in his family. God has His own methods of bringing us back into a fellowship with Him. The problem is we either blame God, refuse His chastisement, or run from His correction and counsel.

Do you think David had any idea this was going on in his family? I want to give him the benefit of a doubt. I wonder though. How connected are we with our family? Do we have such a relationship that problems like this can be addressed? We should have a relationship with our heavenly Father that we can bring these feelings to Him. If we are not one of His children we have no relationship and certainly no fellowship.

I hope you're not one of those who are saying, "This could never happen to me." That is an open door for Satan to come in and prove you wrong. The devil's tricks are so deceiving that if we are not on our guard it can be fatal! Never assume you have complete control of your thoughts and feelings. Never forget Adam and Eve. They had a "perfect" environment, but Satan told them there was more! Stay close to God!

And Jonadab said unto him, Lay thee down on thy bed, and make thyself sick: and when thy father cometh to see thee, say unto him, I pray thee, let my sister Tamar come, and give me meat, and dress the meat in my sight, that I may see it, and eat it at her hand. So Amnon lay down, and made himself sick: and when the king was come to see him, Amnon said unto the king, I pray thee, let Tamar my sister come and make me a couple of cakes in my sight, that I may eat at her hand. Then David sent home to Tamar, saying, Go now to thy brother's house, and dress him meat. (2 Samuel 13:5-7)

One nice thing about reading the Bible, you can skip those parts you don't want to read. That is impossible in life. We have had to deal with situations that we wish we didn't have to deal with. We can ask all kinds of questions at this point.

I guess the biggest question is, "How can this be?" There are a lot of things that go on in this world that we know nothing about. There are things we don't want to know anything about. They are in secret! God knows about everything. So why doesn't God intervene? God has turned those choices over to us. I'm sure He is not happy about the choices we make. But, they are our choices. I think the big message from the previous story was that there will be consequences. We just never seem to consider those consequences when we make the choices we make.

I wonder, for how many, this is the first time they have read this passage? Maybe you have heard about it but never read it. Maybe a pastor had referred to it but never covered it. No wonder. It's not something you want to preach on. Nevertheless, it was included by God in this story of David. In my study Bible, there is a list of David's wives and their offspring. It lists eight wives. Each with children. We can't begin to imagine the atmosphere in that household. The discipline, etc. We don't know how much of this story had to do with their upbringing.

Is it any wonder that Satan is referred to as "The father of lies"? From the Garden of Eden that has been his method of deceit. "Just this one little lie, it won't hurt anyone." One lie leads to another, soon there is no escape. Maybe the first lie is to ourselves that this is okay. We find ourselves in so many hurtful situations by telling ourselves, "this is okay." First, we begin by lying to ourselves, then it is easier to lie to others, isn't it?

To be honest I was surprised that David was deceived. I'm sure it seemed like an honest request. But where was the Holy Spirit in David at this point. Once we have grieved the Spirit it can be muted in our thoughts. Maybe David heard it, but chose to ignore it. That happens to us sometimes, doesn't it? We are warned but choose to ignore it. To our peril!

We have just seen the opening act to this scene in David's family. It is no accident that it follows right after David's ordeal with Bathsheba and God's judgment. Don't miss the thread here. Don't forget God's judgment. We will see it acted out through the rest of David's life. Some worse than others. This is one harsh judgment from God because it lasts and lasts. I think we can get a glimpse why in this verse:

> "*However, because by this deed you have given great occasion to the enemies of the Lord to blaspheme, the child who is born to you shall surely die.*" (2 Samuel 12:14) (NKJV).

David's sin reflected on God. That must be dealt with. As a child of God our testimony is precious to God and should be to us. We take it lightly when we go forward in our church and proclaim that we are saved, then leave and live like the devil. God will not wink at that. You have made a claim to be one of God's children, then live otherwise. That reflects on God, not on you. God will not take that lightly, just as He says here to David. It wasn't so much, taking Uriah's life as the soiling of God's testimony. I have heard it said that if a "professing" Christian refuses to give God glory, God will take him home rather than soil His name. Think about it!

So Tamar went to her brother Amnon's house; and he was laid down. And she took flour, and kneaded it, and made cakes in his sight, and did bake the cakes. And she took a pan, and poured them out before him; but he refused to eat. And Amnon said, Have out all men from me. And they went out every man from him. And Amnon said to Tamar, Bring the meat into the chamber, that I may eat of thine hand. And Tamar took the cakes which she had made, and brought them into the chamber to Amnon her brother. (2 Samuel 13:8-10)

Did you hear the other day where our Vice-President was chided for stating that he would not be in a room alone with a woman other than his wife? He was made fun of. Did you notice what Amnon did when the food was ready? He asked the "witnesses" to leave. It has always been an unspoken rule in the ministry to never be in a closed room with a woman other than your wife. At least leave the door open. If possible have someone else present. That's sad today but VERY necessary!

We can't relate to this story. Today, I would think the sister would at least be suspicious. In those days though women were not treated as today. Thank God! We must always be aware of the culture of the day.

I get this picture of the spider and the fly luring the fly into the trap. We know what's going to happen. I don't believe Tamar did. She trusted her brother. I don't know if she was aware of his affections for her.

Can you see the devil at work here? Innocent request. But a trap built on lies, deceit, lust. Oh, Amnon would have us believe it was because he loved Tamar, but love doesn't act this way. It was pure lust.

My wife and I attended a wedding just recently, the minister read from 1 Corinthians 13. The Love Chapter. I have used the passage myself. It certainly doesn't apply here. I doubt that Amnon had anything resembling marriage in mind. It is sad, but our culture is moving in that direction today. Too many young people, forgoing marriage and living together. It would be interesting if they spent some time in this chapter of 2 Samuel. Lust is a poor substitute for love, and many times lasts about as long.

Here might be a good case of being aware of your surroundings. Again, when Amnon suggested moving to the bedroom, today the warning bells would go off. In this scenario Ammon was supposed to be sick. It might make sense, but again warning bells should go off. It's hard sometimes to relate to a different culture. Do you think something like this would work today? Not likely.

Again, we must ask ourselves, why would God include these details? When we can know Satan's game plan, in advance, we can be prepared, we won't be caught off guard. Just like the night David walked out on that balcony. The lure was set. The fish doesn't have to bite. Amnon didn't have to follow through with his lust. David didn't have to send for Bathsheba. You see the tactic here? Beware!

I think it is interesting that John deals with this weakness in 1 John,

> For all that is in the world—the lust of the flesh, the lust of the eyes, and the pride of life— is not of the Father but of the world. (1 John 2:16) (NKJV)

Did you notice that two of the three deals with "lust", desire? Lust of the flesh, lust of the eyes. Both at play here in this story of Amnon. God has given us a Holy Spirit to deal with those lusts. To convict us, to warn us, beware you are headed into danger. It would benefit us greatly to heed those warnings!

And when she had brought them unto him to eat, he took hold of her, and said unto her, Come lie with me, my sister. And she answered him, Nay, my brother, do not force me; for no such thing ought to be done in Israel: do not thou this folly. And I, whither shall I cause my shame to go? And as for thee, thou shalt be as one of the fools in Israel. Now therefore, I pray thee, speak unto the king; for he will not withhold me from thee. Howbeit he would not hearken unto her voice: but, being stronger than she, forced her, and lay with her. Then Amnon hated her exceedingly; so that the hatred wherewith he hated her was greater than the love wherewith he had loved her. And Amnon said unto her, Arise, be gone. (2 Samuel 13:11-15)

Did you notice the three 4-letter words here? Love, lust, hate. Lust is not love. Lust can lead to hate. Lust is so prevalent today. Whether for things or for sex. It is so amazing to me today how living together outside of marriage is so acceptable. To me, that is lust not love. Love is a commitment to one another that cannot be broken by lust or love.

I have been married for over fifty years. I know where of I speak. Love comes and goes. Lust comes and goes. Commitment, which is what marriage is, is permanent.

Amnon thought what he felt was love. So many today are fooled the same way. So, they move in together and think that will satisfy. As soon as the lust is gone, like Amnon, then the love is gone. Our definition of love today is so shallow. Love is a commitment. Look what Jesus said,

> "For God so loved the world that He gave His only begotten Son, that whoever believes in Him should not perish but have everlasting life". (John 3:16) (NKJV)

That's commitment. Here is another definition of love:

> "Husbands love your wives, just as Christ also loved the church and gave Himself for it," (Galatians 5:25) (NKJV)

I have used the Galatians passage in weddings. It illustrates the commitment a husband should have toward his wife. Just as Christ has toward His church.

I could stand on this soapbox a long time. I hate to see where marriage is going today. Kids don't even consider marriage until they have lived together for years. That is NOT God's plan!

That is what we see here with Tamar and Ammon. Pay close attention. Amnon loved Tamar so much it made him ill. Once he had her, he hated her. Really? Is that the definition of love? That's the world's definition. No commitment. If you make me happy, we will live together, as soon as you don't, you're gone, really?

Tamar tried to point out how wrong it was. When there is lust involved there is no reason, just lust. No common sense, no commitment, just satisfaction, then hate! Remember that!

Again, as we will see, there are consequences. Lust blinds us to the consequences of our actions. Lust takes over our common sense, it controls our minds. We are singularly focused on the object of our lust.

I remember as a teen. I wanted a speedometer for my bicycle so bad. I went around the house and pouted for three days. Finally, my parents gave in. I got the speedometer and put it on my bike. In a couple of weeks, it was invisible. I forgot that it was even there. My lust for that thing, just took control. Fifty years later I still remember how I acted, and am ashamed. It will always be with me. I knew I was wrong, but I had to have that object of my lust. Lust doesn't always mean sex. It can be anything we want so bad that we don't care how we get it.

This is such a sad episode. It doesn't involve David, yet! It involves his family. It involves God's judgment on David for his lust after Bathsheba. A lust so strong that David had a man killed. Lust is a powerful force. It is an evil force, that can easily take control of our better judgment. How do we control it? First, we must stay close to God. We must pray, and we must listen to the promptings of God's Spirit within us. He will shout in our ear, "This is not right". It still comes down to our obedience.

And she said unto him, There is no cause: this evil in sending me away is greater than the other that thou didst unto me. But he would not hearken unto her. Then he called his servant that ministered unto him, and said, Put now this woman out from me, and bolt the door after her. And she had a garment of divers colours upon her: for with such robes were the king's daughters that were virgins apparelled. Then his servant brought her out, and bolted the door after her. And Tamar put ashes on her head, and rent her garment of divers colours that was on her, and laid her hand on her head, and went on crying. And Absalom her brother said unto her, Hath Amnon thy brother been with thee? But hold now thy peace, my sister: he is thy brother; regard not this thing. So Tamar remained desolate in her brother Absalom's house. (2 Samuel 13:16-20)

This, of course, is one of those events we would love to skip. Like it didn't happen. The problem is, that is the approach today. If we ignore it, it will go away. It will take care of itself. Just let it be. I have seen issues in the church that were dealt with that way. All they do is fester, and when they are finally dealt with it's too late. Let this story be a lesson.

I'm not sure, at what point David became aware of what happened. In our next segment, we will talk about David. Here is a perfect example of "I don't get mad, I get even." Can you imagine telling your sister, after she had been raped, to just keep cool, ignore what happened. That seems cruel, doesn't it? Wait a minute! Don't forget we are dealing with a totally different culture. All these individuals are related to the king. He has ultimate authority, etc. I guess it would be like walking on egg shells.

Don't forget! Where is God in all this? Do you think God has no idea what has happened? Be serious. So why doesn't He do something? Isn't that our natural response when something bad happens? Now suppose God stepped in, when Amnon asked Tamar to come to the bedroom, God steps in and blocks her. That's what your asking isn't it? Then we become puppets only moving and acting only as far as God will allow. Then we would have a "perfect world" right? Not hardly. Like I said, we would simply be puppets. God hopes that we will act according to His standards, but He refuses to FORCE us!

I hope you don't think God is not aware of what happened. God is totally aware. The same as when David sent his servant to bring Bathsheba. He also allows us to make huge mistakes, because He wants us to follow Him freely! To walk in His path not our own. We want God to do something here, but don't interfere in MY affairs. Right?

We all feel sorry for Tamar, sure! How about those around us that are suffering do to no fault of their own. Trapped in a bad relationship. Unless you have a ton of lawyers you can't get involved today. That is a sad case of affairs. That is where we have come. God's people are so afraid to get involved, we just pray. I'm not putting down prayer, Please! We should pray. We also need to do what we can to remedy the situation. That is a great ministry for the church. A haven for those who don't know what to do!

You see, we can read this story. We know the beginning and the end. We know the outcome. It makes it easy for us to judge and criticize. I doubt that Tamar had any idea what was going to happen when she entered that bedroom. Her brother was "sick" it seemed logical to bring the food to him. Hind-sight is 20/20 isn't it. The deed is done, now what? Is Absalom's answer, the right one? Just be still I will deal with it later. Does that solve the problem? No way!

I have found very early that it is better to deal with a problem head-on, up front, than to let it fester. It can be painful at first but the healing begins, while it can still be healed. If it is allowed to fester it can cause the loss of a limb, maybe even death. It must be dealt with.

Maybe that is why God chose to tell us this story. How NOT to deal with something? Because later we will see the results!

But when king David heard of all these things, he was very wroth. And Absalom spake unto his brother Amnon neither good nor bad: for Absalom hated Amnon, because he had forced his sister Tamar. And it came to pass after two full years, that Absalom had sheepshearers in Baal—hazor, which is beside Ephraim: and Absalom invited all the king's sons. (2 Samuel 13:21-23)

Are you asking yourself, how can this be? How long have you carried a grudge against someone until you had opportunity to get even? This is not that unusual, is it? How about, when you were little, people saying you won't amount to much. Your nothing but a failure. You will never make it. Especially if your handicapped in some way. Because of those words you are determined to prove them wrong. You spend your whole life, working hard, 60 to 70 hours a week just to prove to some people who are not around anymore that you "can do it!" Getting even never works! The only one you need to impress is God. God is very easy to impress, He just wants your fellowship and love.

Did you notice that this first line is the only given response from David? *"he was very angry."* Really? Okay, let's ask, "What would you do?" Let's put ourselves in David's shoes. He is the king. All the parties are your children. How would you respond? What would you do. I can't answer that, I wasn't there. All we have is this written account. We haven't lived in the culture of the day. The point I want to make is, unless your personally involved you have NO right to judge. Only God has that right. And God will deal with it in His time, in His way.

There is that dreaded word "Hated". That word has caused so much heartache in this world. It must be one of Satan's great weapons. Do you see or hear about it all around us today? Rich vs poor, black vs white, male vs female, educated vs uneducated, you name it and there is another group to hate or be hated by. Did you notice how long Absalom carried this hate? Two full years. Just waiting for the right opportunity to get revenge.

Do you remember when Joshua conquered the Promised Land? After dividing up the land between the tribes. They established twelve "Cities of Refuge". What is a "City of Refuge?" (Numbers 35. These were cities where you could run to, if you had killed someone "accidentally" and you could run there to keep from being killed by someone seeking revenge. No trial, no justice, you had to run. God forbid if you got caught. Tamar went to her brother, Absalom. Absalom said, "Just keep cool, I'll take care of it." Revenge!

Hatred, revenge, all tools of Satan. Do you remember Amnon's response to Tamar after he had raped her? Look back at verse 15,

> *Then Amnon hated her exceedingly, so that the hatred with which he hated her was greater than the love with which he had loved her. (2 Samuel 13:15) (NKJV)*

That is a powerful emotion, hate. It is far too prevalent today. I remember how so many used to revile Rodney King, when he said, "Can't we all just get along?" It was the butt of jokes for years. That's sad.

There are many lessons to learn from this episode in David's life. The sad part to me was David's response. It is so easy to be "angry" about something but so hard to really do anything about it. To face it and deal with it. We have already talked about ignoring it. I think it's funny that the hardest part about solving an issue is "talking" about it. We would rather get on "social media" and vent instead of dealing with the person face to face. Let's tell the world, but not the person offended or offending. If you notice that is what happened here. Absalom simply kept it to himself. David didn't bother to investigate and issue punishment, whatever that might be. Again, put yourself in David's shoes. What would you do?

And Absalom came to the king, and said, Behold now, thy servant hath sheepshearers; let the king, I beseech thee, and his servants go with thy servant. And the king said to Absalom, Nay, my son, let us not all now go, lest we be chargeable unto thee. And he pressed him; howbeit he would not go, but blessed him. Then said Absalom, If not, I pray thee, let my brother Amnon go with us. And the king said unto him, Why should he go with thee? But Absalom pressed him, that he let Amnon and all the king's sons go with him. (2 Samuel 13:24-27)

I wonder if David gave this invitation any thought? Remember he turned Absalom down at first. Notice that ALL the king's son attended. I guess this was a big celebration. Amnon invites the king and all the family. Did he know what he was going to do? Of course, he did. He had been planning this for two years. He carried that hate and desire for revenge for two whole years. It's interesting that there is no further mention of Tamar as far as what she was doing.

Tamar must have been a popular name. Remember back in Genesis 38? The daughter-in-law of Judah who tricked Judah into giving her a child, her name was Tamar.

Can you read the deceit in the words above? Probably not. That is the problem with writing things on "social media" it can be interpreted so many ways. Myself, I much prefer face-to-face. Many times, I would rather drive to the store or the person I want to talk to, rather than text, or even call them on the phone. I much prefer one-on-one!

Does it surprise you that Absalom waited two years? It shouldn't. Many people carry hate for much longer time periods. Years and years. Eating away at them. One day the opportunity comes to get your revenge. Does it make you feel better? Not likely. Hopefully, by this time God has gotten a hold of your heart and brought some light into it! God's light is a great change-agent!

Would that we would put as much planning and effort into godly pursuits. But then, we are human. Is that an excuse? The thing is we don't take the time to talk it out with God, do we? I have done this. If you present your arguments to God, ask for His direction and input, you might be surprised at the response. But as I have said so many times, we know so much more than God, don't we?

If David had said no, Absalom would have found another time, another situation, another opportunity. He was determined to get his revenge. To what end? Would it help Tamar any? Would Amnon's death solve anything. It might make him feel better but it would destroy his relationship with his father David. It just doesn't serve any purpose. Can we ask that same question? Take that question to God. What purpose would this revenge serve? Think about it!

And it came to pass, while they were in the way, that tidings came to David, saying, Absalom hath slain all the king's sons, and there is not one of them left. Then the king arose, and tare his garments, and lay on the earth; and all his servants stood by with their clothes rent. And Jonadab, the son of Shimeah David's brother, answered and said, Let not my lord suppose that they have slain all the young men the king's sons; for Amnon only is dead: for by the appointment of Absalom this hath been determined from the day that he forced his sister Tamar. (2 Samuel 13:30-32)

It's over, right? Not by a long shot. Anytime you take justice in your own hands there are consequences, as we will see. Again, do you see God in any of this. You would think these were children of Saul rather than David. Because of David's sin with Bathsheba, God has taken His hand off of David and his family. When you stray from the will of God there are consequences!

Rumors can be so devastating. Gossip as well. Stories told by people, either with evil intent or just misinformed. It never hurts to find the truth before jumping to conclusions, please! How many terrible mistakes have been made because of false information. That includes the internet!

I think it is interesting that Jonadab knew what had happened. It seemed that David's family knew what was going on, but David didn't. We saw earlier that when David heard he was furious. So, what did he do? Apparently, nothing. It passed.

It's just like Bathsheba. It is traced back to one mistake, one wrong move outside of God and the consequences just seem to snowball. It quickly gets out of control. When nothing is done to remedy the wrong, the devil will continue to fester the wrong into many, many other wrongs. Deal with it.

Did you catch that phrase, *"this has been determined"* Determined by whom? Certainly not God. Determined by a grieving brother. I asked earlier what would you do? Is there a solution? I know it sounds trite but you might try praying first. I remember when David used to "inquire of the Lord". Is that not appropriate here? Oh, only before going into battle. Any time you face a challenge your first step must be to pray.

Next you might want to get the facts. Get the story from all involved. Also, you might want to pray that God will reveal the truth. Not all of the stories will be accurate. Trust that God will lead you to the truth. That assumes you have the Holy Spirit living within you to guide you. If not you're on your own. Once you have all the facts you pass sentence, NO! You're not their judge, you could be their counselor. Pray and seek God's judgment, not yours! God will guide you to the right solution.

The wrong that has been done cannot be changed. That fact must be dealt with. The guilty, of course, must be punished, then there must be forgiveness. Forgiveness? Yes, without that you will have revenge. All parties must come together and resolve the wrong. If God is not in the solution it will never work.

The great wrong that this incident will achieve will be a rift between David and his son Absalom. Because of the wrong by Amnon, who is now dead, this will fester and create a huge divide between David and Absalom. When we sin, there will be consequences. Some may last for years and years. It must be dealt with, both with the parties involved and with God. We can't change the sin, we can repent and turn it over to God.

Now therefore let not my lord the king take the thing to his heart, to think that all the king's sons are dead: for Amnon only is dead. But Absalom fled. And the young man that kept the watch lifted up his eyes, and looked, and, behold, there came much people by the way of the hill side behind him. And Jonadab said unto the king, Behold, the king's sons come: as thy servant said, so it is. And it came to pass, as soon as he had made an end of speaking, that, behold, the king's sons came, and lifted up their voice and wept: and the king also and all his servants wept very sore. (2 Samuel 13:33-36)

From grief to joy. Would, that were the message at every funeral. Only Amnon is dead. It ought not to have been. But it is done. The deed is done by Absalom, he has fled, one dead, another gone. David's family being torn apart because of his lust. How many homes and families are torn apart because of the influence of this world's morals. Sad!

If this passage, and the previous ones, this whole sordid story, doesn't get your attention you deserve the consequences. I cannot stress this lesson enough. Of course, today there is no marriage so infidelity isn't an issue, really? Two people put their "faith" in each other. One breaks that trust, oh well. That is so sad!

I will keep hammering this point through this passage. I am so disappointed in our world today. The total lack of respect for the sacredness of marriage. As a former pastor and a husband of over fifty years. It hurts me deeply to see where our morals have come to. Even in the movies it is no big deal if a couple sleeps together before they are married. That is not God's way!

At one point David had thought he had lost all his sons. Then he comes to find out that only one had died. It's interesting how easily we can be distracted from the real message. It wasn't that Amnon was dead, it was that his brother killed him. We are missing the warning signs.

The warning signs are all around us today. Pre-marital sex, same-sex marriage, vulgar language and nudity on TV. I think the thing that stands out the most to me right now, is the total disregard for the truth. Lying is an art form now. No one is held accountable, let alone called out for it. Truth has been lost in our society. Okay, I'll get off my soapbox.

The truth of the Word of God still stands out. Why do you suppose God thought it was necessary to include this sordid episode in the life of David? Maybe, by the sheer horror of it He might get our attention to the consequences of sin. Yes, lying is a sin, or used to be. It still is in God's judgments. There will always be a payment due when we lie. In one form or another.

David has just begun to feel the wrath of God. There is a payment due. Sometimes, I think we have the idea that if we confess, and ask God's forgiveness, that it will relieve us of responsibility. No, there are consequences. God will not wink at sin. Maybe we need to be refreshed in the words of the Ten Commandments. Ten, simple "commands" that will change our perspective on our walk with God. The first four dealing with our vertical relationship with God. The remaining six, with our horizontal relationship with each other. Don't discard these because we are in New Testament times. Jesus condensed them into two commandments. (Matthew 22:37-40). No less important!

Love God with all your heart, and love each other. Maybe sometimes we make it TOO simple. Whether it is ten or two, Jesus said,

> *"If you love Me, keep My commandments" (John 14:15).*
> (NKJV)

I guess that is the question, do you love God? If you love Him, do what He tells you. Ten simple rules, why are they so hard to follow? How is your relationship with God today?

But Absalom fled, and went to Talmai, the son of Ammihud, king of Geshur. And David mourned for his son every day. So Absalom fled, and went to Geshur, and was there three years. And the soul of king David longed to go forth unto Absalom: for he was comforted concerning Amnon, seeing he was dead. (2 Samuel 13:37-39)

So, you think this episode is over. We are dealing with an interesting situation. One son has killed the other. What could possibly be going through David's mind. Again, I want to point out there is no mention of God here. Tragedy, heartbreak, misunderstanding, but no God. I wonder why that is? What does it take to look up? How far down do we must get, before we seek God?

It took me a while to discover these verses. They always come to my mind when I think of being comforted. Look in 2 Corinthians,

> *Blessed be the God and Father of our Lord Jesus Christ, the Father of mercies and the God of all comfort, who comforts us in all our tribulation, that we may be able to comfort those who are in any trouble, with the comfort with which we ourselves are comforted by God. (2 Corinthians 1:3-4). (NKJV)*

Mark these in your Bible. These truths are so profound. Memorize if you will, at least the address!

He says that David was comforted but it doesn't say how. We are going into some interesting verses in the next chapter. Verses I struggle with. We will walk through them together. There must be something there that God wants us to learn. They would not be there if He didn't have something for us.

Absalom fled because, maybe, he expected a response from David. He was angry earlier, because of Tamar. Maybe Absalom misunderstood David's reaction. Here is something we may want to take note of. How many relationships have been destroyed by misunderstandings. Things not said, that should have been said. Things said that were misunderstood, etc. That's why I am not a supporter of "social media" for communication. It must be face-to-face.

I am glad they included the time here, three years. It helps to get a perspective. Imagine how long three years is. A long time to think, to stew, to imagine all kinds of things. Instead of talking, their imagination is going crazy. Instead of understanding there is conjecture. Not good!

I wonder if some of David's remorse is because Absalom took a hand where it should have been David's responsibility. Guilt can be a powerful emotion. It says, *"King David longed to go to Absalom."* (v. 30). What was stopping him? David was king, he was free to go to battle but he could not go after his son? Pride, guilt, shame, who knows. Interesting dilemma. What would you do?

Here again, no mention of God, prayer, counsel, advice from Nathan. How long have you stewed about something because you were afraid to take the first step? "They have to come to me." That sounds like pride to me. So many emotions get in our way from doing the right thing, don't they? How about just getting on our knees, admit we need help, ask God to show us what to do. I know why we don't. We don't want to hear the answer. Just leave it alone it will heal itself. Good luck with that. I have never heard of a cancer that healed itself.

I can't begin to know where you're at in your family struggles. I am not an expert. I know who is. At this point I am very serious, pray it through. Don't just offer up a simple sentence prayer then move on. Keep praying until God gives you an answer. He will, but He wants to know you're serious here! Don't just pray and leave it! Keep praying until you get an answer. That is "praying through" something. That is, if you seriously want an answer. Maybe you don't want an answer. It might mean you would have to do something you don't want to!

COFFEE BREAK

I was thinking about this last night. Think about David's life. From defeating Goliath, to his battles as the general of Saul's army. Then Saul gets jealous and runs David off. Then Saul decides to chase him and kill him. David moves to Achishs' land with the Philistines. He lives in Ziklag. Later his home is invaded and his family taken away. He defeats the Amalekites and rescues his family. In 2 Samuel David goes from king of Hebron to king of Israel. Along the way he picks up Michal and Abigail as wives. He finds Mephibosheth, Jonathan's son, and brings him to live with David the king.

Do you get the picture? David is always serving. Whether leading his men in battle or setting up his kingdom in Israel. There is always something to do. He offers to begin building the temple for the ark of God, which he has moved to Jerusalem. God denies his offer and David is okay with that. Oh, don't miss his great prayer in 2 Samuel 7, about David being God's servant, etc.

Here is where I am going. Look at 2 Samuel 11,

> It happened in the spring of the year, at the time when kings go out to battle, that David sent Joab and his servants with him, and all Israel; and they destroyed the people of Ammon and besieged Rabbah. But David remained in Jerusalem. (2 Samuel 11:1) (NKJV)

First, we noted that David was not where he ought to be. We got that.

I retired at age 62. I wanted to be healthy enough to enjoy my retirement. In September, I will have been retired for ten years. I remember my last day at work. I remember thinking, "Now what do I do." I had been "working" for forty years. There were no clear prospects ahead. I really didn't know what I was going to do. Money was not a problem at the time.

God has managed to keep me busy for these past ten years. It seemed there was always something. I was active in my church. God always seemed to have a ministry for me. Later I gave up the Sunday School Ministry. The young ones were coming along and it was time to pass that ministry on. Up to this time I had a "Newsletter" ministry. I sent anniversary cards, etc. I kept busy.

Do you see where I'm going? David had responsibilities and duties. There were places and things to do. He took the time off. Even in the Garden of Eden God had duties and chores for Adam and Eve, even in a "perfect" environment. The same is true for us today.

God has never intended for us to be idle. Just sit around. To be honest, God has a ministry for every one of His children! There is so much to do in His kingdom that there is plenty to go around.

One lady in our church thought that there should be regular visits to those who can't gt out and come to church. She told some others and our Homebound Ministry was formed. Even after she could no longer do the duties, someone else stepped up, and it is going great. Another lady felt that our "New Members" were being overlooked. She formed a group and we have regular dinners to welcome our new members, and she prepared a notebook to help explain our ministry at First Baptist.

Has God laid something on your heart? Tell someone. The motto of our church is "Connecting People to God and People to People." That's what ministry is all about. There is always a place to serve in God's house and His people. Pray about it!

The few moments that David was idle, not where he should have been, Satan moved in and distracted him from his primary calling, "God's servant". God has never intended for His children to "sit around" occupying a pew. We are to be busy at the Lord's work! Are you serving God in some way? Why not?

2 Samuel 14

Now Joab the son of Zeruiah perceived that the king's heart was toward Absalom. And Joab sent to Tekoah, and fetched thence a wise woman, and said unto her, I pray thee, feign thyself to be a mourner, and put on now mourning apparel, and anoint not thyself with oil, but be as a woman that had a long time mourned for the dead: and come to the king, and speak on this manner unto him. So Joab put the words in her mouth. (2 Samuel 14:1-3)

Now it's Joab instead of Nathan. Why is it easier to tell someone something using a "parable" than to come right out and say it? Using the word parable may not be the best choice. Maybe we get the impression that a parable is a "fairytale." In some cases, it may be. Jesus used parables a lot in teaching His truths. The book of Luke has most of them. They are a teaching method quite effective!

Nathan confronted David about Bathsheba using a story. Now Joab wants to convict David about his son Absalom. Story telling is a great method of teaching truths. We can understand better when there is a personal application. We can put ourselves into the situation and better understand what we need to learn. We use this method more than we think.

Joab is getting involved in "family" matters. That can be dangerous. He sees how David is treating Absalom, he wants to help. He knows the whole story behind Absalom killing his brother Amnon. That is such a critical decision to make. Do I get involved or stay out of it? I think I like Joab's approach. Tell this story and gauge David's response. I wouldn't recommend it! But, God has decided to include this episode for our benefit. Let's see what we can learn.

God sends different people into our lives. These individuals, seem to pass through. We may get to know them, and maybe not. Some we may not even know their names. They pass through our lives for a reason. Either they are to teach us something, or we may be the ones making an impact on their lives. We may never know.

For over four years I prepared a monthly newsletter. Other than a few articles most of it was copying from my favorite books. At one point my mailing list consisted of over 400 names. Most I knew from church. Each month I sent thirty newsletters to names I took from a local phone book. If they came back I would scratch them and add another. The names from the phone book I never met. Maybe, God willing I might meet someone in heaven who received my newsletter and gave their life to Christ. What a glorious day that will be.

We all have opportunity to touch someone's life. What kind of mark we leave on their life is up to us and God. God can use a simple comment to touch someone when they need it the most. God can use a brief story about how God changed our life to bring someone to a saving knowledge of the Lord Jesus Christ. That may be the sole reason you passed through their life. You just never know.

Here is a woman, recruited by Joab to take a message to the king. Joab told her what to say. She was willing to be a messenger to the king. We can be a messenger for our King. We can tell others the story of our salvation. Share your story.

And when the woman of Tekoah spake to the king, she fell on her face to the ground, and did obeisance, and said, Help, O king. And the king said unto her, What aileth thee? And she answered, I am indeed a widow woman, and mine husband is dead. And thy handmaid had two sons, and they two strove together in the field, and there was none to part them, but the one smote the other, and slew him. And, behold, the whole family is risen against thine handmaid, and they said, Deliver him that smote his brother, that we may kill him, for the life of his brother whom he slew; and we will destroy the heir also: and so they shall quench my coal which is left, and shall not leave to my husband neither name nor remainder upon the earth. (2 Samuel 14:4-7)

Do you think about your heritage any? What you are leaving behind to the next generation. Okay, you have no children, you have other relatives, family connections. How do you wish to be remembered? I think someone wrote a book once on the notations people leave on their headstones in cemeteries. Is that all you want to leave behind?

Joab has hired this woman to try and patch up a misunderstanding between David and his son Absalom. Absalom has killed his brother Amnon for raping his sister Tamar. Sorry for the details. It's important we keep the scene in tack. Absalom runs away fearing his father's retribution. David, knew of the attack on Tamar, but really did nothing. It's a mess. The family is divided! Joab is trying to repair the situation. It can be very dangerous to interfere in family matters. Sometimes necessary.

There are a lot of families today torn apart for a lot less reasons. We have lost, in our culture, the meaning of "family". The closeness that we enjoyed as children. Sometimes family members move away. Sometimes they just lose contact. They are still "family". That must be the mindset of Joab here. He wants to try to bring the family back together.

Do you know who I'm thinking about during this? Solomon. He must be around five or so. It's hard to tell, when the Bible doesn't keep us up on time periods. We do know that it has been three years since Absalom killed Amnon (v. 38). Solomon is growing up in this environment. We hardly ever think of the imprint these episodes may leave on the children. No one should have to grow up in a divided family. Again, the concept of "family".

We see in verse 39 of the previous chapter that David feels no ill-will toward Absalom. Yet it took Joab hiring an actress to convey the idea of reconciliation. Sad. David won't make the effort, Absalom won't reach out. Isn't that the way it is today? We have all this social media, but no communication. Weird!

This whole episode with Absalom will take some interesting and strange twists later. When we get deeper I want you to keep the beginning of this in mind. What's that line in a Paul Newman movie? "What we have here is a failure to communicate" that is so true.

When was the last time you talked to God? How often do you talk with your heavenly Father? Is it a one-way conversation? You do all the talking. Do you spend any time in meditation, listening for God's response? A conversation involves two parties. Maybe you have a relationship with God like Absalom and David. You are thinking God has given up, or abandoned you, and because you feel that way, you refuse to talk with God. Does that solve anything? Talk to Him!

I stressed "family" earlier. There is also the family of God. I thought I was the only one who felt this but I have heard from others that say, "I am closer to my church family than my own family." Why is that? For one, we spend more time together. Another reason is that they seem to care more than our own family. Misconceptions? Probably, but why is that? Social media is NOT the answer to "family" ties. It's sad to say that is the way of the world today!

And the king said unto the woman, Go to thine house, and I will give charge concerning thee. And the woman of Tekoah said unto the king, My lord, O king, the iniquity be on me, and on my father's house: and the king and his throne be guiltless. And the king said, Whosoever saith ought unto thee, bring him to me, and he shall not touch thee any more. Then she said, I pray thee, let the king remember the Lord thy God, that thou wouldest not suffer the revengers of blood to destroy any more, lest they destroy my son. And he said, As the Lord liveth, there shall not one hair of thy son fall to the earth. (2 Samuel 14:8-11)

This doesn't make a lot of sense if you're not familiar with the "Cities of Refuge" set up after Joshua conquered the Promised Land. The establishment of these six Cities of Refuge takes place in Numbers 35:6-34. When a relative is killed the kinfolk will appoint someone (avenger of blood) to take revenge on the killer. If that killer can reach a "City of Refuge" before that, he is spared. That is what this woman is referring to. Strange laws for a strange time.

There was a period in our culture where, if you were a fugitive and sought refuge in the church you were spared until justice could be done. Not that familiar with it, I just know of it. Today it is totally perverted in the term "Sanctuary City". I won't go there. In a sense, it's the same principle.

Have you noticed that David has no clue that the story the woman is relating mirrors his own situation? Sometimes the hardest sin is the one right in front of us in the mirror. It's easy to point out the sin of others. I like this verse in the New Testament:

Judge not, that you be not judged. For with what judgment you judge, you will be judged; and with the measure you use, it will be measured back to you. (Matthew 7:1). (NKJV)

I might have known it would be in the Sermon on the Mount. Such a powerful warning to us today.

The Cities of Refuge and the Avenger of Blood were the justice system of the day. The one running may have killed someone accidentally. No trial, no jury, no justice. If he could make it to a City of Refuge before the Avenger of blood tracked him down and killed him, he would be spared. This was the law set up in the book of Numbers.

I think it is ironic. Do you see David's outrage? *"Whoever says anything to you, bring him to me, and he shall not touch you anymore."* (v. 10) (NKJV). How about this,

> *So, David's anger was greatly aroused against the man, and he said to Nathan, "As the Lord lives, the man who has done this shall surely die!" (2 Samuel 12:5). (NKJV)*

This was David's response to Nathan's tale.

It's easy to be self-righteous when we think it was someone else. Don't overlook that verse above by Jesus about judging. Meditate on that verse a while. Surely you have not pre-judged someone without the facts. Surely, you have not judged someone based on a "story". It is never a wise thing to judge anyone without the facts. Then we are to leave the consequences up to the Great Judge, God Almighty!

Here, again the use of an illustration to make a point to David. I just realized something. Have you ever sat on a jury? What does the prosecution do? They present a "story" of how this crime took place. They present witnesses, and evidence. They are telling a story. It is up to you to decide how much is true and how much is made up. Then you render a verdict based on the "evidence" presented. Much like David does at the end of this woman's story. The problem is the story is not true. It is made up to make a point. That is your job as a jurist. If you have never served on a jury it is one of life's experiences that no one should miss. It will give you a whole new perspective on the judicial system. You will never forget it!

Maybe this story by this woman can give David some clarity about the way he has treated his family, especially Absalom. We will see. David is going through some tough times right now. You might want to note the absence of God, or reference to Him.

Then the woman said, Let thine handmaid, I pray thee, speak one word unto my lord the king. And he said, Say on. And the woman said, Wherefore then hast thou thought such a thing against the people of God? For the king doth speak this thing as one which is faulty, in that the king doth not fetch home again his banished. For we must needs die, and are as water spilt on the ground, which cannot be gathered up again; neither doth he devise means, that his banished be not expelled from him. (2 Samuel 14:12-14)

There are passages in the New Testament, especially in Romans, where I made it a point to underline "Therefore". You should always ask yourself, "What is that therefore, there for?" It refers to the previous statements. Because, of the previous statement you should...! Always be on the lookout for "therefore".

Based on the illustration I previously gave you, here is my real message. Why are you treating your son as though he were exiled? I don't remember any place where David "banished" his son Absalom. I think it is what Joab had interpreted. I don't know if he has talked to Absalom, either. That was how Joab saw it. Getting in the middle without knowing the facts, we talked about this earlier. Look at this verse:

> *And King David longed to go to Absalom. For he had been comforted concerning Amnon, because he was dead. (2 Samuel 13:39) (NKJV)*

David had accepted the reason Absalom felt it necessary to kill Amnon. David grieved for Absalom. David wanted to make amends. But he chose to do nothing. Isn't that the way we deal with those situations today. We expect the parties involved to read our minds. We expect them to "understand" without a word from us. I hate to point this out, but again, no reference to God here!

Unless, maybe God is working through Joab. I have my doubts. Either way, it should be David to send for Absalom. To make amends, to resolve the misunderstanding. There needs to be some movement. Given David's spiritual condition right now, God may be speaking to him, and he is not listening.

The relationship between God and His children is so precious! God will not "push" Himself on us. The relationship is ours for the asking, BUT, we must seek it. Once we have that relationship it is ours to maintain. Our sin, our disobedience, our lack of faith, can weaken that relationship. God gets harder and harder to hear. We lock the Holy Spirit away in a closet and we only listen when it is convenient for us. Most of the time, at this point, it is not convenient.

The verse said David "longed" for Absalom. What did he do about it? God's Spirit lays something on your heart, what do you do? You respond! It may be hard, it may be embarrassing, trust God and do it! God has already gone ahead of you and prepared the way. If it's making amends to a family member, etc. You may need to make the first move. If it fails, it is their fault not yours. You have done what God asked you to do. The rest is in God's hands.

We think this scenario is strange. In the culture of the day, if this woman offends David she could be put in prison or killed. She was taking her life in her hands just coming to David. Remember this whole story is made up by Joab, to get the king's attention. She is scared to death, yet she has the courage to confront the king.

I would be curious to know how long David waited before this woman confronted him. How long he "longed" for Absalom. You know the longer you put these things off, the easier it gets to ignore it. But, if it is not dealt with early, it festers, it gets worse and worse. Soon there is no mending, it's too late. Never let hurt go unattended to. Deal with it now, it's easier!

Now therefore that I am come to speak of this thing unto my lord the king, it is because the people have made me afraid: and thy handmaid said, I will now speak unto the king; it may be that the king will perform the request of his handmaid. For the king will hear, to deliver his handmaid out of the hand of the man that would destroy me and my son together out of the inheritance of God. Then thine handmaid said, The word of my lord the king shall now be comfortable: for as an angel of God, so is my lord the king to discern good and bad: therefore the Lord thy God will be with thee. (2 Samuel 14:15-17)

Does it seem we are "slow-walking" through these verses? Maybe. The point of this treatise is to "walk" with David throughout his walk with God. Did you catch those last few words? *"And may the Lord your God be with you."* Of course, He is with David. I am wondering, through this time with

Absalom how many times God's words would echo in his mind? *"Thus, says the Lord, 'Behold, I will raise up adversity against you from your own house; . . . "*(12:11). How many times will those words echo in David's mind.

Do you think the Lord has left David, as He did with Saul? I don't think so. When God pronounced His judgment, it was over as far as God was concerned. Oh, there are consequences, we know that. It's the relationship that is what we want to watch. It's important to remember this quote from the book of Acts:

> *"And when He had removed him (Saul), He raised up for them David as king, to whom He gave testimony and said, 'I have found David the son of Jesse, a man after My own heart, who will do all My will.'" (Acts 13:22) (NKJV)*

This from the Apostle Paul. Paul's reference was from the Hebrew books he studied as a Pharisee. Paul gave testimony of God's relationship with David.

How is your relationship with God? Have you checked it lately? Are you "walking" with God or have you left Him somewhere along the path? I think David is walking with God, but his attention is on himself right now. David is too wrapped up in "Woe is me" syndrome right now.

We get that way, sometimes don't we? We get so wrapped up in our own trials and tribulations we forget that God is walking right beside us and wants to comfort and encourage but we are too distracted to even know He is there.

Joab is trying to get David back on track with this lady he chose to bring this story, this illustration to reach David. God uses so many different methods to get our attention, to get us back on tract. One of the many reasons I won't miss church on Sunday. Sometimes God will use the pastor just like Joab used this lady. The pastor will tell a story, use an illustration, even a passage of Scripture will bring my focus back on God. A kindly word from a friend at church. A Sunday School lesson that reminds me that God is still there and cares about me. Any number of ways God can get our attention. Sadly, most of the times it can be through trials as well.

Have you ever noticed that God rarely attends "Pitty-Parties"? Those are strictly reserved for those who have taken their eyes off the blessings and presence of God. We start looking inward instead of upward.

Again, when was the last time you checked your walk with God? I used this illustration in my last book, THE PATH. We are walking a path. The moment we become a child of God, we begin this journey with God. In Jeremiah 29:11 we see that God has this plan for our life. God wants to walk with us and guide us through this life. The hard part is staying on that path with God. Too many times we want to be distracted from the path. We think we know a shortcut, a "better way". The further we stray from that path the harder it is to hear God. Sometimes we get so far down that path, we fall into a pit. Then we look around and God is nowhere to be found. Then we have to backtrack and find where we left God. He is right there waiting!

Then the king answered and said unto the woman, Hide not from me, I pray thee, the thing that I shall ask thee. And the woman said, Let my lord the king now speak. And the king said, Is not the hand of Joab with thee in all this? And the woman answered and said, As thy soul liveth, my lord the king, none can turn to the right hand or to the left from ought that my lord the king hath spoken: for thy servant Joab, he bade me, and he put these words in the mouth of thine handmaid. To fetch about this form of speech that thy servant Joab done this thing: and my lord is wise, according to the wisdom of an angel of God, to know all things that are in the earth. (2 Samuel 14:18-20)

Caught! I don't know, for sure, how David realized that it was Joab. Maybe a combination of two+two and the work of the Holy Spirit. Not sure. Maybe it was conviction about the way he had treated Absalom. It is interesting that the woman recognized the wisdom of God working in David.

Why are we so hard-headed sometimes? I knew this lady. She had been dating this guy since high school. Everyone kept telling her he was the wrong guy. She eventually married him and one year later was divorced. Godly counsel is great, but it must be heeded before it is useful.

We rarely if ever really get away with something. Be sure you will be found out. I don't think Joab really thought he would fool David. He simply wanted us to get to recognize his treatment of Absalom. That's the way God works in our lives as well. Someone will cross our path that will help point out a misdeed. It's how we respond to the revelation, that matters to God.

There are two responses! The first and most popular is to blame it on someone or something else. It's not your fault! Right? Of course, the better one is to say, "You're right, I was wrong, I'm sorry." Why is that so hard? David has been confronted with his attitude. I am not sure I want to call it a "sin". He is confronted, convicted of neglect. How does he respond? We will see.

I think it is interesting that Joab chose this way to address David. Nathan the prophet also chose this method of confronting David. Could he not handle the truth? Interesting question, why God chose to approach David this way. Could it be, that God speaks to us the same way? He puts people in our path, with a story that is meant to get our attention? God has so many ways of getting our attention. Friends, family, circumstance, sermons in church, church acquaintances, etc. He will use what is necessary to get the message across.

I think it is important not to look past this lesson. What does it take to convict you of a wrong doing? Then, what do you do when you see it? How do you respond to being caught? We talked about that. Maybe we think if we can ignore it, there won't be any consequences. I learned the hard way that if you try to hide it, once you're caught it is worse. The consequences are rough.

Okay, it's time to move on. You get the message. David has been confronted with his relationship with Absalom. Let's clean this up and move on. Easy to say. It's not that easy. There will always be consequences, I hate that word! Payment due! There is always a time when things need to be made right. Let's see what David does.

And the king said unto Joab, Behold now, I have done this thing: go therefore, bring the young man Absalom again. And Joab fell to the ground on his face, and bowed himself, and thanked the king: and Joab said, To day thy servant knoweth that I have found grace in thy sight, my lord, o king, in that the king hath fulfilled the request of his servant. So Joab arose and went to Geshur and brought Absalom to Jerusalem. (2 Samuel 14:21-23)

Maybe it's me, I don't really recall Joab approaching the king about Absalom. He sent a maidservant to tell him a story. I don't recall Joab saying anything. Interesting. How might you respond to someone who sent someone else to ask your permission to do something. I remember as a kid, my brothers, who were younger than I, would have me approach our parents for permission to do something. They knew, as the oldest, I was more likely to get the right answer.

Maybe that's what happened here. I was thinking about something this morning. Are you keeping a personal journal? Recording events daily, your thoughts, etc. I want you to consider this seriously. We have the Bible, a journal if you will, to reflect on. To be reminded of the whole process of events to bring us to this point. Do you remember, for instance, that Joab was once Saul's general? Do you remember David chastising Joab for allowing David to enter their camp and possibly killing their king? Later, Joab became David's general after killing Abner.

Anyway. I want to encourage you to seriously think about keeping a journal. When you find yourself in a storm, as you surely will. I want you to look back in that journal and observe then events until you find the "beginning" of this trial, this storm. Notice how it all started. Maybe there is a lesson to learn there. I could to do that once, I thought I knew God's will, I made some mistakes, big mistakes. When I reflected I realized that I had gotten ahead of God and thus eliminated all chances of achieving what I thought was God's will. Reflection can be very valuable!

Remember where this all started? When David gave Tamar permission, at Amnon's request, to come to Amnon's house and nurse him. Even faking his illness. Look at the snowball that has been growing and growing. It's not over yet.

There is also a little lesson we might want to take note. It is such a hard call today. Something that requires MUCH prayer. How much do you get involved in family matters that are not your own? We must pray! God may be doing something that you might be interfering with. You may be able to help, of course, but, like I said, it requires much prayer!

Joab has taken it on himself to try to patch the differences between David and his son, Absalom. Joab is the friend of Absalom. David was the friend of Jonathan as well. As friend's we must be real sure how much we want to get involved in family problems. Just a thought!

There never really was anything between David and Absalom, misunderstanding. I think David realized why Absalom did what he did. He was hurt but not mad at Absalom. Absalom misunderstood how

David responded. This happens so many times. Personally, when I am upset I shut up! I won't talk. I hate confrontation. So, I just keep quiet. Many people misunderstand this as anger. I can't help the way I respond. Misunderstanding!

We also need to keep in mind that this whole episode is part of God's judgment on David for his sin with Bathsheba and Uriah. So how does David deal with it in that regard. Prayer, of course. Seeking God's direction, His peace, His will. God can use any situation to His glory. Never forget Romans:

> *For we know that all things work together for good to those who love God, to those who are called according to His purpose. (Romans 8:28) (NKJV)*

We know that David loves God. We also know that David was called according to God's purpose. We know that there are consequences to sin. God will use this to bring glory to Himself!

And the king said, Let him turn to his own house, and let him not see my face. So Absalom returned to his own house, and saw not the king's face But in all Israel there was none to be so much praised as Absalom for his beauty: from the sole of his foot even to the crown of his head there was no blemish in him. And when he polled his head, (for it was at every year's end that he polled it: because the hair was heavy on him, therefore he polled it:) he weighed the hair of his head at two hundred shekels after the king's weight. And unto Absalom there were born three sons, and one daughter, whose name was Tamar: she was a woman of a fair countenance. So Absalom dwelt two full years in Jerusalem and saw not the king's face. (2 Samuel 14:24-28)

Have you ever heard the expression, "If you ignore it, it will go away?" That seems to be the method David is using. So, Absalom named his daughter after his sister whom Amnon raped. Then Absalom killed Amnon to avenge his sister.

David allows, or invites Absalom to return to Jerusalem, but will not see him, or speak to him. That will solve everything. Have you ever dealt with a problem that way? Surely not.

To be honest I wish I understood David at this point. Granted there is a big cultural difference in those days. He is the king, Absalom his son. We can't relate. So, we ask ourselves why did God think it important to include this in his narrative? What benefit does it do for us the read this story? Most importantly, how can we learn from this story. I think I hit on it at first. Ignoring something or someone does not make the problem go away. Eventually it must be dealt with!

Did you notice the transition? *Now in all Israel there was no who was praised as much as Absalom.* We went from Absalom not seeing David's face for two years, to how handsome Absalom is. There is an interesting transition from verse 24 to verse 25. Even the Bible is ignoring the subject. Just kidding! It is like a scene change in a movie.

God is now laying a foundation for what is about to happen. Do you think there was some amount of arrogance in Absalom when he decided to kill Amnon for his treatment of his sister? Maybe that is something else that might have been addressed in the beginning. In any family, there is a "pecking" order. Imagine the chaos in David's family with up to eight wives, eight mothers, eight children, wondering who is first in line, etc. It breeds jealousy unless the parents address it. And when I say parents I'm talking TWO!

I was the oldest of six boys and two girls. I married a lady from a family where she was the youngest of six boys and two girls. We have a lot of birthday cards and Christmas cards to mail each year. We can relate to a "pecking" order. Imagine the confusion and disharmony that went on in David's family.

Most of the names of the offspring are never mentioned again. I wonder how old Solomon is at this point. He is already recognized as the heir to the throne. Can you hear the talk now? Maybe Absalom thinks he is more qualified because of his looks, his long hair, etc. Maybe we will find out later. If you have read the story don't tell anyone, it's our secret.

Interesting, do you remember what God told Samuel when he went looking for a king to replace Saul? Look:

> But the Lord said to Samuel, "Do not look at his appearance or at his physical stature, because I have rejected him (Eliab). For the Lord does not see as man sees, for man looks at the outward appearance, but the Lord looks at the heart. (1 Samuel 16:7). (NKJV)

A biblical principle to store in the back of your mind when you "size" up someone you just met.

It appears that Absalom has the credentials but what is in his heart. God knows what is there. God will deal with it accordingly. This was one of the early traits of David that God liked. David had a pure heart. David had a heart for God. Of course, he fell, he made mistakes. God knew his heart. Does He know yours? Do you?

Therefore he said unto his servants, See, Joab's field is near mine, and he hath barley there; go and set it on fire. And Absalom's servants set the field on fire. Then Joab arose, and came to Absalom unto his house, and said unto him, Wherefore have thy servants set my field on fire? And Absalom answered Joab, Behold, I sent unto thee, saying, Come hither, that I may send thee to the king, to say, Wherefore am I come from Geshur? It had been good for me to have been there still: now therefore let me see the king's face; and if there be any iniquity in me, let him kill me. So Joab came to the king, and told him: and when he had called for Absalom, he came to the king, and bowed himself on his face to the ground before the king: and the king kissed Absalom. (2 Samuel 14:29-33)

What does it take to get your attention? Maybe you happen to attend your local church one day. The pastor preaches a message that hits you right in the heart. It is time to decide. What do you do? Nothing. You put it away in the back of your mind. Do you think God will allow it to stay there? I think not. Suppose you walked forward in the invitation time. You profess to have accepted Jesus as your Savior. You go home and forget all about it. Do you think God will let you just ignore that profession?

Then God begins to get your attention. He will bring His words to your mind. Others may drop hints here and there. Things will begin to happen in your life that remind you of that commitment, that profession of faith. Maybe it will be hard to sleep some nights. God works in a lot of different ways. All to remind you of that decision you made. Maybe even burn your field of barley. Just saying.

What does it take to do the right thing? You have already made that "walk". Now God is supposed to leave you alone. Let you go on with your life. It doesn't work that way. If you have asked Jesus into your life, God sends His Holy Spirit to dwell in you till you graduate to heaven. This Holy Spirit has work to do. He brings a gift with Him. This gift is to help you serve God and glorify God. It is meant to be used.

Absalom, even fearing the king, took a chance and returned to Jerusalem from Geshur. He just wanted to confront the king and see where he stood. What was his relationship to the king. Did the king blame him for Amnon? Did he know what happened? He wanted to understand what his relationship was. The king refused to see him. Years went by. Where do I stand?

I wonder how much Absalom's arrogance played in this. He is "demanding" to see the king. He finally convinces Joab to bring him to the king. The king kissed him. All is well? We will see. There is an interesting picture here. How many verses have we read to get to this point? This meeting, this reconciliation. It took a long time. It took forgiveness.

Are you reconciled with God? Have you made amends and become a child of God? The sad part is that all God wants is your attention. Your commitment, your seeking His face. To come into His presence and ask His forgiveness. Absalom hasn't done that. Absalom is forcing King David to make amends, to accept what he did.

Absalom got David's attention. He forced himself into David's presence. God always has His door wide open. He is ready whenever you are, to make amends. To bring you into His family. A very simple verse,

> If, you confess with your mouth the Lord Jesus and believe
> in your heart that God has raised Him from the dead, you
> will be saved. (Romans 10:9). (NKJV)

God simply asks that you believe that God sent His very own Son, to pay for your sins on the cross of Calvary. By putting your faith in that payment on the cross, you can be a child of God.

When you make that decision and then turn your back on God, it hurts Him so much. God wants to use you in a great way. He will need to get your attention, won't He?

2 Samuel 15

And it came to pass after this, that Absalom prepared him chariots and horses, and fifty men to run before him. And Absalom rose up early, and stood beside the way of the gate: and it was so, that when any man that had a controversy came to the king for judgment, then Absalom called unto him, and said, Of what city art thou? And he said, Thy servant is of one of the tribes of Israel. And Absalom said unto him, See, thy matters are good and right; but there is no man deputed of the king to hear thee. (2 Samuel 15:1-3)

These are hard verses to understand. Oh, we understand what Absalom is doing, sure enough. We just don't understand why. Does he hate his father that much that he would try to steal the hearts of God's people away from David? That is surely what he is doing. I'm sure you have probably dealt with people like this, especially in the work force.

Revenge? Not sure what it is about. Remember how we ended the last chapter, *"Then the king kissed Absalom."* It would seem they had made up. Forgiveness, etc. I'm not sure I want to know what is in Absalom's heart. Darkness, unforgiveness, hatred, who knows. It just doesn't make sense to me.

No, I'm not going to use the excuse that it was God's plan. This was even foretold to David through Nathan after David's sin with Bathsheba (2 Samuel 12:10). Still, we can't just chalk it up to God's vengeance, God's punishment. God had to have a willing participant! I'm not altogether sure but that this wasn't Absalom's plan from the time he ran off to Geshur. We don't know.

Let's ask that question. What does God want to reveal in this passage? Betrayal? Revenge? He almost reminds us of Judas in the New Testament.

This is a tough passage for me. I just can't imagine anyone betraying someone like this. It is obvious what Absalom is doing. I wonder if David is aware? We will see shortly.

Is this passage to reveal to us the heart of Absalom? Absalom, David's third son, Amnon being his first born. Don't know if this factors in. Honestly, it's just a mystery. Maybe Absalom knew how David felt about him. We don't know what words transpired after their last meeting. Maybe Absalom knew that Solomon would be the heir to the throne and was trying to usurp Solomon. It won't be last time it's tried. We will see later.

If God wanted us to know why, He would have told us. We are left to use this passage to examine our own hearts. To what lengths are we willing to go to, to accomplish our desires? Who are we willing to destroy to reach our goals? Even family members?

"A man after God's own heart". Let's take a minute and imagine that heart. I am sure there is not a minute that goes by that King David says in his heart, "Why did I do it?"

His first-born son, Amnon, is dead. Killed by his third son, Absalom, because he raped his sister. Absalom is now turning God's people against their king. It seems his whole world is turned upside down.

In the evening King David sits at his dinner table. Across from him is Mephibosheth, who by custom, should be dead. Maybe David sees a little of Jonathan, his father, in his face. Maybe at the end of the table sits a small boy. The child of the king and Bathsheba, his name is Solomon. His son will one day build the temple that David so desired to build.

David has asked God for forgiveness, and received it. He is determined to restore his relationship with his heavenly Father.

> "Restore to me the joy of Your salvation, and uphold me
> by Your generous Spirit. (Psalm 51:12) (NKJV)

Absalom said moreover, Oh that I were made judge in the land, that every man which hath any suit or cause might come unto me, and I would do him justice! And it was so, that when any man came nigh to him to do him obeisance, he put forth his hand, and took him, and kissed him. And on this manner did Absalom to all Israel that came to the king for judgment: so Absalom stole the hearts of the men of Israel. (2 Samuel 15:4-6)

We are about three months from the mid-term elections. You can imagine the rhetoric that is being broadcast. Absalom is the "perfect" politician. Promise you "justice" all the while undermining the king. I feel for David. How do you combat this tactic? I would think that David hasn't much to brag on. David does have something that Absalom does not. A relationship with God the Father. Tarnished a bit but still "a man after God's own heart."

I think I mentioned this before. We not only have the passage prior to David's anointing, we also have the testimony of the Apostle Paul in Acts 13:22. How is your relationship with the Father? He knows you have made some mistakes, we all have. Have you asked His forgiveness and moved on? Oh, but God can't forgive what I have done. Really? Did you kill someone? David did. I Believe there is nothing God can't forgive, EXCEPT, rejecting the conviction of the Holy Spirit of God. That means you have rejected the work of His Son on the cross of Calvary. God cannot forgive that.

Look at the last part above, "So Absalom stole the hearts of the men of Israel." That is what Satan is doing every day with his lies. He slips in and steals the word of God right from our hearts and leaves us empty. Especially if you are lost. Look at this passage in Luke 8,

> Now the parable is this: The seed is the word of God.
> Those by the wayside are the ones who hear; then the
> devil comes and takes away the word out of their hearts,
> lest they should believe and be saved. (Luke 8:11-12).
> (NKJV)

These men that Absalom has drawn away from David have had the testimony of their godly king pulled out of their hearts.

Slowly, on purpose, Absalom drew the hearts of David's people away from David. That is happening so much today! Our lives have gotten so busy, so hectic, so distracted that the devil has slowly and methodically removed the truth of God's love from our hearts. We are so focused on "keeping up" we don't have time to reflect on what God has done in our lives.

Tonight, is a good example. We had a regular Wednesday night prayer meeting. We sing a couple of songs, then we take the prayer concerns from the congregation. There were at least three testimonies of what God has done to heal them, miracles! Too many times we want to bring our requests for healing and neglect to thank God for His healing. We need a "Praise List" as well as a "Prayer List." God is still in the healing business.

I mentioned keeping a journal before. We need to be reminded of what God is doing in our lives. Of course, that takes time. We don't have fifteen minutes each day to reflect on what God has done in our life today? That is time you can't get back. Those are memories, if not recorded, can be lost in the fog of old age. Don't let Satan and this world "Steal your heart" from God's presence. Seek His fellowship each night or morning. I love beginning my day with my "quiet time" Read some Bible, read a devotion (The Path) and pray for family, the sick, our church, the lost, etc. I can't think of beginning my day any other way!

I think those last few words just have struck a chord! Satan desires to steal our joy, our fellowship with God. Keep our minds on anything but God. Satan cannot steal our relationship if we are children of God. That is sealed through God's Holy Spirit. He can steal our fellowship. That's what Satan did with David when he tricked David into his sin with Bathsheba. David is restoring that fellowship, slowly, day by day.

And it came to pass after **forty years**, that Absalom said unto the king, I pray thee, let me go and pay my vow, which I have vowed unto the Lord, in Hebron. For thy servant vowed a vow while I abode in Geshur in Syria, saying, If the Lord shall bring me again indeed to Jerusalem, then I will serve the Lord. And the king said unto him, Go in peace. So he arose, and went to Hebron. (2 Samuel 15:7-9)

Isn't it easy to invoke the name of the Lord in our language? Do you think God will hold us guiltless for such a deed? How important is a vow to you? Today we would call it a promise. Maybe we don't say, "I promise" as such, but the meaning is clear. When you tell someone, you will do something you must try to keep your promise.

We talked about this in our Sunday School class. The dangers in making vows, or promises. The biggest danger to me is, you are not in control of tomorrow, God is. God may have other plans that do not include your promise. You might add a clause, "if I can, I will. . ."! Our word, anymore, is almost meaningless. Contracts are only valid depending on the number of lawyers you enlist.

Absalom is using this as an excuse to leave Jerusalem. He lies to David, in order to travel to Hebron. Why Hebron? That is where David started first as king, and then moved to Jerusalem, and thus king of Israel. Absalom has the same goal in mind. Let's see, other than invoking the name of the Lord, do you see any reference to God? Did a prophet, Nathan perhaps, anoint Absalom king? I think not. God is not in this whole process. There is a great lesson to learned here. If God is not in it, it will surely fail.

Did you notice a phrase Absalom used? *"then I will serve the Lord."* I wonder if Absalom believes that God is in this? Isn't it interesting the contrast between David and his son, Absalom? David would not lift a hand against God's anointed king, Saul. Here, Absalom is conspiring to dethrone the king whom God anointed. The contrast in the reverence for God's authority. Interesting.

Did you notice the method Absalom used, whether true or not? Absalom threw out a fleece. The method Gideon used to determine God's will. "If" the Lord brings me back to Jerusalem. I wonder how effective this method is. Suppose, you had an idea something was going to happen. Then you told God that if it happened it was a sign that God wanted you to do something. The point is that this method can often be manipulated. The best way to determine God's will is to pray and ask God to open the door, not you!

To be honest, I have yet to understand why Absalom is doing this. Pride? Arrogance? Maybe sensing Solomon will be the next king. Did you catch the time span? Forty years later. Forty years, Solomon is of age. Forty years for David to let down his guard. Forty years to forget God's judgment on David's family.

This is a sad commentary on today. We think because God doesn't chastise us today or this week, that we have gotten away with something. That God has "forgotten" our sin and we escaped judgment. God doesn't need a "smart-phone" to remind Him of our transgressions, our unrepentant transgressions. He is simply working out the appropriate response. Now if we take it to God, ask His forgiveness and repent, God will forgive and forget it.

Look at this verse. This was the first verse my wife and I memorized as new Christians:

If we confess our sins, He is faithful and just to forgive us our sins and to cleanse us from all unrighteousness. (1 John 1:9). (NKJV)

That is a promise from God. It isn't mentioned but I'm sure implied, repentance. Just "confessing" is not the point. We can admit to all our sin, but if it is without repentance, it is simply hollow words. God knows our heart! Don't forget that!

But Absalom sent spies throughout all the tribes of Israel, saying, As soon as ye hear the sound of the trumpet, then ye shall say, Absalom reigneth in Hebron. And with Absalom went two hundred men out of Jerusalem, that were called; and they went in their simplicity, and they knew not any thing. And Absalom sent for Ahithophel, from his city, even from Giloh, while he offered sacrifices. And the conspiracy was strong; for the people increased continually with Absalom. (2 Samuel 15:10-12)

We are in the middle of an election season. About three months from now are the mid-term elections. The time of selecting Congressman and Senators from each state. The reason I'm bringing this up is, that is what I am seeing here. I am so thankful for our system of government. Did you know that at the end of Washington's term some tried to convince him to become king? It's true. Washington could have accepted the appointment as king, but refused.

I think the thing that hurts me most is who is doing this. David's son. I have already speculated as to his motives. I think it is interesting how he goes about this. He wouldn't dare confront David openly, David is too popular. Instead, Absalom resorts to trickery, and sneaky tactics. Like I said it reminds me our election season today. Truth, is the last thing that is used in our elections any more. Integrity? Very rare.

I mentioned that it says that it has been forty years since Absalom lived in Jerusalem. I keep thinking about Solomon. He is in his forties or older. Absalom must know by now that David (and God) have selected Solomon as the heir to the throne. This could be his attempt to circumvent that process. Again, I point out, God is not in this scenario. All through the process of David becoming king we could see God's hand. Not here!

Have you noticed how the people are fooled, those following Absalom? I am amazed today how few people I know are aware of our political process. The three branches of government, how they interact with each other. I am still amazed at what our Founding Fathers developed that is still the envy of the world. It checks the three branches of government while maintaining our freedom to choose our leaders.

Don't forget the process Absalom used forty years ago. He stood outside the gate and one-by-one convinced each person that he could give them what the king would not. That's what goes on today. I heard the other day that someone thinks every person should get a paycheck from the government. No one ever answers the question, "Where does the money come from?" I wonder what Absalom promised the people besides an ear to their grievances.

We are so easily fooled today because we refuse to be informed. So long as I am doing okay, that's all that matters. When Absalom raises his army and challenges the king, he needs to remember one thing, God is on David's side. With that you have a majority!

Every four years I go and vote. Then I watch the returns. Who is elected tells me the spiritual condition of our country. Where we are headed, and what is important to our country. Who they choose to lead our country gives me insight into the morals, the priorities, the culture of our great land. To me it is a barometer of the spiritual condition of our country. I have also noticed one more thing. When we have drifted so far away from God, He steps in and corrects our course. Much like He does in our private lives. God will only allow us to drift so far, then He will act. That is what is happening here with Absalom. God has allowed Absalom to go so far, soon God is going to take a hand. David is STILL "a man after God's own heart!"

And there came a messenger to David, saying, The hearts of the men of Israel are after Absalom. And David said unto all his servants that were with him at Jerusalem, Arise, and let us flee; for we shall not else escape from Absalom: make speed to depart, lest he overtake us suddenly, and bring evil upon us, and smite the city with the edge of the sword. And the king's servants said unto the king, Behold, thy servants are ready to do whatsoever my lord the king shall appoint. And the king went forth, and all his household after him. And the king left ten women, which were concubines, to keep the house. And the king went forth, and all the people after him, and tarried in a place that was far off. (2 Samuel 15: 13-17)

How do you handle getting out of your "comfort zone"? Do you fight it, accept it, roll with flow, or do you ask God what is going on? It is never easy. We have our routines and a disruption is just not welcome! Mark, it down, it will happen.

Did you notice that it has been forty years since David accepted Absalom back into Jerusalem, back into the family, if you will? Forty years of "comfort zone." Suddenly, here is this rebellion and David is faced with running. Something David is familiar with, although not recently. How does David handle it?

First notice the commitment of those around him. "We are your servants, ready to do whatever my lord the king commands." I was thinking the other day. Were their "rumors" of what Absalom was doing. Surely there must have been some stories circulating. Maybe David couldn't believe that his son would do anything this bad.

How often have you been in this routine, daily, basically the same routine? Have you ever tried to change things or do you just enjoy the peace and "sameness?" How about vacations? That is the point of a vacation to "break" the routine. We think of them as a rest but I think we work harder on "vacations" than in our daily routine. When we get home from our vacation we look forward to going back to work, to restoring our routine. We need change.

Whether David knew what was coming or not David was used to running. All those years running from Saul. Now he is running from his own son. Surely there is some hurt there that your own son, whom you have forgiven for killing your first born, would not do this to you, his father.

That is not the culture of the day. I keep coming back to this picture of Solomon and Absalom living in the same house. Knowing that God told David that Solomon would be the next king. Can you accept that?

After forty years we are beginning another phase in David's life. If you have read ahead, you know what's coming. The point of the story is to glean two things: (1) Why did God think it was important for this passage, this episode to be revealed? (2) Then how can we apply the principles taught in this passage to our own lives. Believe me, it is not unimportant. It was put here to teach us a lesson that can be applied to our own lives. Always remember that.

Rebellion is coming. I know many, many homes have to deal with this. You raise your children, you provide for them, you feed them, clothe them, then one day they think they know much more than you. Then you deal with rebellion. There is a great Country son by Trace Adkins entitled, "Your Gonna Miss This." It shows a teenager who basically says, "I can't wait to leave home and make my own decisions." Then Trace says, "You gonna miss this." We will all deal with rebellion in our life, and family. How do you deal with it? Some lessons are best learned the hard way. It is painful to the parent, but it is necessary. Be patient, trust God and allow them to learn.

I trust that God is in the picture. That that teenager has a relationship with God the Father. He will go a long way to guiding that teen in the right direction, to opening their eyes to truth!

And all his servants passed on beside him; and all the Cherethites, and all the Pelethites, and all the Gittites, six hundred men which came after him from Gath, passed on before the king. Then said the king to Ittai the Gittite, Wherefore goest thou also with us? Return to thy place, and abide with the king: for thou art a stranger, and also an exile. Whereas thou camest but yesterday, should I this day make the go up and down with us? Seeing I go whither I may, return thou, and take back thy brethren: mercy and truth be with thee. (2 Samuel 15:18-20)

Loyalty. Interesting word. Did you notice? *"Six hundred men who had followed him from Gath."* That was the army that David had raised in Ziklag. It's been forty years (15:7) since David was a young king. Forty years later the same six hundred men continue to follow their king. To me that is fantastic!

David is now leaving, being chased by Absalom, along with his household. He is also leaving behind his concubines, and who knows how many staff. He must run from Absalom, who would be king. You see that is how it is done in Israel of the day. You want to be king, you raise an army and you defeat the current king, then you become king.

Absalom forgot one simple thing. God must be in it. We saw a great example between David and Saul. God's hand was David, and God removed His hand from Saul (1 Samuel 28:6). Nothing will succeed without God's hand on it.

Did you notice that David did not "inquire of the Lord" whether to leave or not? I don't think that was necessary. David knew, or remembers, what God told him through Nathan the prophet.

> *Behold, I will raise up adversity against you from your own house. (2 Samuel 12:11). (NKJV)*

Do you not think those words, still, ring in David's ears? It was just a matter of time and circumstance.

David had compassion on those who would follow him. He knew this was God's doing. God holds all the cards. We can read on ahead, maybe figure out what might happen. David doesn't know what God is up to. Neither do we.

Is God dealing with you about something? Do you recognize God's hand in the events taking place? What is your response? Ignore it? I hope not. It must begin with prayer. Pray through the situation. Find out what God is trying to show you, or teach you. I know, for a fact, He will show you, or put in your mind what He is trying to accomplish. If you never know why, God is wasting His time. If He is trying to show you, or teach you something, do you not think He wants you to know what that is?

It begins with prayer! Ask God to show you, or reveal His will in this chaos. The next thing is the hardest. If He is trying to teach you something, you must apply this lesson to your walk with Him. If He is showing you something in your life that needs correcting, do it!

God has just disrupted David's "comfort zone." I don't think David needs to ask God, he knows. So, what does David do? He continues to follow God's leading. Okay, God is doing something here. My response is to continue to walk with God through this process and see where God is leading. David knows this is for a past sin. God has forgiven him but there are still consequences. David simply wants to follow where God is leading.

How about you? Do you rebel against God's leadership? Are you determined to have it your way? If you are fighting God, let me give you a hint, you lose! When you surrender and seek God's direction and guidance then you win. The longer you continue to fight against your heavenly Father the longer you will be miserable. Just put life in neutral, take your hands off the wheel, and allow God to bring you to the point where He wants you to be.

When you allow God to have His way in your life, it will amaze you where God will take you. Remember He is your heavenly Father! He wants only the best for you. You must let Him have complete control, stop fighting!

And Ittai answered the king, and said, As the Lord liveth, and as my lord the king liveth, surely in what place my lord the king shall be, whether in death or life, even there also will thy servant be. And David said to Ittai, Go and pass over. And Ittai the Gittite passed over, and all his men, and all the little ones that were with him. (2 Samuel 15:21-22)

Look at these verses in the Gospel of Mark:

> *But he spoke more vehemently, "If I have to die with You, I will not deny You! And they all said likewise. (Mark 14:31). (NKJV) Then they all forsook Him and fled. (Mark 14:50). (NKJV)*

I don't know why this passage came to mind when I read the passage above. David's troops did not "forsake" him. They stood with him through this whole ordeal.

If memory serves me, the Brook Kidron is just outside the city of Jerusalem. It is also mentioned in the Gospel of John,

> *When Jesus had spoken these words, He went out with His disciples over the Brook Kidron, where there was a garden, which He and His disciples entered. (John 18:1). (NKJV)*

It was within walking distance of the city of Jerusalem. This was David's escape route.

David is running from his throne which God had given him. There is something I want you to think about in this passage. I think it can be applied to our Christian walk. I will be doing some meddling so beware.

David's men were committed to him. To follow him, to fight for him, to do whatever David needed. I am amazed today how little commitment there is to following Jesus. It would be interesting if we could see into the hearts of those who make a "profession" of faith. It's like they have their ticket to heaven, now I will go and live my life, apart from God, then present my ticket when the time comes. Is that what God had in mind? If that were the case why did Jesus bother to institute the church? This has always bothered me. When you give your life to Christ I would think you would want to know more about that commitment.

I love the latest definition of some "Christians". It's called C.E.O. Christians. Christmas and Easter Only. Is that what they think of their salvation? The salvation that was bought on the cross of Calvary. Really.

Look at the commitment of these six hundred soldiers that followed David. It's been forty years since they might have fought in a battle. Yet, the alarm goes out and they are there. It might be forty years since some Christians have attended church. This has always been a problem for me. I would think that when Christ came into your heart, receiving God's Holy Spirit, would change your conception of church. I just don't understand.

The commitment of David's family and army just amazes me. There should be the same commitment today, for God's people to be in God's house on the Lord's day. The day that Jesus instituted the church, when He arose from the grave on "the first day of the week". If it was not that important, why did Jesus think it important enough to establish it while He was here.

Let me give you another verse from the New Testament:

> *Husbands, love your wives, just as Christ also loved the church and gave Himself for her. (Ephesians 6:25). (NKJV)*

Jesus gave Himself on the cruel cross of Calvary for His bride, the church. But we can't manage to find two hours on Sunday morning to worship the One who bought our salvation at Calvary.

Okay, I will get off my soapbox. I just think it isn't something to just forget about.

David is running from Absalom. It doesn't say here, but do you think it is an accident that David was alerted, and now has time to flee? I think not. We need to get in the habit of meditating on those events in our life, that can change our life!

And lo Zadok also, and all the Levites were with him, bearing the ark of the covenant of God: and they set down the ark of God; and Abiathar went up, until all the people had done passing out of the city. And the king said to Zadok, Carry back the ark of God into the city: If I shall find favour in the eyes of the Lord, he will bring me again, and shew me both it, and his habitation: But if he thus say, I have no delight in thee; behold, here am I, let him do to me as seemeth good to him. (2 Samuel 15:24-26)

Do you have that much faith in God's will and purpose in your life? This must be one of the key reasons David is "A man after God's own heart." God wants our faith in His plan for our life. Nothing short of that will work. Look at this verse, one of my favorites:

> *But without faith it is impossible to please Him, for he who comes to God must believe that He is, and that He is a rewarder of those who diligently seek Him. (Hebrews 11:6). (NKJV)*

Chew (meditate) on this verse a minute. Is that not what David is saying here?

David recognizes all that has happened in his life. He also recognizes that God is in control of his life. Therefore, like I said before, David has put his life in neutral and taking his hands off the wheel has turned all future events over to God. Including running from Absalom, his son.

Did you notice how David acknowledges his relationship with God? Look at these words, *But, if He (God) says thus: "I have no delight in you"* here *I am.* This is awesome. David knows he has disappointed God. Let Him down. He has put his life in God's hands. I think these words demonstrate David's intimate relationship with God. David just says, "I'm yours Lord". Whatever You chose to do to me is fine with me. I trust You to do whatever You think is best. Even to overthrowing the kingdom. Can you say that?

I can't pass it up. I need to mention another favorite verse of mine pertaining to faith.

> *The He touched their eyes, saying, "According to your faith be it unto you." (Matthew 9:29) (NKJV)*

Can you measure faith? According to this verse you can.

One of the first things I do when I buy a new Bible is set down and go through the entire New Testament and underline the word faith. This word is so important to me. Think about it, it is what gets us to heaven, faith in the Lord Jesus Christ and what He did on the cross, and His resurrection!

I think David just gain some points with God. David has been, the last forty years, licking his wounds from the judgment concerning Bathsheba, then his ruckus with Absalom. Here he has a chance to demonstrate to God that He is still a man after God's own heart. You want to reach God's heart? Maybe it can be reached through that simple five letter word: Faith!

David doesn't know what is going to happen. I mentioned before that either we know how the story ends or we can read ahead. David must deal with it each day, each hour, he is running from Absalom who wants to kill him. That is how Absalom becomes king, he must kill his father. He has already killed his brother. When you have no connection with God, murder is no big thing.

Did you notice that they just automatically brought the ark along? Got to have our "good luck charm" with us. I'm sorry, I don't know their hearts but it just seems to me that they treat this holy thing as a charm. Maybe it represents the presence of God. I don't see that. Cheers for David for telling them to take it back where it belongs. David constructed the tabernacle for the ark, until the temple could be built. David seeks God's presence, not a box with some stone tablets.

How about you? Do you feel God's presence? If you're not a child of God the only thing you feel is God's Spirit tugging at your heart to accept Jesus Christ as your Lord and Savior. Read Romans 10:9. Then pray and ask Jesus into your heart today!

The king said also unto Zadok the priest, art thou a seer? Return into the city in peace, and your two sons with you, Ahimaaz thy son, and Jonathan the son of Abiathar. See, I will tarry in the plain of the wilderness, until there come word from you to certify me. Zadok therefore and abiathar carried the ark of God again to Jerusalem: and they tarried there. And David went up by the ascent of mount Olivet, and wept as he went up, and had his head covered, and went barefoot: and all the people that was with him covered every man his head, and they went up, weeping as they went up. (2 Samuel 15:27-30)

The wilderness. We talked about this before. Have you been to the wilderness? That time of searching the heart of God. What is God doing in your life. How much of your life does God have? A lot of questions. Let me refer you to Jesus' time in the wilderness. Satan attempted to throw God's plans off track. I think it is interesting that Jesus went to the wilderness right after He was baptized. Satan's greatest opening for distracting a new convert is right after they have accepted Jesus as their Savior.

I remember the night I was saved. The pastor had led my wife and I in the sinner's prayer. After he left I went into the living room and picked up a Bible I had laying there. I hadn't spent any time in it. We had been attending church and I was reading a little here and there. That night I read Third John. I was so excited that I had read a whole book in the Bible and I haven't lost my appetite since. It's interesting that when Jesus was tempted by Satan in the wilderness His defense was the Word of God.

David, in this passage, is ascending the Mount of Olives. The same Mount of Olives that Jesus ascended to pray with His disciples before His arrest. There is a time in a child of God's life when he must make this ascent. He must come before God, and place his or her life in God's hands. This was years after the wilderness experience. Jesus had performed countless miracles. God had blessed Him greatly. Then there comes that time to put "everything" in God's hands. Jesus wanted to change the game plan. He knew what was about to happen. Look what Jesus says,

He went a little further and fell on His face, and prayed, saying, "O My Father, if it is possible, let this cup pass from Me, nevertheless, not as I will, but as You will." (Matthew 26:39). (NKJV)

Did you catch that critical word? "Nevertheless" there is our will and there is God's will.

We have our "wilderness" experience when we have accepted Jesus as our Savior, and our task is to get in God's Word and learn how to defend ourselves against the tricks of Satan. Then there must be a "Mount of Olives" experience where we simply say, "Not my will, but Your will, Father."

David has had an experience with God the Father. He was confronted with his sin, and God passed judgment. Now David is learning the consequences. He is willing to walk whatever path God has laid out. Can you do that? Accept God's will for your life? Do you even know what God wants to do in your life? If you haven't taken that "Mount of Olives" walk you need to now. Put your life in God's hands and say those words from your heart, "Not my will, but Your will be done."

David has sent the ark back to Jerusalem. He will not use a "thing" to represent God. He will get on his knees in his "Mount of Olives' trip and search God's heart. David is a "man after God's own heart." Right now, he wants to know that heart. Notice how he words this,

> "If I find favor in the eyes of the Lord, He will bring me back and show me both it His dwelling place. (2 Samuel 15:25b). (NKJV)

David is searching and waiting to hear from God, and His will for him. David is having his "Mount of Olives" experience. What is God's will for his life. If you haven't had your "Mount of Olives" experience, what are you waiting for. You have asked Jesus into your heart, now make Him Lord of your life. Put Him in control, let Jesus lead you down the path of God's will and purpose for your life!

And one told David, saying, Ahithophel is among the conspirators with Absalom. And David said, O Lord, I pray thee, turn the counsel of Ahithophel into foolishness. And it came to pass, that when David was come to the top of the mount, where he worshipped God, behold, Hushai the Archite came to meet him with his coat rent, and earth upon his head. Unto whom David said, If thou passest on with me, then thou shalt be a burden unto me: But if thou return to the city, and say unto Absalom, I will be thy servant O king; as I have been thy father's servant hitherto, so will I now also be thy servant: then mayest thou for me defeat the counsel of Ahitophel. (2 Samuel 15:31-34)

Did you catch that? David prays and here is the answer to his prayer. Interesting. Notice what David prays. He simply asks God to turn Ahithophel's counsel to foolishness. I am sure the devil has attempted that a lot today. Where do you get your "counsel"? From whom do you get your counsel?

Did you notice that David knew Absalom would get his counsel from men? So, David asked God to give him false counsel. If Absalom's counsel were from God, David wouldn't be here. I guess that is my thinking. David knew he could influence Absalom's counsel with a man of his own influencing Absalom.

I wonder where David got this idea? You know as well as I do, from God. In the process of writing this book, many times I have set down to write and I read the scripture passage and God just begins giving me these words. When I am finished I stand amazed at what He has written. I claim no special credit, please. I am as amazed as the reader. God has laid this idea on my heart and I pray I give it the effort He has requested.

There is that phrase again, *"Now it happened."* If we really noticed, in our life, how many things "just happen", how many people just happened in our lives, etc. Nothing is by accident. We have talked about this before. There is another reason to keep a journal. Note the different people who pass through our lives, some for good, some for bad.

As a parent, especially, we need to be aware of the individuals our children "associate" with. They are passing through their lives, what influence will they have? How will they affect the path our children take? Another good reason to be conscious of regular church attendance. Granted, not all who attend church are saints, but neither are those they hang with in school. The odds are better in church.

There is a battle going on right now. Our country is being divided on which "counsel" to listen to. The counsel of God or the counsel of the world. Much like the battle that David knew would be going on in Absalom's world. Who would Absalom listen to? What advice would he obey? Do you see the parallels? Of course, we know that God will win out. I wonder sometimes, if we let our guard down because we know God will win out. That is dangerous. God expects our participation, our involvement, our impact. If we just set by and leave it up to God, we may be in for a rude awakening. God uses us to make a difference!

Does anyone remember when you had a prayer from the principles, office before you began the day. Do you remember when we could say the Pledge of Allegiance without controversy? There are a lot of battles that we have lost, because we refused to get involved. David is sending someone into Absalom's camp to offer an alternative, to defeat Ahithophel's counsel. Are we arguing God's counsel today? Are we standing up for godly principles and God's message in our world today?

David would have been defeated if it were not for Hushai's counsel. We need to get our side heard, to make a difference.

And hast thou not there with thee Zadok and Abiathar the priests? Therefore it shall be, that what thing soever thou shalt hear out of the king's house, thou shalt tell it to Zadok and Abiathar the priests. Behold, they have there with them their two sons, Ahimaaz Zadok's son, and Jonathan Abiathar's son; and by them ye shall send unto me every thing that ye can hear. So Hushai David's friend came into the city, and Absalom came into Jerusalem. (2 Samuel 15:35-37)

I think it is interesting that David used the priest, and their sons to carry the message to David. Such as it is today. God uses His ministers to bring His message to us today. A message of warning. A message of salvation. So, it has been from the very early days of scripture. We can start with Aaron. God gave the Ten commandments to Moses but it was Aaron that God chose to make the first priest. Throughout history God has had His messengers to bring His message.

Now, suppose, these messengers bring David all the details of what Absalom is going to do. Play by play. Then David says, "Okay, that's great but here is what I am going to do." Completely ignoring the message from the priests to David. Sounds crazy, doesn't it? That is what we are doing today. One distinction today. The message isn't from the "priest" it's from God in His Holy Word! You might ignore the messenger but you can't ignore the message.

David would be flying blind without these messages from the priests, Abiathar and Zadok. Much as we are today. The blessing that we have today is that we have the very Word of God in our hands. Of course, that depends on how much time we spend in it. Now confess, if you did not go to church and hear the Word of God preached, you would know next to nothing about is in God's Word. Besides, if God thought all we needed was the Bible He would not have instituted the concept of the church through His Son Jesus. Think about that one. (Matthew 16:18)

Did you notice that David was not even thinking of fighting back? His concern right now is just staying alive. Sounds like his years of running from King Saul. First things first! The same is true for us. First, we must become a child of God. That is accomplished by asking Jesus to forgive us of our sins and then to come into our hearts. When we have done that, God will send the third person of the Trinity, the Holy Spirit to dwell in our hearts and begin the process of establishing a fellowship with God the Father. That relationship is established once we become a "child" of God. It's that fellowship with our heavenly Father that takes time and prayer, and studying God's word, and learning to walk with God. There is the fellowship.

Now that David has established his lines of communication. He can now keep track of Absalom and how he plans to remove David as king. So long as David is alive, he is a threat to Absalom. I'm sure Absalom feels he is the "rightful" heir to the throne. Being one of David's oldest sons. I'm also sure, the time Absalom spend hanging around David's house, he discerned that the plan is to make Solomon the next king. If he doesn't act now, he will miss his chance.

Did you detect any reference to God in Absalom's plan? Neither did I. Absalom is working and planning by the flesh, David is operating by the Spirit. Who do you think will win out? I still think it's interesting that the "priests" are involved in the communication lines. Just as they are today. Bringing, on Sunday morning, a word from God, that God has laid on their hearts during the week. Our pastor is currently working through the gospel of John. An awesome study. A book we might spend a few hours reading through. Here the pastor is taking us, step by step through this awesome gospel, one of my favorites.

If you are a young Christian and not sure where to start in your Bible reading, let me recommend the gospel of John. The thing that is interesting to me. The last half of the gospel takes place in the "upper room" just prior to His crucifixion. His last words, if you will, before He departs. Parting words, if you will, I think that is significant!

2 SAMUEL 16

And when David was a little past the top of the hill, behold, Ziba the servant of Mephibosheth met him, with a couple of donkeys saddled with loaves of bread, and an hundred bunches of raisins, and a hundred of summer fruits, and a bottle of wine. And the king said unto Ziba, What meanest thou by these? And Ziba said, The donkeys be for the king's household to ride on; and the bread and summer fruit for the young men to eat; and the wine, that such as be faint in the wilderness may drink. And the king said, And where is thy master's son? And Ziba said unto the king, Behold, he abideth at Jerusalem: for he said, To day shall the house of Israel restore me the kingdom of my father. Then said the king to Ziba, Behold, thine are all that pertaineth unto Mephibosheth. And Ziba said, I humbly beseech thee that I may find grace in thy sight, my lord, O king. (2 Samuel 16:1-4)

Ziba! You remember Ziba? *And there was a servant of the house of Saul whose name was Ziba.* (2 Samuel 9:2a). Ziba was the one who brought Mephibosheth to David's attention and eventually became his servant. David had instructed Ziba to tend to Mephosheth's affairs while he lived in David's house and ate at his table.

Here we see Ziba transporting some supplies to David. Personally, and it doesn't say in the text, but I think he was taking them to Jerusalem to Absalom.

Did you notice something in the third verse? Notice the supposed words of Mephibosheth, *"Today the house of Israel will restore the kingdom of my father to me."* This is interesting. Did Mephibosheth think that Absalom was going to make him king? I think not. Absalom was not related to Saul but to David. I'm not sure what he meant.

You might want to make a note in your margin: 2 Samuel 19:7-30. David has another run-in with Ziba later. That is why I am suspicious here.

Mephibosheth disappoints me here. David has done everything he could to make the rest of his life comfortable. Then, at the first opportunity he rejects David's kindness. But, then, we do the same thing with our relationship with God. I mentioned earlier that I wasn't saved until I was thirty-five. I can look back at the countless times I could have died. I spent a year in Vietnam in the United States Air Force. Many times, driving for United Parcel Service. The point being, I believe God spared me to have the opportunity to become a child of God.

So, how do we treat this God, who asked His Only Son, to give His life on the cross of Calvary just so we could eat at God's table? God offered His Son as a sacrifice for our sins, to allow us access into His presence. And how do we treat Him? INDIFFERENCE? Really?

I have heard stories from our classmates in Sunday School of how, even the common courtesy of saying "thank you", is all but forgotten in our culture. How about thanking God for a blessing we might receive during the week. If anything, the Sunday worship is all about "thank you, God" isn't it?

There are far too many Mephibosheth's in the world today. Taking the blessings of God for granted! I think the worse thing is taking our salvation for granted. "I have my ticket, now I can ignore God." I don't think it works that way. We will see, later.

And when king David came to Bahurim, behold, thence came out a man of the family of the house of Saul, whose name was Shimei, the son of Gera: he came forth, and cursed still as he came. And he cast stones at David, and at all the servants of king David: and all the people and all the mighty men were on his right hand and on his left. And thus Shimei when he cursed, Come out, come out, thou bloody man, and thou man of Belial: The Lord hath returned upon thee all the blood of the house of Saul, in whose stead thou hast reigned; and the Lord hath delivered the kingdom into the hand of Absalom thy son: and, behold, thou art taken in thy mischief, because thou art a bloody man. (2 Samuel 16:5-8)

There is such an important principle here. How do you respond to a "spanking" from God? It's that simple. Mark this down for David, and another reason David is "a man after God's own heart." David acknowledges his sin. Acknowledges that God has dealt with him about it. Acknowledges that it was his mistake, and his punishment to take. What about you?

Our response? Remember Adam and Eve in the Garden?

> *Then the man said, "the woman whom You gave to be with me, she gave me of the tree, and I ate." (Genesis 3:12) (NKJV)*

How about Eve, what was her response?

> *And the Lord said to the woman, "What is this you have done?" The woman said, "The serpent deceived me, and I ate." (Genesis 3:12-13). (NKJV)*

It's not my fault! I was tricked! Adam knew it was wrong and did it anyway!

So, again, how do we respond? Does anyone remember a comedian named Flip Wilson? He does a whole comedy routine, "The devil made me do it." Ever tried that excuse? How about using that one with God? I don't think it will work. Do you remember Saul's response to God's judgment? God took His Spirit from Saul. What does Saul do? He searches out a "witch". (1 Samuel 28). What is David's response when Nathan confronts him about Bathsheba?

Then Nathan said to David, "You are the man." (2 Samuel 12:7) (NKJV)

> *So, David said to Nathan, "I have sinned against the Lord." And Nathan said to David, "The Lord also has put away your sin; you shall not die." (2 Samuel 12:13). (NKJV)*

Do you see the contrast?

Here is another response. "It's all God's fault" (like Adam in the Garden). It's God's fault that I messed up. I will never talk to God again. I refuse to go to church, that will punish God. Really? Blaming God has never solved anything except put a wedge between you and God the Father, who simply wants to correct His child and put them back on the right track. The same as a father corrects his children, to protect them and teach them right from wrong.

David recognizes that here. He accepts the cursing, the stones and the hatred. He knows the man is right. Did you notice his reference? "Bloodthirsty man" Do you remember the reason God told David that he could not build the temple that David wanted to build? David is a warrior; his battles will continue throughout his reign. God promised David that his offspring would build His temple. When David has established peace in Israel.

David recognized God's hand in this cursing. The man was simply voicing what David felt in his heart. Understand something here. David still had God's Spirit within him. God was still alive and well in David's life. If David had responded by attacking him, he would not be the man after God's own heart.

I don't know how to explain this. I guess with my original question, "How do you respond to God's chastisement? Look at this:

My son, do not despise the chastening of the Lord, nor detest His correction; for whom the Lord loves He corrects, just as a father the son in whom he delights. (Proverbs 3:11-12). (NKJV)

If you endure chastening, God deals with you as sons; for what son is there whom a father does not chasten? (Hebrews 12:7). (NKJV)

When God sees fit to correct us, just as our earthly father, understand that it is done in love. It's interesting that this same principle is in the Old Testament (Proverbs) and the New Testament (Hebrews). Think about it!

Then said Abishai the son of Zeruiah unto the king, Why should this dead dog curse my lord the king? Let me go over, I pray thee, and take off his head. And the king said, What have I to do with you, ye sons of Zeruiah? So let him curse, because the Lord hath said unto him, Curse David. Who shall then say, Wherefore hast thou done so? And David said to Abishai, and to all his servants, Behold, my son, which came forth of my bowels, seeketh my life: how much more now may this Benjamite do it? Let him alone, and let him curse; for the Lord hath bidden him. It may be that the Lord will look on mine affliction, and that the Lord will requite me good for his cursing this day. And as David and his men went by the way, Shimei went along on the hill's side over against him, and cursed as he went, and threw stones at him, and cast dust. (2 Samuel 16:9-13)

Did you catch that? *"See how my son who came from my own body seeks my life."* And who would that be? Absalom! His son is trying to kill his father in order to take the throne. Mephibosheth, Jonathan's son whom David rescued from Lo Debar now is encouraged that David will lose his throne in revenge for his father's death. How would you feel?

We need to think about something here. I touched on it earlier. David recognizes where this is coming from. God is reminding David of his disobedience and the fellowship that David broke with God. How do you respond to God when He is trying to deal with you about rebellion? Do you shake your fist at God and say, "I will no longer follow you!" I will never go to church again, "that will show You". Really? And you're going to punish God? Think about it.

Now, I have been through several trials at one time, I did ask God WHY? I remained active in my church. I continued to serve in the Sunday School ministry. I didn't shake my fist at God. I just kept asking why. A year later God responded. "I wanted to see if you would remain faithful." Does God test us? I think so. Let's see, what does James say?

> "My brethren, count it all joy when you fall into various trials, knowing that the testing of your faith produces patience. But let patience have its perfect work, that you may be perfect and complete, lacking nothing." (James 1:2-4). (NKJV)

God wants to use you. But God also must know how much He can trust you. He will send tests in your life to gauge your commitment, your faithfulness. If you pass the test God will begin to use you more and more. The greater the test the greater the blessing. The greater God will use you to accomplish His will and touch other lives around you. It begins with trust and obedience. There is a great hymn in our hymn books, "Trust and Obey" for there is no other way to be happy in Jesus but to trust and obey.

David is about to go through a tough period. A test that might determine how much God is going to use him. Remember, God has already denied his request to build a temple. But, God also told him that his son would build the temple. No consolation for what he is going through. His other son wishes to kill him. How do you deal with that? You trust God.

There is no point in punishing someone who is pointing out your faults. How do you respond to someone who, by God's grace, points out something you know in your heart to be true, but it is tough to admit? Our first response is rebellion. We must learn to seek God's hand in this. Pray, "God what do I need to do?" "What is the lesson here?"

I have said it before. God had a purpose for including this episode in His Holy Word. There is a message, a lesson, here for all of us. Okay, we messed up. We made a mistake. God has forgiven us. It should go away. Not so! There is a lesson in that mistake. Sometimes we miss the message, we miss what God is trying to teach us. Okay, the sin is taken care of, but the lesson may remain, yet to be learned.

Adultery is one thing, murder is another. God must get across to David the seriousness of his offense. To David and to us as well.

And Absalom, and all the people the men of Israel, came to Jerusalem, and Ahithophel with him. And it came to pass, when Hushai the Archite, David's friend, was come to Absalom, that Hushai said unto Absalom, God save the king, God save the king. And Absalom said to Hushai, Is this thy kindness to thy friend? And Hushai said unto Absalom, Nay; but whom the Lord, and his people, and all the men of Israel, choose, his will I be, and with him, will I abide. And again, whom should I serve? Should I not serve in the presence of his son? As I have served in thy father's presence, so will I be in thy presence. (2 Samuel 16:15-19)

Have you ever wondered why you are in a certain place at a certain time? Of course, in the verses above, David had instructed Hushai to go and join up with Absalom. We see that. How about you? Has God ever sent you on a journey, that you did not understand? Events in your life brought you to this place, and you're asking yourself why? You might want to start with prayer.

Next you want to look around you. Is there a purpose that you might fulfill that will glorify God? Is there a job that you and your spiritual gift may accomplish? How about the people God brings into your life? We talked about this before. Tonight, before you go to bed, ask God, what can you do in this situation.

I had the neatest experience Sunday. I shut the TV off. I had an hour before Evening Worship. I just sat there. I have been trying to work out some priorities in my life. By the end of the hour I believe God had given me an ending point and a plan to get there. We just don't spend enough quiet time listening to God. Oh, I have my "quiet time" with God in the morning. I read and pray, etc. I usually give Him my list during my prayer time. This evening I wanted to "listen" to God. Give Him the opportunity to get my attention. The thing about God is, He will not intrude necessarily, in our directions, unless we allow Him. He is quite content to allow us to go our merry way, struggling with the events in our life, until we take a minute and ask His input.

Hushai would much rather be with David. David asked him to serve the Lord in Absalom's court. Instead of asking God, "Why am I here" you might want to ask, "What am I to do?" God has brought you to this scenario for a purpose. You need to ask God. Listen to the Holy Spirit within you. Sometimes you just need to get to work and God will open the door you're supposed to enter. I learned a long time ago to let God open the doors. If we force the doors open we will be so disappointed.

Do you see the journey we are on? That is why it is so important to keep a journal. When God is through bringing us to where He wants us, we can look back and see how He brought us to this point.

> *Now Absalom would rise early and stand beside the way to the gate. So, it was, whenever anyone who had a lawsuit came to the king for a decision, then Absalom would call to him and say, "What city are you from?" And he would say, "Your servant is from such and such a tribe of Israel." In this manner Absalom acted toward all Israel who came to the king for judgment. So, Absalom stole the hearts of the men of Israel. (2 Samuel 15:2,6). (NKJV)*

Absalom began his rebellion. Now look at the following verse:

> *Now it came to pass after forty years that Absalom said to the king, "Please let me go to Hebron and pay the vow which I made to the Lord." (2 Samuel 15:7). (NKJV)*

Forty years!

Forty years of deceit, trickery, to lure the men of Israel away from David. The time had arrived to remove David from the throne. Remember, we noted earlier, when you removed a king, he and his family must be killed. David's life is in danger.

David needed to know what Absalom's plans were. He sent Hushai to counsel Absalom and lead him away from David. The right place at the right time! How about you?

Then said Absalom to ahithophel, Give counsel among you what we shall do. And Ahithophel said unto Absalom, Go into thy father's concubines, which he hath left to keep the house; and all Israel shall hear that thou art abhorred of thy father: then shall the hands of all that are with thee be strong. So they spread Absalom a tent upon the top of the house; and Absalom went into his father's concubines in the sight of Israel. And the counsel of Ahithophel, which he counselled in those days, was as if a man had enquired at the oracle of God: so was all the counsel of Ahithophel both with David and with Absalom. (2 Samuel 16:20-23)

First, let's deal with prophecy. Do you remember Nathan's words after God pronounced judgment on David after Uriah's death?

> *Thus, says the Lord: "Behold I will raise up adversity against you from your own house; and I will take your wives before your eyes and give them to your neighbor, and he shall lie with your wives in the sight of this sun. For you did it secretly, but I will do this thing before all Israel, before the sun." (2 Samuel 12:11). (NKJV)*

The advice from Ahithophel,

> *"So, they pitched a tent for Absalom on the top of the house, and Absalom went in to his father's concubines in the sight of all Israel." (2 Samuel 16:22) (NKJV)*

God's judgments are sure!

I wonder about Absalom. Was it not Joab, who tried to patch things up with David? He encouraged Absalom to return to Jerusalem. Now Absalom is seeking advice from Ahithophel, who tells him to disgrace the king in this way, to demonstrate his authority. I'm curious. Where do you get your counsel? When you have a decision to make, where do you go for advice? It is a very critical question! The advice we receive can mean the difference between life and death.

Where do you go for counsel on eternity? Eternity? You do know that we will ALL live forever, don't you? God created us for eternity. The decision that we need counsel on is, where we will spend that eternity. There are two options. One, we can spend eternity in heaven with God, or, we can spend eternity in Hades with the devil and his angels. Two choices, two futures, two options. A decision must be made before you leave this world! So, how do you make that decision?

Absalom, sought Ahithophel for counsel as to what to do once he arrived in Jerusalem. David has left, So Absalom thinks he can just move in. Remember the custom of the day. Absalom must kill David, his father. His throne will never be secure until David is dead. What a culture.

So, Absalom seeks counsel. Ahithophel advices Absalom to demonstrate his authority over David by disgracing David's family. Great advice. Stick it to him. Really?

Let me, again, ask you where you get your advice, your counsel, your decision-making process? How much of the word of God do you know? How much time do you spend in prayer. How close is your walk with God? All of these can help determine your decision-making process. Each can contribute to you making the decision that will honor God and not Satan. Including your eternity!

You know that verse in the Romans Road.

> "That if you confess with your mouth the Lord Jesus and believe in your heart that God raised Him from the dead, you will be saved." (Romans 10:9) (NKJV)

Did you catch that one little two-letter word? "IF" You see, it's your choice. God will not make you do anything you don't want to do. It's all on you! It's your choice. So, it was in the very beginning. At the creation of man. God gave Adam and Eve the choice to obey Him or not. They chose to rebel against God's instructions. It has always been the choices we make in life.

The older we get the more our choices should be based on the wisdom we have acquired through the years. That "wisdom" will depend on where we get our counsel, of whom we get our counsel. Bad counsel, bad results. Think about it.

One last thing. Did you notice that Absalom never "inquired of the Lord"? Interesting.

2 Samuel 17

Moreover Ahithophel said unto Absalom, Let me now choose out twelve thousand men, and I will arise and pursue after David this night: And I will come upon him while he is weary and weak handed, and will make him afraid: and all the people that are with him shall flee; and I will smite the king only: And I will bring back all the people unto thee: the man whom thou seekest is as if all returned: so all the people shall be in peace. And the saying pleased Absalom well, and all the elders of Israel. Then said Absalom, Call now Hushai the Archite also, and let us hear likewise what he saith. And when Hushai was come to Absalom, Absalom spake unto him, saying, Ahithophel hath spoken after this manner: shall we do after his saying? If not; speak thou. (2 Samuel 17:1-6)

Did I miss it? Maybe the original translators missed it. Did you see it in the text? The words, "And they inquired of the Lord". No, it isn't in there. A son of David, who was raised in David's home from birth.

This is interesting. If you read through the books of First and Second Kings, I want you to notice something. First, none of the Northern kings were godly kings. For the most part, most of the Southern kings were godly kings, with a few exceptions. The thing that fascinates me the most is how a godly king will be followed by one of the worst, ungodly kings, and then his offspring will be a godly king. I don't get it.

Of course, that can very well be the case today. Both my wife and I can't really say our parents were godly parents. I think they "reverenced" God, but as far as attending church or exhibiting godly characteristics in the home, they didn't. They offered no prayers, etc. Yet my wife and I have both been saved and serving the Lord. I really don't understand. I can understand my wife and my situation but to be raised in a godly home and have your children reject God, that I don't understand.

Just a reminder about godly counsel. I think it is interesting that Absalom hears Ahithophel's counsel and then seeks Hushai's counsel. Do you think God was in that? Of course, He was. The thing is that Ahithophel's counsel would have done David in. He would have been captred and probably killed. Yet God intervened. I am sure it was God! Remember how Hushai came to be in Absalom's presence? (15:32-34). Of course, all this just happened by accident.

Absalom consulted Ahithophel, Absalom consulted Hushai, did Absalom consult a priest? Did Absalom pray? Did Absalom "inquire of the Lord, search for an ephod? No, to all these. We talked earlier about our source of counsel. You notice I didn't say "godly" counsel. Most of the time we seek no counsel at all. We already know the right thing to do why ask someone else, how foolish!

Did you notice how many men Ahithophel wanted to take with him. If memory serves David's loyal army consisted of six hundred men. Sounds even to me. Again, the power is not in the number but if God is in the army. Ahithophel could have had ten times that number, if God's not in it they will be defeated. If God is not in your plans they will be defeated. Absalom was doomed to fail the day he decided to take vengeance into his own hands and kill Amnon.

Have you discussed your plans with God lately? Do you have plans for the future? Do they include God? It's funny how we make all these plans, then God says, "Today your life will be required of you." Think about it!

And Hushai said unto Absalom, The counsel that Ahithophel hath given is not good at this time. For, said Hushai, thou knowest thy father and his men, that they be mighty men, and they be chafed in their minds, as a bear robbed of her whelps in the field: and thy father is a man of war, and will not lodge with the people. Behold, he is hid now in some pit, or in some other place: and it will come to pass, when some of them be overthrown at the first, that whosoever heareth it will say, There is a slaughter among the people that follow Absalom. And he also that is valiant, whose heart is as the heart of a lion, shall utterly melt: for all Israel knoweth that thy father is a mighty man, and they which be with him are valiant men. (2 Samuel 17:7-10)

I wonder if Hushai was surprised at his argument. David knew what he was doing when he sent Hushai to change the counsel of Ahithophel. You don't suppose God put those words in his mouth? I am always amazed at the power of the Holy Spirit.

When I was a pastor I learned this first hand. There were Sunday's (more than I care to count) when I just felt so inadequate in the pulpit. I might skip an illustration. I might miss read a passage, nervousness most of the time. I would say the closing prayer and be so discouraged that I had not done what God wanted me to do. After the invitation and closing prayer I would go back by the front door and greet the people as they left. Person after person would say how much they were moved by the message. How it spoke to their hearts, etc. I'm thinking did you hear the same sermon I heard? Then I learned a very valuable lesson. God can take our efforts and turn them into a message to glorify God. The people hear what God wants them to hear, not what we say. It is amazing, I saw it many, many times. I would be so disappointed in "my" efforts but God would use that to touch hearts.

I don't know if Hushai felt that way. What he said was just what God wanted him to say. He was able to turn the counsel of Ahithophel and help protect David in his escape.

This concept also works in witnessing. First let me be clear. One of the most powerful weapons a child of God has in witnessing, aside from the work of the Holy Spirit, is their personal testimony. Telling others what God has done in your life is indisputable. They can't argue with your testimony because it is YOUR testimony. I like what a pastor once said, "Sharing the gospel is like telling a starving person where to find bread." God will put the words in your mouth and He will put the right words in their heart. Trust Him.

I think Hushai had some help as well. David's testimony. Absalom knows the battle stories of David, from his defeat of Goliath to his victories against the surrounding nations. Absalom knows of David's fighting ability. Absalom, whether he wants to admit it or not, also knows his father's relationship with God. Hushai reminded Absalom of the fierce fighter his father is. You might say Hushai put the "fear of God" in Absalom.

You come to a fork in the road of your life. How do you decide which way to go? Let me remind you of one of my favorite verses:

*For I know the **plans** that I have toward you, says the Lord, **plans** of peace and not of evil, to give you a future and a hope. Then you will call upon Me and go and pray to Me, and I will listen to you. And you will seek Me and find me, when you search for Me with all your heart. (Jeremiah 29:11-13). (NKJV)*

Are you at the fork in the road? You're not sure which road to take. Chew on these verses, then ask God. If you are following God you, simple go where He is going. He will never lead you astray. If you're not a child of God don't take one more step! Stop right now and pray and ask Jesus to come into your heart and make you a child of God. It is that simple! If you have a Bible turn to Romans 10:9. Read and believe and God will make you one of His children and then you can claim Jeremiah 29:11-13 for your very own. You can't go wrong there!

Therefore I counsel that all Israel be generally gathered unto thee, from Dan even to Beersheba, as the sand that is by the sea for multitude; and that thou go to battle in thine own person. So shall we come upon him in some place where he shall be found, and we will light upon him as the dew falleth on the ground: and of him and of all the men that are with him there shall not be left so much as one. Moreover, if he be gotten into a city, then shall all Israel bring ropes to that city, and we will draw it into the river, until there be not one small stone found there. And Absalom and all the men of Israel said, The counsel of Hushai the Archite is better than the counsel of Ahithophel. For the Lord had appointed to defeat the good counsel of Ahithophel, to the intent that the Lord might bring evil upon Absalom. (2 Samuel 17:11-14)

The one thing David needed was time. Hushai convinced Absalom to take the time to raise an army. If they had followed Ahithophel they would have caught David tired and defenseless. Isn't it interesting how God works. Absalom is trusting in the counsel of men. David, as we have seen, "Inquires of the Lord."

The neat thing about reading these episodes in the Bible is that we can see the end from the beginning. Of course, Absalom will take the advice of Hushai rather than Ahithophel, we know the outcome, it's easy.

How about tomorrow? Do you know what is going to happen next week? Of course not! I know who does! God has this plan. You are the key to this plan. Just like in Jeremiah 29:11b, *"to give you a future and a hope."* God knows where we are going and that His plan is to bless us. Now, the problem is, we know better than God, don't we? We want to take this road that looks, at first, so promising, it looks great! God says, "trust Me" take the "road less traveled by". You have heard that phrase before. But we want to follow the crowd. We want to go where everyone else is going. Do you know what is in the future? Of course not! God does!

I am in my seventies now. There was a time I didn't think I would see forty. I asked the same question, maybe, some of you asked when you retired, "Now what?" We have been working according to someone else's plan for decades. Now we are free. Really? One day God said, you need to take your perspective on the Bible, your daily reading plan and put it in a devotional. So, I got started. When I sat down I thought, "365 pages, really?" That book has been published. Now He has me working on this book. Remember I'm over seventy. Nice time to start.

The point being, that God has a road for us to travel. We can either follow "closely" behind God or we can go our own way. That is your choice. Before you go making choices just remember Adam and Eve in the Garden of Eden. Anyway, there is also one other thing, as I mentioned before, God knows what is going to happen next week, next year, ten years from now, do you? So, it is a no-brainer which you must follow.

Remember this verse,

> "But without faith it is impossible to please Him, for he who comes to God must believe that He is, and that He is a rewarder of those who diligently seek Him. (Hebrews 11:6) (NKJV)

Don't miss that word "diligently" in this verse. If you approach God haphazardly, why would He not treat you the same? Think about it.

David and Absalom are at a disadvantage. They don't know the outcome. In a sense we are like God, in that we know the outcome. Sometimes it's hard to grasp the situation because we DO know what the outcome is. Keep in mind these men do not! It gives it a whole new prospective. We can understand them when we consider that we are in their circumstance, not knowing what will happen next. For all David knows God has decided to remove him from being king. For all Absalom knows he is to be the next king. He IS heir to the throne, right? I like what Charles Stanley is always saying, "Trust God, leave all the consequences to Him." Good advice!

Then said Hushai unto Zadok and to Abiatha the priests, Thus and thus did Ahithophel counsel Absalom and the elders of Israel; and thus and thus have I counselled. Now therefore send quickly, and tell David, saying, Lodge not this night in the plains of the wilderness, but speedily pass over; lest the king be swallowed up, and all the people that are with him. Now Jonathan and Ahimaaz stayed by En-rogel; for they might not be seen to come into the city: and a wench went and told them; and they went and told king David. (2 Samuel 17:15-17)

I remember as a young boy, we had a phone number that consisted of HA-3456 (example). Not long after that it became HA-1-3456. Later it became 324-3456. (the HA stood for Harrison). Do you remember the times when you had these special phone numbers where your long distance would only 10 cents a minute? We have come a long way in communications.

The episode above reminds me of the spies sent into the Promised Land who were hidden on a rooftop by Rahab (Joshua 2). Anyway, the point being to communicate the information that David needed to know concerning Absalom's intentions. Without this information David was vulnerable to attack. Communication is so important today as it was then

Where am I going? You hold in your hand God's communication with mankind in the form of a letter. The Bible is God's total revelation of His will and purpose for His creation. Imagine that! Everything that God wants us to know, everything we need to know is wrapped up in these 66 books. All written by the Spirit of God, the third person of the Trinity.

I did an article once about the silver or gold you have in your house that can determine your relationship with God. Do you remember when you bought your new Bible? How some of the pages were stuck together? Do you remember the coating on the pages as your Bible was closed? It was either gold or silver. Is that coating still there? Why? I even found a typo in one of my Bibles, how? I read it! (That typo is SO rare!)

If you want a really fascinating study, try studying the history of the

Word of God. From the Qumran scrolls, to the Geneva Bible, to the King James and on and on. It is really fascinating. What is even more astonishing is how God preserved His word for thousands of years. Do we have the original manuscripts? No. There is a great story in the Bible as to why we do not have the original texts. Look at Numbers 21:8 "Nehushtan" then look at 2 Kings 18:4. Man would have made the original texts into an idol.

Okay. Why so much time on communication? How important is this message from Hushai to King David? It saved his life. How important was Hushai's input to Absalom that changed his course of action against David?

How important is God's Word to you? How much time do you spend seeking God's mind and heart concerning your life? He is the One who created you! He is the One, if you're a child of God, that has a plan for your life and a desire that your life would prosper. Speaking of which, one of my favorite verses on this subject:

> *This Book of the Law shall not depart from your mouth, but you shall meditate in it day and night, that you may observe to do according to all that is written in it. For then you will make your way prosperous, and then you will have good success. (Joshua 1:8). (NKJV)*

You would do well to remember this verse!

Suppose, the messenger from Hushai was ignored by David. Oh, I don't need that message. I am smart enough to make my own decisions. I'm a king I don't need any help. I have a strong army and I can handle anything that comes my way. Really? David had the foresight to plant Hushai in Absalom's camp. He would not have done that if he planned to ignore the message. Are you ignoring God's message in His word? To your own peril, my friend. The more time you spend in His Word to more you will understand the mind and heart of God. He loves you and wants only the best for His children!

Nevertheless a lad saw them, and told Absalom: but they went both of them away quickly, and came to a man's house in Bahurim, which had a well in his court; whither they went down. And the woman took and spread a covering over the well's mouth, and spread ground corn thereon; and the thing was not known. And when Absalom's servants came to the woman to the house, they said, Where is Ahimaaz and Jonathan? And the woman said unto them, They be gone over the brook of water. And when they had sought and could not find them, they returned to Jerusalem. And it came to pass, after they were departed, that they came up out of the well, and went and told king David, and said unto David, Arise, and pass quickly over the water: for thus hath Ahithophel counselled against you. (2 Samuel 17:18-21)

This reminds me of the episode in Joshua with Rahab.

I don't think there is a pastor or missionary you would not have a story of divine intervention. An incident where God made Himself known. Mine occurred several years ago at my home church. Our youth group was on their way to a youth camp in Bowling Green, Kentucky from Independence, Missouri. We had a school bus with twenty-five youth and five adults. Our bus was also pulling a U-Haul trailer behind it.

We had packed up and we left the church and had just pulled onto 7-Highway going south. I was driving. I thought I had shifted up as we were picking up speed. I didn't realize I had down-shifted. As I let the clutch out the bus lunged forward. Then suddenly it began heading toward a ditch on the side of the road. I spun the steering wheel like a top, no control at all. All I could do was hold on.

When the bus came to a stop leaning in the ditch, we checked and no one was hurt. We all piled out of the bus. When we got out we saw that the front AXLE had broken off and by some miracle was behind the bus between the bus and the trailer. The whole axle, wheels and all had traveled the length of the bus and somehow wound up behind the bus.

We obtained another bus and finish our trip. All along the route we would say, "What, if it happened here?" I can never explain how that axle and wheels got under the rear wheels and wound up behind our bus. God was truly watching over us that day!

God was watching over these two messengers. You may want to note these instances through the Bible. God has a habit of making Himself known throughout the Bible. That has always been an important part of my prayer life. I pray, "Lord make yourself known to_____." Especially if it's a lost person I am praying for. God can and will manifest Himself to others. Don't forget what Hebrews says,

"Do not forget to entertain strangers, for by so doing some have unwittingly entertained angels. (Hebrews 13:2). (NKJV)

You never know.

I think it's interesting that here the name of the woman isn't given. She is just called "servant" while in Joshua she is named Rahab. Of course, Rahab marries into the line of Jesus. Matthew 1:5. You never know how God will use you if you are open and willing to be used. God accomplishes His will on this earth through the hands and feet and mouth of His children. The trick is to trust God to do what He asks you to do. Most of us are too scared.

When I took the pastor's job at Freeman Baptist I had not been to seminary, no college, my only training was serving in my home church. I had become Associate Pastor. It was totally a step of faith that led me to Freeman. I can truly say that I had never seen God so powerful than in those two and a half years in Freeman. Those years will always be the highlight of my ministry!

If you will allow God to use you, you will see more miracles than you can imagine. You must be willing to trust God and walk in His will and in the power of His Holy Spirit. Be obedient and watch God work!

Then David arose, and all the people that were with him, and they passed over Jordan: by the morning light there lacked not one of them that was not gone over Jordan. And when Ahithophel saw that his counsel was not followed, he saddled his donkey, and arose, and gat him home to his house, to his city, and put his household in order, and hanged himself, and died, and was buried in the sepulchre of his father. Then David came to Mahanaim. And Absalom passed over Jordan, he and all the men of Israel with him. And Absalom made Amasa captain of the host instead of Joab: which Amasa was a man's son, whose name was Ithra an Israelite, that went in to Abigail the daughter of Nahash, sister to zeruiah Joab's mother. So Israel and Absalom pitched in the land of Gilead. (2 Samuel 17:22-26)

Suicide. How do you respond? Have you thought about it? What about as a Christian? Then what? First off, let me remind you that suicide is NOT the unforgivable sin, rejecting the Holy Spirit is! So how do you deal with suicide. Suicide is murder, can we agree on that? Okay, David committed murder. God punished him, but he was still known as a "man after God's own heart." This is probably one of the toughest subjects for a Christian to deal with. First, let me say that as a Christian you should be the LAST person to consider suicide. But, we know that it happens.

Let me give you my take. I think a person who commits suicide will stand before God. He will give an account for his or her "shortened" life! Next, I think God will show them what their life would have been had they not shortened it. The people who might have been impacted by them, for the good. If you want an idea take a look at "It's A Wonderful Life." That might give you an idea of the lives you might affect by "not being here!" Suicide is not a Christian option.

Have you noticed in the verses above how "the stage is set?" All the principle actors are in place. Absalom's desire for power, his deceit and desires have brought him to the point of going to war with his own father. David, partly because of his murder of Uriah and his sin with Bathsheba has brought David to this point. There is one difference between David and Absalom. Absalom is led by self-desire, David by his desire to serve God. Granted, David had a fall, but he has restored his relationship with God.

Have you ever asked yourself, "How did I ever get here?" Sometimes a good situation, sometimes a bad situation. Still, "How did I get here?" Think. Do you remember that fork in this road of life you are walking? That time when you had to decide. You chose one way. That choice brought you here. Good or bad, it was because of a choice you made. You need to think back to that fork, that decision that brought you on this road. Life is made up of choices.

David is our study. David made some great choices in his life, and some not so great. The day he challenged Goliath, and trusted God. The day he was to lead his army in battle and decided to stay home. We need to think back to that fork. It may be that you left God at that fork and chose your own path. If so, you need to return there and find God. He is waiting right where you left Him.

We know what will happen. David doesn't know, and Absalom doesn't know. Now put yourself in their shoes. What might be going through your mind? Did you notice that up till now the Bible hasn't said the size of the armies? Because it doesn't really matter. It depends on whose side God is on.

We will come to many a fork in the road of life. How will you determine which path to take? We have two examples, I have already stated their cases. How about you? How will you determine which path to take? I hope it begins with prayer. Then you need to look around and find out which fork God has taken. Follow Him. The minute you put your faith in your own resources you will fail. Be it knowledge, resources, prestige, peers, wealth, etc. Anything other than what God wants for you, you will fail. Mark it down! When you get to the end of that path you chose, you will find NOTHING!

2 SAMUEL 18

And David numbered the people that were with him, and set captains of thousands and captains of hundreds over them. And David sent forth a third part of the people under the hand of Joab, and a third part under the hand of Abishai the son of Zeruiah, Joab's brother, and a third part under the hand of Ittai the Gittite. And the king said unto the people, I will surely go forth with you myself also. But the people answered, Thou shalt not go forth: for if we flee away, they will not care for us; neither if half of us die, will they care for us: but now thou art worth ten thousand of us: therefore now it is better that thou succour us out of the city. And the king said unto them, What seemeth you best I will do. And the king stood by the gate side, and all the people came out by hundreds and by thousands. (2 Samuel 18:1-4)

The time had come for David to battle his son. It could not have been a pleasant thought. Did you notice that, maybe, David had learned his lesson from Bathsheba? He wanted to go to battle rather than stay home. But the people understood his worth would be in Jerusalem.

I remember this scene from "The Longest Day" the troops were landing in Normandy and the generals were watching from the towers on the ship. Feeling helpless I'm sure. That was probably the feeling David had as these troops set to battle his son, Absalom. Much like the feeling parents have went their sons and daughters enlist in the military, especially in times of conflict. A lady in our church has bought a bunch of toy soldiers and put them in a box. She asks everyone to take a soldier to remind us pray for our military every day! Fantastic idea!

I think it is interesting that God doesn't see fit to tell us how many men are going to battle. Earlier we know that David had 600 men while he was running from Saul. There are no numbers here.

Just a thought, I think you might want to note. Did you know our system of government is demonstrated, maybe influenced, by a passage in Exodus 18 from Jethro, Moses' father-in-law?

> *Listen now to my voice; I will give you counsel, and God will be with you: Stand before God for the people, so that you may bring the difficulties to God. And you shall teach them the statutes and the laws, and show them the way in which they must walk and the work they must do. Moreover, you shall select from all the people able men, such as fear God, men of truth, hating covetousness; and place such over them to be rulers of thousands, rulers of hundreds, rulers of fifties, and rulers of tens. And let them judge the people at all times. (Exodus 18:19-22a). (NKJV)*

Did you know that in the beginning the House of Representatives CHOSE the Senators from each state? Check it out. Do you see our system of government? Did you notice God's role?

David is a battle hardened general. I wonder how much Absalom knows about fighting? This wisdom will come in handy later. Wisdom that God has given David through many years of fighting. The point that God made to him about constructing His temple. God has blessed each of us with certain gifts. I'm not talking about the Holy Spirit here. I'm talking about talents given us when God created us in the womb. I have always wished I had a voice to sing. I don't! My daughter has. A gift from God. The other daughter has a gift of learning. She is using that great talent. My wife has a great gift of "friendship" she can meet a stranger and in ten minutes be the best of friends. It's wonderful to behold!

What are you doing with the gifts God has given you, aside from His Holy Spirit. The Holy Spirit is a spiritual gift, God has given you talents as well to use for His glory!

And the king commanded Joab and Abishai and Ittai, saying, Deal gently for my sake with the young man, even with Absalom. And all the people heard when the king gave all the captains charge concerning Absalom. So the people went out into the field against Israel: and the battle was in the wood of Ephraim; Where the people of Israel were slain before the servants of David, and there was there a great slaughter that day of twenty thousand men. For the battle was there scattered over the face of all the country: and the wood devoured more people that day than the sword devoured. (2 Samuel 18:5-8)

Did you notice who is fighting? Brother against brother, father against son. Reminds me of the Civil War our country fought. Absalom's forces against David's forces, all Israelites! Don't miss this. Rebellion is never pretty, necessary sometimes, but never pretty.

There was a song on an album I have by John Wayne. Did you know John Wayne did a record album? I don't know if it is still available. Anyway, the song had to do with a hyphen. The song decried the use of a hyphen in our heritage; African-American, Hispanic-American, Italian-American, etc. You get the point. I got to thinking about this. It reminds me of a fraction, the numerator and the denominator. A fraction denotes less than whole. America is a WHOLE nation. One nation under God. We are not a fraction.

Let me stir your thinking a little more. As a casual observer, I like to listen sometimes at the conversation when family members gather together. What is the main topic of conversation? You guessed it, other family members, usually negative. That ought not to be. I would rather talk politics than gossip. Both can be as explosive. One last thing, what is your conversation about on Sunday after you leave church, headed to lunch? Church people? I hope it is all positive.

I think it is interesting the narrator makes it a point to notice that most of the deaths were brought about by the trees, the forest and not each other. It doesn't help the fact that countrymen were fighting each other. One of the greatest arrows in Satan's quiver is "division" whether it is a country, a family, or a church. If he can divide he will conquer. Think about that at your next gathering.

God does mention the number who were killed, twenty thousand, all in rebellion. The battle takes place in Ephraim, a member of the original twelve tribes that settled the Promised Land. I believe Ephraim was one of the largest tribes. The point being that it was a "family" fight. Jew against Jew. Just to demonstrate God's reason for David not building the temple of God. When there is peace God can accomplish so much more, God is the author of peace not calamity!

Here are a couple of verses in Corinthians for you:

For God is not the author of confusion, but of peace, as in all the churches of the saints. (1 Corinthians 14:33). (NKJV)

Let all things be done decently and in order. (1 Corinthians 14:40). (NKJV)

Do you know how to tackle an enormous endeavor? You break it down into small pieces and you tackle them "in order". It's scriptural!

David approached this battle methodically. Dividing his troops into three armies, each making their perspective attacks. The system worked, he attained a great victory that day, at what cost? We will see soon. Civil War never ends well. The casualties can be far more than human lives. Our country still cannot put that conflict behind us. In a sense, we are still a divided country if we continue to use "hyphens". One of the most dangerous mindsets today is to not become assimilated into our culture. We can't seem to remove the "hyphen" until we can do that we will continue to be a divided country, so many pieces of the whole, never becoming ONE nation under God.

And Absalom met the servants of David. And Absalom rode upon a mule, and the mule went under the thick boughs of a great oak, and his head caught hold of the oak, and he was taken up between the heaven and the earth; and the mule that was under him went away. And a certain man saw it, and told Joab, and said, Behold, I saw Absalom hanged in an oak. And Joab said unto the man that told him, And, behold, thou sawest him, and didst not thou smite him there to the ground? And I would have given thee ten shekels of silver, and a girdle. And the man said unto Joab, Though I should receive a thousand shekels of silver in mine hand, yet would I not put forth mine hand against the king's son: for in our hearing the king charged thee and Abishai and Ittai, saying, Beware that none touch the young man Absalom. (2 Samuel 18:9-12)

Do you see the lesson here? I have mentioned it before. Good time to stress it again. "Integrity". This soldier isn't even named. Joab says, "Why didn't you kill him?" The servant says, "The king said not to." Plain and simple. I like the part where the servants said, "*Though I were to receive a thousand shekels of silver and a belt.*" I don't care what the price is I would not disobey my conscience. Can we say that?

I talked earlier about having "convictions" in our life. Standards that we simply will not cross over. Where do we get these "limits"? Some of course are passed down from our parents. Long before I read the Bible I remember my dad telling there are three things we must not do. Lie, cheat and steal. Basic convictions taught very early, I still can see my dad telling me these. Interesting that these are also in the Ten Commandments.

Next, as a Christian the more we learn from the Word of God the more we will insert these convictions into our own life. The closer we walk with God the more of His character we will absorb into our own lifestyle. Church is a big component of this growing process. You wondered when I would get to the church part. As a former Sunday School Director, I know the critical importance of beginning early, bringing up our children in Sunday School. Our public schools have hours every day to teach our children about the world. We have one hour on Sunday morning to teach them godly principles. A little lopsided. Of course, that doesn't include the godly influence from godly parents. I hope it is frequent!

Anyone remember where Joab first appeared? Joab was the general of Saul's army. Now he has become a general in David's army, just saying. I wonder if there might have been some hard feelings that David also appointed two other generals and split his army into three parts? Who knows?

Did you notice that the "villain" in this scenario wasn't captured or killed by David's forces? He just "happened" to be caught in a tree by his hair. His hair? Yes, remember this passage:

> And when he cut the hair of his head—at the end of every year he cut it because it was heavy on him—when he cut it, he weighed the hair of his head at two hundred shekels according to the king's standard. (2 Samuel 14:26). (NKJV)

God has His ways.

The point I want to make in this passage is not Absalom's hair but the integrity of this servant. There was no cost to his integrity. I think the movie is "Courageous". In it this employee is offered a better job and higher wages if he would just "bend" the rules a little and change some numbers in his inventory. The employee wrestled with his choice. He and his family needed the job badly. He chose to sacrifice his job rather than cheat on the numbers. It was a test from the employer. I don't know if you caught the bosses remark as the employee was leaving. You were the "sixth" one we asked, we were beginning to give up hope. That is scary.

What is the price of your integrity? It seems to be getting cheaper and cheaper every day. Where do you draw the line? My dad taught me, "Do not lie, cheat or steal" what are your "standards" in today's world?

Otherwise I should have wrought falsehood against mine own life: for there is not matter hid from the king, and thou thyself wouldest have set thyself against me. Then said Joab, I may not tarry thus with thee. And he took three darts in his hand, and thrust them through the heart of Absalom, while he was yet alive in the midst of the oak. And ten young men that bare Joab's armour compassed about and smote Absalom, and slew him. And Joab blew the trumpet, and the people returned from pursuing after Israel: for Joab held back the people. And they took Absalom, and cast him into a great pit in the wood, and laid a very great heap of stones upon him: and all Israel fled every one to his ten. Now Absalom in his lifetime had taken and reared up for himself a pillar, which is in the king's dale: for he said, I have no son to keep my name in remembrance: and he called the pillar after his own name: and it is called unto this day, Absalom's place. (2 Samuel 18:13-18)

And what kind of monument will you erect in your memory? What a sad story. Joab will answer for his life later. But, Absalom, David's son. Instead of following in his father's footsteps he decided to be king. Again, I know I'm redundant here, but, where is God in Absalom's life. Granted he didn't have a stellar role model but still. I am sure he had to know about God.

I wonder if the monument is still there today? Doesn't matter. We have his story in the Word of God. How would you like to have this story recorded for eternity?

Let's see, Amnon, David's oldest son, was killed by Absalom, his third son, (his number two son was Chileab the son of Abigail). Amnon, raped

Absalom's sister, and on it goes. Again, where is God in all this? We should ask the question ourselves at times. Especially when we have lost our way.

Do you remember, a while back, how I got tired of talking about Saul? Now, it seems, we can't get rid of Joab. How many people pass through our lives? Some with a good impact some not so good. I'm sure we could make a lengthy list on both sides. We talked about this already. And their impact on our lives depends on what? YOU! David could have been rid of Joab a long time ago.

Not only the people who pass through our lives, but those who "impact" our lives. Those who leave a lasting mark on our life. Parents, teachers, neighbors, friends, peers, co-workers, etc. They impact our lives because we allow them to.

Dr. Dobson made this observation once. You have twins. They will both be raised, exactly the same, one will become a doctor the other a criminal. The parents impacted both the same yet they turned out different. The same for students who sit under the same teachers, yet many will go different paths. God created us each unique.

I used to wish I could preach like Dr. Stanley or Dr. Swindoll. If I could, one of us would be unnecessary. God doesn't create "duplicates". He made us each unique to serve a specific purpose in our lifetime. Our challenge is to find that purpose and follow God's plan.

Absalom had the same opportunities as Solomon, yet Absalom chose not to take it, while Solomon searched for direction and guidance. We were talking earlier about our distinct talents that God has given us. I think God put in Solomon the talent to be an architect. While his father, David, was a warrior, a shepherd, a king.

You have talents and gifts that God has given you from when He created you in your mother's womb. Those talents and gifts were given to you for a reason. Of course, once you become a child of God you also receive a "spiritual" gift that is unique to you. Others may have the same gift, but your opportunities to exercise your gift will be unique. The point is, what are you doing with what God has given you? You might want to consider Jesus' parable of the talents in Matthew 25.

Then said Ahimaaz the son of Zadok, Let me now run, and bear the king tidings, how that the Lord hath avenged him of his enemies. And Joab said unto him, Thou shalt not bear tidings this day, but thou shalt bear tidings another day: but this day thou shalt bear no tidings, because the king's son is dead. Then said Joab to Cushi, Go tell the king what thou hast seen. And Cushi bowed himself unto Joab, and ran. Then said Ahimaaz the son of Zadok yet again to Joab, But howsoever, let me, I pray thee, also run after Cushi. And Joab said, wherefore wilt thou run, my son, seeing that thou hast no tidings ready? (2 Samuel 18:19-22)

This is an interesting segment. Ahimaaz thought he knew all he needed to know and couldn't wait to tell David that Absalom was dead. The Cushite, given the message from Joab was also sent. Granted I am not a fan of Joab. There is a principle here that I think we might want to look at.

Have you memorized the Roman's road? How about Revelation 3:20 and John 3:16. So now you are ready to tell someone about Jesus? You share all these verses, you open your Bible you even have them read the Bible. Their response, "I don't believe the Bible." So, they don't believe your resource for truth. What do you do?

"You don't believe the Bible?" "Let me tell you what Jesus has done in MY life!" They might argue the validity of the Bible but they "cannot" argue what God has done in your life. Do you have a testimony? As a young Christian, it might be hard. The stronger you grow in your faith, in your walk with God the more you have to share with an unbeliever. Your testimony is your greatest asset in winning people to the Lord.

The Cushite had the authority of one of David's commanders behind his message. Ahimaaz had only what he had seen or heard, as his authority. As a Christian we have, not only our own testimony, the authority of scripture, but also the power of the Holy Spirit in our message, and working on the one we are witnessing to. We have the authority of God behind our message.

We are bombarded every day with "facts", with all kinds of messages from every kind of source. How do we determine what is true and what is not? We "consider the source" I love this phrase whenever I hear outrageous comments purported to be fact. "Consider the Source." Great advice today. If you cannot verify the message, discount it. Lying has become an art form today.

I don't know how much these guys have read their Bible. I would be a little leery about bringing a message to David. I'm not sure what David's response would be. I don't think I would be so eager to run to David and tell him his son was killed in battle, especially how he was killed. I think I would leave that message to Joab.

What message do we have to share with others? Can we tell them that God loves them? Can we share what God has done in our life? Maybe, we are mad at God, so we don't have a message. You need to take that to God. Your message must be clear. Granted, not everyone believes in the Bible, that's sad. It is a "proven" source. It has outlasted thousands of alternative messages. Even cults are based on partial or perverted forms of the Bible.

Every morning, in my prayers, I ask God to put someone in the path, of those who don't know Jesus as their Savior, to share with them the gospel of Jesus Christ. Everyone should have the "opportunity" to know Jesus. How can they know unless someone share the message of the "good news" of the gospel of Jesus Christ, God loves them and wants to come into their life and bring them into the family of God as a child of God!

But howsoever, said he, let me run. And he said unto him, Run. Then Ahimaaz ran by the way of the plain, and overran Cushi. And David sat between the two gates: and the watchman went up to the roof over the gate unto the wall, and lifted up his eyes, and looked, and behold a man running alone. And the watchman cried, and told the king. And the king said, If he be alone, there is tidings in his mouth. And he came apace, and drew near. And the watchman saw another man running: and the watchman called unto the porter, and said, Behold another man running alone. And the king said, He also bringeth tidings. (2 Samuel 18:23-26)

This is such a critical concept, you need to think about what is going on here. I don't want to take away from the historical picture. These two messengers are bringing news of Absalom's death. The death of David's son. I have already cautioned about reading too much into the context. I am not doing that. But, there is a spiritual principle that is too important to ignore!

The principle that there are two messages being brought today. We must be discerning about which message we believe and follow. Let me give one example from the Old Testament then one from the New Testament.

Do you remember the message in the Garden of Eden?

And the Lord God commanded the man, saying, "Of every tree of the garden you may freely eat; but of the tree of the knowledge of good and evil you shall not eat, for in the day that you eat of it you shall surely die." (Genesis 2:18-19). (NKJV)

That was God's message to Adam, whether he shared it with Eve we will never know. Now look at the message of Satan:

Then the serpent said to the woman, "You will not surely die. For God knows that in the day you eat of it your eyes will be opened, and you will be like gods, knowing good and evil." (Genesis 3:4-5). (NKJV)

Do you see the contrast in the messages? I love the false promise of Satan, *"you will be like gods."* The promise Satan has fooled us with throughout history. You want to know Satan's heart? Look at these verses:

For you have said in your heart: I will ascend into heaven, I will exalt my throne above the stars of God; I will also sit on the mount of the congregation on the farthest sides of the north; I will ascend above the heights of the clouds, I will be like the Most High. (Isaiah 14:13-14). (NKJV)

Do you see? The same heart of Satan is what he preached to Eve.

Two messages, one from God the other from Satan. Now let's see what method, or message, we get in the New Testament:

For all that is in the world—the lust of the flesh, the lust of the eyes, and the pride of life— is not of the Father but is of the world. (1 John 2:16-17). (NKJV)

Note these three modes of attack. Do you see the last one, "pride of life" as the one used in the Garden? Satan uses the same weapons, but, they have gotten more sophisticated in these times.

There is a battle going on today. Look what Paul says in Galatians:

For the flesh lusts against the Spirit, and the Spirit against the flesh; and these are contrary to one another, so that

you do not do the things that you wish. (Galatians 5:17)
(NKJV)

Two messages, two battles. The lust of the flesh was another attack that Satan used in the Garden, look at this verse:

So, when the woman saw that the tree was good for food, that it was pleasant to the eyes, and a tree desirable to make one wise, she took of the fruit and ate. She also gave to her husband with her, and he ate, (Genesis 3:6). (NKJV)

There are two messages today. Obey God and have a relationship and fellowship with our heavenly Father. Disobey God, seek the things of this world, they are pleasant to look at, they will make you like gods. It's your choice which message you believe, which message you follow. Much of Galatians speaks of this battle between the flesh and the Spirit of God. It is your choice which message you listen to and heed. Just consider the consequences!

And the watchman said, Me thinketh the running of the foremost is like the running of Ahimaaz the son of Zadok. And the king said, He is a good man, and cometh with good tidings. And Ahimaaz called, and said unto the king, All is well. And he fell down to the earth upon his face before the king, and said, Blessed be the Lord thy God, which hath delivered up the men that lifted up their hand against my lord the king. And the king said, Is the young man Absalom safe? And Ahimaaz answered, When Joab sent the king's servant, and me thy servant, I saw a great tumult, but I knew not what it was. And the king said unto him, Turn aside, and stand here. And he turned aside, and stood still. (2 Samuel 18:27-30)

Do you see what happened? Ahimaaz had a "half-message" to bring to David. He knew there was a victory but David wanted to know about his son. Maybe Ahimaaz thought it was what David wanted to know about. Hard to say. He only had half of the news.

From the very beginning of my walk with God, I have loved the Sunday School Ministry. Even as pastor I worked closely with the Sunday School. It was my passion, and I believe my calling. Even today I firmly believe that most Christians only have half of the message! We know, usually, that in the end we win. At least, I hope we have that assurance. Just read the book of Revelation. Several years after I had accepted Jesus Christ as my Savior I asked myself, one day, "Why did Jesus have to die on the cross?"

When I was saved I acknowledge that Christ died for my sins. John 3:16 is clear that God "gave" His only begotten Son. Just one day I asked, Why?

As a student of the Bible I had some "pieces" that I needed to connect to fully understand the complete message that God has given us in His Word. Look at some pieces I found. We begin in Exodus,

> Your lamb shall be without blemish, a male of the first year. You may take it from the sheep or from the goats. (Exodus 12:5). (NKJV)

Why this sacrifice? This is the final plague of the "first born" that God will bring upon Egypt to free His people from bondage. Look at this verse:

> "Now the blood (lamb) shall be a sign for you on the houses where you are. And when I see the blood, I will pass over you; and the plague shall not be on you to destroy you when I strike the land of Egypt." (Exodus 12:13) (NKJV)

We need to understand. Some of the plagues affected Egypt only, Israel was spared. In this plague if a Jew did not apply this blood to their door posts and lintels, their first born would have died as well. If an Egyptian applied the blood they would have been spared. This was later called "The Passover" which is still observed today.

> The next day John saw Jesus coming toward him, and said, "Behold! The Lamb of God who takes away the sin of the world!" (John 1:29). (NKJV)

Look at this verse:

> But when they came to Jesus and saw that He was already dead, they did not break His legs. For these things were done that the Scripture should be fulfilled, Not one of His bones shall be broken. (John 19:33,36) (NKJV)

Fulfilling the requirement in Exodus 12:5.

It's not important that you understand all of the particulars. If you have asked Jesus into your heart by faith, you are a child of God. I just wanted to know why it had to be this way. It didn't have to be by a cross. The sacrifice had to be made for our sin. That sacrifice was God's only Son. This was a principle that God established when He freed Israel from Egyptian bondage.

I love the picture here. You see, when God looks at my life in judgment He will not see all the sins I have committed, God will see the blood of His Son Jesus and I will be allowed into His presence. Only because of what Jesus did for me, nothing I could have done on my own. One more verse if you will:

> *For by grace you have been saved through faith, and that not of yourselves; it is a gift of God, not of works, lest anyone should boast. (Ephesians 2:8-9). (NKJV)*

You see? It is strictly by the grace of God on the cross of Calvary! That is the "complete" message!

And, behold, Cushi came; and Cushi said, Tidings, my lord the king: for the Lord hath avenged thee this day of all them that rose up against thee. And the king said unto Cushi, Is the young man Absalom safe? And Cushi answered, The enemies of my lord the king, and all that rise against thee to do thee hurt, be as that young man is. And the king was much moved, and went up to the chamber over the gate, and wept: and as he went, thus he said, O my son Absalom, my son, my son Absalom! Would God I had died for thee, O Absalom, my son, my son! (2 Samuel 18:31-33)

There is something interesting here. Let's look at an earlier verse:

> *And he said, "While the child was alive, I fasted and wept; for I said, 'Who can tell whether the Lord will be gracious to me, that the child may live?' But now he is dead; why should I fast? Can I bring him back again? I shall go to him, but he shall not return to me." (2 Samuel 12:22-23). (NKJV)*

I don't hear anything like that here, do you? Is David not planning on meeting his son in heaven? One can only guess. There is nothing of that "reuniting" etc.

Grief can be so hard. I have noticed an attitude that hurts me greatly. I mentioned it before. The attitude that "we must blame someone, or something, i.e. the church, or God. Does that relieve the pain? I'm curious. There is a far better attitude that I have noticed at funerals lately. "Let's celebrate that life". Do you like that one? I do.

Wait a minute, how can you "celebrate" a life, if you're not sure where they are going? The grieving family members, who know where their loved one is going has reason to celebrate! Like David they know one day they will be reunited, with his infant son, anyway. Not so sure about Absalom.

Do you see the contrast? Not only in David's two sons, but in our response as well. Could that be the determining factor? If we are not sure where they are going, maybe we NEED to blame someone, or something.

I love to watch the Hallmark Channel. At least I can be sure I will not hear "GD". Anyway, I have noticed something, especially around Christmas time. How many plots can you remember where this person no longer celebrates Christmas? They broke up with someone, their spouse died, their pet died, a parent died, etc. So, because of their grief they are going to blame Christmas, really?

It's no different than blaming God for your loss. And how do we manifest this? We refuse to go church anymore. That will punish God! That will show Him. Really? Who loses out? You do of course. You have broken that fellowship with God because you need someone or something to blame for your grief. Does it help? I think not. You have broken fellowship with the one Person who could help you with your grief.

The funeral of a child of God SHOULD be celebrated, for many reasons. A lot of times we pray for someone who is ill, or in pain that God would heal them. When He takes them home we think God didn't answer our prayer. God did even better, He relieved their pain and took them home to be with Him. Of course, we will miss them. We can also celebrate, like David, that we will be reunited again. David has that peace with his infant son. Not so with Absalom.

I heard there are seven stages of grief that we can go through. To me, the first stage must be to give it to God. Death is God's timing, not ours.

We can have a peace about that. Of course, if they are not a child of God, there is reason to grieve! So, take care of that right now! If you're not sure where you're going when you die, you can settle that right here, right now. Pray, ask God to forgive you of your sins and ask Jesus to come into your heart. He will give you a peace about where you're going to spend eternity!

2 Samuel 19

And it was told Joab, Behold, the king weepeth and mourneth for Absalom. And the victory that day was turned into mourning unto all the people: for the people heard say that day how the king was grieved for his son. And the people gat them by stealth that day into the city, as people being ashamed steal away when they flee in battle. But the king covered his face, and the king cried with a loud voice, O my son Absalom, O Absalom, my son, my son! (2 Samuel 19:1-4)

I can't begin to understand David's grief. I don't try. It just seems to me that David has lost his focus. Granted he has lost his son. I understand, but, as I said before, "Where is God in all this?" It is so easy to do this. We are hurt, in so many different ways. We set up the decorations, get out the balloons and throw a huge "pitty-party". I can't feel sorry for David. This is the same son, had he the opportunity, would have killed David to become king. If not Absalom, surely his troops.

Why is it, when adversity strikes we look everywhere but up? Somehow God isn't invited to our "pitty-party". I don't believe He would accept the invitation if offered. God doesn't deal in that emotion. God is the God of all comfort (2 Corinthians 1). But, in order to be comforted we have to lean on Him.

Here, I think is a good example of the need for a journal. You see we can look back a few chapters in our Bible and see how this whole thing got started. David can't. Right now, he is not even capable of "remembering" the past. His grief has distracted him from thinking clearly. He is not only distracted but has demoralized his friends and fellow soldiers and the nation that stood beside him. He has dragged them down with him.

So, how do we deal with grief? I know there is the seven-steps of grief. I have no idea what they are. The problem is we can't all fit into a plan. God has created us all different. So, we must come the One who created us. God knows our heart. We pray, we meditate, we look to God for comfort (2 Corinthians 1). God will bring the appropriate memories to our mind. He will walk with us through this time.

I want to point out, again, something I mentioned earlier. Perhaps the reason David is so grieved is that he may realize that he may not see him again. Remember his "peace" when the child of Bathsheba died? He does not have that peace here. Interesting.

Just that fact, can go a long way in relieving our grief. If we know that we will see that loved one again. It becomes just a temporary absence, not a permanent separation. Maybe that is part of David's grief here. Did I mention that David is human? We must be reminded of that once in a while. Be careful not to put David on a pedestal. David can also be a great teacher. By observing how David responds we can learn how God works. Remember these words we have read are what God wants us to know. So, we can learn from David's response or lack of focus on God.

I wonder, if in David's grief, he might remember the judgment from God, after his sin with Bathsheba. God said that a sword would pass through his family. (12:10-11). But we don't want to be reminded of our own transgressions. The consequences of our sin, though they are forgiven, can be lifelong. In the eyes of God, they are covered by the blood of Christ, but that does not negate the consequences.

And Joab came into the house to the king, and said Thou hast shamed this day the faces of all thy servants, which this day have saved thy life, and the lives of thy sons and of thy daughters, and the lives of thy wives, and the lives of thy concubines; in that thou lovest thine enemies, that hatest thy friends. For thou hast declared this day, that thou regardest neither princes nor servants: for this day I perceive, that if Absalom had lived, and all we had died this day, then it had pleased thee well. Now therefore arise, go forth, and speak comfortably unto thy servants: for I swear by the Lord, if thou go not forth, there will not tarry one with thee this night: And that will be worse unto thee than all the evil that befell thee from thy youth until now. (2 Samuel 19:5-7)

Isn't it interesting who or how God gets our attention. I believe that is one of the biggest reasons people stay away from church. I heard Dr. Stanley tell his story of how God changed his message on Sunday morning. There is someone in the congregation who needed to hear a different message. God works that way.

As a young preacher, I used to get so discouraged when I felt I didn't deliver the message God wanted me to, or do my best at the time. As I stood at the door as the congregation would leave, I would hear, "Great message pastor!" "That rally spoke to my heart, pastor." And I'm thinking, did they hear the same message I preached? They heard what GOD wanted them to hear. I was just the instrument of delivering His message.

God can use, and often does, any number of ways to get our attention. It can be a "near miss" while driving or any number of ways. I was headed to work on a snowy morning. I lost control of my car and it went into a ditch. Sarcastically I said, "Thanks Lord!" Two minutes later a car with two college kids drove by, lifted my car out of the ditch (it was a Gremlin) and I wasn't even late for work. I still remember that incident fifty years later. God got my attention.

God is using Joab to get David's attention. We talked earlier about our "focus", David was looking inward instead of looking upward. Joab had to remind him who he was. He is the King of Israel. You have a duty and responsibility to your people. David even forgot just who Absalom was. He was not only his son, but he also led a rebellion against his father the king. Too many times our focus is on our own personal needs or wants and forget that we are also responsible for those around us, be it a family, or our co-workers, or even our church family.

This is so important, I need to spend all this time on it. It's basic, sure, but so important. We can use David as a barometer, a gauge to examine our "focus" to remind us to look up not at our circumstances but finding that path again that God has for us to walk. He doesn't want us sitting on the roadside saying, "Woe is me". He wants us up and following His lead in the path of life.

I don't know about you. it irritates me to no end that it is Joab who chastises David for his reaction. It was Joab who killed his son. This isn't over yet, but still. Why not Nathan, or Abiathar, or someone like that. Why does it have to be Joab? Only God knows. We are simply observers of this history. And God decided to tell it this way for a reason. We can't choose who God will use to get our attention. The challenge for us is to listen!

Be walking so close to God that His mind is our mind. His thoughts and desires are ours. His "heart" is our heart. Our focus must be on Him, not on self!

David has a lot to deal with. We can sympathize, but we also must gain some insight into how God gets our attention, how God gets us back on track. That is the work of God's Spirit, if we are listening. If we are a child of God, He wants only the best for us. He doesn't want us sitting on our heart and pouting. He wants us focused on Him, listening for His leadership and guidance!

Then the king arose, and sat in the gate. And they told unto all the people, saying, Behold, the king doth sit in the gate. And all the people came before the king: for Israel had fled every man to his tent. And all the people were at strife throughout all the tribes of Israel, saying, The king saved us out of the hand of our enemies, and he delivered us out of the hand of the Philistines; and now he is fled out of the land of Absalom. And Absalom, whom we anointed over us, is dead in battle. Now therefore why speak ye not a word of bringing the king back? (2 Samuel 19:8-10)

GET UP! I can hear God right now. How many of God's children, knocked down by Satan's tricks, are still lying in their helpless estate? Far too many I'm afraid. God does not want us idle and useless. God called David to be the king of Israel. God did some mighty deeds through David. David, like us, made a mistake. Now Satan has rendered him helpless, really? Only by David's choice. God never intends for us to "give up" He shouts to us, "GET UP" I am not through with you yet!

The only time God can't use us, is when we refuse to be used by God. We are the ones who forget God's grace, God's plan for our life. If I may, let me reprint these fantastic verses:

> *For I know the thoughts that I have toward you, says the Lord, thoughts of peace and not of evil, to give you a future and a hope. Then you will call upon Me and go and pray to Me, and I will listen to you. And you will seek Me and find Me, when you search for Me with all your heart. (Jeremiah 29:11-13). (NKJV)*

Did you catch that last part? *And you will seek Me and find Me.* Who is doing the seeking and finding? Only if you get up and start looking for Him.

I have used the picture of walking along a path with God. You come to a fork in the road. You decide to go left. God stops, "Don't go that way". You decide to go anyway. God is not following, He certainly isn't leading. You leave Him at the fork. You travel on your merry way, then you realize you have made a mistake. What do you do? You sit down and cry? NO, get up and go back to where you left God last. You say you're sorry, then you resume your walk WITH HIM!

That's where David is at. He has been straightened out by Joab. He has been reminded of his responsibility to God and country. When we get down, we think God has abandoned us. He's there waiting where you left Him. You just must get up and return to Him. What a picture here. You may stray off the course God has set for you, God will never leave you or forsake you.

> *Let your conduct be without covetousness; be content with such things as you have, For He Himself has said, "I will never leave you nor forsake you." (Hebrews 13:5)* (NKJV)

Have you given up on God? He hasn't given up on you! David took his eyes off God and focused on Absalom. Focused on his loss, instead of his relationship with God the Father. We do this all the time. I'm sure you have heard, "If all else fails, pray!" Really? So where does that put God, at the tail end?

David gives us a great lesson here. Oh, it will be a slow process. It's a long way back up that path to where he left God waiting and watching. You remember the parable of the Prodigal Son? Do you know how long he was gone? Apparently, he had a long road back to his Father. So, have we. Sometimes we must travel a long distance down the wrong road before we realize our error. Just be assured, God is waiting, right where you left Him. Waiting for you to return and get back on the plan He has for your life.

Don't miss this part of Jeremiah 29:11-13, *to give you a future and a hope.* I want to challenge you to meditate on these three verses. Chew on them, absorb them, memorize them. At least the address, Jeremiah 29:11-13! I think this is one of the great promises in God's Word for us today. The more you incorporate these verses into your mind and heart, the closer to God!

And king David sent to Zadok and to Abiathar the priests, saying, Speak unto the elders of Judah, saying, Why are ye the last to bring the king back to his house? Seeing the speech of all Israel is come to the king, even to his house. Ye are my brethren, ye are my bones and my flesh: wherefore then are ye the last to bring back the king? And say ye to Amasa, Art thou not of my bone, and of my flesh? God do so to me, and more also, if thou be not captain of the host before me continually in the room of Joab. And he bowed the heart of all the men of Judah, even as the heart of one man; so that they sent this word unto the king, Return thou, and all thy servants. (2 Samuel 19:11-14)

Did you notice the method David used? *"So, he swayed the hearts of all the men."* That is what God wants more than anything. He wants your heart. It is amazing, really, if you did a "word search" on your computer for the word heart. It is amazing how many different "hearts" are in the Bible. God deals in hearts. For example, remember Romans 10:9? It is one of the key verses in the Roman's Road:

> *That if you confess with your mouth the Lord Jesus and believe in your **heart** that God has raised Him from the dead, you will be saved. (Romans 10:9) (NKJV)*

Did you notice it said nothing about intellectually? Head knowledge!

Someone once said that many people will miss heaven by eighteen inches. The difference between their head and their heart. They will certainly know WHO Jesus is. They may even have read the whole Bible. But, until He is in your heart, you will miss heaven. David reached the hearts of his people. Just as God must reach your heart.

The book of Proverbs talks a lot about knowledge and wisdom. You can know a lot of "facts" but until you put them into practice, that is all they are, knowledge. The wisdom comes from rightly applying those facts to everyday life. There is the challenge. Just like the Ten Commandments. You can post them all over your house, but until you follow them, they are just plaques on a wall.

Notice, that even with all of David's faults, it's the hearts of the people that bring them back. That encourages them to follow him. He could sight all the battles he's won, beginning with Goliath, and the defeat, eventually, of the Philistines. His accomplishments, etc. That's not why the people follow David. They know, and we know, it's because David is a "man after God's own heart." Oh, there's that word heart again.

David broke God's heart with his affair with Bathsheba. David knew that and now is working to restore that fellowship with God. David, more than ever before, knows the pain of betrayal. Absalom, his son, betrayed him. Much as David did with Bathsheba.

Do you suppose God will work that way in your life? The thing you hold dear, the thing most precious to you, other than God, God may use to bring you to Him. Remember, that is what we are looking at, the heart. What or who occupies your heart, fills your heart, other than God? You must search and find out. God is a jealous God look at this verse,

> "For the Lord your God is a consuming fire, a jealous God." (Deuteronomy 4:24). (NKJV)

Or this verse in the Ten Commandments:

> You shall not make for yourself a carved image—any likeness of anything that is in heaven above, or that is in the earth beneath, or that is in the water under the earth; you shall not bow down to them nor serve them. For I, the Lord your God, am a **jealous** God, visiting the iniquity of the fathers upon the children to the third and fourth generations of those who hate me. (Exodus 20:4-5). (NKJV)

Don't miss that last part, "of those who hate me." God does not carry our sin into the next generations. Only the relationship we have with God, our testimony, our children and grand-children observe and are likely to repeat. We each are responsible for our own sin, it is not transferred. Many times, it's the consequences that are passed down. Our attitude toward God can be transferred as well. Think about it!

So the king returned, and came to the Jordan. And Judah came to Gilgal, to go to meet the king, to conduct the king over Jordan. And Shimei the son of Gera, a Benjamite, which was of Bahurim, hasted and came down with the men of Judah to meet king David. And there were a thousand men of Benjamin with him, and Ziba the servant of the house of Saul, and his fifteen sons and his twenty servants with him; and they went over Jordan before the king. And there went over a ferry boat to carry over the king's household, and to do what he thought good. And Shimei the son of Gera fell down before the king, as he was come over Jordan; (2 Samuel 19:15-18)

That is interesting. David is returning to Jerusalem, a victor from a war he didn't fight. Joab, Abishai and Ittai, his generals fought that battle, Joab killed Absalom, the ring leader. But, David is the one the Jews are welcoming home as the victor. They are celebrating! That's an interesting picture.

You know, when we get to heaven, assuming you have asked Jesus into heart and made Him your Savior, we will be welcomed the same way. The same way, because of the battle someone else fought for us. The victory at the cross of Calvary where our Lord defeated Satan in the battle over death. Look at this verse:

O Death, where is your sting? O Hades, where is your victory? The sting of death is sin, and the strength of sin is the law. But thanks be to God, who gives us the victory through our Lord Jesus Christ (1 Corinthians 15:55-57). (NKJV)

You see, because of Christ's victory over death we can enjoy the promise of God expressed by the Apostle Paul,

To be absent from the body is to be present with the Lord. (2 Corinthians 5:8). (NKJV)

What a great promise only because Jesus paid our sin-debt on the cross.

David is celebrating in a victory he had not taken part in. This was one battle he wanted to join but, his commanders and the people restrained him. If I were David I would not want to sit home any more either!

Speaking of victories in battles we never fought. I am in such awe of our Founding Fathers. The cost they paid for us to live in this great country. Those who fought in subsequent battles to maintain the freedoms we enjoy to this day. There are many battles that we did not fight but we enjoy the fruit of the victory.

There is another battle that rages on. Once we become a child of God, Paul talks about the constant battle within us, the battle of flesh over Spirit. It is a battle that will be fought until we go home to be with the Lord. Our general, who is fighting this battle alongside us? The Holy Spirit of God. The same Holy Spirit that takes up permanent residence within us to engage the enemy, the flesh, and help us gain the victory. But, we must learn to listen to that General! Obey, that General, to get the victory.

Battles are all around us, as children of God we have an Advocate to stand before God and present our case to God Almighty (1 John 2:1). He is our lawyer, our judge, and our Savior. Because we are on the right side. We have signed up for the winning side. God has already won, just read the Book of Revelation, God wins!

Are you fighting a battle right now? Do you know who is on your side? This assumes you have asked Jesus into your heart and trust Him as your Savior. Otherwise, you're on your own in a world that will devour you, top to bottom! You can enlist in God's army or go it alone. It has always been your choice to make. God will not "draft" you. You must volunteer!

And said unto the king, Let not my lord impute iniquity unto me, neither do thou remember that which thy servant did perversely the day that my lord the king went out of Jerusalem, that the king should take it to his heart. For thy servant doth know that I have sinned: therefore, behold, I am come the first this day of all the house of Joseph to go down to meet my lord the king. But Abishai the son of Zeruiah answered and said, Shall not Shimei be put to death for this, because he cursed the Lord's anointed? And David said, What have I to do with you, ye sons of Zeruiah, that ye should this day be adversaries unto me? Shall there any man be put to death this day in Israel? For do not I know that I am this day king over Israel? (2 Samuel 19:19-22)

Is this scene familiar? Remember when Nathan confronted David about his sin? David admitted his sin, acknowledge he had sinned, accepted God's judgment, the death of his child. In many ways, this is the path we take, on our salvation road. I have been using the analogy of walking on a road with God. As long as we walk with Him, follow closely alongside God, we will be in His will, and walking the path He has chosen for us.

Sunday our pastor shared this verse that really illustrates what I am getting at.

> *And when he brings out his own sheep, he goes before them; and the sheep follow him, for they know his voice. (John 10:4).* (NKJV)

In this chapter of the Gospel of John, Jesus is portraying Himself as "The Good Shepherd" and His relationship to his followers, the sheep. We know His voice and we follow Him. That is the picture I want to draw. How closely we follow His will, will determine our daily walk.

Shimei, confessing to David how wrong he was, and now wishes to follow David. Let's take a trip on another road that we find in Romans. The first step is:

> *"For all have sinned and fall short of the glory of God."* *(Romans 3:23)* (NKJV)

Until you acknowledge your spiritual condition you cannot get well. The same is SO true in our physical world. For years my doctor had been trying to get me to have a colonoscopy. I kept putting it off. I finally gave in and he found a tumor on my colon wall. It was cancerous. Thank God, they got to it in time. I am cancer free. Until I recognized I might be sick, then only could it be addressed. Until we acknowledge our sinful condition we cannot be healed!

Here is another verse along this road:

> *For the wages of sin is death, but the gift of God is eternal life in Christ Jesus our Lord. (Romans 6:23).* (NKJV)

There is only one result for sin. Eternal condemnation. Eternally separated from God. God made this promise to Adam and Eve in the Garden:

> *"And the Lord God took the man and put him in the garden of Eden to tend and keep it. And the Lord God commanded the man, saying, "Of every tree of the garden you may eat; but of the tree of the knowledge of good and evil you shall*

not eat, for in the day that you eat of it you shall surely die."
(Genesis 2:15-17) (NKJV)

You will note that this command was given BEFORE He created Eve. The consequences of disobeying God, is spiritual death. Every human being since Adam and Eve are under this condemnation. God needed to provide a way for His creation to restore their relationship with a holy God.

In Romans, we read:

> *But God demonstrates His own love toward us, in that while we were yet sinners, Christ died for us. (Romans 5:8) (NKJV)*

Only the life of God's Son was holy enough and precious enough to pay for our sins, past, present and future. Only the blood of the sacrificial Lamb of God could be enough to allow us into God's presence again. Without that blood, we are forever condemned to an eternity in Hades. You notice that there was nothing we could do to restore that relationship? *"While we were yet sinners."*

Look at this verse in Ephesians:

> *For by grace you have been saved through faith, and not of yourselves; it is the gift of God, not of works, lest anyone should boast. (Ephesians 2:8-9). (NKJV)*

There is nothing for us to do. God has done it all! Why would God do that for me? I know you know this verse:

> *"For God so loved the world that He gave His only begotten Son, that whosoever believes in Him should not perish but have everlasting life. (John 3:16). (NKJV)*

How did God give His son? On the cruel cross of Calvary. Jesus willingly offered His life so that we may have a relationship with our heavenly Father!

So, how do I get my sins erased, and my relationship with a holy God achieved? Look at this verse:

If you confess with your mouth the Lord Jesus and believe in your heart that God has raised Him from the dead, you will be saved." (Romans 10:9). (NKJV)

Saved from what? Spending eternity in Hades, separated from God. Notice where this decision must originate!

For with the heart one believes unto righteousness, and with the mouth confession is made unto salvation. (Romans 10:10). (NKJV)

Okay, one day, when I get around to it, I will ask Jesus into my heart. And you know how long you're going to live? Really? Let me share one more verse, one of my favorites!

Behold, I stand at the door and knock. If anyone hears My voice and opens the door, I will come in to him and dine with him, and he with Me. (Revelation 3:20). (NKJV)

The invitation is there! It's your choice to open that door or not. When you stand before God and say, "Okay, I believe now, I will accept Your Son as my Savior." IT IS TO LATE! It must be done now, right now. You have no guarantees!

If you follow this road, acknowledge you're a sinner, believe that Christ died for your sins, ask Jesus to come into your heart right now. You can begin a walk with God that will simply amaze you. Once you have asked Jesus into your heart, you will receive a "Helper" to guide you along this road. The Holy Spirit will come into your heart and guide you along this walk.

One more thing, your relationship with God will change. Look at this verse:

For as many as are led by the Spirit of God, these are sons of God. For you did not receive the spirit of bondage again to fear, but you received the Spirit of adoption by whom we cry, "Abba, Father." The Spirit Himself bears witness with our spirit that we are children of God. (Romans 8:14-16). (NKJV)

When you ask Jesus into your heart, you become a child of God. It's up to you!

Therefore the king said unto Shimei, Thou shalt not die. And the king sware unto him. And Mephibosheth the son of Saul came down to meet the king, and had neither dressed his feet, nor trimmed his beard, nor washed his clothes, from the day the king departed until the day he came again in peace. And it came to pass, when he was come to Jerusalem to meet the king, that the king said unto him, Wherefore wentest not thou with me, Mephibosheth? And he answered, My lord, O king, my servant deceived me: for thy servant said, I will saddle me a donkey, that I may ride thereon, and go to the king; because thy servant is lame. And he hath slandered thy servant unto my lord the king; but my lord the king is as an angel of God: do therefore what is good in thine eyes. (2 Samuel 19:23-27)

Do you remember when David encountered Ziba as he was leaving Jerusalem, running for his life from Absalom? Remember what Ziba told David?

> And Ziba said to the king, "Indeed he is staying in Jerusalem, for he said, 'Today the house of Israel will restore the kingdom of my father to me.' "(2 Samuel 16:3). (NKJV)

Ziba lied to David, he was simply covering because he had been caught stealing Mephibosheth's goods. I can't imagine how hurt David was, hearing these words.

Now, he sees Mephibosheth, and the truth comes out. Isn't that always the way it is? The truth will show itself at one time or another. The problem today is, there are no consequences to lying!

Not so in David's time, as we will see.

I think it is interesting that Mephibosheth calls David an "angel of God". Ever been called an "angel of God?" Why do you suppose Mephibosheth called him that? Remember what lengths David went through, to find Mephibosheth? Then he allowed him to sit at his table the rest of his life. A special blessing to Mephibosheth no doubt!

Don't you see it? This is the same situation we face every day. If we have not accepted the Lord as our Savior we are like Mephibosheth in the wilderness of Lo Debar (2 Samuel 9:5). We have been rescued from the wilderness of sin, our fleshly lusts, and invited to sit at the King's table. Jesus bought that privilege with His death on the cross. Now, if we have accepted Jesus as our Savior, we have the right to sit at the King's table, as children of God. (Romans 8:15). I love the comparison of these two pictures!

Now David has found out the truth. From the mouth of Mephibosheth, the lie has been revealed. I'm curious what Ziba did with all the goods he had. Did he sell them, I think the implication was that he gave the supplies to Absalom's army? Who knows. Did you notice the neglect of Ziba?

> *"And he had not cared for his feet, nor trimmed his mustache, nor washed his clothes, from the day, the king departed until the day he returned in peace." (2 Samuel 19:23) (NKJV)*

I think it is a good thing Ziba was not within reach of David. As much love as David showed to Mephibosheth, to have Ziba neglect him this way is shameful. David won't forget it.

David has returned to Jerusalem, I'm not sure he would consider it a triumphal return. He has been told Absalom is dead, but not how he died. That will come later. I mentioned it before but sometimes we need to be forced out of our "comfort zone." It helps to give us a new perspective, a new purpose, maybe. If you just realized your stuck in a "comfort zone" you need to shake things up a bit. Try something new, it won't kill you. As a child, we all hate to try new foods. When I was little my mother always fixed broccoli with cream cheese, I hated it, refused to eat it. After I got married my wife simply boiled it and I loved it! Get out of your "comfort zone", you never know what you might find.

David was running for his life. His son was taking his kingdom away, and threatened to kill him. The same son who had killed David's oldest son. Now he is back in Jerusalem, another opportunity, to begin a-new. We will see.

For all of my father's house were but dead men before my lord the king: yet didst thou set thy servant among them that did eat at thine own table. What right therefore have I yet to cry any more unto the king? And the king said unto him, Why speakest thou any more of thy matters? I have said, Thou and Ziba divide the land. And Mephibosheth said unto the king, Yea, let him take all, forasmuch as my lord the king is come again in peace unto his own house. (2 Samuel 19:28-30)

Will you indulge me? I love the picture here! These could very well be our words as Jesus welcomes us into His kingdom. This whole episode with Mephibosheth reminds me of Jesus words in Matthew 25:

> *Then the King will say to those on His right hand, 'Come, you blessed of My Father, inherit the kingdom prepared for you from the foundation of the world: For I was hungry and you gave Me food; I was thirsty and you gave Me drink; I was a stranger and you took Me in; I was naked and you clothed Me; I was sick and you visited Me; I was in prison and you came to Me.' Then the righteous will answer Him, saying, 'Lord, when did we see You hungry and feed You, or thirsty and give You drink? When did we see You a stranger and take You in, or naked and clothe You? Or when did we see You sick, or in prison and come to You?' And the King will answer and say the them, 'Assuredly, I say to you, inasmuch as you did it to one of the least of these My brethren, you did it to Me.'" (Matthew 25:34-40). (NKJV)*

I wonder if David knew this principle? He used it with Mephibosheth.

This is such a picture of heaven to me. Imagine, because we are children of God we will be allowed to sit at the table with the King of Kings. Our "relationship" with God the Father will grant us access to the table of God. We will feast with the King!

Maybe we might relate a little to how Mephibosheth might feel. Totally unworthy, yet because of our lineage in the family of God, we can join Him at the table for bread. I don't think I need to remind you of Romans 8:15.

Do you see the pieces returning in David's life? Many times, after we have come through a storm, God will gradually restore the pieces of our life. That is, if we keep our focus on Him. I love the illustration of a farmer plowing a field, hundreds of yards across. In order to plow a straight line, he focuses on a tree or a pole or something on the other side of the field.

He simply plows toward that mark. It will keep his furrows straight. That is how God gets us through the storms. We fix our focus on God. And we travel, through the storm, toward that mark. That is what David has done.

Let me remind you of something David said when he left Jerusalem,

> *Then the king said to Zadok, "Carry the ark of God back into the city. If I find favor in the eyes of the Lord, He will bring me back and show me both it and His dwelling place. But if He says thus: 'I have no delight in you,' here I am, let Him do to me as seems good to Him." (2 Samuel 15:25-26). (NKJV)*

Do you see it? David's focus was on God. Even after God had judged him, and is punishing him. David said, "My life is in God's hands. My future is in God's plan." David still trusted God for direction and courage, and provision. Have you ever said, "The Lord willing?" To trust God completely for the outcome of any trial. I love the way Dr. Stanley puts it: Because God is All-knowing, He knows where you are at in the storm. Because God is Omni-present, He is with you in the storm. Because God is All-powerful He will bring you through the storm." Is that not awesome?

David has that kind of relationship with God. We know he is not perfect, neither are we. What kind of relationship do you have with your heavenly Father? Are you walking close enough that you can sense His presence? Does God have His hand on you? Are you in His word every day? Do you talk to Him every day in prayer? Important questions to ask.

And Barzillai the Gileadite came down from Rogelim, and went over Jordan with the king, to conduct him over Jordan. Now Barzillai was a very aged man, even fourscore years old: and he had provided the king of sustenance while he lay at Mahanaim; for he was a very great man. And the king said unto Barzillai, Come thou over with me, and I will feed thee with me in Jerusalem. And Barzillai said unto the king, How long have I to live, that I should go up with the king unto Jerusalem? I am this day fourscore years old: and I can discern between good and evil? Can thy servant taste what I eat or what I drink? Can I hear any more the voice of singing men and singing women? Wherefore then should thy servant be yet a burden unto my lord the king? (2 Samuel 19:31-35)

Time, it goes so fast, and it takes so long! I understand that this is a line from a song. I will be celebrating my seventy-second birthday next month, God willing! Where has the time gone? We can all say that at one point or another. In the verses above, this fellow, who is eighty, confronts David. Here is another individual that passes, briefly, through David's life. I think there is a lesson here.

In the Psalms it says, my *times are in Your hand;* (Psalm 31:15a). I love the verse in Galatians where the apostle Paul writes:

But when the fullness of time had come, God sent forth His Son. (Galatians 4:4a). (NKJV)

And in Psalm 90 we read:

The days of our lives are seventy years; and if by reason of strength they are eighty. (Psalm 90:10). (NKJV)

There are a lot of verses in the Bible pertaining to time.

I get the idea from the words above from this guy that he thinks his time is up. Let's say he thinks his "usefulness" is past. Do you think that? Of course, I don't know how old you are. Do you think that life has past you by, that there is no more for you to do? You're not walking with God then. God always has work for us to do.

Do you think God wants us sitting around idle? Do you remember what Adam and Eve were told in the "perfect" Garden of Eden? Look here:

Then the Lord God took the man and put him in the garden of Eden to tend and keep it. (Genesis 2:15). (NKJV)

I have always thought it was interesting that God created man "outside" the garden then put him in it! I wonder if there were any "poison ivy" in the Garden? Adam would have been immune anyway. The point is he was given a task to perform. He wasn't to sit around and eat. There was work to be done.

How about you? I remember as a kid, we had none of these computers and games. We would go outside and "invent" things to do. Back when coffee cans were metal we would use the lid as a "frisbee". Years before they made the plastic ones. The point of course, be creative FIND something to do. Pray! God is there a ministry I could be involved in? Is there a need I could help provide? You are never too old to "do something!"

It sounds like this guy has given up. He thinks about what he can't do, instead of what he can. He could have encouraged David. He could have offered to be of "service". Don't forget how David got into so much trouble! Instead of going to battle, like he was supposed to, he was at home, DOING NOTHING! It cost him his intimate relationship with God at the time. I think David is slowly restoring that fellowship.

Once, I loved listening to country songs on the radio. I began to keep a notebook of titles and artists. I kept alphabetizing the lists. Good practice! At one point, I had over one-thousand songs. I sent the notebook to a local radio station. The Program Director made me the secretary to his fan club. You can always find something to do. Be creative. Get your face out of that computer and ask God for some direction. That's assuming you and He are on speaking terms. Are you a child of God? Why not?

Thy servant will go a little way over Jordan with the king: and why should the king recompense it me with such a reward? Let thy servant, I pray thee, turn back again, that I may die in mine own city, and be buried by the grave of my father and of my mother. But behold thy servant Chimham; let him go over with my lord the king; and do to him what shall seem good unto thee. And the king answered, Chimham shall go over with me, and I will do to him that which shall seem good unto thee: and whatsoever thou shalt require of me, that will I do for thee. And all the people went over Jordan. And when the king was come over, the king kissed Barzillai, and blessed him; and he returned unto his own place. (2 Samuel 19:36-39)

David escapes Jerusalem, ahead of Absalom's army. First, he hides in the wilderness until he receives word from Zadok. Absalom is building an army to take the throne by defeating David in battle. David raises an army and divides it into three sections, with three generals to lead it. Joab, one of the generals eventually kills Absalom, contrary to specific instructions from King David not to harm him. David and his household have crossed the Jordan prior to the battle.

The battle is over. David has been informed of the victory and the loss of his son, Absalom. He is now returning to Jerusalem, the rebellion defeated, so he returns with his household back across the Jordan. On the way he meets two men, Barzillai and Chimham. Barzillai is eighty years old and laments his old age and simply wants to go home and die (19:37). Then David meets through Barzillai a man named Chimham. Now look at the attitude of Chimham. Verse 37, the tail end. *let him cross over with my lord the king, and do for him what seems good to you.* Barzillai puts his servant Chimham in David's hands and tells David, "do what seems good to you."

I have talked often about the people God puts in our lives. They pass through and most of the time seem to have little or no impact. I am wondering why God saw fit to include the story of these two men, who pass through David's life right now. They don't seem to make an impact. Yet, God saw fit to relate the story, passing through David's life on his way back to Jerusalem.

I mentioned earlier about an older gentleman who offered to sit in our children's Sunday School class to bring order. This same fellow, later, took it upon himself to sit down and write a very encouraging note. He put it in the mail. I received the note one day at home. He could have just handed it to me at church, but he mailed it. It was such a blessing at a time when I needed a blessing. I have never forgot that show of kindness and support. That may be the reason God chose to include these gentlemen here in David's story.

Did David need encouragement? Of course, he did. I just related the events above. One other reminder. When David left Jerusalem, running from Absalom, do you remember the guy who followed along for a stretch and cursed and threw stones at David? Maybe this was God's way of telling David that God was still there in his corner. That God had not given up on him. God accepted his repentance and would always be there when David sought Him.

How is your list coming? I asked earlier, to make a list of those people who have "passed" through your life. If they impacted your life their name will come to your memory. Those who encouraged you, etc. I still remember a teacher I had in 9th grade, Mrs. Stenson. I didn't know her personally, but she impacted my desire to learn, especially American history. I think we have all had teachers that made a special mark in our lives. Remember them? Write then down.

These two men in David's life might seem insignificant here. But God included them in this stage of David's life for a reason. Those who pass through your life, touch your life for a reason, they made a mark on your life. Was it a positive mark, or negative? Has God made an impact on your life? Something to think about!

Then the king went on to Gilgal, and Chimham went on with him: and all the people of Judah conducted the king, and also half the people of Israel. And, behold, all the men of Israel came to the king, and said unto the king, Why have our brethren the men of Judah stolen thee away, and have brought the king, and his household, and all David's men with him, over Jordan? And all the men of Judah answered the men of Israel, Because the king is near of kin to us: wherefore then be ye angry for this matter? Have we eaten at all of the king's cost? Or hath he given us any gift? And the men of Israel answered the men of Judah, and said, We have ten parts in the king, and we have also more right in David than ye: why then did ye despise us, that our advice should not be first had in bringing back our king? And the words of the men of Judah were fiercer than the words of the men of Israel. (2 Samuel 19:40-43)

As many times, as I have read the Bible, I missed this. Such is the miracle of Scripture. I missed the fact that the division between the Northern Tribes and the Southern two tribes begins here. The real split doesn't happen until after Solomon's reign. Solomon's son Rehoboam is confronted by the Northern tribes. They request a more peaceful relationship. Solomon's reply to the request is, it will get worse. So, the Northern ten tribes separate and become Samaria or Israel. The Southern tribes become Judah or Jerusalem. But during Solomon's reign there is peace just as God promised. Solomon is indeed allowed to build the temple.

This is funny. Is it not the way of the world today? Who is the closest to the powers that be? "He's my friend! No, he's my friend," etc. If you want to be close to the throne, consider the throne of God! What kind of relationship do you have with the King of Kings?

Now that the fighting is over. Absalom is defeated we all want credit or "let by-gone's be by-gone's" So what, if you chose to fight with Absalom, you won now we want to be on your side. I think this is so interesting. The same is true today, isn't it? Never mind what I said or did yesterday, today is what counts. I wonder how that would go over in front of God? Never mind what I did or said on earth Lord, I am here and I want in heaven, now I believe. I don't think so!

God will hold us accountable for our life on this earth. Just ask David. David paid for his sin here on earth. He made amends with God. He made mistakes, he broke fellowship with God. He never broke his relationship with God the Father. The same can be true with us. The question is, do you have a "relationship" with God? A relationship established through the shed blood of Jesus Christ on the cross of Calvary. That is the foundation of our relationship with God.

Now our fellowship with God is broken by disobedience. Much the same, as a child to his father. The child disobeys, the father corrects. Does that change the fact that he is your child? No! It doesn't change the relationship only the fellowship. They are two completely different status.

Do you remember the consequences of the ten Northern tribes? They never had a godly king. King after king rejected God. They built their idols and God eventually had them taken out of Israel through the nation of Assyria. The Southern tribes did have some godly kings. They, nevertheless, had a payment due to God. They had not let the land rest one in seven years so they built up a "past due" payment to God. God removed the Southern kingdom by way of Babylon for 70 years.

I think, if we got anything from this past chapter it should be that there are consequences for sin. It is how we deal with those consequences and how we respond to God that will determine our fellowship with God. If we have the right "relationship," to God, as our heavenly Father, we will respond accordingly. If we are not in God's family, the consequences can be dire, ask Saul and Absalom. What is your "relationship" with your heavenly Father?

2 Samuel 20

And there happened to be there a man of Belial, whose name was Sheba, the son of Bichri, a Benjamite: and he blew a trumpet, and said We have no part in David, neither have we inheritance in the son of Jesse: every man to his tents, O Israel. So every man of Israel went up from after David, and followed Sheba the son of Bichri: but the men of Judah clave unto their king, from Jordan even to Jerusalem. And David came to his house at Jerusalem; and the king took the ten women his concubines, whom he had left to keep the house, and put them in ward, and fed them, but went not in unto them. So they were shut up unto the day of their death, living in widowhood. (2 Samuel 20:1-3)

Again, a divide. Good and evil, God and the world, right and left, etc. Why must it ever be so. That is what we are dealing with in our world today. I have mentioned several times about coming to a "fork" in the road. Which way do I go? We talked about making that decision. Here is David. He no sooner, wins a victory over his own son, when this guy Sheba shows up.

Do you ever feel that way? Just when you think you are on the right track, things are going great, BOOM, here comes a road block, a stumbling block, the door is closed. You want to give up, don't you? I have worked too hard to get here, now look. Do you think that might be going through David's mind about now? Has David been here before? Yes! What was his response? Maybe we can learn from how David responded.

Do you remember a phrase we noted early in David's walk with God? "He inquired of the Lord," do you remember that phrase? I love the saying, "When life gives you lemons, make lemonade." When these road blocks show up you need to start by asking God what is going on. God may very well have sent them to change direction, get your attention, or simply get you to look up. Just a thought:

Have you considered my servant Job? (Job 1:8) (NKJV).

We need to always keep "biblical" principles in mind. God put this book and these pictures in His Word for a reason! One thing to note in the book of Job. Satan could do NOTHING except God allowed it. Oh, Satan talked a good argument, but he could do nothing that God did not allow.

So then, this thing, this obstacle in your way. What are you doing about it? What do you think David might do with Mr. Sheba? We will soon see. How did he deal with Absalom? He trusted God to bring His outcome from the situation, didn't he? He instructed his generals not to harm Absalom, did they do that? No. David will deal with that soon, as well.

I think, what I have learned in the past few years is to, WAIT! A lot of times we want to rush in and correct the situation in our own strength, in our own wisdom. That is NOT how God deals with these road blocks. Sometimes, we need to take a step back. The first thing to ask is, "What can I do to affect the outcome?" Most of the time the answer is "nothing!" I know it's hard! A lot of times if we simply step back and wait, God will work it out to our benefit. The neat thing is we will see God work! Too many times we try to fix things, when God just wants us to "watch Him work." Pray! If God lays on your heart to get involved, then ask Him what to do. Do NOTHING apart from God's leading. Remember David?

Therefore, David inquired of the Lord. (1 Samuel 23:2). (NKJV)

That should always be our first step when these "road blocks" appear. God is at work! You want to take the road God is walking on, not your own separate way!

Then said the king to Amasa, Assemble me the men of Judah within three days, and be thou here present. So Amasa went to assemble the men of Judah: but he tarried longer than the set time which he had appointed him. And David said to Abishai, Now shall Sheba the son of Bichri do us more harm than did Absalom: take thou the lord's servants, and pursue after him, lest he get him fenced cities, and escape us. And there went out after him Joab's men, and the Cherethites, and the Pelethites, and all the mighty men:

and they went out of Jerusalem, to pursue after Sheba the son of Bichri. (2 Samuel 20:4-7)

With all these names, there is a name I have not seen in a while, Nathan. The last time we saw Nathan was when he confronted David about Bathsheba. Interesting. Now they are coming at David from all sides. Amasa, Abishai, Joab, Sheba. One after another. I like this old line, "You can't tell one villain from another, without a program." Abishai, is the one I trust. The others, not so much, especially Joab. I can't figure him out. He strikes me as a guy only interested in Joab!

Notice where Amasa gathered David's troops? The men of Judah. We need to pay attention to this term. Do you remember who Judah was? Judah was the fourth son born to Jacob through Leah (Genesis 29:35). What else is significant about Judah? This is the lineage of the Messiah. Genesis 38, Ruth 4, David is from the line of Judah. It all fits together.

First, David sends Amasa to assemble the troops. Why do you suppose David said, *"within three days?"* Amasa was late so, David sent Abishai to see what was going on. It seems David is not sure who to trust around him. Joab gathers David's "mighty men" and goes after Sheba. Do you remember these guys? The same six hundred that have been with David since his problems with Saul. That is a loyal army!

I wonder if David learned a lesson from Ahithophel and Zadok? Ahithophel counseled to go right after David, pursue him immediately. Zadok cautioned that they should raise an army first. This, in order, to save David. Now, here, David says let's go now. As soon as possible, raise my army and let's go! He saw the wisdom of Ahithophel vs. Zadok. Notice his reasoning: *lest he find for himself fortified cities."* Let's get him before he can find a defensive position.

Has God ever asked you to do something and you ignored Him or put it off, delayed a response? Why? Oh, you can find all kinds of reasons, can't you? Do you think God was pleased with you ignoring Him? The interesting thing is, God will accomplish His will, whether with you or someone else. The problem is, YOU missed the blessing. If anything, the blessing of being where God wants you to be when He wants you to be there.

Another problem. If you're not where God wants you to be, God will think twice before asking you to do something else for Him. Do you remember what happened to David when he wasn't where he was supposed to be? Can you say, Bathsheba?

Did you notice the different attitude of David here? David's not running, trying to stay alive. David is back in charge, leading his people again. He has crossed the Jordan. When he crossed the other way, he was running from his son, Absalom. Now he is headed back to Jerusalem to take back his throne. He may well be in Jerusalem by now. The point is David is king again.

When we are walking with God, where we are supposed to be. When we know that God has His hand on us. Guiding, directing our steps, we are confident of His leadership in our life, we are confident and walk accordingly. When we have that intimate fellowship with God, we can be confident in our decisions, confident in our words and actions. God is in control.

When we can't feel God's presence we need to stop right there. Pray, ask God what is between us. What do I need to correct, it may be that absence, when God asked you to do something and you didn't do it? You need to restore God's confidence in you, to be obedient to the leadership of His Spirit!

When they were at the great stone which is in Gibeon, Amasa went before them. And Joab's garment that he had put on was girded unto him, and upon it a girdle with a sword fastened upon his loins in the sheath thereof; and as he went forth it fell out. And Joab said to Amasa, Art thou in health, my brother? And Joab took Amasa by the beard with the right hand to kiss him. But Amasa took no heed to the sword that was in Joab's hand: so he smote him therewith in the fifth rib. So Joab and Abishai his brother pursued after Sheba the son of Bichri. (2 Samuel 20:8-10)

Have you heard the term "inner circle"? Jesus had an "inner circle" of disciples, Peter, James and John. This James is not the one who wrote the epistle of James. The James who wrote the epistle was Jesus' half-brother. We all have an "inner circle". Those we frequently see, talk to, maybe ask counsel. Amasa, Joab, Abishai, etc, were part of David's "inner circle". They are mentioned frequently. Amasa just shows up here but he is part of David's army.

Do you think your "inner circle" says anything about you? Think about it. How much do you do as a group? Is your family included in that "inner circle"? In my family, we have two daughters. I think of the four of us as an "inner circle." We also have a group of friends at church, our "inner circle". Who is in your "inner circle"? What types of activities do you enjoy as a group.

For the most part, David's "inner circle" consists of military men, I think I mentioned earlier that we have not seen Nathan mentioned since the Bathsheba incident. This could be telling. Also, this is an example of why God did not want David to build His temple. David is a "warrior," God wanted it built during a time of peace. Interesting though, Solomon is raised in this "conflict" environment.

Many times, how we are raised causes us to rebel in later years. I think that is especially true in our concept of the church. Not always, but I have seen too many teens reject church attendance later because, "our parents made us go." Of course, their relationship with God had nothing to do with it, really?

Speaking of "inner circle" is God in your "inner circle"? Is He a part of your daily routine? Maybe you only "think" of Him on Sunday, maybe? We have degrees of circles in our life. Those we frequently talk with, eat with, fellowship with. Then there are those we see only once or twice a year. Friends, but distant, but still friends. Regularly thought of but rarely seen. Then there is that circle, mostly family, that we rarely see or hear from, maybe at funerals or weddings, etc. Where does God fit into these circles. How often do you connect with God? Is Sunday the only time you think of God?

I have talked often about a relationship and/or a fellowship with God. There is a difference. It saddens me so much to see those who walked the aisle, professed Jesus as their Savior, get baptized, then rarely enter the church again. It's like they have their ticket, that's all that matters. They have a relationship with God. They are part of the "family". They have never thought about a fellowship with God, a daily walk, having God in their "inner circle". That is such a shame. They are missing out on so much!

I question some of the individuals in David's "inner circle". They just don't seem to have David's best interest at heart. Have you noticed that since Bathsheba, David's fellowship with God has seemed to cool? Maybe it's just me. I don't seem to see the references to God as much as before. Maybe God has moved to the outer circle of David's priorities. He is no longer in the "inner circle". That is such a shame.

Just a question. Where is God? Is He in your "inner circle"?

Look at this verse in Hebrews:

> *And according to the law almost all things are purified with blood, and without the shedding of blood there is no remission of sin. (Hebrews 9:22). (NKJV)*

When Adam and Eve rebelled against God in the Garden of Eden they committed sin. That sin must be atoned for. Do you remember reading this verse in Genesis?

> *Also for Adam and his wife the Lord God made tunics of skin, and clothed them. (Genesis 3:21). (NKJV)*

Who made the tunics? God did. God provided the "sacrifice" that was required for their sin.

Wait a minute. This was long before the books of Exodus and Leviticus. The books that gave the details for the different "sacrifices" to atone for our sin. Yes! The principle was established from the very beginning. So, how does this apply to my sin? We don't make sacrifices today. How can this "blood" thing apply to me?

Take a close look at these verses in Exodus. I once asked myself, why did Jesus have to die on a cross? Look at these verses:

> *For the Lord will pass through to strike the Egyptians; and when He sees the blood on the lintel and on the two doorposts, the Lord will pass over the door and not allow the destroyer to come into your houses to strike you. (Exodus 12:23-24). (NKJV)*

One more verse here in Exodus.

> *Now the blood shall be a sign for you on the houses where you are. And when I see the blood, I will pass over you; and the plague shall not be on you to destroy you when I strike the land of Egypt. (Exodus 12:13). (NKJV)*

Both passages were a warning to Israel.

The interesting thing is, if an Egyptian believed the warning and had put the blood on their doorposts and lintel the "death angel" would have passed their home as well. If God was focused on the Egyptians he would have done it differently. Another thing, if a Jew refused, and didn't believe the warning he and his family would have died. The power is in the blood NOT who they were. The power is in faith in the warning, the faith to believe what God said!

The same is so very true today! We will all stand before God one day. That is clear in the Bible. When we stand there before God with our dollar bills dripping out of our pockets, our stacks of diplomas, God will be looking for just one thing: The blood of His Son, applied by faith in His Son, to our hearts! It's just that simple. The theme throughout the Bible: The payment for sin is blood. That is why Jesus was called "The Lamb of God" in John 1:36. The sacrifice has been made, the blood is available, you must apply it to your heart for God's judgment to "pass over" you!

A bloody passage, yes! Maybe it will remind us of the value of God's precious blood, shed by His Son, Jesus. I hope so. Never forget the price God the Father paid for your disobedience, His Son's death on the cross of Calvary allows you to come into God's presence. Best of all! This blood shed by Jesus allows us to be called "children of God". That describes our relationship to God the Father. Purely based on what Jesus Christ did on that cross in Jerusalem over two thousand years ago. You are a child of God!

And they came and besieged him in Abel of Beth-maachah, and they cast up a bank against the city, and it stood in the trench: and all the people that were with Joab battered the wall, to throw it down. Then cried a wise woman out of the city, Hear, hear, say, I pray you, unto Joab, Come near hither, that I may speak with thee. And when he was come near unto her, the woman said, Art thou Joab? And he answered, I am he. Then she said unto him, Hear the words of thine handmaid. And he answered, I do hear. Then she spake, saying, They were won't to speak in old time, saying, They shall surely ask counsel at Abel: and so they ended the matter. I am one of them that are peaceable and faithful in Israel: thou seekest to destroy a city and a mother in Israel: why wilt thou swallow up the inheritance of the

Lord? So Joab answered and said, Far be it, far be it from me, that I should swallow up or destroy. (2 Samuel 20:15-20)

That is an interesting study. I remember reading about this method in high school. When you "besiege" a city, you surround it and not allow anyone to enter or leave the city. Basically "starving" them into surrender. Joab's troops have tracked Sheba to this city. They surrounded the city, waiting for Sheba to come out.

Do you remember David's admonition earlier? Look at this verse:

> *And David said to Abishai, "Now Sheba the son of Bichri will do us more harm than Absalom. Take your lord's servants and pursue him, lest he find for himself fortified cities, and escape us." (2 Samuel 20:6)* (NKJV)

That may be the reason Joab killed Amasa when he found him. He allowed Sheba to escape. Who knows?

I think it is interesting how so many times the innocent, are caught in the sins of others. That is a sad fact of life. Remember Bathsheba?

There is an interesting comment here we might overlook. Did you notice how this woman is referred to? "Then a wise woman cried out from the city." I wonder how they knew? Remember this book is being written by God's Holy Spirit through the prophet Samuel (my guess). My Bible says: Author: unknown. Well, the author is God's Holy Spirit. He calls her a "wise woman". So, we have this woman who goes to David with a story about her son, to convict David of his treatment of Absalom. Here we have a wise woman who wishes to talk to Joab about his mission.

Wise women, beginning with our mothers, often are used by God to raise up godly children. It is the wise man who recognizes this fact in raising their family! Did you notice how many "women" are mentioned in the lineage of Jesus? Matthew 1: *Tamar,* (the mother of Perez and Zerah by Judah (Genesis 38). *Rahab,* (the lady in Jericho, that hid the spies that spied out the Promised Land for Joshua. *Ruth,* (The pagan that was in the linage to King David. Ruth 4). That is the interesting thing about each of these women. ALL were Gentiles, pagans Yet God included them in His lineage. Important to note!

For me, it was my godly grandmother. Don't misunderstand me. My grandmother was far from perfect, she had her mistakes. My grandmother, as far back as I can remember, made it a point that her grandchildren were going to church on Easter. The only exposure we had to church and the gospel message. Our parents didn't go. She also encouraged me later as I was saved and went into the ministry.

I know, if you have heard any messages on Mother's Day you have this passage:

> When I call to remembrance the genuine faith that is in you, which dwelt first in your grandmother Lois and your mother Eunice, and I am persuaded is in you also. (2 Timothy 1:5). (NKJV)

God is always using godly women to reach the next generation with the gospel of salvation through Jesus our Lord!

Another one of those people who pass through our lives and tend to leave a mark that will last a lifetime. Are there any women impacting your life right now? Pray for them!

The matter is not so: but a man of mount Ephraim, Sheba the son of Bichri by name, hath lifted up his hand against the king, even against David: deliver him only, and I will depart from the city. And the woman said unto Joab, Behold, his head shall be thrown to thee over the wall. Then the woman went unto all the people in her wisdom. And they cut off the head of Sheba the son of Bichri, and cast it out to Joab. And he blew a trumpet, and they retired from the city, and every man to his tent. And Joab returned to Jerusalem unto the king. (2 Samuel 20:21-22)

"The woman in her wisdom." Did you catch that? What an awesome description. The book of Proverbs has so much to say about knowledge and wisdom. Just to refresh your memory. The difference between knowledge and wisdom: Wisdom is the correct application of knowledge. I have said this many times. I have known people with a wall full of degrees and not a lick of "common" sense. This lady recognized the situation and notice she *"went to the people."* Notice, it seems she was the spokesperson for her city.

Do you know the difference between wisdom and knowledge? It has been said, and I totally agree, that a person can miss heaven by eighteen inches. The difference between the head and the heart. I know you might get tired of hearing that. Most of the time the person who uses that logic doesn't know how flawed it is. You can be a Bible scholar, a professor of Biblical studies, and miss heaven. It's not much you know, it's who you know.

This concludes another sordid tale. I do not care for Mr. Joab. there is nothing I can put my finger on. I don't want to focus on him. He really reminds me of King Saul. There just seems to be no connection with God in his life and conduct. I could do some research and note how many he has killed. Let's just say, David needs to take inventory of his "friends".

I guess it is one thing to know the right thing to do, still another to do it. I guess that's where wisdom comes in. Let's try this verse in Proverbs:

> *The fear of the Lord is the beginning of knowledge, but fools despise wisdom and instruction. (Proverbs 1:7).* (NKJV)

We talked before about the meaning of the term, "fear of the Lord." It's not fear as we know it, it's more of a "reverence" if you substitute "reverence" for fear it would make more sense. Look at the last part of that verse: *fools despise wisdom and instruction.* Is that the attitude of the "knowledgeable"? Those who have all this book learning but can't change a light bulb.

What is your attitude toward old people? Do you discount their "wisdom"? I hope not. That would include the wisdom of your parents. I learned the hard way to pay attention to the wisdom of your elders. I even told my dad once, "I am going to do what I want, but I would like your opinion." I could kick myself now. Thank heaven I don't remember what it was about. That is such a foolish attitude, but, it very well could be the attitude today.

They have the Internet, Facebook, Twitter, etc. Really? Have you ever "fact-checked" anything you read on those web-sights? Of course, we Googled it! Really? What is your source for information? I just quoted a verse from Proverbs. Have you ever read any of Proverbs? Let me encourage you to take a few minutes and read through the book of Ecclesiastes. Solomon, had all the wealth he could possibly want. He had four-hundred wives. If you read the book you will see his attempt to "try" everything under the sun. He had the ability to try everything that came to his mind. In chapter 12, he came to this conclusion:

Let us hear the conclusion of the whole matter: Fear God and keep His commandments, for this is man's all. For God will bring every work into judgment, including every secret thing, whether good or bad. (Ecclesiastes 12:13-14). (NKJV)

Wisdom, I believe, is a gift from God. Every day I pray, I ask God for His wisdom to do what God wants me to do. Look at one more verse:

If any man lacks wisdom, let him ask of God, who gives to all liberally and without reproach, and it will be given him. (James 1:5). (NKJV)

Wisdom is born of experience and walking with God!

2 SAMUEL 21

Then there was a famine in the days of David three years, year after year; and David enquired of the Lord. And the Lord answered, It is for Saul, and for his bloody house, because he slew the Gibeonites. And the king called the Gibeonites, and said unto them; (now the Gideonites were not of the children of Israel, but of the remnant of the Amorites; and the children of Israel had sworn unto them: and Saul sought to slay them in his zeal to the children of Israel and Judah.) Wherefore David said unto the Gibeonites, What shall I do for you? And wherewith shall I make atonement, that ye may bless the inheritance of the Lord? (2 Samuel 21:1-3)

The Gibeonites. In Joshua 9, the Gibeonites came to Joshua just after Israel had defeated Ai. They dressed like they had come from a far country. Joshua signed a treaty with them. Look at these two verses:

> Then the men of Israel took some of their provisions; **but they did not ask counsel of the Lord**. So, Joshua made peace with them, and made a covenant with them to let them live; and the rulers of the congregation swore to them. (Joshua 9:14-15). (NKJV)

Later, when Israel found out who they were, they were put into bondage. While Saul was chasing David, some priests provided aid to David (1 Samuel 21:6). In First Samuel 22, the priests of Gibeon were murdered by Saul's army for helping David.

God revealed to David that this famine is the result of what Saul did to these priests. It has been awhile since we have seen these words from David, *David inquired of the Lord*. That is so encouraging. For one thing, it means that God has not taken His hand off of David. It also means David still has fellowship with God the Father.

David has been through some trying times these last few years. Absalom, Amnon, Tamar, Joab, Amasa, etc. Ever since Bathsheba, David has been wrestling with "life". Have you been there? Does it seem like forever since you and God had a conversation? That is assuming you have asked Jesus into your heart and you are a child of God. If you haven't done that, that must be the first step. The only thing God will hear from an unbeliever is "Lord, save me!" That must be the first step.

Did you catch the scenario here? God brings a famine. David asks God, why? God reveals a sin that has not been addressed. David addresses the sin. Mark that process down. When you are going through a storm, a trial, the first thing you must do is seek God. Is there something that God is trying to correct? Maybe there is danger up ahead and God is trying to get you to change course. Ask Him!

Next, there may be something that needs to be corrected. Offended someone, took something that didn't belong to you, anything that hinders your fellowship with God. It must be corrected. Have you noticed how many times God uses "famines" to lead someone, or get their attention? What might be the equivalent today? Loss of income? Disease? Hospitalized? God has so many ways of getting our attention. The thing is, are you listening? Do you chalk it up to "bad luck" I hope not!

It would seem David has "re-connected" with God. God hasn't gone anywhere, but David has lost his focus, his direction, his reliance on God's leadership. It is so easy to do today. We must work daily on our fellowship with our heavenly Father!

And the Gibeonites said unto him, We will have no silver nor gold of Saul, nor of his house; neither for us shalt thou kill any man in Israel. And he said, What ye shall say, that will I do. And they answered the king, The man that consumed us, and devised against us that we should be destroyed from remaining in any of the coasts of Israel, Let seven men of his sons be delivered unto us, and we will hang them up unti the Lord in Gibeah of Saul, whom the Lord did choose. And the king said, I will give them. (2 Samuel 21:4-6)

Thank God for the cross! Talk about a "blood" sacrifice. Notice this passage in First Samuel:

> And the king said to Doeg, "You turn and kill the priests!"
> So Doeg the Edomite turned and struck the priests, and
> killed on that day eighty-five men who wore the linen
> ephod. (1 Samuel 22:18) (NKJV)

These priests were Gibeonites. Under Saul's reign this event happened. Can you blame the Gibeonites for wanting revenge?

Maybe you wonder why I said, "Thank God for the cross?" The cross is God's way of achieving what David must deal with here. Sin's payment. God has paid for our sin on the cross of Calvary. I am not sure I am getting across what I want. We talked about the "Cities of Refuge" and the "Avenger of Blood" in the Levitical law. This was set up to save innocent lives. Six cities were established in the Promised Land as "Cities of Refuge.

> "Now among the cities which you shall give the Levites
> (42) you shall appoint six cities of refuge, to which the
> manslayer may flee. And to these you shall add forty-two
> cities (Numbers 35:6). (NKJV)

The Levites were given forty-eight cities in the Promised Land, since the tribe of Levi received no inheritance. Of those forty-eight, six were set aside as cities of refuge.

Numbers 35 gives the details. The point being, we have no need of such things in the New Testament. Christ is our refuge. When we have sinned, we can go to Him for an advocate between us and God. If we are a child of God, Jesus will present our case before God. God will then determine the sentence. I have pointed out before—there are consequences to sin! Look at this verse in First John:

> My little children, these things I write to you, so that you
> may not sin. And if anyone sins, we have an advocate with
> the Father, Jesus Christ the righteous. (1 John 2:1). (NKJV)

Here, the Gibeonites come to David as their advocate. David is to right a wrong done by Saul in 1 Samuel 22. It is interesting to me what we think we can get away with. This is over forty years later. Remember after David sent for Absalom, Absalom came to Jerusalem, just before he rebelled against the king.

> *Now it came to pass after forty years that Absalom said to the king, "Please let me go to Hebron and pay a vow which I made to the Lord." (2 Samuel 15:7) (NKJV)*

This is a key verse to keep in mind as to the time frame we are looking at.

God has no time limit on making things right. Just when we think we have gotten away with some sin, God chooses the right time and the right circumstance to make things right. We need to walk close with the Lord and be aware of things that will displease God. Of course, as we noted above, we have a Lawyer pleading our case before God. The neat thing about our Lawyer is that He is related to the Judge. I like the odds!

Not to miss the fact that the payment for this atrocity is "blood". Notice what the Gibeon's said in verse 4: *And the Gibeonites said to him, "We will have no silver or gold from Saul or from his house...."* Nothing but the blood! God established that price in the Garden of Eden. He could have allowed Adam and Eve to leave the garden in their "fig leaves". But that was insufficient! The theme carries throughout the Bible, all the way to the cross.

It is so important that we make a special effort to walk daily with God our Father. Walk together on this path of life. Seeking His guidance and direction!

But the king spared Mephibosheth, the son of Jonathan the son of Saul, because of the Lord's oath that was between them, between David and Jonathan the son of Saul. But the king took the two sons of Rizpah the daughter of Aiah, whom she bare unto Saul, Armoni and Mephibosheth: and the five sons of Michal the daughter of Saul, whom she brought up for Adriel the son of Barzillai the Meholathite. And he delivered them into the hands of the Gibeonites, and they hanged them in the hill before the Lord: and they fell all seven together and were put to death in the days of harvest in the first days, in the beginning of barley harvest. (2 Samuel 21:7-9)

Does the name Michal sound familiar?

> *Then David returned to bless his household. And Michal the daughter of Saul came out to meet David, and said, "How glorious was the king of Israel today, uncovering himself today in the eyes of the maids of his servants, as one of the base fellows shamelessly uncovers himself!" (1 Samuel 6:20).* (NKJV)

One more verse:

> *Therefore, Michal the daughter of Saul had no children to the day of her death. (1 Samuel 6:23).* (NKJV)

Look at these verses:

> *So, David sent messengers to Ishbosheth, Saul's son, saying, "Give me my wife Michal, whom I betrothed to myself for a hundred foreskins of the Philistines." And Ishbosheth sent and took her from her husband, from Paltiel the son of Laish. (2 Samuel 3:14-15).* (NKJV)

Michal had no children by David but she was "married" to another guy before David sent for her.

Interesting that the Gibeonites request "seven' men to pay for what Saul's men did, namely Doeg. (1 Samuel 22:18).

Why do you suppose the writer made such a point to mention the harvest time? Remember what brought this all about? 21:1a, *Now, there was a famine in the days of David for three years.*

There was a famine. What better time to make things right with God than at harvest time.

There is something else here, I think, that shows why David was a man after God's own heart. Did you notice, *because of the Lord's oath between them, between David and Jonathan.* David made an oath to Jonathan that David would not destroy the line of Saul through Jonathan. That is why God spared Mephibosheth. David kept his promise to his friend.

This isn't the first time David needs to atone for a mistake in judgment.

Not to mention Bathsheba. There is a census coming up that cost Israel greatly. Let me just say, "consequences!"

Someone remarked in our Sunday School class, "Why can't these guys have names like, George, Frank, or Steve? The obvious answer is that they are Jews. I think it's interesting that most of the time when they give a person's name they link them someway with a father, son, daughter, etc. They just don't use their name they give their lineage. I am Lonny son of Earl, son of Charles, etc. Interesting.

Do you have any loose ends in your life? Maybe someone you have wronged, spoke evil of, cheated, etc. I mentioned earlier that this episode goes back over forty years. There are some things I wish I could apologize to my parents for, both are deceased now. It's too late in this life. That is sad. When I was younger I made so many mistakes, mostly out of ignorance, but that is no excuse. Have you burned any bridges you wish you had not? Just saying.

David, here, makes amends for a wrong done to the Gibeonites over forty years ago. Don't forget what else is said in the first verse of this chapter. We talked about the famine, look at David's response: *And David inquired of the Lord. And the Lord answered.* (21:1). Did you catch the fact that God responded to David's inquiry?

Take a minute now, ask God if there is anything in your past that is "undone". Is there some unfinished business with someone that needs to be dealt with? God will lay them on your heart. Then it is up to you to resolve the situation. If not possible, lift them in prayer, and yourself as well.

Now Rizpah the daughter of Aiah took sackcloth and spread it for herself on the rock, from the beginning of harvest until the late rains poured on them from heaven. And she did not allow the birds of the air to rest on them by day nor the beasts of the field by night. And David was told what Rizpah the daughter of Aiah, the concubine of Saul, had done. Then David went and took the bones of Saul, and the bones of Jonathan his son, from the men of Jabesh Gilead who had stolen them from the street of Beth Shan, where the Philistines had hung them up, after the Philistines had struck down Saul in Gilboa. So, he brought up the bones of Saul and the bones of Jonathan his son from there; and they gathered the bones of those who had been hanged. They buried the bones of Saul and Jonathan his son in the country of Benjamin in Zelah, in the tomb of Kish, his father. So, they performed all that the king commanded. And after that God heeded the prayer for the land. (2 Samuel 21:10-14) (NKJV)

Is this not a great picture? David is bringing closure to some bad memories for Saul's family. He brought the bones of Saul, Jonathan and those of his relatives that were hung, all together and gave them their final resting place. The Philistines thought they had a victory by desecrating Saul's remains. David got the final victory!

The final resting place. What a thought. Let me contribute a beautiful verse if I may.

> So, we are always confident, knowing that while we are at home in the body we are absent from the Lord. For we walk by faith, not by sight. We are confident, yes, well pleased rather to be absent from the body and to be present with the Lord. (2 Corinthians 5:6-8). (NKJV)

Do you remember what Jesus said to the thief being crucified next to Him on the cross?

> "Assuredly, I say to you, today you will be with Me in Paradise." (Luke 23:43). (NKJV)

It is great that David gathered the bones of Saul's family. They are already in heaven. We can only hope that Saul was reunited with his family. The point being, this is a wonderful promise God gives each of His children. "To be absent from the body is to be present with the Lord." That is one the great promises we have as God's children.

Remember, Kish is Saul's father. This is a family tomb. David has reunited Saul's family. And they are also buried with their grandfather, Kish. I know it can be hard sometimes, but when was the last time you visited the graveside of a loved one? We like to shy away from those memories don't we. They are simply reminders of those who have gone on before us.

I love this picture in Hebrews:

> Therefore, we also, since we are surrounded by so great a cloud of witnesses, let us lay aside every weight, and

the sin which so easily ensnares us, and let us run with endurance the race that is set before us. (Hebrews 12:1). (NKJV)

One year, I was able to borrow some posters of past missionaries. I put them up on both sides of the sanctuary. Then I preached a series on Hebrews 11, The Hall of Faith chapter in Hebrews. A reminder of those who had gone on before us. They didn't have to be missionaries, but those who lived their Christian life making a difference in someone else's life.

After what God had led David to do for Saul's family, this was a time to bring his family together. To show them that God cares about them. David, being the catalyst to bring peace and a conclusion to Saul's resting place. I know he blessed his family and especially Rizpah, who was grieving the loss of her family members.

What can you do for someone grieving? Just be there! Do what you can to bring comfort. Remember 2 Corinthians 1:3-6. This was a great picture in David's life. I doubt it went unnoticed by his army, friends, and those gathered. I sense that David is gradually reconnecting with God. He is restoring his fellowship with the One who called David, "A man after My own heart."

When the Philistines were at war again with Israel, David and his servants with him went down and fought against the Philistines, and David grew faint. Then Ishbi-benob, who was one of the sons of the giant, the weight of whose bronze spear was three hundred shekels, who was bearing a new sword, thought he could kill David. But Abishai the son of Zeruiah came to his aid, and struck the Philistine and killed him. Then the men of David swore to him, saying, "You shall go out no more with us to battle, lest you quench the lamp of Israel." (2 Samuel 21:15-17) (NKJV)

At this point I am assuming David is getting along in years. I mentioned before, when there is a battle David is determined to lead. He learned his lesson with Bathsheba. Here is another example. His men recognize his condition. Guess who the enemy is? You guessed it, the Philistines. It's like a bad cold that won't go away.

Is there a sin in your life that you can't seem to get a victory over? You fight, and pray, and ask God, it just won't go away. I know someone else who had to deal with something in his life. Many think it was a physical ailment, I'm sure that was the case. But look at this:

> And lest I should be exalted above measure by the abundance of the revelations, a thorn in the flesh was given to me, a messenger of Satan to buffet me, lest I be exalted above measure. (2 Corinthians 12:7). (NKJV)

Did you notice the author of this affliction? Satan. The Apostle Paul, who God has blessed beyond measure, was afflicted with "something" that would keep him humble.

Do you remember the opening of the book of Job? Do you remember that Satan could do "nothing" to Job other than what God would allow? God "allowed" this thorn in Paul for a purpose! We all need to be humbled occasionally. In the book of Acts Paul gives his testimony at least three different occasions. Do you remember how Saul of Tarsus was saved? That would be something to boast about, would it not? God took care of that.

God will always assist you! Ishbi-benob was there, saw the need and jumped in. Now remember this is the same type of giant that David faced in 1 Samuel 17. He was dealt with as well. I learned the hard way, you don't have to fight all your battles by yourself. I heard the funniest illustration once. This person believes we have two guardian angels. Their names are "goodness" and "mercy". Look at this verse in the Psalms:

> Surely goodness and mercy shall follow me all the days of my life; and I will dwell in the house of the Lord forever. (Psalm 23:6). (NKJV)

There is also a Baptist hymn that uses these words. Make of it what you want.

I think it is funny that they describe Goliath the same way. By the weight of his weapons. Really? I guess that is impressive. Of course, David used a sling and a stone. That's how God works. One of my favorite verses is in 1 Corinthians:

> But God has chosen the foolish things of the world to put to shame the wise, and God has chosen the weak things of the world to put to shame the things which are mighty. (1 Corinthians 1:27). (NKJV)

Does that not describe David and Goliath?

What about you? Are you wrestling with a huge problem? Have you asked God? Have you turned it over to God? Why not? Oh, I know, it's beyond God's ability. You need to handle this yourself. One of the most frustrating things for me, as a Christian, is how believers put God in a box! If you can't figure it out, it can't be fixed. God is "limited" by your faith. You need to spend more time in the Gospels. Notice how much Jesus praises faith, and chastises His disciples for their "lack" of faith. Jesus puts tremendous stock in a person's faith. How much are they willing to "trust" God?

Maybe some of David's faith rubbed off on Ishbi-benob. He took on the giant, just as David did. Maybe not with a sling and a stone but he was willing to take him on. Maybe he heard the exploits of David.

Now it happened afterward that there was again a battle with the Philistines at Gob. Then Sibbechai the Hushathite killed Saph, who was one of the sons of the giant. Again, there was war at Gob with the Philistines, where Elhanan the son of Jaare-Oregim the Bethlehemite killed the brother of Goliath the Gittite, the shaft of whose spear was like a weaver's beam. Yet again there was war at Gath, where there was a man of great stature, who had six fingers on each hand and six toes on each foot, twenty-four in number; and he also was born to the giant. So, when he defied Israel, Jonathan the son of Shimea, David's brother, killed him. These four were born to the giant in Gath, and fell by the hand of David and by the hand of his servants. (2 Samuel 21:18-22) (NKJV)

Let me refresh your memory about something very early in David's story:

> Then he (David) took his staff in his hand; and he chose for himself **five** smooth stones from the brook, and he put them in his shepherd's bag, in a pouch which he had, and his sling was in his hand. And he drew near to the Philistine. (1 Samuel 17:40). (NKJV)

Do you remember? Have you ever heard any comments about WHY five stones? In my Bible, next to this verse I noted this verse:

These four were born to the giant in Gath, and fell by the hand of David and by the hand of his servants. (2 Samuel 21:22) (NKJV)

David was ready and willing to take on Goliath's whole family!

Ishbi-benob, Saph, 24 digits, Goliath, and another not named. The point being, again, David was prepared to take on FIVE giants! Here his army helped, but in the beginning, it was just David and the giant (Goliath) and his sons.

One of my favorite authors wrote a chapter on these five stones. Each was given a Christian characteristic. If I may, I would like to give my own version.: Stone #1: Relationship. I have explained earlier but I want to make myself clear. Sometimes I will enter-change the two words, Relationship and fellowship. Relationship refers to the act of becoming a child of God. I refer you to Romans:

For you did not receive the spirit of bondage again to fear, but you received the Spirit of adoption by whom we cry out, "Abba, Father" (Romans 8:15) (NKJV)

When we have opened our heart and asked Jesus to come in and save us, we become children of God. NOTHING can dissolve that "relationship."

Stone #2: Fellowship. We cannot break that relationship, but we CAN break our fellowship. This will not keep us out of heaven but we will no longer have God's hand on our life. God will not be walking with us on this path He has for us. Much like David did with Bathsheba. David broke "fellowship" with his heavenly Father, but not his relationship! I hope you understand!

Stone #3: The Holy Spirit. When we become children of God, we receive the Holy Spirit who will dwell within every believer. He will guide us, instruct us, and He also brings a spiritual gift. Look what Jesus said in John:

And I will pray the Father, and He will give you another Helper (Holy Spirit), that He may abide with you FOREVER—the Spirit of truth, whom the world cannot receive, because it neither sees Him nor knows Him; but

you know Him, for He dwells with you and will be in you.
(John 15:16-17). (NKJV)

Stone #4: The Word of God. This is critical. Through the guidance of the Holy Spirit when you open and read the Word of God you get to know your heavenly Father more intimately. Through reading how God responds to situations in the Bible, especially watching the works of His Son Jesus. You will discover how God thinks and his priorities.

Stone #5: His church. You thought I was going to say prayer, didn't you? Prayer is part of maintaining that fellowship, reading His word, etc. The church is so important in improving our walk with God. We must have the support and encouragement of fellow believers. (Hebrews 10:25). Sunday is a natural part of that worship experience. It helps us each week to remember God has a purpose for our lives and helps to maintain that fellowship!

2 SAMUEL 22

Then David spoke to the Lord the words of this song, on the day when the Lord had delivered him from the hand of all his enemies, and from the hand of Saul. And he said:

The Lord is my rock and my fortress and my deliverer; The God of my strength, in whom I will trust; My shield and the horn of my salvation, my stronghold and my refuge; My Savior, You save me from violence. I will call upon the Lord, who is worthy to be praised; So, shall I be saved from my enemies. (2 Samuel 22:1-4) (NKJV)

Interesting. This is only the second psalm from David in this narrative (1 & 2 Samuel). We meet David in the sixteen chapter for First Samuel. After Saul's death David relates his first psalm in this narrative. (2 Samuel 1). Now, after God has given David, finally, complete victory over the Philistines, David shares another psalm. Remember these "psalms" are Hebrew songs.

My study Bible says David is credited with 73 psalms of the 150 in the book of Psalms. Almost half of these beautiful songs of praise are attributed to David. Can you see it? In the verses above, David has renewed his fellowship with God. It has been a long road from Bathsheba to this point. I don't think God ever lost his "trust" in David. It was David who took a separate road from God, when he had Uriah killed. From then on, it seemed God just waited at that fork in the road until David returned to Him.

Let's see, when does David first encounter the Philistines? You know, with a fellow named Goliath. 1 Samuel 16, David is bringing lunch to his brothers on the battlefield, under King Saul. You remember the story! God so blessed David from then until he wasn't where he was supposed to be. He should have been on the battlefield with his troops. Instead, he arose one night and saw Bathsheba bathing. That event broke the fellowship David had with God. Ten months later (more or less), Nathan, by direction from God, confronted David about his sin, including the arranged death of Uriah, Bathsheba's husband.

In these first few verses David is acknowledging the power and strength of God. God had just given him a huge victory over a longtime enemy. This will go a long way to establishing the peace in Israel that God required for Solomon to build Gods temple. Just a note. You might want to take a minute and read Psalm 51. Many believe this psalm was written around the time, or just after the whole Bathsheba affair. Take a minute and see if you can see David's heart in that psalm.

What about you? Is there something between you and God? Have you taken a separate road than the one God wants you on? Did you leave God at the crossroad and taken your own road? Do you feel God's presence in your life? Why not? First you need to pray and ask God to show you where He is at. Maybe God asked you to do something you didn't think you could do. Maybe God told you NOT to do something, you went on and did anyway. Anything that defies God's will, neglects His leadership, can cause a silence between you and God. Don't let it linger, return to that fork in the road where you left God.

Look at this verse,

> *When the Philistines were at war with Israel, David and his servants with him went down and fought against the Philistines; and David grew faint. (2 Samuel 21:15). (NKJV)*

We are nearing the end of David's reign. He is much older than when he fought Goliath. This is a precious psalm. Spend some time and meditate on the words!

When the waves of death surrounded me, the floods of ungodliness made me afraid. The sorrows of Sheol surrounded me; the snares of death confronted me. In my distress, I called upon the Lord, and cried out to my God; He heard my voice from His temple, and my cry entered His ears. (2 Samuel 22:5-7) (NKJV)

In case you're wondering, I think David knows a little about death. Do you remember this verse?

> "But now he is dead; why should I fast? Can I bring him back again? I shall go to him, but he shall not return to me. (2 Samuel 12:23). (NKJV)

This was David's comment after the death of his child born to Bathsheba. David understood about death. Do you?

It is such an "avoided" subject. That's a shame. As a Christian, it is probably one the best subjects to get someone to grapple with the hereafter. I have said before, one of the best places to give the gospel message is at a funeral. The attention of those attending is on "death."

You do know, when we are created by God in the womb of our mother, we will live forever? Every person that God creates has a purpose, God established your purpose from the beginning. The only question you must answer in this life is, "Where will I spend that eternity?" There are two options. One of course is to spend that time in heaven with God. I love the last line of "Amazing Grace." "When we've been there ten thousand years, bright shining as the sun. We've no less days to sing God's praise, than when we first begun." Just a picture of "eternity".

Of course, there is the alternative. It's called Hades. The Bible says that Hades was prepared for the devil and his angels. Hades was NOT prepared for God's creation, meaning us. But, if we choose to reject the offer of God's Son as our Savior, we have then decided to reject heaven as well. God has given us a gift to allow us to enter heaven, imperfections and all. You know this verse:

> For God so loved the world that He gave His only begotten Son, that whoever believes in Him should not perish but have everlasting life. (John 3:16). (NKJV)

Did you catch those last words? "Everlasting life" that means eternity!

Did you notice that this psalm was not written at someone's funeral? David is celebrating his victory over the Philistines. In a sense, he may be celebrating God's victory over death. If I may, one more verse:

*O death, where is your sting? O Hades, where is your
victory? The sting of death is sin, and the strength of sin
is the law. But thanks be to God, who gives us the victory
through our Lord Jesus Christ. (1 Corinthians 15:55-57).
(NKJV)*

David's confidence of where he would spend eternity is in his relationship
with God the Father. Do you remember, when he was first anointed by
Samuel from the shepherd's field, it says?

*Then Samuel took the horn of oil and anointed him in the
midst of his brothers; and the Spirit of the Lord came upon
David from that day forward. So, Samuel arose and went
to Ramah. (1 Samuel 16:13). (NKJV)*

We have the same promise and the same "seal" for our salvation, the
Holy Spirit. I know I said one more verse, I lied!

Do you fear that moment when God's time for you has run out? As a
Christian, that ought not be so. As a child of God, we have the promise from
God, that to be absent from the body is to be present with the Lord! There
should be a peace in our soul about that day. Look at this verse:

*Now He who has prepared us for this very thing is God,
who also has given us the Spirit as a guarantee. So, we
are always confident, knowing that while we are at home
in the body we are absent from the Lord. For we walk by
faith, not by sight. We are confident, yes, well pleased
rather to be absent from the body and to be present with
the Lord. (2 Corinthians 5:5-8). (NKJV)*

Do you have that Spirit of confidence? Why not?

Most of us avoid this subject. Well and good, if you have made
arrangements with Almighty God. Have you accepted Jesus Christ as your
Savior? Better think about it.

Then the earth shook and trembled; the foundations of heaven quaked
and were shaken, because He was angry. Smoke went up from His nostrils,
and devouring fire from His mouth; coals were kindled by it. He bowed
the heavens also, and came down with darkness under His feet. He rode

upon a Cherub, and flew; and He was seen upon the wings of the wind. He made darkness canopies around Him, dark waters and thick clouds of the skies. From the brightness before Him coals of fire were kindled. (2 Samuel 22:8-13) (NKJV)

Do you see the contrast? David, a warrior, is describing the God of the Old Testament. Mount Sinai, the burning bush, the destruction of Jericho, the parting of the Red Sea, etc. The Old Testament prophets talking about God's judgment on Israel. David gives us that picture here in his psalm. The psalm of victory over the Philistines. David could relate! David understood this kind of God.

Of course, we do see glimpses of a kinder God through the Old Testament, for the most part this is the God we recognize in the Old Testament. You might also remember this God in the book of Revelation. It's judgment time! Not just Israel but for the whole world. The reason I bring this up is to contrast the "God" of the Old Testament with the "God" of the New Testament. Both the SAME God! Don't miss this!

I love these words, a little confusing but SO profound:

> *In the beginning was the Word, and the Word was with God, and the Word was God. He was in the beginning with God. All things were made through Him, and without Him nothing was made that was made. (John 1:1-3). (NKJV)*

Now look at this verse:

> *And the Word became flesh and dwelt among us. (John 1:14). (NKJV)*

Without verse fourteen, the previous verses might not make sense. Basically, God became flesh and visited His creation. Don't miss that!

The reason I want to point this out, I believe God gave us a "picture" of two personalities. I told you about the Old Testament. THE SAME GOD visited us in the person of Jesus Christ. Please! Don't miss that. It wasn't two separate God's. John 1:1-3. God is judgment AND He is also love. A good picture is the epistle of First John. Even in John 3:16, *"For God so loved the world. . . "*God loves us so much that in order to keep us out of Hades, God was willing to allow His Son to die on the cross of Calvary just so we could establish a relationship with God Almighty!

God gave us the option, but it is up to us to receive or accept it. Again, don't mistake the gentle Jesus for He is the God of the Old Testament as well. Don't forget this same "gentle" Jesus is the one who authorized the 21 plaques in the book of Revelation. It is Jesus who opens the seal and releases the judgments.

> *So, I wept much, because no one was found worthy to open and read the scroll, or to look at it. But one of the elders said to me, "Do not weep. Behold, the Lion of the tribe of Judah, the Root of David, has prevailed to open the scroll and to lose its seven seals". And they sang a new song, saying: "You are worthy to take the scroll, and to open its seals; For You were slain, and have redeemed us to God by Your blood out of every tribe and tongue and people and nation, and have made us kings and priests to our God; and we shall reign on the earth." (Revelation 5:4-5,9-10). (NKJV)*

Don't think I am talking about two Gods. Almighty God and Jesus are one and the same God. God simply took a different tact in the New Testament. Jesus also did miracles, but miracles of healing, and casting out demons, etc. God wanted to show us that the Old Testament God was more than just fire and brimstone. God did many loving acts in the Old Testament, but it seems we have a "mighty warrior" picture of God, much as David presented. That is the picture David is giving us here. David also knew the softer side of God when he spared his life. How do you perceive God? Are you walking with the God of the universe today?

The Lord thundered from heaven, and the Most High uttered His voice. He sent out arrows and scattered them; lightning bolts, and He vanquished them. Then the channels of the sea were seen, the foundations of the world were uncovered, at the rebuke of the Lord, at the blast of the breath of His nostrils. (2 Samuel 22:14-16) (NKJV)

Did you notice the reference in these verses? "The channels of the sea" God thousands of years before explorers discovered currents in the seas, God made note of it. Columbus used charts of these currents to find America. Here is another quote:

> *It is He who sits above the circle of the earth, and its inhabitants are like grasshoppers. (Isaiah 40:22a)* (NKJV)

Thousands of years before man "discovered" that the earth wasn't flat, God wrote it in His word. Just saying!

David understood the power of God. David didn't put God in a box. In his psalms, he recognizes the awesome power of God. When David was walking with God, he recognized where the victories came from. Where the power came from.

How about you? To what do you attribute your blessings? Luck, happenstance, right place, right time, providence? If you are walking with God, you have no problem recognizing God's hand in your blessings. How do you think God feels, when He blesses you with a healthy child and you give all the praise to your doctor or your genes? That's sad. When you get up in the morning you should thank God you have another day to witness His miracles! David knew!

I touched on this before. I see it a lot today. A total lack of faith. I describe it as putting God in a box. That is, He can do no more than what we can grasp. If we can't figure it out, God can't do it. Have you seen the efforts to explain the parting of the Red Sea? How about Jesus feeding five thousand? If we can destroy these miracles then we have succeeded in putting God in a box. Do you have an issue you are praying about? Have you told God how He could accomplish it? I hope not! Because God will accomplish His perfect will in an extra-ordinary way to prove He can do it.

God is always trying to show Himself to us, in ways that only He can. I am sure there are things that happened in your life you can't explain. Think about it a minute. You might want to write them down. They will help your faith!

Let me share a couple of verses:

> *But they constrained Him, saying, "Abide with us, for it is toward evening, and the day is far spent." And He went in to stay with them. Now it came to pass, as He sat at the table with them, that He took bread, blessed and broke*

it, and gave it to them. Then their eyes were opened and
they knew Him; and He vanished from their sight. And they
said to one another, "Did not our heart burn within us while
He talked with us on the road, and while He opened the
Scriptures to us?" (Luke 24:29-32) (NKJV)

I love this story. God was walking with them and they didn't even realize
it until He left. God may have visited you. Would you recognize Him?
Here is another favorite:

Then He said to Thomas, "Reach your finger here, and
look at My hands; and reach your hand here, and put it
into My side. Do not be unbelieving, but believing." And
Thomas answered and said to Him, "My Lord and my
God!" Jesus said to him, "Thomas, because you have
seen Me, you have believed. Blessed are those who have
not seen and yet have believed." (John 20:27-29) (NKJV)

Another awesome illustration.

It has become my practice during the week between Christmas and
New Years to reflect on the past year and remember, with the help of a
journal, what God has done in the past year. Most importantly to look
forward to what God is going to do in the New Year. We should, daily, look
forward to what God is going to do each day. God desires to make Himself
known to us every day. It strengthens our faith and encourages our daily
walk with Him.

He sent from above, He took me, He drew me out of many waters. He
delivered me from my strong enemy, from those who hated me; for they
were too strong for me. They confronted me in the day of my calamity, but
the Lord was my support. He also brought me out into a broad place; He
delivered me because He delighted in me. (2 Samuel 22:17-20) (NKJV)

Do you see where David is coming from? Think about the scenario I
have been putting forth. We need to walk this path with the Lord. David
did great at first. When Samuel called David out of the shepherd's field,
anointed him, the Lord and David walked this same path. God blessed him,

protected him. David, when in doubt, "inquired of the Lord." They were both on the same path.

Then one night the Lord goes to battle with the troops. David takes a different fork. He stays home and sees Bathsheba. To compound the situation, he takes an even worse path and has Uriah, Bathsheba's husband, killed. At this point David is so far off the path that it cost him dearly, for years.

After the death of Absalom, we see David finding his way back on the path that God was walking. Look at this verse:

> Then the king said to Zadok, "Carry the ark of God back into the city. If I find favor in the eyes of the Lord, He will bring me back and show me both it and His dwelling place." (2 Samuel 15:25) (NKJV)

I believe this is where David met up with God on the right path. David had put his life back in God's hands. I believe this is the first mention, since his confession to Nathan, that David acknowledges his trust in the Lord.

Did you catch the last part of the verses above? *He delivered me because He delighted in me.* The fellowship has been restored. I think what David did with the Gibeonites also helped. It is a tough thing to realize that you have traveled so far down this path and God has left you at the fork. Sometimes it's tough to find your way back. David had the Holy Spirit within him to guide him back to where he left God.

"He delivered me from my strong enemy" How long has David and Israel been fighting the Philistines? God has given David the victory. David gives God the glory! That is so critical. We have talked about this before. We need to open our eyes to the miracles God performs for us every day. When I am trying to think of a person's name, they come to my memory I say, "Thank you, Lord." When something happens that averts a problem, it doesn't have to be major, I say, "Thank you, Lord." When I have a great worship experience at church on Sunday or Wednesday. I say, "Thank you, Lord". Do you know what that does? It reminds me that God is walking with me on this path called life. He is still there, daily!

That's why David is pausing here to write or sing this psalm. David wrote it, so he is singing it. Wouldn't you love to know how David sounds when he sings? He is praising God, and God is back walking with him. I would be excited enough to write a song as well. You can feel it in his words. He can't say enough about God's provision. David recognizes it! How about you. Do you think to thank God during the day when He does something out of the ordinary? The older I get the more forgetful. When I can bring a name or an incident to my memory I praise God that His Spirit brought to my mind.

Do you need a lift sometimes? You don't know what to say to God, how to express your gratefulness? Read the psalms! There is so much praise in those 150 psalms. Israel was all about praising God, obedience, not so much, but praise, YES! That should be our response. We will praise God if we are walking with Him on this path of life. We notice what God is doing in our life, we acknowledge His presence and His hands guiding us step by step. When you come to that fork, you start praying. Looking for God's direction.

The Lord rewarded me according to my righteousness; according to the cleanness of my hands He has recompensed me. For I have kept the ways of the Lord, and have not wickedly departed from my God. For all His judgments were before me; and as for His statutes, I did not depart from them. I was also blameless before Him, and I kept myself from my iniquity; Therefore, the Lord has recompensed me according to my righteousness. According to cleanness in His eyes. (2 Samuel 22:21-25) (NKJV)

Is this David? The same David we have been walking with through these pages? It doesn't sound like it, does it?

Do you remember what it was like when you were first saved? The day you your heart to God and became a child of God? That assumes you are a child of God. That, one day, you asked Jesus into your heart. Do you remember what it was like? I think David can relate to a verse in Corinthians,

> *Therefore, if anyone is in Christ, he is a new creation; old things have passed away, behold, all things have become new. (2 Corinthians 5:17). (NKJV)*

That is the picture of David here.

We have just traveled through the extent of David's life to this point. Of course, he made mistakes. Have you noticed that since Nathan confronted David about Bathsheba and Uriah, there have been no "mistakes"? He has basically suffered from that point till now. Do you remember what Nathan told David?

> So, David said to Nathan, "I have sinned against the Lord."
> And Nathan said to David, "The Lord also has put away
> your sin; you shall not die." (2 Samuel 12:13) (NKJV)

Did you catch that first part? "The Lord has put away your sin." God didn't put it in a drawer somewhere to be brought out later. By "put away" He means "forgotten!" Erased!

That is the attitude and picture we see here with David. You remember earlier we talked about that "reuniting" time when David goes back to the fork in the road and reunites with God? That is the picture David gives us here in this portion of this "praise" psalm. David recognizes the truth of 2 Corinthians, "all things have become new". His fellowship with God has been restored. Are the "judgments" over, not really. But David can face them from a new perspective.

Back to our first question: "Do you remember when you were first saved?" How is your walk now? Is there something between you and God? Have you left God at a fork in the road and traveled your own course? Can you feel God's presence? If not, why? You may want to use David's words, "I Have sinned against you, Lord" Confession begins the healing process. (1 John 1:9)

David is ready to begin a new phase in his life. That is the feeling we get when we make things right with God. Keep that Corinthians verse in mind. We (you and God) are continuing the path that God has chosen from the beginning. You took a detour, you learned a valuable lesson (hopefully) now it's time to get back on track. The exciting thing about getting back on track is the anticipation of what God is going to do in your life from now on. Unless you take another fork in the road.

I am not going to argue with David's attitude in this portion of this psalm. Don't read more into it than what is there. David is simply excited that he and God are back on the same path. David recognizes he has been separated from God's direction but God has still been beside him all this time. In his defeat of Absalom, David saw God's hand working things out.

I think he began to see that God had not given up on him. Remember his word's earlier when he sent the priests back to Jerusalem with the ark of God? At that point David put his life in God's hands.

Can you praise God right now for what He has done in your life? Are you and God on the same path? Maybe you left Him a while back and took another fork in the road. Do you even recognize His absence? Let's do a "heart check" right now. Come to God in prayer and ask God if He is walking there beside you, then listen!

With the merciful You will show Yourself merciful; with a blameless man; You will show Yourself blameless; with the pure You will show Yourself pure; and with the devious You will show Yourself shrewd. You will save the humble people; but Your eyes are on the haughty, that You may bring them down. (2 Samuel 22:26-28) (NKJV)

Do you see it? David recognizes where the justice and mercy comes from. Six times David says, "You". Notice some of the attributes of God that David points out: mercy, blameless, pure, shrewd, etc.

In this treatise, where we have followed King David from the shepherd's field, Goliath, Saul, Jonathan, Uriah and Bathsheba, Absalom, and Joab. Watching how David walks with God. Of course, he is human, as we are human. He has made mistakes, he has also "inquired of the Lord" which is a trait we need to take note of. As we watch David, we can learn from his mistakes and rejoice in the praises of God.

You know the phrase by now, "A man after God's own heart." Did you notice something about that phrase? We can not only know David's heart we can learn something about God's heart. I think a great example is with Bathsheba. The penalty for sin is death. There are always consequences. Sometimes we don't always understand those consequences. But don't overlook the fact that their next child was "Solomon". Solomon, who would eventually complete the building of the greatest temple to God in history. God's grace.

I don't know what version of the Bible you are reading. In my Bible, this "psalm" is arranged differently so that you recognize that it is "different". The other psalm for Saul and Jonathan was the same way. The point I want to make is that this "variation" makes it easy to ship. Oh, just another psalm of David's. It is not part of the storyline so we will skip it. Don't do that. This psalm as well as the previous one, I think, shows David's heart.

I mentioned before how David has managed to find his way back to a personal relationship with God his Father. It has been a long journey. We can read it in a few minutes but over forty years have passed. It doesn't say how old David is but don't miss those few words,

> *When the Philistines were at war with Israel, David and his servants with him went down and fought against the Philistines; and David grew faint. (2 Samuel 21:15).* (NKJV)

I don't think that was included as an aside remark. David is getting older, much older. His weakness is such that his own soldiers implored him to stay out,

> *"lest you quench the lamp of Israel." (2 Samuel 21:17).* (NKJV)

David is there king. To lose their king would be devastating to the country. Their leader, who has led them in countless victorious battles. Must remain king. Such is the love the people had for David.

One of my favorite times in the worship service is the singing of the old hymns. With the medicine, I have been taking I get hoarse easily. So, I can't really sing. I do mouth the words. I must sing from my heart. The message of the old hymns is "priceless!" They can lift me just mouthing the words. Such is the message of these psalms in David's time. They bring hope, praise, encouragement, worship, and a devotion that inspires all of Israel. Remember it was David who wrote this psalm. His divinely inspired words from God to His people are no less inspiring than the hymns of our day. The hymns bring us closer to God. The hymns bring us into His presence in an attitude of worship!

> *Speaking to one another in psalms and hymns and spiritual songs, singing and making melody in your heart to the Lord. (Ephesians 5:19)* (NKJV)

Just imagine you walk into church. No music, no piano or organ. You sit down. Someone opens in prayer and the preacher begins. I doubt that would last long. The hymns bring our hearts to focus on God and His presence. When our hearts are ready God will open to our hearts His word for us that day. The music brings us to a time of worship, an attitude of worship!

For You are my lamp, O Lord; the Lord shall enlighten my darkness. For by You I can run against a troop; by my God I can leap over a wall. As for God, His way is perfect the word of the Lord is proven; He is a shield to all who trust in Him. (2 Samuel 22:29-31) (NKJV)

That is interesting. My Bible doesn't say whether David wrote psalm 119. Look at this verse:

> Your word is a lamp to my feet and a light to my path. (Psalm 119:105). (NKJV)

I love this portion of the psalm above. *"For You are my lamp"* We have talked quite a bit about this path we are walking with God.

That is interesting. I was thinking that Jesus was called the "Light of the world." Look at these verses from the Sermon on the Mount:

> You are the light of the world. A city that is set on a hill cannot be hidden. Nor do they light a lamp and put it under a basket, but on a lampstand, and it gives light to all who are in the house. Let your light so shine before men, that they may see your good works and glorify your Father in heaven. (Matthew 5:14-16) (NKJV)

Here is another verse:

> Then Jesus spoke to them again, saying, "I am the light of the world. He who follows Me shall not walk in darkness, but have the light of life." (John 8:12). (NKJV)

So how important is light? Our pastor said, in his study of the gospel of John, "Light and darkness cannot occupy the same space." How profound, think about it! It sounds simple but we think we can walk around in a world of darkness and not need a light. We think we can walk this "path of life" without any light, really? How dangerous is that?

"As for God, His way is perfect; The word of the Lord is proven; He is a shield to all who trust in Him." (2 Samuel 22:31). (NKJV)

Has God's word been "proven" in your life? Have you "tested" it? If you haven't tested it, you haven't proved it. If you don't know it you can't test it! The best way to "know" God's word is faithful attendance to God's house, both worship AND Sunday School. We need godly instruction, Spirit led instruction! You could spend a year just in the book of Proverbs and still not glean near what it contains. Look at Proverbs:

Trust in the Lord with all your heart, and lean not on your own understanding; in all your ways acknowledge Him. And He shall direct your path. (Proverbs 3:5-6) (NKJV)

Have you TESTED those words? Do you believe those words?

I don't suppose you noticed those last few words? *"And He shall direct your path."* That is what we are talking about! Light on your path of life. Direction at those crossroads when you need to know what decision to make. You need God's light on the right path to take. Don't forget what Jesus said in Matthew. "You" are a light carrier. There is a catch. You MUST have the light within you, before you can share it with others. Without the Lord Jesus Christ, in the person of the Holy Spirit, living within you, you have NO light!

Look at the end of verse 29, *The Lord shall enlighten my darkness.* That is where our light comes from. David has come through some tough times, some dark times. We have walked with him through these last few chapters. We have seen what he has endured. Could you go through that path? Remember, David is no different than you or me. He is human, he has his failures. Yet David has found his way back to God's light. This psalm, to me, demonstrates the renewed fellowship with his heavenly Father. These words are so encouraging to me.

David has returned to God's path, God's direction. No, I haven't read ahead. I have read this passage several times, but I don't know what's coming. I am walking this journey along with you. I have learned so much about David on this journey. It has been a blessing to me. I hope it has blessed you as well. I do know that David has a few more trials ahead. He is nearing the end of his life. Watch with me, glean as much as you can from the remaining verses, truths that we can incorporate into our walk with God. Have you found anything that might shed some light on why God refers to David as "A man after God's own heart." Acts 13:22 and 1 Samuel 13:14

For who is God, except the Lord? And who is a rock, except our God? God is my strength and power, and He makes my way perfect. He makes my feet like the feet of deer; and sets me on my high places. He teaches my hands to make war; so that my arms can bend a bow of bronze. You have also given me the shield of Your salvation; Your gentleness has made me great. You enlarged my path under me; so, my feet did not slip. (2 Samuel 22:32-37) (NKJV)

That is an interesting picture: *the shield of Your salvation*. I wonder why David equates his salvation to a shield. Of course, you remember the Armor of God in Ephesians. I get the Fruit of the Spirit (Galatians) and the Armor of God confused as to location. Look what Paul says in Ephesians,

> *Finally, my brethren, be strong in the Lord and in the power of His might. Put on the whole armor of God, that you may be able to stand against the wiles of the devil. For we do not wrestle against flesh and blood; but against principalities, against powers, against the rulers of the darkness of this age, against spiritual hosts of wickedness in the heavenly places. (Ephesians 6:10-12). (NKJV)*

Paul goes on to describe the various parts of this armor. In Paul's message, he refers to the "shield of faith". David calls it the "shield of salvation". Both and the same. You cannot be saved without faith in the Lord Jesus Christ!

Notice that David recognizes, (1) from where his strength comes from. This is more than physical strength, it can also be spiritual strength, as Paul relates in Ephesians 6. (2) David recognizes that God is Lord. That is important and significant. How about you? Is God Lord of your life? Is He in control? We have talked about walking this "path" of life. Who is in the lead? When it comes to making a decision, who determines the path you take?

Did you catch that last part? *"You enlarged my path under me; so, my feet did not slip."* Another reference to a path. I don't think this concept is too far out of reach. We are all traveling a path. From childhood to old age. A path that may take us to, God knows where, have you heard that expression before? Of course, God knows. The thing I am stressing is, that God also gives us the "option" to choose our own path. God has given us that option from the Garden of Eden. It's our choice. We are also responsible for the choices we make. ask Adam and Eve!

Notice in verse 35, *He teaches my hands to make war.* The talents and gifts we enjoy are straight from our Maker. There are so many things on my "Bucket List" that I wish I could do, but that is only a wish. There are things I am not meant to do. God didn't make me that way. God gave me certain talents and it's His plan for me to use them. Many times, I set in church and wish I could sing in the choir, I love the hymns so much, but I CAN'T SING! So, I enjoy what God has given me!

Many times, those gifts God has given us are wasted. We might use them for evil, we might discard them and go our own way. Many years I wished I could preach like Chuck Swindoll or Charles Stanley. I can't, that doesn't mean God can't use the talents I DO have to spread God's wonderful word of salvation through His Son Jesus!

I think the point of this section of this psalm is that David recognizes where his warrior abilities come from. Because of these abilities God has asked that David pass on his desire to build a temple. Pass that desire on to his son Solomon. David accepts the talents that God has given him, and uses them to accomplish "God's" purpose, and God's glory! How many ballplayers have you seen, when they get a hit, point to the sky. That used to annoy me, I thought it was for show. Not so much anymore. David is doing the same thing here. In this psalm, he has written, he is pointing to the sky, after David's victory over the Philistines.

Do you remember to thank God daily for the victories He brings into your life? A simple praise, "Praise God" will suffice. Of course, you could really praise God by going to church!

I have pursued my enemies and destroyed them; neither did I turn back again till they were destroyed. And I have destroyed them and wounded them, so that they could not rise; they have fallen under my feet. For You have armed me with strength for the battle; You have subdued under me those who rose against me. You have also given me the necks of my enemies, so that I destroyed those who hated me. They looked, but there was none to save; even to the Lord, but He did not answer them. Then I beat them as fine as the dust of the earth; I trod them like dirt in the streets, and I spread them out. (2 Samuel 22:38-43) (NKJV)

We can't relate to David's praise for giving him victory in battle. There is a lady in our church who bought a bunch of toy soldiers. She put these in a box and put a sign that says: "Pick a soldier, Pray for them." How often do we think to pray for our military? Unless you have someone in the military it really doesn't cross your mind. We need a reminder that apart from our military we would be a communist country today. Beginning with World War II, our military has kept those communist dictators away from our shores. Remember Pearl Harbor? What if that had gone the other way? We need to pray for our military daily. When I lift up this fellow I know in the military, I went to his wedding, I also pray: "If there is anyone who doesn't know Jesus as their Savior, I pray You would put someone in their path to share with them the gospel of salvation through Your Son Jesus." Pray for our military!

David knew and recognized where his victories came from. All the way back to his battle with Goliath. Look at this verse:

> Then all this assembly shall know that the Lord does not save with sword or spear; **for the battle is the Lord's**, and He will give you (Goliath) into our hands." (1 Samuel 17:47). (NKJV)

Can you relate to that statement? Probably not, you haven't battled Goliath or any other giant lately. You are facing challenges in your daily life. So, when do you let God into your battle?

We face "battles" every day. Whether in our school environment, our workplace, or even in our social life. We will always have the battle of "flesh" vs "Spirit". Paul talks a lot about his struggles with the same battles. It's not new. The challenge is, are you recruiting God into this battle. David did! Where is your strength to engage in these daily battles? In God, through His Spirit. Of course, if you are not a child of God you are defenseless! You will go with the flow, with your peers, and trust their leadership. That's sad. That can lead to all kinds of problems, and consequences that you don't want to know. You need the guidance of God's Holy Spirit in your life.

David had problems. We have been slowly walking with David throughout this whole scenario. Have you learned anything? I think the first lesson I learned was: "Inquire of the Lord" when you are not sure what to do. Next, be where you are supposed to be when you're supposed to be there. Don't shirk your responsibilities. Next, when you have sinned, confess and ask God's forgiveness (1 John 1:9). Maintain that fellowship with your heavenly Father. Lastly, with this psalm, it is very important that we recognize where the victories come from, and praise God for His strength and deliverance. The best place to praise God is in His house on the Lord's day. Recognize Jesus mandate to gather and worship in His church!

As we finish up this psalm of David's I want to think back to where David was, then reflect on where he is. I guess that might be an unspoken theme here. I have mentioned on several occasions about keeping a journal. Just a personal journal of your walk with God. Times you may not be where God wanted you to. Times when you strayed from His path, and the results, will help you later. Times when God has blessed your socks off! We especially want to note those special times when God, through His blessings, strengthens our faith and walk with Him. That needs to be written down and reflected on in times of trial.

You have also delivered me from the strivings of my people; You have kept me as the head of the nations. A people I have not known shall serve me. The foreigners submit to me; as soon as they hear, they obey me. The foreigners fade away, and come frightened from their hideouts. The Lord lives! Blessed be my Rock! Let God be exalted, the Rock of my salvation! It is God who avenges me, and subdues the people under me; He delivers me from my enemies. You also lift me up above those who rise against me; You have delivered me from the violent man. Therefore, I will give thanks to You, O Lord, among the Gentiles, and sing praises to Your name. He is the tower of salvation to His king, and shows mercy to His anointed, To David and his descendants forevermore." (2 Samuel 22:44-51) (NKJV)

I have already pointed out how many references to David there are through the books of First and Second Kings. I ran across this verse in my reading this morning:

Of the increase of His government and peace there shall be no end, upon the throne of David and over His kingdom. (Isaiah 9:7a). (NKJV)

I miss my Bible program. I know the throne of David is mentioned in Revelation. Can't find it right now. The point being that David, as the seed of Jesus Christ, "lineage" is mentioned several times in the New Testament.

He wasn't perfect, was he? Neither are you! God can, and will, use whoever is willing to be used of God. He delights in changing lives and using those who are least likely, even shepherds out tending their flocks. I know you remember, who were the first ones God chose to announce the arrival of His Son in Bethlehem. (Luke 2:8). God will use anyone who is "willing" to be used of God.

Did you notice how many times David mentions salvation in this psalm? I counted four, (v. 3, 36, 47, 51). Just a quick scan. You might find more. The point is that David recognized where his "salvation" came from. David was speaking in the sense of victory in a battle. You can use the same principle. There is a battle going on today in our world. The battle for the souls of men. Satan knows his time is short and he will do everything he can to persuade as many as he can to follow him and deny Christ! The battle of the flesh and the Spirit. You can win the victory, the salvation, by putting your trust in Jesus Christ. Pray and ask Jesus into your heart right now.

Do you remember early in David's walk with God, when he received the Spirit of God?

*Then Samuel took the horn of oil and anointed him in the midst of his brothers; and the **Spirit of the Lord** came upon David from that day forward. So, Samuel arose and went to Ramah. (1 Samuel 16:13). (NKJV)*

This was the beginning of David's walk with God.

Your walk can begin right now. Open your heart to salvation through Jesus Christ and God will "anoint" you with the same Holy Spirit that He gave to David. The same power to win those battles over the lies of Satan. The Holy Spirit will help you know God's will for your life. Help you in your daily walk with God. Help you to stay on His path, His will and purpose for your life. He will help you discern between the wrong path and the right path that God wants you to walk. This Spirit is only present in a true child of God. It's yours for the asking. Look at this verse:

> "Behold, I stand at the door and knock. If anyone hears My voice and opens the door, I will come in to him and dine with him, and he with Me. (Revelation 3:20). (NKJV)

God is knocking on your hearts door right now. It is up to you to open that door and invite Him in. It is that simple.

David has traveled a long way since his sin with Bathsheba and Uriah. His own son, seeking to kill him and take his throne. God denied him the right to build His temple. But, passed that honor to his son, born of Bathsheba. His fleeing from his son. The betrayal of Joab, yet to be dealt with. In the process, as we see with this psalm, David has grown in his fellowship with God. You can see that in his giving God all the glory for the peace that Israel enjoys now, with the defeat of the Philistines!

2 SAMUEL 23

ow these are the last words of David. Thus, says David the son of Jesse; thus, says the man raised up on high, the anointed of the God of Jacob, the sweet psalmist of Israel: The Spirit of the Lord spoke by me, and His word was on my tongue. The God of Israel said, The Rock of Israel spoke to me: He who rules over men must be just, ruling in the fear of God. And he shall be like the light of the morning when the sun rises, a morning without clouds, like the tender grass springing out of the earth, by clear shinning after rain. (2 Samuel 23:1-4) (NKJV)

Have you heard this? "I, being of sound mind and body, spent all the inheritance? There are some jokes about the word "inheritance." There is a show on Fox Business called, "Strange Inheritance" narrated by Jamie Colby. Jamie has made a career out of telling the stories behind "strange inheritances." Interesting show. The words of David, beginning this chapter reminds me of "inheritances." What are we leaving behind when we go to meet the Lord?

We have been so wrapped up in David's psalm that he wrote, that we might forget about the seventy some psalms he has written. I mentioned before that it would be interesting to know at what point in his life he wrote each individual psalm. What was he dealing with. Most assume he wrote Psalm 51 just after his affair with Bathsheba. Maybe the 23rd Psalm early in his life, just out of the shepherd's field. We don't know.

I have a bunch of books, some DVD's and journals I am leaving behind. There is one thing that is impossible to leave behind. Salvation in Jesus Christ. Did you know you cannot leave that behind? You can leave a "testimony" you can leave the story of your walk with god, etc. The decision to follow Christ is totally up to the individual. It is the responsibility of each of God's creation to decide for themselves who they will follow. There are only two choices. It must be made BEFORE you stand before God on judgment day.

I have mentioned before, the fascinating thing about the books of Kings. You can have a godly king who followed God faithfully and his son will be one of the worst ungodly kings in the Bible. It is not passed down. Likewise, you can have an ungodly king and his heir will walk with God throughout his reign. It is amazing to me. Like I said it is not inherited.

Will I be held accountable for the choices the next generation makes? No. I can pray, I can encourage, I can exhort, but the choice is theirs, the consequences are theirs. There are things we can do, I just stated, but in the end, it is their choice. I have heard so many stories of parents and grandparents that have prayed for their offspring for years. Faithfully lifting their names before God. Some get to see the fruits of their prayers, some may not know till they get to heaven.

We can impact the next generation in so many ways. The older generation that put all their time, effort and resources into the construction of a little country church have no idea the lives that effort may impact. In Matthew 13 Jesus tells of a "sower" who sowed the word of God. That is all we can do. We are not responsible for the crop only sowing the seed, God takes care of the rest. Are you faithfully sowing the word of God?

As a longtime Sunday School Director, I would always encourage our teachers to encourage their students, "Invite people to Sunday School." Just get them under the word of God. God will do the rest!

Although my house is not so with God, yet He has made with me an everlasting covenant, ordered in all things and secure. For this is all my salvation and all my desire; will He not make it increase? But the sons of rebellion shall all be as thorns thrust away, because they cannot be taken with hands. But the man who touches them must be armed with iron and the shaft of a spear, and they shall be utterly burned with the fire in their place. (2 Samuel 23:5-7) (NKJV)

"An everlasting covenant." That is what God has with us. The seal to this covenant? The presence of God's Holy Spirit living within us. Look at these verses:

And do not grieve the Holy Spirit of God, by whom you were sealed for the day of redemption. (Ephesians 4:30). (NKJV)

In Him you also trusted, after you heard the word of truth, the gospel of your salvation; in whom also, having believed, you were sealed with the Holy Spirit of promise, who is the guarantee of your inheritance until the redemption of the purchased possession, to the praise of His glory. (Ephesians 1:13-14). (NKJV)

That is the seal of this everlasting covenant. David also had that assurance as we have pointed out at his anointing he received that same Holy Spirit!

David is also dealing with "sons of rebellion." These thorns, in New Testament times, being the battles we fight over the desires of the flesh. Remember what John said,

For, all that is in the world—the lust of the flesh, the lust of the eyes, and the pride of life— is not of the Father but is of the world. (1 John 2:16-17). (NKJV)

David had the same struggles we face today. David has the same remedy we have today, the power of the Holy Spirit within us. But we enjoy this "sin for a season" so we ignore that prompting from God's Spirit, until we are in so deep, like David!

There are great lessons to be learned from David. That is why we are taking this journey together. Hopefully we can learn and apply these principles to our daily walk. When you take your eyes off of God, you are not where you ought to be, you are looking for a fall. Someone once gave the analogy of walking on a path with no opposition. If you are not facing opposition then you are walking WITH the devil. While you are going his way, he will not oppose you. When the devil starts whispering in your ear, and setting up road blocks to God's will, then you know you are walking contrary to the devil's tricks.

We are nearing the end of our walk with David. This journey will travel to the second chapter of First Kings. Then Solomon will take the throne. We could go on but this study is about David. What made David known, both in the Old and New Testaments as, "A Man After God's Own Heart!" I hope this journey has opened some areas in your life that you might not have thought of before. We still have a way to go yet, but we have traveled far and learned much. I hope these lessons will remain in your heart and help you walk a closer walk with God.

Let me close this portion with another of David's psalms:

You will show me the path of life; in Your presence is fullness of joy; at Your right hand are pleasures forevermore. (Psalm 16:11). (NKJV)

I found this verse after I had completed my first book, THE PATH. Meditate on this verse a bit. Chew on it, think about it. Pray about it. Maybe write this address next to Jeremiah 29:11-13. If I may, let me give you one more of my favorite verses. These all come to mind at various times. This one is in Joshua:

This book of the Law shall not depart from your mouth, but you shall meditate in it day and night, that you may observe to do according to all that is written in it. For then you will make your way prosperous, and then you will have good success. (Joshua 1:8). (NKJV)

It wouldn't hurt to note this in the flyleaf of your Bible, along with the other two. You will have a great foundation to begin your own list of verses that speak to you in a special way and help you in your daily walk with God.

These are the names of the mighty men whom David had. (23:8a) (NKJV)

And David said with longing, "Oh, that someone would give me a drink of the water from the well of Bethlehem, which is by the gate!" So, the three mighty men broke through the camp of the Philistines, drew water from the well of Bethlehem that was by the gate, and took it and brought it to David. Nevertheless, he would not drink it, but poured it out to the Lord. And he said, "Far be it from me, O Lord, that I should do this! Is this not the blood of the men who went in jeopardy of their lives?" Therefore, he would not drink it. These things were done by the three mighty men. (2 Samuel 23:15-17) (NKJV)

I was going to skip this passage. It mostly consisted of listing those in David's army. But I couldn't pass up these verses. These are the kind of men that followed David. Servants, every one of them.

I want to use this to recognize some other servants that have blessed me countless times in my thirty years in the Sunday School ministry. The Sunday School teachers! What a fantastic group of people. Their dedication and time spent in the word of God and then to bring that study every Sunday to their class is amazing. They are not paid. They are servants of the Lord. I guess I can't pass up the chance to share one of my favorite verses as a Sunday School teacher:

> If anyone speaks, let him speak as the oracles of God. If anyone ministers, let him do it as with the ability which God supplies, that in all things God may be glorified through Jesus Christ, to whom belong the glory and the dominion forever and ever. Amen. (1 Peter 4:11). (NKJV)

I cannot begin to number the times that I have asked or persuaded a young Christian to take on a Sunday School class. They, question their own ability, doubt they could do it, but are willing to try it. Six months later you could not get them to quit.

I had not been saved for six months. My Sunday School teacher told us, in our class, that the pastor was teaching a class of teenage boys. He didn't think the pastor should have to teach a class. I volunteered. I didn't know Genesis from Revelation but I offered to try. Thirty years later, the Sunday School ministry has been my calling. Even when I pastored for two and a half years I focused on the Sunday School.

If you want to get to know the Bible better, volunteer to teach a class.

I also know, first hand, the hours of study and preparation that goes into preparing a lesson each week. While other members may attend church occasionally your Sunday School teacher is one of the most faithful in the church, next to the pastor, of course. They not only prepare a lesson, they pray for their class member's needs. Maintain a relationship with them. The Sunday School is the "outreach" arm of the church. Most new members begin by attending Sunday School first.

I especially applaud the preschool and children's department. You not only have to teach the Bible you must entertain them as well. I am sure there is double the preparation in those departments compared to youth and adult classes. A lot of people don't think of the nursery as a Sunday School class—it is! You begin very early telling that little baby that God loves them. God cares about them, the parents, most of the time, need to hear this as well. It is sad to me that a lot of young parents wait so long before putting their children in the nursery. Those are the most dedicated servants and want only the best for your little ones.

Are you praying about how God might use you? Why not try the Sunday School ministry? You will grow so much just with the commitment to teach others. Even I enjoy sitting in a class with a novice teacher. We can all learn something from others, if we are willing to listen. As director, I enjoyed sitting in the various classes and marvel at the creativeness of each teacher. That can only be Spirit led teaching! Thank you from the bottom of my heart!

2 SAMUEL 24

Again, the anger of the Lord was aroused against Israel, and He moved David against them to say, "Go, number Israel and Judah." So, the king said to Joab the commander of the army who was with him, "Now go throughout all the tribes of Israel, from Dan to Beersheba, and count the people, that I may know the number of the people." And Joab said to the king, "Now may the Lord your God add to the people a hundred times more than there are, and may the eyes of my lord the king, see it. But why does my lord the king desire this thing?" (2 Samuel 24:1-3) (NKJV)

As a Sunday School Director, I was always focused on the numbers. I got teased a lot about it. I even would counter with, "There is a book, entitled 'Numbers.'" I had to wrestle with getting too focused on numbers and forgetting what Sunday School was all about. I also reminded them that these "numbers" represented visitors to our church and potential commitments.

In my study Bible, there is a cross-reference to 2 Samuel 21:1

> *Now there was a famine in the days of David for three years, year after year; and David inquired of the Lord. (2 Samuel 21:1) (NKJV)*

I didn't see anywhere in the verses above where David "inquired of the Lord." If I may, let me share one more verse from James,

> *My, brethren, count it all joy when you fall into various trials, knowing that the testing of your faith produces patience. (James 1:2-3). (NKJV)*

God is always in the process of "growing" our faith. Our faith in His leadership. David had the right response when God brought the famine. Here, not so much. Even our buddy Joab counseled against it.

Did you notice the first words of this chapter? *Again, the anger of the Lord was aroused against* **Israel**. It wasn't against David. David had the option of "inquiring of the Lord" but chose not to. It will cost him. It doesn't say why God was angry at Israel. Notice how God works!

Has God brought a "storm" into your life? No mistake! As we have seen, it's God that brings the storms. Check out the first couple of chapters of Job. Satan can do nothing but what God allows. Job is a great book when things are happening in your life you don't understand. The next question is WHY?

I shared this before but it is a great illustration of this very truth. As a young Christian, in one month, my father passed away from cancer. I had a terrible wreck driving with U.P.S. coming back from Wichita. I had laid my big-rig on its side. I wasn't hurt but I was suspended. In the same month, my daughter came home from college, pregnant. All of this in the span of thirty days. I asked God why! Almost every day I asked why? I offered to resign as deacon. My pastor would not hear of it. I didn't blame God, or the church. I just kept asking God, why! This went on for a year. One morning I was driving to work, again, I asked God why. As clear as day God said, "I wanted to see if you would be faithful." I cried all the way to work. God puts trials in our life for a "specific" reason. It is usually a test, NOT a temptation, but a test. It is up to you what you do with that test.

I love the way Dr. Charles Stanley explains it: Because God is all-knowing, He knows where you are at in the storm. Because God is ever-present, He is with you in the storm. Because God is all-powerful He will bring you through the storm. IF you are walking with Him in the storm. He is there, don't let go, don't blame God, trust Him. There is a lesson to be learned. Now when a storm arises I ask, "Okay Lord, what is the lesson you have for me now?"

Nevertheless, the king's word prevailed against Joab and against the captains of the army. Therefore, Joab and the captains of the army went out from the presence of the king to count the people of Israel. And they crossed over the Jordan and camped in Aroer, on the right side of the town which is in the midst of the ravine of Gad, and toward Jazer. Then they came to Gilead and to the land of Tahtim Hodshi; they came to Dan Jaan and around Sidon; and they came to the stronghold of Tyre and to all the cities of the Hivites and the Canaanites. Then they went out to South Judah as far as Beersheba. (2 Samuel 24:4-7) (NKJV)

I guess I must have missed it, in the previous chapter. I saw all the praise for David's "mighty" men, and rightly so, but I missed any mention of the Lord. Did I miss something? There is a great lesson here, I hope David is paying attention. When you fail to acknowledge God's hand in any achievement, you're looking for a reminder from God. David needs to be reminded where his victories come from. Granted the judgment is on "Israel" but David represents Israel. Israel will pay, as they always have for ignoring God's part in their victories!

How about you? Is there some great achievement in your life? Have you won a victory over some sin, some habit you have wanted to break, even a relationship you needed to deal with? If you have won a "victory" you need to recognize God's hand in that victory. It's just like prayer. Prayer is the "last resort" when we are in a fix. And God is the last one, if ever, that we thank when we have a victory. That's sad!

I am really puzzled about David's reference to Joab. Either he hasn't learned of his role in killing Absalom, or he is waiting for the right moment to confront him. If memory serves, Joab is dealt with at one point, in the book of 1 Kings.

So, David sends out his generals to take this census. From Gad to Beersheba trying to get an accurate count of the Israelites. Did you catch how this came about again?

Again, the anger of the Lord was aroused against Israel, and He moved David against them to say, "Go, number Israel and Judah." (2 Samuel 24:1) (NKJV)

Did you notice he separated Israel and Judah? This is important later, remember those two distinctions in the books of First and Second Kings.

Don't miss the method God uses here. God was mad at the nation Israel. He uses David to accomplish his wrath against them. God can and does use whatever means He sees fit to bring about His judgment. He also can use any means to get our attention, to turn us around, or get us to look up. We can see that so clearly, especially in the Old Testament.

I think it is interesting. Have you ever served in the military? Even though the generals didn't like this "order" they carried it out. See this here *"But why does my lord the king desire this thing?"* Do you remember David's response? There was none. David doesn't have to explain to his generals when he gives them an order. God doesn't have to "explain" to us when He is trying to get our attention. Our response? PRAY! Ask God, He doesn't have to explain but you can ask!

Do you remember the last time God got Israel's attention? I mentioned it before. He sent a famine for three years. That was to right a wrong that Saul had committed on the Gibeonites. God will correct wrongs. The time is of no importance to Him. The scales will be balanced! God will make things right. Look at this verse in the New Testament:

> *Beloved, do not avenge yourselves, but rather give place to wrath; for it is written, "Vengeance is Mine, I will repay," says the Lord. (Romans 12:19) (NKJV)*

That is interesting. That quote is referenced to an Old Testament verse:

> *Vengeance is Mine, and recompense their foot shall slip in due time; for the day of their calamity is at hand, and the things to come hasten upon them. (Deuteronomy 32:35). (NKJV)*

Do you see what I see? The timing is the Lords. How and when belong to God, the promise is "vengeance is MINE!" (Deuteronomy 32:35) (NKJV)

So, when they had gone through all the land, they came to Jerusalem at the end of nine months and twenty days. Then Joab gave the sum of the number of the people to the king. And there were in Israel eight hundred thousand valiant men who drew the sword, and the men of Judah were five hundred thousand men. And David's heart condemned him after he had numbered the people. So, David said to the Lord, "I have sinned greatly in what I have done; but now, I pray, O Lord, take away the iniquity of Your servant, for I have done very foolishly." (2 Samuel 24:8-10) (NKJV)

If you have a minute, I encourage you to turn to Psalm 51 and read that psalm of David. Here are a couple of verses I have bracketed:

> *Restore to me the joy of Your salvation, and uphold me by Your generous Spirit. Then I will teach transgressors Your ways, and sinners shall be converted to You. (Psalm 51:12-13).* (NKJV)

> *Create in me a clean heart, O God, and renew a steadfast spirit within me. Do not cast me away from Your presence, and do not take Your Holy Spirit from me. (Psalm 51:10-11).* (NKJV)

Four awesome verses. Do you see David's heart here? He craves a right relationship with his heavenly Father.

Did you notice in verse 11: *and do not take Your Holy Spirit from me?* In the Old Testament, as we have pointed out before, God can remove His Spirit from anyone he chooses. Saul went looking for a medium because God had withdrawn His Spirit from Saul (1 Samuel 16:14). Today, as a child of God, once we have accepted Jesus as our Savior we are given the Holy Spirit to dwell with us forever, as a seal of our salvation.

Look at these two verses:

> *Who has sealed us and given us the Spirit in our hearts as a guarantee. (2 Corinthians 1:22).* (NKJV)

> *Do not grieve the Holy Spirit of God, by whom you were sealed for the day of redemption. (Ephesians 4:30).* (NKJV)

The day we receive Christ into our hearts we become children of God and that assurance is sealed in us by the presence of God's Holy Spirit. We cannot lose that relationship. Of course, my favorite is Romans:

> *For you did not receive the spirit of bondage again to fear, but you received the Spirit of adoption by whom we cry out, "Abba, Father." The Spirit Himself bears witness with our spirit that we are children of God. (Romans 8:15)* (NKJV)

David recognized the necessity of retaining God's Spirit. That assured him of his relationship with God. After his affair with Bathsheba he was afraid he might lose that relationship. You see that in the 51st Psalm. I think, in this one instance, David came so close to God's wrath. Of course, he did pay a price for his sin, as he will here as well. There are always consequences to sin. The question is, how will we respond to the "spanking?"

Have you ever told your parents, "I hate you" after being disciplined? That is not the response God wants. Far too often it is our response. God is looking for the same response of David, *I have sinned greatly in what I have done.* The same response was given Nathan when he confronted David about Bathsheba, *"I have sinned."* That is the response God is looking for! That is the response of a "Man After God's Own Heart."

I think it's interesting that as soon as Joab gave him the numbers he knew he had sinned. Sometimes we may need God to point ours out to us. To convict us, that is the work of the Holy Spirit within us. Notice what happened, *And David's heart condemned him.* The Holy Spirit resides in our heart. When we have sinned against our heavenly Father, the Spirit within us begins to stir and eventually God will get our attention. If we think we can ignore that prompting from His Spirit, God will find other means to get our attention.

For a man after God's own heart David has a lot of struggles. How about you? Is God dealing with you about something? How are you responding? That is a sure sign of "standing in the need of prayer!"

Now when David arose in the morning, the word of the Lord came to the prophet Gad, David's seer, saying, "Go and tell David, 'Thus says the Lord: "I offer you three things; choose one of them for yourself, that I may do it to you"'. So, Gad came to David and told him; and he said to him, "Shall seven years of famine come to you in your land? Or shall you flee three months before your enemies, while they pursue you? Or shall there be three days' plague in your land? Now consider and see what answer I should take back to Him who sent me." (2 Samuel 24:11-13) (NKJV)

It is all about choices, isn't it? God has given David three options to punish Israel. God is always giving us choices. Where we will spend eternity is a "choice". How we live our lives are choices we make every day. Someone once said that we make over three-thousand choices every day. I hate going to buffets, too many options! We live in a world full of choices. How do you determine your choices?

I mentioned earlier that my daughter got pregnant in college. When she came home we went to a crisis pregnancy center. First the counselor took our daughter through the "options" available. She followed each to its logical conclusion. Our daughter chose life. Today that little girl is a Registered Nurse and a surrogate mother. She has brought several little ones into this world. What a blessing! It is all about choices!

How we choose to spend our Sunday's, is a choice. What we do with our money, is a choice. Our lifestyle, is a choice. Who we hang around with, is a choice. Our occupation, is a choice. And, finally, where we spend eternity, is a choice.

I once preached a sermon on "Choices". Adam and Eve had a "choice" in the Garden of Eden. Even Jesus in the Garden of Gethsemane had a choice:

> *saying, "Father if it is Your will, take this cup from Me; nevertheless, not My will, but Yours be done. (Luke 22:42). (NKJV)*

Jesus knew what was ahead. In order to fulfill the Father's will He would need to go to the cross.

David is given a choice. Of the three options, which one would you have taken? I think like David, "Let's get it over with." God can do a lot of damage in three days. As you noticed before, I have tried to figure out what made God do this judgment. In verse one of this chapter we saw: *Again, the anger of the Lord was aroused against Israel.* It doesn't say. I surmised, from the previous chapter that Israel, and/ or David were reveling in their "mighty" army and forgetting about the role God played in their victory. Not sure, just my guess.

Do you remember any other place in the Bible where we are given "options' other than where we will spend eternity? I can't think of any. If we remember that God is all-knowing we know that God already knows the option that David will take. Maybe God knows the impact it will have on David and that is the purpose of the whole exercise. God will put obstacles and trials in our life to guide and teach and correct things in our lives that need correcting. Sometimes they are just to get us to look UP!

I think David is going to learn a valuable lesson in this ordeal. You do know that the greatest lessons we learn come through trials, not blessings, don't you? Think about all the lessons we have learned as children growing up. They usually came from the consequences to things we tried and failed. Failure is a good thing! It teaches many valuable lessons. Just remember the "mistake" that David made and the lesson from that mistake. Sometimes the lesson can just be to "trust God".

Dr. Charles Stanley's favorite quote is: "Obey God, and leave all the consequences to Him." There is that word consequences again. When we are walking with God down the path He has chosen for us we can be assured that God will have only the best for us. It is when we take those detours that we run into trouble.

David must make a choice. I wonder if he "inquires of the Lord."

And David said to Gad, "I am in great distress. Please let us fall into the hand of the Lord, for His mercies are great; but do not let me fall into the hand of man." So, the Lord sent a plague upon Israel from the morning till the appointed time. From Dan to Beersheba seventy thousand men of the people died. And when the angel stretched out His hand over Jerusalem to destroy it, the Lord relented from the destruction, and said to the angel who was destroying the people, "It is enough; now restrain your hand." And the angel of the Lord was by the threshing floor of Araunah the Jebusite. Then David spoke to the Lord when he saw the angel who was striking the people, and said, "Surely, I have sinned, and I have done wickedly; but these sheep, what have they done? Let Your hand, I pray, be against me and against my father's house." (2 Samuel 24:14-17) (NKJV)

The judgment is in. The plague has been implemented. The mercy of God spares Jerusalem. Did you notice David's response in verse seventeen? *Surely, I have sinned, and I have done wickedly; but these sheep, what have they done?"* Isn't it ironic that David, toward the end of his life, is talking about sheep? The "shepherd" of Israel. Again, concerned about the sheep. He is taking his plea to God.

Let's think for a moment. This treatise was to examine David's life, find out what it is in his life that would cause God to call him, "A man after God's own heart." I hope you have picked up some traits, some examples in his life that you might consider for your own walk with God. We have also seen the mistakes that David has made and the consequences of those mistakes. That is a lesson here.

There is one concept I want to explore here. When we are first saved we are babes in Christ. Look at these words in Hebrews:

> *For though by this time you ought to be teachers, you need someone to teach you again the first principles of the oracles of God; and you have come to need milk not solid food. For everyone who partakes only of milk is unskilled in the word of righteousness, for he is a babe. But solid food belongs to those who are of full age, that is, those who by reason of use have their senses exercised to discern both good and evil. (Hebrews 5:12-14). (NKJV)*

Do you get the picture? As a newborn (born again) Christian there is a growth process that must take place. The problem today is, that a lot of Christians have been "baby" Christians for decades!

The Christian walk is not a train headed for heaven and you are just along for the ride. The Christian walk is a "growing" process. Each day, hopefully, we will grow stronger and deeper in our faith and our walk with God. If you read the gospels you will note that Jesus is often surprised at the faith of the Gentiles and chastises His disciples for their lack of faith. Faith is something that must grow as a Christian. Another great verse in Hebrews:

> *But without faith it is impossible to please Him, for he who comes to God must believe that He is, and that He is a rewarder of those who diligently seek Him. (Hebrews 11:6). (NKJV)*

It is a growing process, growing our faith and trusting God.

We can see the progress that David has made in his walk. Of course, early in his walk he had great faith. He defeated Goliath and several times, "inquired of the Lord." But David got off the path. God needed to work on David's walk with God. Through various trials, challenges, God has brought David to this point in his life.

One more thing, did you notice how much God spoke with David through his pastor? First it was Nathan, and now Gad, earlier the priest Abiathar and the ephod. Priests that God uses to communicate with David. The same is true today. God lays a message on the pastor's heart to communicate to His children. It is an essential part of our growth as Christians. So many of God's people on still on milk! It is time to grow some Christians!

And Gad came that day to David and said to him, "Go up, erect an altar on the threshing floor of Araunah the Jebusite." So, David, according to the word of Gad, went up as the Lord commanded. Now Araunah looked, and saw the king and his servants coming toward him. So Araunah went out and bowed before the king with his face to the ground. Then Araunah said, "Why has my lord the king come to his servant?" And David Said, "To buy the threshing floor from you, to build an altar to the Lord, that the plague may be withdrawn from the people." (2 Samuel 24:18-21) (NKJV)

Do you see a pattern here? Maybe it is something for us to take a closer look at. First, do you remember the famine?

> *Now there was a famine in the days of David for three years.* (2 Samuel 21:1a). (NKJV)

The result of that famine was that the Gibeonites received restitution for the killings that Saul had committed. The restitution being the hanging of seven of Saul's descendants. So, God brings a trial, a storm, something to get David's attention to correct a wrong.

In the previous chapter (23) we suggested that Israel was giving the "glory" of their victories to the "mighty men" of David with no mention of God. God had to get their attention. He "moved" David to take a census, for which David would pay. He gave David the choice of three things. In the verses above David is to build an altar to the Lord. He is to "acknowledge" God now, when he didn't earlier. Cruel? Maybe. God is always, as I stated earlier, in the process of growing us as Christians. David had to be reminded of where his strength came from.

We must learn the same lesson. The minute we start thinking that our blessings, our wealth, our soft living, if you will, was all because of our efforts, we are looking for trouble, especially as Christians.

Here David receives word from his pastor that he was to build an altar. Do you see all the questions David asked of Gad? Why? Where? How much? How big? David simply did as his pastor told him to do. That is what God is looking for in us. Obedience through faith. David did plead the cause of Israel's people but in the end accepted the judgment. Have you argued with God lately about what He is doing your life? Surely not!

Just to continue what I was talking about earlier. God wants to do a work in your life. To do that He must grow your faith to the point of complete obedience. If you want to study an example, look at Abraham. God told him he would have a child of his own. They couldn't wait. Sarah persuaded Abraham to have a child by Hagar. Later when Abraham finally had a child by Sarah, what did God do? He told Abraham to take the child up on a mountain and sacrifice him. From Abraham's disobedience God had to make sure Abraham's faith was back 100% on God. He took Abraham right to the brink of killing his son. He tested Abraham after his earlier disobedience.

God is always testing our faith, our obedience to see how much He can use us. The greater our faith, the greater our obedience, the more God will use us. I saw this in my own life. I was totally blown away when God allowed me to pastor a church for two and a half years. I saw God do some fantastic things in that ministry. I was by no means qualified. I was willing to trust God and walk where He had called me. It wasn't until I took my eyes off of God and started looking to my own desires that I failed God.

I hope you have noticed the slow change in David's attitude from Bathsheba till now. It has been a long time. I think David's walk with God has grown stronger. I think his plea for the people in 24:17 indicates a stronger relationship with God.

We are drawing to the close of David's life. David reigned in Jerusalem thirty-three years and over Israel for forty (seven years in Hebron) (1 Kings 2:11). A growing process. Some pain, some praise, much to learn about the man who was called, a man after God's own heart.

Now Araunah said to David, "Let my lord the king, take and offer up whatever seems good to him. Look, here are oxen for burnt sacrifice, and threshing implements and yokes of the oxen for wood. All these, O king, Araunah has given to the king." And Araunah said to the king, "May the

Lord your God accept you." Then the king said to Araunah, "No, but I will surely buy it from you for a price; nor will I offer burnt offerings to the Lord my God with that which costs me nothing." So, David bought the threshing floor and the oxen for fifty shekels of silver. And David built there an altar to the Lord, and offered burnt offerings and peace offerings. So, the Lord heeded the prayers for the land, and the plague was withdrawn from Israel. (2 Samuel 24:22-25) (NKJV)

Here is a trivia question for you: Do you know when the first sacrifice (offering) was made?

> *And in the process of time it came to pass that Cain brought an offering of the fruit of the ground to the Lord. Abel also brought of the first-born of his flock and of their fat. And the Lord respected Abel and his offering. (Genesis 4:3-4). (NKJV)*

No, it wasn't in Exodus or Leviticus. It is said that Job is one of the earliest Old Testament books. Look at this verse:

> *So, it was, when the days of feasting had run their course, that Job would send and sanctify them, and he would rise early in the morning and offer burnt offerings according to the number of them all. For Job said, "It may be that my sons have sinned and cursed God in their hearts." Thus, Job did regularly. (Job 1:5). (NKJV)*

This practice goes all the way back to the beginning. The idea of an altar, I assume would be just as old. It was a way of expressing worship and praise to God. The principle of offering blood to atone for sin goes to Genesis 3:21.

I have verse 24 underlined in my Bible. There is another 24 that is significant in the Bible. Joshua 24:15. Just saying. This is an important principle that also translates to today's culture. David had enough integrity to account for the offering he was making to God. If it's free it would mean just that to God.

I would like to offer a suggestion to those who can't seem to make it to church on Sunday. Not those who are physically unable but those who would rather "sleep-in". To my way of thinking, just the "extra" effort it takes to disrupt your weekend routine. Get up, clean up, and dress up to go to church to worship God would fit in the cost of worship. We won't even go there about your tithe.

I wonder if we would even think about the cost, if it were offered free? We would accept the "gift" and proceed to offer it to God. Exactly who would be making the offering?

Let's try one more. Suppose Jesus had chosen not to go to the cross. He knew the pain and suffering that lay ahead. Remember He approached God in the Garden and asked if there were any other way. Jesus knew the "cost" of our salvation. Suppose He walked away. We would die in our sins, separated from God, forever. There was no other way to cover our sins. Check this verse out:

> "To what purpose is the multitude of your sacrifices to Me?" Says the Lord. I have had enough of burnt offerings of rams and the fat of fed cattle. I do not delight in the blood of bulls, or of lambs or goats. (Isaiah 1:11). (NKJV)

Why would God say that? Because these "offerings" have come to be meaningless to Israel, and to us for that matter.

We go to church and offer the "sacrifice of praise" that's great. What has it cost you?

David has made a great point here. When we bring our sins, our repentance, our confessions to the cross, what has that cost us? Nothing. It is what God PAID for us to even have the opportunity to come to a Holy God and offer our lives to God. Let me close with one of my favorite verses:

> I beseech you therefore, brethren, by the mercies of God, that you present your bodies a living sacrifice, holy, acceptable to God, which is your reasonable service. (Romans 12:1). (NKJV)

You talk about an offering that cost something, how about your life?

1 KINGS 1

Now King David was old and advanced in years; and they put covers on him, but he could not get warm. Therefore, his servants said to him, "Let a young woman, a virgin, be sought for our lord the king, and let her stand before the king, and let her care for him; and let her lie in your bosom, that our lord the king may be warm. So, they sought for a lovely young woman throughout all the territory of Israel, and found Abishag the Shuammite, and brought her to the king. The young woman was very lovely; and she cared for the king, and served him; but the king did not know her. (1 Kings 1:1-4) (NKJV)

I don't understand this. Why don't they just go down to Walmart and buy an electric blanket? You know why! I have mentioned in the past that you are watching a movie. Suddenly, they focused on a pair of scissors on the table, then the camera goes back to the main characters. Now why would they show those scissors? If your Columbo, you know that those scissors are the murder weapon, etc. The same principle applies here. Later, this lady will play a significant role in who will reign in Israel.

Here is an interesting idea for an in-depth Bible study. We pick up David in the sixteenth chapter of First Samuel. You can start there or at the beginning of First Samuel. Start making a list of names and places. As you make this list, add certain facts you discover as you read the text. Significant events, locations, interactions with others, i.e. Tamar and Absalom, etc. Then as you read and run across these names you can check your resource and fill in the background. Makes for increased Bible knowledge. The neat thing is you will see the thread of each character as they weave through this narrative. Try it!

We surely can't relate to these verses in our culture. It was probably common place for the kings of the day. Assuming they lived long enough to need the benefit. Do you remember the book of Esther? The king simply "retired" his wife and sought a new wife. One of the key principles of Bible study is to remember the culture you are reading in. It helps understand certain acts that would be unthinkable today.

I think it is interesting that in the next chapter it says,

> *The period that David reigned over Israel was forty years; seven years he reigned in Hebron, and in Jerusalem thirty-three years. (1 Kings 2:11). (NKJV)*

It doesn't say how old he was when he died. That is unusual. Assuming he was a teen as a shepherd he would be over sixty. Who knows. He was old enough to need help staying warm. I am seventy and I keep a blanket at my chair because my legs are always cold.

Also notice the extent of their efforts to keep the king comfortable, of course, he is the king. I think it is interesting that it says, *the young woman was very lovely.* I am glad they also stipulated, *but the king did not know her.* Like I said earlier all these details are given for a reason. This is not something God would include just to inform us.

You would think with David in this kind of shape there would be little or no more intrigue in his household. Think again. Here is where that notebook would come in handy. A new name enters the scene, Adonijah. Zadok shows up again. Just a note. Mr. Joab also appears again shortly. My buddy Joab, in the second chapter of First Kings.

> Then Adonijah the son of Hagith exalted himself, saying, "I will be king"; and he prepared for himself chariots and horsemen, and fifty men to run before him. (And his father had not rebuked him at any time saying, "Why have you done so?" He was also very good looking. His mother had born him after Absalom). Then he conferred with Joab the son of Zeruiah and with Abiathar the priest, and they followed and helped Adonijah. But Zadok the priest, Benaiah the son of Jehoiada, Nathan the prophet, Shimei, Rei, and the mighty men who belonged to David were not with Adonijah. (1 Kings 1:5-8) (NKJV)

Does this sound familiar?

> *You have said in your heart: I will ascend into heaven; I will exalt my throne above the stars of God; I will also sit on*

*the mount of the congregation on the farthest sides of the
north; I will ascend above the heights of the clouds. I will
be like the Most High. (Isaiah 14:13-14). (NKJV)*

The familiar quote attributed to Satan. I see this in Adonijah and if it
is familiar it is almost the same attitude as his brother, Absalom.

Look at this verse:

*After this it happened that Absalom provided himself with
chariots and horses, and fifty men to run before him. (2
Samuel 15:1). (NKJV)*

That must have been the custom.

I am confused. These are all children of David, granted they each
had a different mother, you would think, if they were raised in the same
household they would know that God had chosen Solomon as the next
king. You would think.

This kind of reminds me of stories I have heard of what happens when
someone passes away. The family descends on their belongings to get what
they "think" belongs to them. So many sad stories, fights, disagreements,
hurt feelings, etc. Such is the way of this world. The funny thing is these
items will end up in an attic somewhere, never to be seen again. Is it worth it?

Did you catch that phrase? *And his father had not rebuked him at any
time.* This is the same response of David when he heard of Amnon raping
Tamar, "he was angry," really? (2 Samuel 13:21). These family problems
may be part of God's judgment against David for Bathsheba and Uriah
but there must be a better response from David. He is still the head of the
household. It is interesting that he can command a great army but cannot
control his own house.

In a sense, maybe, we can understand Adonijah. Don't forget he also
has Joab whispering in his ear. He will get his soon. Adonijah as well as
Absalom were "heirs" to the throne. They were both sons born to David
through different wives. Amnon was the son of Ahinoam, Absalom was the
son of Maacah, Adonijah is the son of Haggith. If this doesn't support the
principle of one woman, one man I don't know what will. Of course, David
is their father, hence the problem. The interesting thing is GOD chose
Solomon, the son of Bathsheba to be the next king. It was God's choice.

Being God's choice brings up another question about this family. How much was God talked about? More accurately the "will" of God. Has David told his family, shared with them God's plan for Solomon. Would it have made a difference? I wonder. The quest for power, the "pride of life" can blind us to God's working in our life.

I believe David will deal with Abiathar as well.

I am so glad we don't have to deal with kings and these family problems today, right? There are always family problems. So what might be done to solve some of these problems. I am surely no expert. I have heard that even families that go to church together are not immune. Is there an answer. I do remember a passage in the book of Acts:

> *And he brought them out and said, "Sirs, what must I do*
> *to be saved?" So, they said, "Believe on the Lord Jesus*
> *Christ, and you will be saved, you and your household."*
> *(Acts 16:30-31). (NKJV)*

Don't get the wrong impression. Just because the father was saved that didn't include the household. The whole "household" had to believe in Jesus Christ. But because of what had happened they all came to accept Christ.

And Adonijah sacrificed sheep and oxen and fattened cattle by the stone of Zoheleth, which is by En Rogel; he also invited all his brothers, the king's sons, and all the men of Judah, the king's servants. But he did not invite Nathan the prophet, Benaiah, the mighty men, or Solomon his brother. (1 Kings 1:9-10) (NKJV)

I am sitting here, looking at this story. Been there, done that. I'm thinking why is God telling basically the same story. we know the ending, we know Solomon is going to be the king, why are we doing this? I am looking at it through a microscope instead of a telescope. Of course, we know the end. God put this in here for a reason. God chose to include this story, to last thousands of years for a reason. What is He getting at?

God is in charge. We were told at the birth of Solomon that God had chosen him to be the next king after David. Then we see Absalom raise up and challenge for the throne. Now we see Adonijah doing the exact same thing. They were both raised in the same household as Solomon. They all three had the same father. Adonijah saw what happened to Absalom. Yet, still he follows the same "pride of life" that John talks about in 1 John 2:16-17. We are scratching our heads wondering why the repeat?

You see, God has already charted the course. It's the same in our life. God, as we see in Jeremiah 29:11, has a specific plan, IT WILL BE DONE. The question is, will we be a willing participant or go off on our own road and miss heaven. The course has been set, are you on God's plan or your plan? Think about it!

It seems Adonijah is focused on the throne. He doesn't notice Joab, the one who killed his brother Absalom, he is totally focused on what he thinks belongs to him. He is off the road God has planned. You would think that Adonijah would have heard at some point that GOD had chosen Solomon to be the next king. Maybe it didn't matter. Of course, you would never do that with God? You wouldn't argue with God about His plan for your life verses your plan, surely not?

Do you know who Joab reminds me of? Satan. He is the one whispering in our ear that God doesn't know everything. God is trying to keep you from having what is rightfully yours. Do you remember the Garden of Eden?

> *Then the serpent said to the woman, "You will not surely die. For God knows that in the day you eat of it your eyes will be opened and you will be like God, knowing good and evil." (Genesis 3:4-5). (NKJV)*

I can hear Joab now whispering in Adonijah's ear, "The throne is rightfully yours, you need to take it!"

Isn't it interesting that Solomon was not invited to this little get together? I think this is the first appearance of Nathan since his last encounter with David. Did you notice that Nathan is a "prophet" as opposed to Zadok who is a priest? Do we have any "prophets" today? If you look at them as bringing the "Word of God" you could look at a pastor as a prophet. The difference being that the pastor already has the word of God. His purpose or calling is to share that with others. As I said earlier God has already determined the future. Today's "prophet" simply is sharing with us that future (Revelation). It is a "call" to get on God's game plan.

We will see that God's plans always come true. We may think we are going our own way, doing our own thing, but God will have His way. The question to us is, what part will we play? Will we be a part of what God is doing or will we be like Absalom and Adonijah? It's your call. Solomon WILL be king. It is so futile to try to change God's plan.

This might be a good place to turn in your Bible to Jeremiah 29:11-13 again. I know I have quoted that passage several times. There is so much meat there, not milk, but meat. Read it, memorize it, let it soak in. Look at this: *And you will seek Me and find Me. . .*

So, Nathan spoke to Bathsheba the mother of Solomon, saying, "Have you not heard that Adonijah the son of Haggith has become king, and David our lord does not know it. Come, please, let me now give you advice, that you may save your own life and the life of your son Solomon. Go immediately to King David and say to him, 'Did you not, my lord, O king, swear to your maidservant, saying, "Assuredly your son Solomon shall reign after me, and he shall sit on my throne"? Why then has Adonijah become king?' Then, while you are still talking there with the king, I also will come in after you and confirm your words." (1 Kings 1:11-14) (NKJV)

Did you notice how Nathan worded this? *"Has become king!"* God made Saul king (1 Samuel 10). God anointed David king (1 Samuel 16). And Adonijah has become king. I didn't see any mentioned of God in any of this process. Oh, it says Adonijah "sacrificed" oxen and cattle, that doesn't mean God is involved. There is Abiathar, the priest, I have questions about him. This would be a good place for that notebook I had mentioned earlier. The main characters that are missing are Nathan the prophet and Zadok the priest. It's like we have a gathering of one "party" without the members of the other "party". God especially.

Evidently the process that Adonijah participated in was not the "official" coronation. Did you notice who is attempting to make things right? Nathan. We have already seen that God speaks through Nathan. God used Nathan to reproach David for his sin with Bathsheba. It is interesting that the prophet who told David about his three choices in 2 Samuel 24, is not mentioned here either. The prophets are the pastors of today. I mentioned this before.

In David's time the prophet's spoke for God. God used them to communicate His message to whom He wanted spoken to. The preachers today are God's prophets. They already have the "perfect" word of God. Their task is simply to tell us. As a former pastor, it always amazes me how God can select a certain passage, a certain message that speaks to the heart of the one God is trying to reach. I saw that so many times in Freeman, where I pastored. Did you notice that God makes a distinction in the Old Testament between prophet and priest?

Someone once pointed out that there are three "offices" in the Old Testament. Prophet, priest and king. NO ONE has ever filled all three. Saul tried and God took His hand off Saul. The only one to fulfill all three offices is the Lord Jesus Christ. He is Prophet, Priest and King!

We can get an idea of the shape of David. Nathan went to Bathsheba with this conspiracy. Yet, the authority still lay with David. The "king" must decree the next king. I think it might have been "understood" in the David household but evidently never publicly proclaimed. That may be why Adonijah took it on himself to "take the throne." You would think he might have noticed something with Absalom. I guess not.

If you tell any preacher that he is a "prophet' he will deny it. They don't think of themselves as such. They already have the word of God. There are no divine revelations as such today. God has already told us everything we need to know, from the beginning to the end. God has called certain men to "proclaim" what the prophets of old had proclaimed. God is sovereign, God is in control, and God has a plan! The question for us? Are we following that plan? Are we on the right track? That is the job of the preacher and the work of the Holy Spirit.

You could put Nathan as doing the "work" of the Holy Spirit here. He is making sure God's plan is being fulfilled and followed. He is talking to the interested parties and bringing the whole plan into fulfillment. That is what God's Spirit does today. He takes the message of the pastor (preacher) and convicts our hearts about what God is trying to get across to us. When we neglect those regular visits to church, we are missing out on what God wants to tell us. Did Bathsheba need Nathan? Bathsheba had no idea what was going on. It took the prophet Nathan to warn her!

So, Bathsheba went into the chamber to the king. (Now the king was very old, and Abishag the Shunammite was serving the king.) And Bathsheba bowed and did homage to the king. Then the king said, "What is your wish?" Then she said to him, "My lord, you swore by the Lord your God to your maidservant, saying, 'Assuredly Solomon your son shall reign after me, and he shall sit on my throne.' So now, look! Adonijah has become king; and now, my lord the king, you do not know about it. He has sacrificed oxen and fattened cattle and sheep in abundance, and has invited all the sons of the king, Abiathar the priest, and Joab the commander of the army; but Solomon your servant he was not invited. (1 Kings 1:15-19) (NKJV)

Have you ever heard the phrase: God said it, I believe it, that settles it? I heard someone later rephrase it: God said it, that settles it. It doesn't matter whether you believe it or not. That is so true. I marvel at the "authority" expressed in these verses. You have Adonijah, who decided he would be king. Of course, he has the "authority" of being the king's son. Maybe he has the "law" on his side. You have Bathsheba, she has the promise of the king. He told her, her son Solomon would be the next king. Her authority was the king's decree. Then you have Nathan. Nathan's "authority"? The word of God. Remember it was Nathan that noticed the deception and came to Bathsheba, then they to the king.

It is all about authority! Who has the right and the power to execute a command. In Basic Training at Lackland Air Force Base in Texas I learned about "authority". We had to learn what different insignia represented. two silver bars represented a "captain" etc. We had to recognize authority. After leaving the Air Force i went to work for U.P.S. There the authority was the "supervisor." He told you what to do. Later, when I went to work for the National Archives I had several "supervisors" each above the next. I had to know the "chain-of-command." The same in the military as well.

Nathan came to Bathsheba, Bathsheba and Nathan went to David, the king. We sometimes miss the chain-of-command in our Spiritual life. Of course, it can get confusing with God the Father, Jesus the Son and then the Holy Spirit. Don't get this wrong! They are all three the same God. There is no "chain-of-command." Each the same God but a different function. You may have three "captains" in the military but each with a different job. I don't want to make this difficult. The point being, who do you follow, who do you obey, where do you get your instructions?

Nathan, Bathsheba each came to the king. Adonijah took it upon himself to proclaim himself king. The same question I have asked throughout this study, WHERE IS GOD? David is the one God chose to be king. You might say "the buck stops there" in earthly terms maybe. God still raises up and sets down whom He chooses. Just ask Saul.

Okay, who is your authority? We have been stuck on this for a while, but it is important to get this. The world around us has so many options, so many alternatives, it can be just like Adonijah or Absalom. Go here, do this, think that, yet who has the "authority" to make those decisions in your life? Of course, if you haven't asked Jesus into your life, you're going to follow the world's lead. If you have become a child of God, then you have the "ultimate" authority in your life. The question then becomes, obedience. David found that out the hard way.

You get the picture that David is weak and helpless, don't you. God can use anyone at any time to accomplish His will. If God had told me a year ago that I would author two books, I would have stood with my jaw to the floor. God has, so, blessed me I am amazed at what He has accomplished. How did I do it? I just obeyed the Holy Spirit that said "write!" I then turned it in to the publisher and put it in God's hands. I did what I was told. The rest is up to the power of God. Obedience to the commands of He who is in charge!

And as for you, my lord, O king, the eyes of all Israel are on you, that you should tell them who will sit on the throne of my lord the king after him. Otherwise it will happen, when my lord the king rests with his fathers, that I and my son Solomon will be counted as offenders." And just then, while she was still talking with the king, Nathan the prophet also came in. So, they told the king, saying, "Here is Nathan the prophet." And when he came in before the king, he bowed down before the king with his face to the ground. And Nathan said, "My lord, O king, have you said, 'Adonijah shall reign after me, and he shall sit on my throne?" (1 Kings 1:20-24) (NKJV)

The words of Genesis keep ringing through my head: "Has God indeed said, "(Genesis 3:1). Satan question Eve on what God told Adam about that tree in the garden.

I have talked at length about this idea of "relationship" verses "fellowship" with God. I am so grateful to God for bringing me along on this walk with David. I have learned so much! This concept intrigues me. I have a new friend. I really love Jeremiah 29:11-13, as I'm sure you have noticed. But

I have referred to this verse several times. As I meditate on it I think it illustrates these two concepts.

> *For as many as are led by the Spirit of God, these are sons of God. For you did not receive the spirit of bondage again to fear, but you received the Spirit of adoption by whom we cry out, "Abba, Father." (Romans 8:14-15) (NKJV)*

I want to stop there. Do you see this first step? You are a child of God when you, led by God's Spirit, have asked Jesus Christ into your heart. When you have made that decision, you are in the family of God. Every Sunday, after our Sunday School lesson we sing, "I'm so glad I'm a part of the family of God. . . "As a child of God, we are in the family of God and have a unique "relationship" with God our Father.

Now look at the rest of Romans 8:15, *by whom we cry out, "Abba, Father."* The meaning of "Abba" in the Greek I understand means "daddy". An intimate name for the God of the Universe. Here is that "fellowship" with God that I am trying to describe. It is one thing to have our "ticket punched" and still another to have that intimate fellowship with our Heavenly Father. That fellowship comes from a regular prayer time and hours in the word of God. You get to know God's heart by spending time in God's word!

If you know God's word you won't have to ask, "Did God say?" You will know. I think we talked before about the reason for this search. I want to find out why David was called: A Man After God's Own Heart? The reverse of this might be, a search for what is in God's heart. If David exemplifies God's heart, we need to understand WHY David has this distinction. We can best understand God's heart by reading and absorbing His word. I hope this journey with David has stirred a new interest in God's word.

Let me finish those verses in Romans:

> *The Spirit Himself bears witness with our spirit that we are children of God, and if children, then heirs—heirs of God and joint heirs with Christ, if indeed we suffer with Him, that we may also be glorified together. (Romans 8:16-17) (NKJV)*

Did you catch that? We are "brothers or sisters" of Jesus. That's what I read. We are PART of God's family. If we, as Christians, ever grasp that "relationship" with our heavenly Father it will change our life, and hopefully our fellowship with God.

They come before King David for the final determination of who will be king. Have you approached God about who is king in your life? Have you asked Jesus to be King of your life? Who oversees your life, you or God? You must one day answer that question. You must decide before you stand before the King of Kings, who is Lord of your life? To wait till you meet the King, is to wait too late! It must be made now!

For he has gone down today, and has sacrificed oxen and fattened cattle and sheep in abundance, and has invited all the king's sons, and the commanders of the army, and Abiathar the priest; and look! They are eating and drinking before him; and they say, 'Long live King Adonijah!' But he has not invited me—me your servant—nor Zadok the priest, nor Benaiah the son of Jehoiada, nor your servant Solomon. Has this thing been done by my lord the king, and you have not told your servant who should sit on the throne of my lord the king after him?" (1 Kings 1:25-27) (NKJV)

Let's take a minute and look at David's journal. First:

> *But when King David heard of all these things, he was very angry. (2 Samuel 13:21). (NKJV)*

What things? Amnon's raping his sister Tamar. Amnon was David's first-born son by Ahinoam. "he was very angry". Really? That was all that was said. Later Absalom killed Amnon in revenge for Tamar his sister.

Second: Absalom ran from Jerusalem rather than face his father. Later, through Joab, Absalom is brought back to Jerusalem.

> *And Absalom dwelt two full years in Jerusalem, but did not see the king's face. (2 Samuel 14:28). (NKJV)*

David arranged for his son's return to Jerusalem but refused to see him. So, what does Absalom do? He arranges a coup against his father. He tries to take his father's throne. After taking the throne and chasing David over the Jordan, Joab kills Absalom. What was David's response?

Third:

Then the king was deeply moved, and went up to the chamber over the gate, and wept. And as he went, he said thus, "O my son Absalom—my son, my son Absalom—if only I had died in your place! O Absalom my son, my son!" (2 Samuel 18:33) (NKJV)

It took Joab to confront David and remind him he is still the king and has a responsibility to his army.

David may have been a great warrior, but was lacking in his parental skills. I point out these events to remind us who we are talking about in these last days. It took Nathan and Bathsheba to remind him of the promise God made to him and Bathsheba about Solomon. Maybe it was his old age, I don't know. He must be weak, if he needs a maiden to keep him warm. He is still the king. I am impressed that they treat him as such, at least his inner circle. Evidently his son, Adonijah doesn't feel the same way.

I wanted to use the "journal" analogy to remind you to seriously consider keeping one of your own. When you seem to be off track, you don't understand why certain things are happening, you might want to pull that journal out and start reading back. You just might run across an event in your life where you turned left on this road and God went right. Who knows?

His wife and prophet don't even know if David has permitted this. They ask him. Maybe it was their way of getting his attention. It still amazes me the lack of communication in David's household. You would think that all of David's sons would know who the next king is. Maybe they know and think they can change the outcome. Have you tried that with God? Maybe you think that if you pray hard enough and often enough you can change God's plan. More than likely God will change your thinking. God always knows best. It is a waste of time to think you can change God's will for your life. Now you can go your own way, to your peril. You can't change what God is going to do.

Suppose David was dead at this point. He couldn't communicate his wishes, etc. Do you think that would prevent Solomon from being king, not hardly? I have shared this before. God will have His way. The question is, will you be a part of the blessing, or be left out in the cold. It's your choice.

That is why it is so important to be on GOD'S path and not your own. You never know what blessing you're going to miss out on.

Then King David answered and said, "Call Bathsheba to me." So, she came into the king's presence and stood before the king. And the king took an oath and said, "As the Lord lives, who has redeemed my life from every distress, just as I swore to you by the Lord God of Israel, saying, 'Assuredly Solomon your son shall be king after me, and shall sit on my throne in my place,' so I certainly will do this day." Then Bathsheba bowed with her face to the earth, and paid homage to the king, and said, "Let my lord King David live forever!" (1 Kings 1:28-31) (NKJV)

Can you, or have you ever used those words? "As the Lord lives." What a neat phrase. What a statement to base your pledge on. There is faith. David is finally taking charge. He has gathered the "appropriate" witnesses, including the priest. He, in a sense, is making his last will and testament. He is righting a wrong he has allowed to fester since Absalom.

That is something I just don't understand. But, then again, how is the communication in your home? Solomon has been in David's home for many years. Surely, the message was sent that Solomon would be the next king, maybe not. We have seen David's communication skills. At the last minute, after a rebellion, David will make things right. The funny thing is, it's not David's will that is being fulfilled here, it is God's!

God has a way of keeping with His divine plan, regardless of the players. I brought this out before. If you think your refusing to go along with "God's" plan will thwart His desires, think again. The only difference is that God will not use YOU to accomplish this plan. God will get the job done one way or another. You simply miss out on the blessing. Have you stood on the sidelines and watched God work in "others" rather than you? Why is that? You must get involved in what God is doing.

The best way to do that is to get involved in your local church. A church where God is reaching people and changing lives. It begins with faithful attendance, more than once a month. Then you keep your eyes and ears open. "Is there a need?" volunteer. Do you know your Spiritual Gift"? Find out what that is. There are questionnaires you can get on the internet, ask your pastor, etc. Find your Spiritual Gift, then use it.

When my wife and I were first saved, we started cleaning the church on Saturdays. I soon learned my gift was teaching. I have been teaching in the Sunday School now over thirty years, in one form or another. I can tell you with full assurance, once you find that gift and begin using it the joy in your life will increase a hundred-fold!

I was thinking earlier about the people of Israel. Can you imagine the confusion? Who, in the world, is king? Who is in charge? Is that what you are saying, in your family, today. If you're not a Christian it is the devil, plain and simple. If you are a Christian, it should be the Holy Spirit, that assumes you are listening to Him. Is their chaos in your life? Who is in charge? Have you "surrendered" to Jesus? Imagine the confusion in Israel, between Absalom, and now Adonijah, I think I would want to know, "Who is in charge?"

Look at this verse: *For God is not the author of confusion but of peace* (1 Corinthians 14:33a). And this one, my favorite: *Let all things be done decently and in order.* (1 Corinthians 14:40). Is there confusion in David's home? Of course, there is, why? David has taken the leadership, to instruct his family in the "will of God." It will always fall to the "head of the household" to take that leadership. God is in the process of bringing order here.

It might be an interesting study, sometime, to research through David's life and see how many times, and in what ways a priest has been involved in David's life. If you remember, early on in his walk, David, "Inquired of the Lord" several times. It was when he got away from that practice he began to make mistakes. How about you? When was the last time you, "inquired of the Lord," before choosing a path to travel?

And King David said, "Call to me Zadok the priest, Nathan the Prophet, and Benaiah the son of Jehoiada." So, they came before the king. The king also said to them, "Take with you the servants of your lord, and have Solomon my son ride on my own mule, and take him down to Gihon. There let Zadok the priest and Nathan the prophet anointing him king over Israel; and blow the horn, and say, 'Long live King Solomon!" Then you shall come up after him, and he shall come and sit on my throne, and he shall be king in my place. For I have appointed him to be ruler over Israel and Judah." Benaiah the son of Jehoiada answered the king and said, "Amen! May the Lord God of my lord the king, say, so too. As the Lord has been with my lord the king, even so may He be with Solomon, and make his throne greater than the throne of my lord King David." (1 Kings 1:32-37) (NKJV)

Did you catch that? Let's look at past verses:

> *After this it happened that Absalom provided himself with chariots and horses, and fifty men to run before him. (2 Samuel 15:1). (NKJV)*

How about this verse:

> *Then Adonijah the son of Haggith exalted himself, saying, "I will be king," and he prepared for himself chariots and horsemen, and fifty men to run before him. (1 Kings 1:5) (NKJV)*

Now compare those with the above verse:

> *The king also said to them, "Take with you the servants of your lord, and have Solomon my son ride on my own mule, and take him down to Gihon. There let Zadok the priest and Nathan the prophet anoint him king over Israel; and blow the horn, and say, 'Long live King Solomon'" (1 Kings 1:33-34). (NKJV)*

Do you see the difference, the contrast?

There is such an important principle here. There is "man's way" then there is God's way. David learned that lesson the hard way when he tried to bring the ark of God into Jerusalem. (2 Samuel 6). I like the way my Bible notes this chapter, "Doing the right thing in a wrong way." There is, as I said, our way and God's way. We see this both in Absalom and Adonijah. So, a simple question, how do we know God's way? How did David learn how to bring the ark of God to Jerusalem? He probably asked the priests. The books of Moses were not widely available. Today we have a copy of God's word in our hands. How much do you know?

Here is a great principle to learn from our study of David. We noted earlier that David, "Inquired of the Lord." We noted that David would confess his sin, when God convicted him of it, usually through a prophet,

Nathan or Gad. David often sought the counsel of his priests. We have seen through these chapters some basic principles that we can apply to our own lives. Oh, this last one, doing things God's way and not the "world's" way. Since both Absalom and Adonijah did the same procedure I am assuming that was the accepted method of becoming king. It wasn't God's will or God's way.

Who is this Benaiah the son of Jehoiada? The first reference I can find is in 2 Samuel 8,

> *Benaiah the son of Jehoida was over both the Cherethites and the Pelethites; and David's sons were chief ministers. (2 Samuel 8:18). (NKJV)*

The best I can determine he was a "servant" of David's. I think it is interesting that he is associated with "David's sons." Maybe he got the memo on who was to be the next king, evidently the sons didn't.

I mentioned earlier that David's story is also relayed in 1 Chronicles. Just like the gospels there are things covered in Chronicles that may not be covered in Samuel and Kings. The story begins in 1 Chronicles 11, with David's anointing as king of Israel. It skips the early years with Saul, etc. We find in 1 Chronicles the reason David was finally able to bring the ark of God to Jerusalem (1 Chronicles 15:13). In 1 Chronicles 22 it tells of David's gathering the materials for Solomon to construct God's temple. This isn't revealed in Samuel. Just a couple of examples of studying 1 Chronicles along with the books of 1 Samuel 16 through 1 Kings 2. Bible study can be so exciting and enlightening. It is a life's work!

So Zadok the priest, Nathan the prophet, Benaiah the son of Jehoiada, the Cherethites, and the Pelethites went down and had Solomon ride on King David's mule, and took him to Gihon. Then Zadok the priest took a horn of oil from the tabernacle and anointed Solomon. And they blew the horn, and all the people said, "Long live King Solomon!" And all the people went up after him; and the people played the flutes and rejoiced with great joy, so that the earth seemed to split with their sound. (1 Kings 1:38-40) (NKJV)

The Three Musketeers! Zadok, Nathan and Benaiah. We need to be aware of the "priests" in David's life. Their impact on David's decision-making process, etc. Both Nathan and Zadok, and, just briefly mentioned, Gad. A lesson for us?

When, how and why are you learning any of the Bible? As a former Sunday School Director for over thirty years, that is my passion and my calling. The more we can incorporate the word of God into our lives, the closer we can walk with God, the more intimate our relationship with the God of this universe, the better off we will be. Should I quote some verses? Let's start with this one:

> *This book of the Law shall depart from your mouth, but you shall meditate in it day and night, that you may observe to do according to all that is written in it. For then you will make your way prosperous, and then you will have good success. (Joshua 1:8). (NKJV)*

A good place to start. This is a challenge and a promise that God made to Joshua just before, finally, entering the Promised land.

Mr. Dave Ramsey, financial expert, quotes several Scriptures in his books on financial wisdom. Here is one of my favorites: *Train up a child. . .* we know that verse. How about the next part?

> *The rich rules over the poor, and the borrower is servant to the lender. (Proverbs 22:7). (NKJV)*

A basic truth that we want to ignore today. We want what we want when we want it. It took me several years to learn this truth! Basic Bible teaching.

Our pastor is teaching through the gospel of John on Sunday morning, the gospel of Mark on Wednesdays and on Sunday nights a study in Angels and Demons. Each service a "helping" of the word of God. Adding to our knowledge, adding to our walk, adding to our fellowship with the Author.

The verses above are simply carrying out what David had said earlier. Do you notice that they carried it out "to the letter"? That is what God wants from us. Not half way, not piecemeal, totally committed to the whole precept of the Word of God.

Let me share a couple more verses, if I may:

You will show me the path of life; in Your presence is fullness of joy; at Your right hand are pleasures forevermore. (Psalm 16:11) (NKJV)

I have just found this recently. After writing a book, entitled THE PATH. It has really become so clear to me that God has this path, established the day He created us in the womb. His desire is that we walk that path. Too many times we stray, just as David, then we must find our way back. The longer and better we make a conscious effort to stay on that path, the better off we will be.

One more, my favorite:

For I know the thoughts that I have toward you, says the Lord, thoughts of peace and not evil, to give you a future and a hope. Then you will call upon Me and go and pray to Me, and I will listen to you. And you will seek Me and find Me, when you search for Me with all your heart. (Jeremiah 29:11-13). (NKJV)

These words have come to mean so much to me. Digest these words. Think about how they may apply to your life. Pray about what God is doing in your life. Is God trying to get your attention about something that needs to change. You may be on one of those side paths, away from God. You need to ask God, let Him help you get back on track, back into His will and purpose for your life.

David is finally fulfilling the promise God made to him, following Solomon's birth. Don't overlook those miraculous circumstances in David's life!

Now Adonijah and all the guests who were with him heard it as they finished eating. And when Joab heard the sound of the horn, he said, "Why is the city in such a noisy uproar?" While he was still speaking, there came Jonathan the son of Abiathar the priest. And Adonijah said to him, "Come in, for you are a prominent man, and bring good news." Then Jonathan answered and said to Adonijah, "No! Our lord King David has made Solomon king. "The king has sent with him Zadok the priest, Nathan the prophet, Benaiah the son of Jehoiada, the Cherethites, and the Pelethites; and they have made him ride on the king's mule." (1 Kings 1:41-44) (NKJV)

What does it take for you to give up? I heard a disturbing comment from the fellow who is leading our "Men's Ministry". He is ready to give up. Why? He doesn't feel it is "growing" or accomplishing what he thinks it should. The problem is, it's not his ministry, it belongs to God. Evidently God has called him to this ministry. He has been the leader for several years. We used to have eight to ten, now we have over twenty coming to our monthly breakfasts. Is he measuring success by his standards or God's.

David could very well give up. He is old, his family, in his eyes, have turned against him. Adonijah has, as far as appearances go, taken over the throne right out from under David. Why fight it anymore? Let him have it! Are you ready to give up? Have you talked to God about it? What did He say?

Let me refresh your memory with some names, Amnon, Tamar, Absalom, Joab, Amasa, Ziba's servant, and finally Adonijah. These are in our notebook of names we are keeping. What kind of notations do you have by each name? I would think, as David reflects on these people and events, David would be ready to give up, except for one thing!

God promised him that Solomon would set on his throne. Of course, David could do like we would, just set back and let God do the work. Have you ever thought of doing that? Do you think that is the way God works? I hope not. God uses His servants to accomplish His will and purpose on this earth. Those who are willing to do God's will receive God's blessing, those who want to just set back, will be ignored by God.

I remember the night that God confirmed His calling to ministry in my life. I was dumbfounded, flabbergasted, amazed. I couldn't believe that He thought He could use someone like me. Then I found this verse:

> But God has chosen the foolish things of the world to put to shame the wise, and God has chosen the weak things of the world to put to shame the things which are mighty. (1 Corinthians 1:27). (NKJV)

Basically, God can use anyone to accomplish His will, if they are willing and obedient!

There is a critical point here in our story. First, remember where David came from? He was a teenager in the fields tending his father's sheep. God called him to be king of Israel. That destination was not easy! There are many different trials and pitfalls David had to struggle through. David had to learn to trust God and most important to follow God's leading. Over forty years later I think he got the memo. Instead of just giving up, David went to work. With the help of Bathsheba and Nathan and Benaiah, David made arrangements for his son Solomon to become king. He called the witnesses, he gave specific instructions, to make it happen. He was determined to do God's will!

How about you? Has God given you a ministry? A calling? Has God laid on your heart a job to do. Maybe it is substitute teacher. Who knows? The question is, are you willing to do what God wants to do in your life? You will have opposition, you will be discouraged, you will question God's wisdom. Let me give you a verse that always gets me back on track:

> *Trust in the Lord with all your heart, and lean not upon your own understanding; in all your ways acknowledge Him, and He will direct your path! (Proverbs 3:5-6) (NKJV)*

So Zadok the priest and Nathan the prophet, have anointed him king at Gihon; and they have gone up from there rejoicing, so that the city is in an uproar. This is the noise that you have heard. Also, Solomon sits on the throne of the kingdom. And moreover, the king's servants have gone to bless our lord King David, saying, 'May God make the name of Solomon better than your name, and may He make his throne greater than your throne.' Then the king bowed himself on the bed. Also, the king said thus, 'Blessed be the Lord God of Israel, who has given one to sit on my throne this day, while my eyes see it!'" So, all the guests who were with Adonijah were afraid, and arose, and each one went his way. (1 Kings 1:45-49) (NKJV)

This scene reminds me of a scene in the movie "Dave" with Kevin Kline. The President's assistant thinks he has managed to unseat the President. He is gathered in a room full of supporters. The President presents a dozier full of evidence that the assistant was the culprit. The camera goes back to the room. . . it is empty, except for the assistant. That is Adonijah here. All his support has vanished once the king is recognized.

I am sure I have shared this before. It is one of my favorite quotes when someone starts talking about "plans." Do you know how to make God laugh? Tell Him your plans. That is what Adonijah is feeling right now. When you start thinking you have it all figured out, God has a habit of reminding you who is in charge!

That may be a lesson David learned that night he should have been on the battlefield but, instead, was watching a girl take a bath. When we are out of God's will, anything can happen, and often does. God has a way of bringing us back to the path we are supposed to be on!

God is not through with Adonijah, or Joab or Abiathar for that matter. That reminds me.

I have been touting the virtues of consulting and listening to the pastor in your local church. Don't get the impression they are "perfect". They are not. Case in point, Abiathar the priest. His relationship with David is much like Joab's. Some good, mostly bad. Just because he is a priest doesn't make him a saint! In our case the first sign is the conviction of the Holy Spirit. We don't have a peace about his teaching and/or preaching. God will warn us right off! The next might be his use of the word of God, if he uses it at all. If your pastor does not quote from scripture or misquotes it, RUN! Find a Bible believing, Bible teaching church. The same can be said for your Sunday School teacher!

David has finally passed on his legacy to his son, Solomon. Solomon is "officially" the king of Israel. You might say David has retired. Such is the "kingship". The king is a concept we in America can't really understand. We fought the Revolutionary War to be out from under a king. To rule by the consent of the people. A totally unheard-of concept in the world prior to the establishment of our government. When I think of the wisdom that those men had at that time, it just amazes me. It could only have come from God.

Judging from the comments of David and his servants we can assume the same is true here. God has set up the next king of Israel. Absalom and Adonijah thought they could "take" the throne that they thought belonged to them. When you leave God out of any equation, you are looking for trouble. How about your plans? Do they include God? Have you prayed and consulted God in your decision-making process? If not you better do it now, before it is too late. Before you get too far down the wrong path. The journey back is not pleasant!

We are nearing the end of David's life. He has established Solomon on the throne, with the help of God, of course! There is still some unfinished business that he must ask Solomon to deal with. How would you characterize the life of David? David, a man after God's own heart. Just what does that phrase mean to you? Can you relate? Have you sought God's heart? How is your relationship with God?

Now Adonijah was afraid of Solomon; so he arose, and went and took hold of the horns of the altar. And it was told Solomon, saying, "Indeed Adonijah is afraid of King Solomon; for look, he has taken hold of the horns of the altar, saying, 'Let King Solomon swear to me today that he will not put his servant to death with the sword.'" Then Solomon said, "If he proves himself a worthy man, not one hair of him shall fall to the earth; but if wickedness is found in him, he shall die." So, King Solomon sent them to bring him down from the altar. And he came and fell down before King Solomon; and Solomon said to him, "Go to your house." (1 Kings 1:50-53) (NKJV)

> "You shall make its horns on its four corners; its horns shall be of one piece with it. And you shall overlay it with bronze. (Exodus 27:2). (NKJV)

The description of the "Bronze Altar" as given to Moses.

Did you catch the words of King Solomon, "*if he proves himself a worthy man*" prophetic words? When you finish reading chapter two. Solomon finally settles the score with Joab, Adonijah, Abiathar and Shimei.

> Thus, the kingdom was established in the hand of Solomon. (1 Kings 2:46b). (NKJV)

That phrase keeps sticking in my head, "*If he proves himself a worthy man*" I can see it now. We have passed away, we are standing before God to determine whether we can enter heaven or not (according to Hollywood). God opens His ledger and counts the good deeds vs the bad deeds, if the good outweigh the bad we can enter heaven. Really? Where does the cross figure in this scenario? It doesn't!

If you spend any time in the Old Testament, God went to great pains to demonstrate the principle of the price for sin. The "deeds" have nothing to do with it. You could be a "saint" on earth and spend eternity in Hades. If you are covered in the blood of Christ your entry into heaven is assured! That is the principle GOD established with the sacrifice of His Son on the cross of Calvary.

Solomon set the rules for Adonijah, the king set the standard. Adonijah couldn't help but betray this trust. He tried to trick his way to the throne. He paid the price. We have covered the "plan of salvation" already, the Roman's Road, etc. We know the truth. The question becomes, what do you do with it?

Suppose you stand before God and God asks, "Did you read My word?" We say, "Oh, just a little, 23rd psalms, the Ten Commandments, a little of John." God replies, "You think that will get you into heaven?" "Yes, I also prayed for my family and friends and the lost." We reply. "So you are listing these spiritual activities and they are supposed to get you in?" God replies. I even went to church a few times, I found some people I saw at my workplace who didn't act like "Christians." Is your response. "So that kept you from worship?" "Yes!"

"What do you think about my Son?" "Who, Jesus?" "Yes!" Your response is, "Great teacher, great stories in the gospels, He did a lot of tricks, miracles." God asks, "Who is He to you?" "A great historical figure, for sure." God says, "Thanks, that is all I need to know." Well, you know the rest, you know where he will spend eternity.

Can I ask you the same question? "What do you think of Jesus?" David didn't "know" Jesus but David was assured he would go to heaven. That's fine prior to the cross. After the cross, there is but one way to heaven. Jesus paid for our sins on the cross so that through Christ we have permission to enter God's presence. There is no other way! Look what Jesus said in the gospel of John,

> Jesus said to him, "I am the way, the truth, and the life. No one comes to the Father except through Me. (John 1:4:6). (NKJV)

1 Kings 2

Now the days of David drew near that he should die, and he charged Solomon his son, saying: "I go the way of all the earth be strong, therefore, and prove yourself a man. And keep the charge of the Lord your God: to walk in His ways, to keep His statutes, His commandments, His judgments, and His testimonies, as it is written in the Law of Moses, that you may prosper in all that you do and wherever you turn; that the Lord may fulfill His word which He spoke concerning me, saying, "If your sons take heed to their way, to walk before Me in truth with all their heart and with all their soul, "He said, "you shall not lack a man on the throne of Israel." (1 Kings 2:1-4) (NKJV)

What would be your last words to those by your bedside? Have you thought about it? Probably not. The scary part is, we don't know how or when we will die. That is up to God. As I mentioned earlier, NOW is the time to prepare, not when you are standing before God, then it's too late!

What do you think of David's last words?

> *Walk in His ways, keep His statutes, His commandments,*
> *His judgments, and His testimonies, as it is written. (1*
> *Kings 2:3a) (NKJV)*

We can stop there, because as a Christian today, we have the New Testament writings as well. I guess the point would be to those standing by, OBEY GOD!

I like the way Dr. Charles Stanley says it, "Obey God, and leave all the consequences to Him." David knows all about consequences.

Does it sound like David had made peace with God? Think about what has happened. The son that was born to him and Bathsheba, after the death of their "first born" has become the king of Israel. His son will build the temple of God. A task David had wished to do, but God asked David to "prepare the way." David assembled all the materials (1 Chronicles 22). I believe I read somewhere that "Solomon's Temple" was one of the "Wonders of the Ancient World". It is interesting how these monuments we build seldom last. It is the truth, that we pass on to the next generation that which will last.

The eleven men that Jesus chose, after praying all night, those eleven and the apostle Paul, later will change the world. The message that was passed down from generation to generation, is still just as powerful today. A message that can change your life! The same message, in a sense, that David is passing on to his son Solomon.

Think about what Solomon has accomplished. Besides building that fantastic temple, he wrote the book of Proverbs, Son of Solomon and Ecclesiastes. Spend some time in these books glean the truths and wisdom from Solomon's writings. Of course, the writings were led by the Spirit of God. We can memorize the book of Proverbs but if we don't apply those truths to our life all we have is "head" knowledge.

It is fitting that, at this point, David is passing on this wisdom to his son, Solomon. The life that David led reminds me, in some ways, of the apostle Paul. Paul was instrumental in another death (Stephen) as David was in Uriah's. Both led stressful and challenging lives. Both maintained that critical relationship with Almighty God. How about your relationship with God? Think about it!

Coffee Break!

The last couple of Bibles I have bought I have turned to John 3:16 and crossed out "world" and wrote my name:

> For God, so loved **Lonny** that He gave His only begotten Son, that whosoever believes in Him should not perish but have everlasting life. (John 3:16) (NKJV)

The Bible is personal. The Bible is God's revealed word for this path we are taking, called life. It is our compass!

I hope this journey with King David has been personal. As we shared in his life events I hope we could sense both his heart and God's heart. That was the motivation for this journey, remember? Why was David referred to as "A Man After God's Own Heart?" We also need to remember, above all else, David is as human as you or I. David made some grave mistakes, but he came back to God! Repented and sought God's forgiveness.

David also shows us that there are consequences for our sin. Some have lifetime results. But God is still there when we search for Him, seek Him with all our heart.

We also see God's faithfulness and His grace. His grace toward Bathsheba, even though she lost the first child, God blessed her with Israel's future king. We were there that night when God took that child, and David shared with us that "he can't come back to me but I can go to be with him." What a fantastic promise we can share.

Then the time David took a census contrary to God's will. God gave David three choices of judgment. Like we would, he chose to end it quickly. Three days of plague. Just before the plague was to destroy Jerusalem, David builds an altar and offers a sacrifice. A sacrifice offered by the owner for free, but David said,

> Then the king said to Araunah, "No, but I will surely buy it from you for a price; nor will I offer burnt offerings to the Lord my God with that which cost me nothing." (2 Samuel 24:24) (NKJV)

Do you know the importance of that simple statement? You see, God made the same statement when it came to covering our sin. Allowing us to come into His presence at a price. That price was the blood of His Son Jesus. (John 3:16). God paid our sacrifice that we may be "allowed" into His holy presence. We could never come close to covering that sin-debt. God covered it with the offering of His Son.

Let me remind you of the question I asked at the beginning of this journey. What word comes to mind when you think of David? My guess is, it would either be Goliath or Bathsheba, maybe Uriah with Bathsheba. I wonder how many remember Uriah's roll in that episode. Hopefully there might be some other words that come to mind.

I was wondering, why were these books not called David 1 and David 2? Samuel was the transition from the time of the Judges to Israel's kings. Samuel was a prophet as was Nathan and Gad. The prophets were the ones God used to bring the word of God to man. Someone once explained it this way: A prophet represents God to man. A priest represents man to God. Interesting. When God needed to convict David of something He chose a prophet to bring the message to David.

Today God has three options to get His message across to us. One: The Holy Spirit of God will convict us, speak to our hearts. Two: The word of God, the more time we spend in God's word the more we understand what God is trying to tell us. Third: The local church and the pastor. Just like the prophets in David's time. Regular church attendance will draw you closer to God than you could possibly imagine. There is one problem with all three of these options. You have to want to listen. Then you need to obey. These are "options"! God will not force us to do anything. It's our choice. It's our call. It's our consequences for not walking with God!

PSALM 37

Do not fret because of evildoers, Nor, be envious of the workers of iniquity. For they shall soon be cut down like the grass, and wither as the green herb. (Psalm 37:1-2) (NKJV)

My study Bible says 73 psalms are attributed to King David. I would love to know at what point David wrote each psalm. Most scholars agree that the 51st psalm was written just after his affair with Bathsheba. Maybe you might guess, according to the content when they might have been written, but it is a guess.

We have finished our walk with David. I hope the walk has been educational and inspirational. Now I would like to finish up our walk with one of my favorite psalms. In the flyleaf of my Bible I noted, "Emergency Sermon" psalm 37. If someone surprises me, and asks me to preach. I could use this psalm with no problem. There is so much here. I hope to share some of my thoughts.

Are you distracted? When you look around and see all the "unfairness" in the world today, doesn't it just frustrate you? Of course, it does! First, you need to remember whose world you are living in, Satan's. Look what Paul writes in Ephesians:

> *And you He made alive, who were dead in trespasses and sins, in which you once walked according to the course of this world, according to the prince of the power of the air, the spirit who now works in the sons of disobedience. (Ephesians 2:1-2). (NKJV)*

Of course, we know from the book of Job that Satan can only do what God allows him to do. So why does God allow so much unfairness? God has pretty much given Satan free rein in the "affairs" of men on this earth. Look what else Paul writes in Ephesians:

> But God who is rich in mercy, because of His great love with which He loved us, even when we were dead in trespasses, made us alive together with Christ (by grace you have been saved.) (Ephesians 2:4-5). (NKJV)

You could almost say that God is allowing Satan to have free reign to drive us to Him.

Are you fed up with the "unfairness"? You need to seek the power that Jesus offers. God will send His Holy Spirit to dwell within you. The Spirit will give you a peace about your relationship with God. Of course, you must ask Jesus to save you and come into your heart by faith. Then you will see this world in a whole new light.

Do you see the promise in the verses above? *For they shall soon be cut down.* Now, understand that "soon" is in God's time, not ours. If you are a Christian you might want to read the book of Revelation. If you're not a Christian it will make little or no sense. Without the Holy Spirit helping to understand it, it will be confusing. The point? We win! The promise of this verse in psalm 37 is fulfilled in God's time in God's way. Our Savior will return and make things right!

Is the world in chaos to you? See what David wrote, *Fret not because of evil doers.* Look what Isaiah tells us about Jesus,

> And His name will be called Wonderful, Counselor, Mighty God, Everlasting Father, **Prince of peace.** (Isaiah 9:6b). (NKJV)

Peace in this world only comes from the relationship with our Heavenly Father. Look at Romans 8:15.

Do you have a relationship with Jesus? You don't know peace until you have given your life to God. Then you need to learn to walk with God, trust Him. God can give you the victories in your struggles with this "unfair" world. Remember, you are only passing through. This is not your home, if you are a child of God.

Trust in the Lord, and do good; dwell in the land, and feed on His faithfulness. Delight yourself also in the Lord, and He will give you the desires of your heart. (Psalm 37:3-4) (NKJV)

Here is one of several verses you could underline in this psalm. "Trust in the Lord" that sounds familiar:

> *Trust in the Lord with all your heart, and lean not on your own understanding; in all your ways acknowledge Him, and He will direct your paths. (Proverbs 3:5-6). (NKJV)*

A couple of verses you need to underline. If you're like me, you have SEVERAL verses underlined! Basic biblical principles to remember and follow.

What do you think it means to "trust in the Lord?" One of my favorite old TV series was Wagon Train. Flint McCullough, the scout for the wagon train would ride out ahead of the train and scout. When he came back he told the Wagon Master what lay ahead, any dangers and land marks to beware of. The Wagon Master (Seth Adams) trusted the direction of the scout. Now, if you knew someone who knew what was going to happen, tomorrow, next week, next year, would you trust him? That's what David is getting at here!

I want to remind you of a phrase David used often, early in his walk with God. David, *Inquired of the Lord.* David sought the counsel of someone he knew would give him good direction. Now, with any advice you have to trust the one giving the advice. Test Him! Of course, you will need a relationship with the God of the Universe. That begins with accepting Jesus as your Savior. Upon that decision, you will receive the Holy Spirit who will guide you along this path that God has chosen for your life. Now the tough part! Just what David and Solomon have said, "Trust in the Lord."

God will give you some strange instructions sometimes. Do you remember Genesis 22? After finally getting the son that God promised to Abraham, God told Abraham to take him up on a mountain and offer him as a "burnt" sacrifice, essentially to kill him. So, Abraham, argued and denied what God had said, and question the wisdom, etc. Look at Abraham's response:

So, Abraham rose early in the morning and saddled his
donkey. . (Genesis 22:3a). (NKJV)

My picture is that he left the next day, or soon thereafter. He did NOT argue, debate or hesitate. Abraham "trusted God" and did as He said. What would you have done?

Here are some words we might miss here: *and feed on His faithfulness.* The more you learn to trust God, be obedient to the promptings of His Spirit the stronger our faith grows. We "feed" on God's faithfulness. Our faith grows, our obedience grows, and our blessings grow.

I don't want to neglect these words: *And He will give you the desires of your heart.* Don't miss what God is saying here. We all have our "wish lists" don't we? "If I had a million dollars" type of thing. That is NOT what God is talking about. Do you remember why we started our walk with David? I wanted to find out why David was called "A man after God's own heart." That is the key. When we are walking with God, we learn the things that please God. We want to please God. The "desires" of our heart are the things that please God. God wants to bless us. If for no other reason than to be a testimony to those around us. We should want the things God wants.

I have the words "trust" and "delight" underlined in this passage. As well as several other words: Commit, Rest, Cease, etc. Twice in this psalm David says, "wait on the Lord." (37:9,34). Not my favorite concept. The hardest thing I have ever learned, (not there yet!) to do with God's plan for my life is to wait on His timing.

There is so much in just these two verses. As we travel through this psalm I hope you will glean the nuggets of truth that will help in your walk with God. That is what life is, or should be, as a child of God. A journey of wonders, as you see God work in your life!

Commit your way to the Lord, trust also in Him, and He will bring it to pass. He shall bring forth your righteousness as the light, and your justice as the noonday. (Psalm 37:5-6) (NKJV)

Not long after I was saved I wanted to go to either a Wednesday night service or Sunday night, not sure which. I asked the family, who wants to go with me? Each had their own excuse. As I was driving to church I was thinking, "I'm not going to do this alone." It wasn't long after I thought that,

that God laid on my heart, to make a commitment. From that night on I made a commitment to God that I would be in His house whenever possible. I have kept that commitment for over thirty years. God has honored that commitment.

I have done a lot of talking all through this treatise about walking with God. Look at the first ten words to this passage: *Commit your **way** to the Lord, trust also in Him.* That is the basic ingredient for the walk I have been talking about. I admit, I have not always walked with God. On a couple of occasions, I have gotten ahead of God. When I have walked with Him AND trusted Him, He has blessed me beyond anything I could imagine!

Just exactly what does it mean to "walk with God." I will share my definition. It means "studying" God's word. It means "praying" every day. It means "seeking" His will when there comes a fork in the road. ALWAYS trying to find God's will every day. Again, how do you do that? I think the answer for me is spending hours in God's word. As a young Christian, I found this schedule for reading through the Bible in one year. I wrote the schedule in my Bible by each chapter. I keep a bookmark by each day's reading. I think I have read through my Bible at least six times, probably more. Each time I read through it, I learn a little more about God's heart.

I don't know how many times I have read the story of David. Working on this study has revealed so much more than I thought I knew. The point? You must get to KNOW God through His word. That's why He gave it to us. Learn the contrast between the Old Testament God and the New Testament God. They are one and the same YET two different personalities of the same God. That is where it must start! Second, when things happen in your life you don't understand, look for God. Ask Him, "Why is this happening? What am I supposed to learn?" God is constantly trying to grow our faith. Strengthen us to do His work in us. The same way we try to teach our children to be better human beings, to grow up and have a better life than we had.

Look at these verses from the Sermon on the Mount:

> *You are the light of the world. A city that is set on a hill cannot be hidden. Nor do they light a lamp and put it under a basket, but on a lampstand, and it gives light to all who are in the house. Let your light so shine before men, that*

they may see your good works and glorify your Father in heaven (Matthew 5:14-16). (NKJV)

Now look what David said, *He shall bring forth your righteousness as the light.* We are called, as children of God, to glorify God. What are you doing to accomplish that? Can people look at you and see Jesus?

Did you catch those words? *and He shall bring it to pass.* What do you suppose God meant by that? Dare I venture to quote my favorite verses:

For I know the thoughts (plans) that I think toward you, says the Lord, thoughts (plans) of peace and not of evil, to give you a future and a hope. (Jeremiah 29:11). (NKJV)

Also 12 and 13. Notice what God's plan is for your life. "Future and hope." God has fantastic plans for your life. BUT you must walk that walk with Him. When you stray you miss the plan, and the blessing.

One of my traditions, when I worked for U.P.S. was to take the week from Christmas to New Years, off on vacation. I would spend that week trying to finish up any loose ends from the past year. I would SO look forward to what God was going to do in the new year, start my journal!

Rest in the Lord, and wait patiently for Him; do not fret because of him who prospers in his way, because of the man who brings wicked schemes to pass. Cease from anger, and forsake wrath; do not fret—it only causes harm. (Psalm 37:7-8) (NKJV)

Twice here, and once previous, the word "fret" appears. Do you know what that brings to my mind? "Buttons". People are funny to watch. I have watched, both my family, and others how people love to push buttons. Once you reveal that there is a button to push, you're are through. Look at verse 8: *Cease from anger, and forsake wrath, do not fret—it only causes harm.* Nothing good ever comes from losing your temper. You are totally out of control.

I used to drink before I was saved. I drank a lot overseas, in the military. Once I was saved I realized that when I drank, I lost control of my tongue, and my thoughts. The same is true with anger. When you lose control of your mind, your thoughts, anything is fair game. How many times have you had to apologize for something you said, "in anger?" More than you care to admit.

Maybe the first words here, help us to defeat "anger."

Rest in the Lord, and wait patiently for Him. (Psalm 37:7). (NKJV)

When we get to the point of "giving it to God" there is such a peace and self-control that comes over us. We can realize, one, that God is watching over His child (assuming you are a child of God) that God will not allow harm to come to His children. Second, anything that God will do will be so much better than what we could devise. God knows "their" weakness as well. Give it to God!

When my wife and I were first married she had a bad temper. I think she got it from her mom. Anyway, in order to fight you must have TWO participants. I refused to argue. When I get mad, I get quiet, I shut up. It is interesting that through the years there are fewer and fewer arguments. Because it takes TWO. We have also learned to give it to God.

I wonder if these words might be part of the problem: *Do not fret because of him who prospers in his way.* Are you jealous? Are you thinking "that's not fair". We talked about this before. I think much of this can be traced to our fellowship with God. Do you believe God should bless you more than someone else? Especially, since you are saved, you should be blessed. Really? I don't believe God works that way.

If we were rewarded based on our works, that is exactly what it would be: Based on works! Then the same questions: How much is enough? What are good works or bad works, by whose criteria? That is a slippery slope. I don't remember any lists in the Bible of what God rewards for what, etc. I do think there is one thing that God rewards: FAITH! All through the gospels Jesus is amazed at who had faith and who didn't. His disciples were the worst.

What do you think it means to *"rest in the Lord"*? Trust, confidence in His will, peace that God is in control, what do you think? You have enough faith to be saved, don't you? That is the faith of a grain of mustard seed that Jesus talks about in Matthew 17:20. Is that enough faith to "rest in the Lord?"

Was David an example of this "resting in the Lord?" Do you remember in 1 Samuel 16 what David did after he was anointed by Samuel? After David was anointed the scene switches to Saul, look at this statement:

> *But the Spirit of the Lord departed from Saul, and a distressing spirit from the Lord troubled him. (1 Samuel 16:14). (NKJV)*

So, Saul and his servants sought for someone to sooth Saul's "distressing spirit". Look at this:

> *Therefore, Saul sent messengers to Jesse, and said, "Send me your son David, who is with the sheep." (1 Samuel 16:19). (NKJV)*

David went right back to the sheep to WAIT for God's next move. David "rested" in the Lord and let the Lord open the next chapter in his life. Are you waiting on the Lord? Are you "resting"?

For evildoers shall be cut off; but those who wait on the Lord, they shall inherit the earth. For yet a little while and the wicked shall be no more; indeed, you will look carefully for his place, but it shall be no more. But the meek shall inherit the earth, and shall delight themselves in the abundance of peace. (Psalm 37:9-11) (NKJV)

Do you recognize those words?

> *But the meek shall inherit the earth. (Psalm 37:11). (NKJV)*

> *Blessed are the meek, for they shall inherit the earth. (Matthew 5:5). (NKJV)*

Of course, the author wrote both verses, the Holy Spirit. One more.

> *But those who wait on the Lord shall renew their strength; they shall mount up with wings like eagles, they shall run and not be weary, they shall walk and not faint. (Isaiah 40:31). (NKJV)*

Don't miss this! God is consistent throughout His word!

I hope, at some point in your life you will make it a priority to read through the Bible at least once. The more you read ALL through the Bible you will notice how God thinks, what is on His heart. How God deals with His children. What God wants and expects from His children. You will also see throughout the Bible how much He loves His children. He loves the whole world, but only those "adopted" into His family (Romans 8:15) will spend eternity with Him.

You want to know the heart of God? You must read His word. That is why He gave it to us. If anyone knew the heart of God, David did. Wait a minute, even after all the mistakes he made? Especially, after all the mistakes he made. He is human just as we are. God didn't create us perfect. He created us with a choice to make. We will spend a lifetime arriving at that choice: Where will we spend eternity? God gave us the ability, the opportunity, to choose Him or Hades. It is our choice!

Does it not frustrate you, when God says, *"For yet a little while and the wicked shall be no more."* A LITTLE WHILE? Yes, I know, it's been thousands of years. I am sure you know this verse:

> But, beloved, do not forget this one thing, that with the Lord one day is as a thousand years, and a thousand years as a day. (2 Peter 3:8). (NKJV)

I did the math once, if I remember, a person who lives to be seventy is about fifteen minutes in God's formula. Basically, time means nothing to God.

The day I retired I took my wrist-watch off and never wore one again. I figured I wouldn't need it. We are SO governed by time it is scary. Even after taking off my watch I am still conscious of time. Church starts at. . . etc. I wonder if God's use of *"a little while"* above is like when we tell someone, "just a minute", and thirty minutes later we show up. Same thing. How about "Wait a second"?

We have God's assurance that it will happen "eventually" don't worry. He will make things right, you can bank on that. That is all we need to know. Just like spending eternity in heaven, we cannot begin to comprehend that length of time. Here is something to add to that thought, *And, shall delight themselves in the abundance of peace.* You know, it will take some getting used to in heaven. "Worries" it will be a struggle at first, until we realize there is nothing further to worry about! Think about that for a minute. We are accustomed so much in this world to worry about things, we INVENT things to worry about. Give us a minute, something will come up. Seriously!

I wonder who David is writing this song to? Probably to himself. When you think of the struggles he endured, especially after Bathsheba, David needed to reconnect with God, be assured that God had not abandoned him, like He did Saul. (1 Samuel 16:14). We have no need of that concern today. Once we become a child of God we are adopted into God's family forever! (Romans 8:15). The more I think about that verse the more I like it. The more I take comfort in God's promise!

The wicked plots against the just, and gnashes at him with his teeth. The Lord laughs at him, for He sees that his day is coming. The wicked have drawn the sword and have bent their bow, to cast down the poor and needy, they slay those who are of upright conduct. Their sword shall enter their own heart, and their bows shall be broken. A little that a righteous man has is better than the riches of many wicked. For the arms of the wicked shall be broken, but the Lord upholds the righteous. (Psalm 37:12-17) (NKJV)

You might see this a lot in the psalms. Have you noticed? The "unfairness" of it all. It seems that the wicked are winning, doesn't it? Does that discourage you? Does it seem David is discouraged? Don't miss these words: *The Lord laughs at him, for He sees that his day is coming.* There is our hope. It doesn't help right now, does it? It depends on your focus. I talked about this before. Where is our focus? Today or eternity? When we look through a microscope, things look bad. We are losing, "what's the use". Then we look through the telescope and we see eternity things are not so bad.

Think about David's picture. He doesn't know about Christ. He doesn't know about the cross. How are our sins paid for by the blood of Christ? David is still looking at the blood of bulls and goats. But David had something that we have as well. Look at this verse:

*Then Samuel took the horn of oil and anointed him in the midst of his brothers; **and the Spirit of the Lord** came upon David from that day forward. So, Samuel arose and went to Ramah. (1 Samuel 16:13). (NKJV)*

David has the same "assurance" that we have. The guarantee of the indwelling Spirit of God.

He is the only one who can give us comfort today. The Holy Spirit is the One who confirms our fellowship with God our Father. He gives us that peace that we are walking with God. If you do not have that peace there are two reasons. One, you have never received Christ as your Savior, therefore you have NO relationship or fellowship with Almighty God. Two, you have strayed so far from God's will, off on a path of your choosing, that you cannot hear God's voice speaking through His Spirit. That is called quenching or grieving God's Spirit.

Just because, as a Christian, you have the third Person of the Trinity living within you doesn't mean He is in control. God will never force His will on us. He may convict us of our misdeed, but He will not cause us to change course. That decision must be of our own free will. That is so important to keep in mind. When God's Spirit starts dealing with you about something you need to get on your knees and pray: "Okay God, what is it that I am doing wrong?" Ask Him! He wants the best for you, the question is, are you willing to listen.

I have quoted Jeremiah 29:11-13 many times. I like the last verse:

> *And you will seek Me and find Me, when you search for Me with all your heart. (Jeremiah 29:13)* (NKJV)

You see? You are the one who must want the answer. God is right where you left Him. Waiting for you to return to Him, and rejoin Him on this path of life. You have to seek Him!

Okay, while we are here look at verse 12:

> *Then you will call upon Me and go and pray to Me, and I will listen to you. (Jeremiah 29:12)* (NKJV)

This is funny! Now I am quoting this verse backwards. However, you look at this truth, it makes no difference, the principle, the truth is the same. God wants a fellowship with His children. He wants us to walk this path of life with Him.

We are on a roll. One more verse:

You will show me the path of life; in Your presence
is fullness of joy; at Your right hand are pleasures
forevermore. (Psalm 16:11). (NKJV)

Same number as the original King James Bible. In order to enjoy those "pleasures forevermore" we must be at His right hand. Isn't that what it says? Not on some path of our choosing, but on God's path, God's plan, for our life. If you are walking with Him, you will experience life like you have never experienced before. Believe someone who has learned that lesson the hard way!

The Lord knows the days of the upright, and their inheritance shall be forever. They shall not be ashamed in the evil time, and in the days of famine they shall be satisfied. But the wicked shall perish; and the enemies of the Lord, like the splendor of the meadows, shall vanish. Into smoke they shall vanish away. (Psalm 37:18-20) (NKJV)

Let's talk about "inheritance" first. Guess what? We are back to Romans eight. Look at these verses:

For you did not receive the spirit of bondage again to fear;
but you received the Spirit of adoption by whom we cry
out, "Abba, Father." The Spirit Himself bears witness with
our spirit that we are children of God, and if children, then
heirs—heirs of God and joint heirs with Christ, if indeed
we suffer with Him, that we may also be glorified together.
(Romans 8:15-17). (NKJV)

If we, as Christians, ever fully grasp that relationship with God, it will change our walk! How many times in the New Testament are we referred to as "children of God?" (1 John). Just grasp that concept. I love that phrase, "Abba, Father." Think about it.

I don't think I covered this in the book of First Kings. I stopped after David's death. As far as David's enemies, let's look:

Then King Solomon swore by the Lord, saying, "May God
do so to me, and more also, if Adonijah has not spoken
this word against his own life. (1 Kings 2:23). (NKJV)

Solomon has Adonijah put to death, for again, trying to trick his way to the throne. And, finally, my buddy Joab,

> *Their blood shall therefore return upon the head of Joab and upon the head of his descendants forever. But upon David and his descendants, upon his house and his throne, there shall be peace forever from the Lord." So Benaiah the son of Jehoiada went up and struck and killed him; and he was buried in his own house in the wilderness. (1 Kings 2:33-34). (NKJV)*

God's time, God's way.

These last few verses in Psalm 37 have been about the wicked not being justly judged. They are and will be. You can rest in that. The thing we must remember is to allow God to do it, in His way, in His time. It works so much better for us!

Did you catch the significance of those first few words? *The Lord knows the days of the upright.* Too many times we think the "good deeds" we do will go unnoticed (1 Corinthians 15:58). That is not true! I want to draw your attention to a fantastic chapter in Jesus' Sermon on the Mount. Matthew chapter 6. I have so marked up this chapter. There are three areas in the Christian life that Jesus gives a clear principle. Fasting, giving, and praying. Now I will admit I don't do the fasting. But the other two are important. Let me give you the key:

> *that your charitable deed may be in secret; and your Father who sees in secret will Himself reward you openly. (Matthew 6:4). (NKJV)*

That is true in all three examples. We do it in secret! God rewards us openly. Matthew chapter six, check it out! The words of Jesus!

It's funny that David should use the phrase," in the days of famine." Do you remember that episode in David's life? The famine in 2 Samuel 21. To get David's attention about something that needed to be corrected. If you read, early in Genesis, famines are mentioned frequently. We have a famine today! Look at Amos 8:

"Behold, the days are coming," says the Lord God, that I will send a famine on the land, not a famine of bread, nor a thirst for water, but of hearing the words of the Lord. (Amos 8:11). (NKJV)

If you have your own Bible you need to spend as much time as you can, absorbing these truths. Apply them to your life. Make them an important part of your walk with God.

If you are attending a church that does not openly preach the Word of God you need to find a church that does. A pastor who preaches from, and teaches about the very Word of God. The famine is coming, if it isn't here already. You need to get to know the God of the Bible who is, hopefully, walking with you every day, guiding your steps!

The wicked borrows and does not repay, but the righteous shows mercy and gives. For those blessed by Him shall inherit the earth, but those cursed by Him shall be cut off. (Psalm 37:21-22) (NKJV)

Are you "blessed" of God? Interesting question. How would you define "blessed"? Are you still breathing? You think that's funny, but every breath you take is a gift from God. In my thirties, I was hurting so bad, and depressed that I told my dad, "I am not going to see my forties." Today I am 71, next week I'll be seventy-two, the Lord willing. A gift from God. I have had blood clots in both my lungs, cancer of the colon, but God has chosen to keep me around a little longer. What does "blessed" mean to you?

Concerning this borrowing thing. Let me just give you one verse:

*The rich rules over the poor, and the borrower is **servant** to the lender. (Proverbs 22:7). (NKJV)*

In 2009 our debt amounted to 70,000 dollars. in seven year's we are debt free. We determined to be debt free when we read Dave Ramey's "Total Money Makeover". The biggest lesson from this was being committed to tithing. If you haven't tried it, don't knock it!

I think it is interesting that David uses mercy along with giving. Let me give you a trivia question: In all the books that the Apostle Paul wrote in the New Testament he begins with basically the same salutation:

Grace to you and peace from God our Father and the Lord
Jesus Christ (Ephesians 1:2). (NKJV)

"Grace" and "Peace" in every book. Not in Hebrews, we are not sure who wrote that book. Now look at the "Pastoral Epistles" and the salutation in those three books (1 & 2 Timothy and Titus). Do you see the difference? I just thought that was interesting.

This may be a strange way to look at these words: "*The wicked borrows but does not repay*" but think of this way. The borrower made a promise, a commitment, to complete a contract. When they do not repay they have broken their word, their promise. Just a thought.

I talked earlier about our inheritance. We talked earlier about being blessed of God. "*Those cursed by Him.*" What would it mean to be cursed by Him? God has taken His hand off your life. There is an emptiness, a loneliness, a hopelessness that you can't shake. I believe, and I have others say the same thing, When God created us, He created us with a piece missing. A piece in our heart that we cannot describe. All of us will spend our whole life looking for that piece. We might try money, sex, adventure, things, etc. A good book to read is Ecclesiastes by Solomon. Solomon had the ability to "try everything under the sun". He came away with one truth:

Let us hear the conclusion of the whole matter: Fear God and keep His commandments for this is man's all. For God will bring every work into judgment, including every secret thing, whether good or evil. (Ecclesiastes 12:13-14). (NKJV)

That "missing" piece? It's God!

Isn't it interesting that David's son, the one God chose to build His temple would write the book of Ecclesiastes? Don't forget that Solomon also wrote the book of Proverbs. Such wisdom can only come from God. You can see Solomon's style in the verses above: The "wicked" vs the "righteous", the "blessed" vs the "cursed". Same style as Proverbs. Like father, like son.

It has been my wish and my goal, beginning with my first book, THE PATH, to encourage you to spend more time in God's Word. The more time you spend reading this wonderful love letter from God the better you will understand what God wants to do in your life. The "miracle" of the

Bible is that each one will read something different. Five people will read the same passage and come away with five different meanings in their life. That is the Holy Spirit revealing God's will in each reader. If you are not a child of God you have no idea what I am talking about. Only a child of God will understand the power of God's written word to His children. Have you asked Jesus into your heart? Why not?

The steps of a good man are ordered by the Lord, and He delights in his way. Though he fall, he shall not be utterly cast down; for the Lord upholds him with His hand. (Psalm 37:23-24) (NKJV)

Not long after I was saved I found this Bible reading schedule. Later I went through every Bible I bought afterward, and at Genesis 1:1 I wrote 1/1, at Genesis 4 I wrote 1/2, at Genesis 7 I wrote 1/3, on throughout my Bible. Then I keep a bookmark at each day as I go through the year. In the morning, all I need to do, is open to the bookmark, read to the next date. In a year, I have read through my Bible. The reason I bring this up is that June 23rd I have this verse bracketed. Oh, later I started "bracketing" a verse for each day that meant something special to me. This is the verse I have for June 23rd. Interesting, our wedding anniversary is June 24th.

Take a minute. Meditate on those first eleven words. *The steps of a good man are ordered by the Lord.* You don't have to count them! What do you suppose that means to you? Have you read Jeremiah 29:11 yet? If you have read this book you probably have. How about Psalm 16:11? I quoted that verse earlier. What is the theme? When God saw fit to create us in our mother's womb God has a plan for our life. He has a plan for every life He has created. So why is the world in such a mess? God also gave us the "option" not to follow His plan. It is our call!

I learned this lesson the hard way. I just thought I knew for sure what Gd wanted me to do. I didn't need to pray, I just knew! I was so sure I quit the church I was pastoring in and went where I thought sure God wanted me. Guess what? He shut that door in my face. It took a while. Eventually I realizes that I had gotten ahead of God. Instead of letting God open the door I was determined to help God out. God doesn't need any help! Are you trying to knock down some doors that God may have other plans?

And He delights in his way. When we are walking the same path that

God is walking there are blessings galore! Oh, we may stumble, may even fall, but God is right there to pick us up, and put us back on our feet. If you get the chance, you need to watch *"Love Comes Softly."* There is a great scene in there that explains what I am talking about. Did you see that in the verses above? *Though he fall, he shall not be cast down* (37:24). That is what I am talking about. We can be walking right next to God and trip and fall. Just ask David!

But like the verse that says, *For the Lord upholds him with His hand.* That is assuming God has His hand on your life. Do you want to know a great place to experience God's presence? In church! If you have ever been in a worship service where God's Spirit is moving you will be amazed! You can feel His presence! It is awesome!

Did you catch the "qualifier"? *The Steps of **a good man** are ordered by the Lord.* So, what constitutes a "good man"? What does God use as a measuring stick. I don't think it is complicated. If you are a child of God you are a "good man". Take a minute and read Romans 8:15-17. I have almost become as fond of these verses as Jeremiah 29:11-13. The more time you spend in God's word the greater God's blessing in verses that speak to your heart and encourage your walk with Him.

Does verse 23 give you some hope and comfort? It should. When I realized that God has a plan for my life I got excited. I wanted to know what that plan was. The exciting thing to me, is watching God work through me. I don't understand it, I can't explain it, I am just flabbergasted that He would even consider me! He can do the same thing for you. I like what Jesus says in John 14,

> *If you love Me, keep My commandments! (John 14:15).*
> (NKJV)

If you want God to "order your steps" you must be willing to follow His instructions. It is that simple.

Just think about what that means. If you are a parent what is your desire for your children? You want them to listen to you and do what you tell them, it's for their good, right?

I have been young, and now am old; yet I have not seen the righteous forsaken, nor his descendants begging bread. He is ever merciful, and lends; and His descendants are blessed. (Psalm 37:25-26) (NKJV)

Cool! That means once I get to be a Christian everything will be smooth sailing from then on. Ask anyone who has been a Christian for any length of time, that is not the way it is. I believe, if I heard right, that all the disciples except John died a martyr's death. Speaking of martyrs, you might want to read a book called "Foxe's Book of Martyrs." Interesting thought.

I had the privilege of portraying Jim Elliot in a play, our church put on, based on the book by Elizabeth Elliott called "Gates of Splendor." Jim and three others were trying to reach a tribe of Auca Indians in South America. They dropped trinkets and tracks to the natives for several days. One day they landed in a field near their village. The natives ran out and killed all four men. Later, Jim's wife, Elizabeth, managed to take the gospel to the same natives who killed her husband.

If you have been a Christian any length of time you know it is not what the "lost" think it is. That is such a paradox to speak about. Our pastor touched on it Sunday. It is so frustrating to be on this side of the glass and know the joys and peace from being a child of God. And to try to explain it to a lost person is so hard! It is like trying to describe heaven. We are on one side of the glass trying to explain to someone on the other side what it is like. Until they experience it, by faith, you just can't put it in words. We can only share the truth and our testimony.

I was not saved until I was thirty-five. I can understand the previous life, verses, the life after I was saved. There were no fireworks and rockets going off. Suddenly, I couldn't get enough of the Bible. That was probably the biggest change in my life. That led to teaching and serving and finally to preaching. It was a "growing" process. God had to take me from where I was (not knowing Genesis from Revelation) to being a pastor. You might say, "God grew me up."

Speaking of martyr's, you might want to take a few minutes and read the book of Revelation. A lot of times we say, "I read the back of the book and we win". That is true. Don't overlook the fact that in the end times, assuming we are here, there will come a time when Christians will have to decide between living and taking the mark of the Beast or dying by beheading. Can you make that choice today? How is your faith in Christ?

How about David? Was his walk with God without bumps? Not hardly. He had his share of bumps. How did he deal with them? He always came back to God. He admitted his sins, asked God's forgiveness and got back on God's path for his life. We know, when we have taken another path, other than God's.

I don't know if you thought about it. I mentioned it at the time. The length of time from the day Bathsheba told David, "I am with child" (2 Samuel 11:5) until Nathan said, "You are the man!" (2 Samuel 12:7). Sure just a few verses later. No, around nine months. God told David the child born would die. (2 Samuel 12:18). Nine months of thinking "I am in the clear. I got away with it." I wonder how many times we think we have pulled one over on God? Don't go there. You might want to consider David.

I have been young, and now I am old. That is me. Over thirty years of watching God do His thing in the people around me, and myself of course. I mentioned earlier that I am a "people watcher" I also like to be a "God watcher" always keeping my eyes open to what God is doing around me. How He is dealing with family and friends and kind of observing their walk with God. Of course, I don't know their heart. It is just interesting to watch how God works!

Depart from evil, and do good; and dwell forevermore. For the Lord loves justice, and does not forsake His saints; they are preserved forever, but the descendants of the wicked shall be cut off. The righteous shall inherit the land, and dwell in it forever. (Psalm 37:27-29) (NKJV)

You can't get used to it, can you? Being referred to as a "saint". Every child of God is a saint in the eyes of God. You might say our "status" has been "upgraded!" Here goes the good vs evil thing again. Solomon must have gotten it from his dad.

That's what life is about isn't it? Good / bad scenario. Really, it's about choices. You don't want to get me started on choices. I preached a whole sermon on "choices." Oh, don't forget the other term David uses here, "righteous." None of us consider ourselves righteous, do we? I think what David realizes and understands, maybe David doesn't, but those terms:

Righteous and saints are what God sees in us because of the work of His Son at Calvary. Without covering our sins at the cross, we don't qualify for those descriptions.

I mentioned choices, sorry, can't resist! Look at the beginning: *Depart from evil, and do good.* So, I hope that doesn't give you the impression that if you do "good" that will get you into heaven or give you the title of "saint?" It doesn't! There is no amount of "good deeds" that will get you into heaven. Look at these familiar verses:

> For by **grace** you have been saved through faith, and that not of yourselves; it is the gift of God, **not of works,** lest anyone should boast. (Ephesians 2:8-9). (NKJV)

It is strictly God's doing.

The minute you begin adding "works" to our salvation you must ask, "how much, for how long, and what qualifies?" I don't recall a list in the Bible that answers these questions, because there isn't any. Wait a minute, there is a verse:

> For no other foundation can anyone lay than that which was laid, which is Jesus Christ. Now if anyone builds on this foundation with gold, silver, precious stones, wood, hay, straw, each one's work will become clear; for the day will declare it. (1 Corinthians 3:11-13a). (NKJV)

One problem! It doesn't say what is gold, silver or hay. The question in these verses is "what is your foundation?" Is your salvation built on "works"? Then what is the foundation? It isn't Jesus Christ!

Our salvation has already been bought. There is nothing that can change that! Jesus death on the cross paid for our sins, past, present and future. You will dilute this truth by trying to add works. Christ has done it all.

So, what does this mean to me? Again, two choices. You can accept that gift from God by receiving Christ into your heart (Romans 10:9). Or you can deny this fact and stand before God condemned, and spend eternity in Hades. It is your choice. I said this before. When you stand before God on judgment day it is too late to say, "Okay, I believe" That "choice" must be made this side of heaven. You must become a "saint" before you stand before God!

Did you catch those four precious words? *They are preserved forever!* Once you have made that decision to ask Jesus into your heart you are a child of God forever. The seal to prove that contract is the gift of the Holy Spirit who comes to dwell within you. The third part of the triune God dwells within all of God's children. He is the Seal of our salvation. (Romans 8:15). It's all in the Bible. It is certainly worth checking into! You might start with the gospel of John.

Just a little note that I find fascinating. The gospel of John has 21 chapters. Half of those chapters take place in the upper room just prior to His crucifixion. It is the last opportunity for Jesus to instruct His disciples. There is so much in those few chapters. Here is a challenge. There are three chapters in the Sermon on the Mount (Matthew 5-7), and these few chapters in John. Meditate on those verses. Absorb the truths in those verses. They will shine a light on the rest of the New Testament. Filter the rest of the Bible through those few chapters. See what you can learn!

The mouth of the righteous speaks wisdom, and his tongue talks of justice. The law of his God is in his heart; none of his steps shall slide. (Psalm 37:30-31) (NKJV)

James chapter three has a great deal to say about the tongue. Proverbs has several verses concerning the tongue. The Bible is full of counsel and illustrations of the damage the tongue can do. I guess the question is, "Who is in control of that thing?" Here is one of my favorites from James:

> *So then, my beloved brethren, let every man be swift to hear, slow to speak, slow to wrath. (James 1:19).* (NKJV)

That has been a goal of mine since I read it. It is amazing what you can learn when your mouth is shut!

Of course, Proverbs also has a lot to say about wisdom. The subject of justice seems to be of great importance today. The problem is we all want to be the arbiter of that justice. We all have our "list" of what is right and wrong. We also have our "priority list". There are things that are worse than others. Here is another piece of wisdom from James:

For whoever shall keep the whole law, and yet stumble in one point, he is guilty of all. (James 2:10). (NKJV)

Justice is in the eyes of God, not in our sinful hearts.

I wonder if we could say what David says here? *The law of his God is in his heart.* Unless we know the heart of God, one of the reasons for this journey, we cannot obey what we do not know. Most people, it is sad to say, know just enough to get into heaven. They couldn't find proof of their salvation if you asked them. They just know, right? Do you know enough to "defend" your salvation if asked? Look at this verse:

But sanctify the Lord God in your hearts, and always be ready to give a defense to everyone who asks you a reason for the hope that is in you, with meekness and fear. (1 Peter 3:15). (NKJV)

Can you "explain" to someone why you are going to heaven?

I have spoken so much about this path we are on. I want to share a brief illustration, that might help. My first book, THE PATH, was written as a challenge from God. I sure had no idea where it was going, I just did what God asked me to do. In the process of writing that devotional I became intrigued with the passages that said, "David is a man after God's own heart." Worded differently, of course, (1 Samuel 13:14 and Acts 13:22). I became so curious that I thought I would read about David and see what I could learn. God said, "write it down." The curiosity sparked this effort. It has blessed me so much! The point of course, God starts us on one road, which will lead to another, and another, etc. I hope this will help you find your path that God wishes you to travel.

I missed that! Did you catch that word? *The law of his God is in his heart.* It is funny that the Holy Spirit here didn't say head. He talked earlier of wisdom. We think of wisdom as knowledge rightly applied. Why would David say, "his heart?" I don't recall any verses that say we must invite Christ into our head, do you? That will be so disappointing when we stand before God and He asks us about Jesus. We will spout all this "historical" knowledge we know about Jesus. We may even quote some scripture. God will say, depart from me, I never knew you.

"Not everyone who says to Me, 'Lord, Lord,' shall enter the kingdom of heaven, but he who does the will of My Father in heaven. Many will say to Me in that day, 'Lord, Lord, have we not prophesied in Your name, cast out demons in Your name, and done many wonders in Your name?' And then I will declare to them, 'I never knew you; depart from Me, you who practice lawlessness!'" (Matthew 7:21-23). (NKJV)

Head knowledge but not in the heart! We did all these great miracles. Yes, but you failed to receive Me into your heart. You might want to read Revelation 3:20.

The wicked watches the righteous, and seeks to slay him. The Lord will not leave him in his hand, nor condemn him when he is judged. (Psalm 37:32-33) (NKJV)

I think I stated earlier that I am a "people watcher", I love to set in my car, while my wife is shopping and watch the people go in and out. This is a totally different kind of watching. As any Christian will tell you the "lost" are constantly watching those who "proclaim" to be Christians. Why? Hoping to find a flaw! If you're like me, they don't have to look too hard. We never claim to be perfect, just forgiven. David is a great example. God used David despite his flaws. God can and will use anyone willing to give their life to God!

Do you see this great promise here? *The Lord will not leave him in his hand, nor condemn him when he is judged.* God won't give up on us, it is usually the other way around. You need to see the contrast. The "wicked" seek to slay us, God will protect us. I love that!

Have you noticed the battle going on today? It is the worst I can remember. It seems the devil is no longer trying to hide what he is doing. He is right out in the open. Satan is doing everything in his power to degrade, diminish, or destroy the Christian influence in our country and world. You do know about this pastor who is held in captivity in Turkey. The leader of the country would rather see his country go bankrupt than release him. Our President has put sanctions on Turkey, but they refuse to release him.

Christians are mocked and ridiculed more than I can ever remember.

It seems Satan is pulling out all the stops. Soon, God will have a choice to make. Of course, as we have seen, God always has the plan in place. Two choices: Jesus returns. After the rapture of His church, God will bring a series of three sets of seven plaques. All for one purpose! To give all those who have rejected Christ "one last chance" to recognize the God of the Universe or perish with the devil and his angels.

Two: This is my hope. It is time for one final great revival. I also see God's people bolder than ever before. Willing to stand up for God. We need God to raise up another Billy Graham, another D.L. Moody, even another Apostle Paul. Someone God's Spirit will enable to reach the hearts of God's people who have long ago given up. Someone to preach the Word of God with the Power of the Holy Spirit. A world-wide Spirit-led revival. Lighting a fire in God's people.

Yes, the wicked are watching. They are no match for the power of God's Spirit working in God's people. Two options. It might be exciting to see which one God will use. As a Christian, I am afraid I won't be here to see what happens, if Jesus returns. If that is the option I will be taken up to heaven in the Rapture. If God decides to send a great revival I will love to see God working in the hearts of God's people. It will be something for the "wicked" to watch! Amen!

Are you one of the "righteous"? I know that seems like a "holy" description of God's people but that is our title. Righteous, because we have chosen "right living" in the will and purpose of God. If we look around our world today, it seems hopeless. Many in our church are saying "end times." I still hold out hope for a real "Holy Ghost" revival in our country. Nothing is impossible with God. If he chooses, if He chooses to extent His grace one more time.

If you want a picture of God's grace just be reminded of David. He not only had an affair with a married woman but he arranged for that woman's husband to be killed. YET! God chose to use David in so many ways "despite" his sin and flaws. Oh, David paid a price. I think the thing that made David, "a man after God's own heart" is that he never gave up on God. He always returned in humble contrition, seeking the forgiveness and return of his fellowship with the God who called him out of the shepherd's field to become King of Israel. David saw many miracles that God worked through him. How about you? Is God working in your life?

Wait on the Lord, and keep His ways; and He shall exalt you to inherit the land; when the wicked are cut off, you shall see it. I have seen the wicked in great power; and spreading himself like a native green tree, yet he passed away, and behold, he was no more; indeed, I sought him, but he could not be found. (Psalm 37:34-36) (NKJV)

This is David's second reference to "waiting on the Lord" (37:9). Of course, my favorite reference:

> But those who wait on the Lord shall renew their strength;
> they shall mount up with wings like eagles, they shall run
> and not be weary, they shall walk and not faint. (Isaiah
> 40:31) (NKJV)

I have numerous pictures of eagles, a cup, even my casket lid, has an eagle on the inside of it. When I discovered this verse, I was struggling with what God was doing in my life. I had acknowledged His call to ministry, and was really searching for "exactly" what did that mean.

We are not a culture comfortable with waiting. Now, with plastic charge cards and debt unbelievable we have basically done away with "waiting". I think the term now is "instant gratification." We don't need to wait any longer EXCEPT on God. God will not be intimidated, or rushed. I learned that the hard way. If you are walking with God you cannot be in a hurry. God will achieve His will in His time, for His glory! No matter how impatient you get.

I love these words in Galatians,

> But, when the **fullness of the time** had come, God sent
> forth His Son, born of a woman, born under the law, to
> redeem those who were under the law, that we might
> receive the adoption of sons. (Galatians 4:4-5) (NKJV)

God doesn't deal in minutes or hours or even years, but centuries! Over two thousand years since God visited us in the person of His Son Jesus Christ.

Do you think God is pacing the floor in heaven wondering when He might choose to send His Son to bring judgment on His creation? I think not. God knows exactly when it will occur and under what circumstances. If God wanted us to know He would have told us through His son.

What does it mean to "wait on the Lord?" Do you have a plan? It is a bad habit I must always be thinking a day ahead. "Okay, tomorrow I need to get this done, and that, and try to get this done." Do you do that? Do you leave any room for "surprises?" I think not. When my "plans" go astray I just grin. "Okay, Lord You made Your point. Now what do you want me to do? Once we decided to buy a house. I know that God wants us out from under this rent and be debt free. We looked at several houses, we tried to buy a few but it seemed every time someone had always beat us to it. It got so frustrating. I realized that we were getting ahead of God.

After a summer of looking and trying, God laid on my heart to write a devotional called THE PATH. I figured that instead of financing a house God would provide the funds to buy a house. Accomplishing His plan, but in His way and His timing. Do your plans seem frustrated? Is it what God wants but it seems long delayed? "Wait on the Lord." If it is His will He will bring it to pass. Do you know what gives us the strength and the will to wait? FAITH. If you believe that God is truly in charge, that you are on His schedule, you can trust God to bring it to pass. That is called faith!

Did you catch the condition to waiting? *and keep His way.* Obedience is always necessary in this waiting process. I shared before that I knew God had called me to ministry. Then He says, "you need to turn in a resume." I hate paperwork. I kept putting it off. Finally, I realized that God would not take the next step until I had been obedient to this step. I asked my daughter to help me, I completed the resume, not long after a church in Freeman, Missouri called me. There are things God wants to do in our life. But, until we are obedient to His instructions we are simply hindering His working in our life. God will not work in our rebellion and disobedience.

Think about the lesson David learned!

Mark the blameless man, and observe the upright; for the future of that man is peace. But the transgressors shall be destroyed together; the future of the wicked shall be cut off. (Psalm 37:37-38) (NKJV)

There is an interesting word that appears twice in these verses. "Future". *For the future of that man is peace.* The future of what man? The blameless and upright man. His future is peace. Not as long as he is in this world. Oh, he will have peace within his soul, but the devil will always be nipping at his heels. As a child of God, we can ignore that and focus on God! There is our peace.

The second "peace" is for the wicked. Do they have any peace? Not likely. They are always looking over their shoulder, scared of being caught. Scared of being "found out" yet God already knows their plight. *The future of the wicked shall be cut off.* Cut off from what? Heaven of course. I think it is physically impossible to be wicked and a child of God. God will not allow His children to soil His name. If they persist God will simply take them home rather than have them defame Him.

I have been struggling with when David might have written this psalm. It is hard to tell sometimes. There was a forty-year period in his life, I think possibly he might have felt the presence of God to write some psalms. Look at this verse:

> Now it came to pass after forty years that Absalom said to the king, "Please let me go to Hebron and pay the vow which I made to the Lord. (2 Samuel 15:7). (NKJV)

Absalom, through the diplomacy of Joab, did return to Jerusalem. It says, earlier, that Absalom began winning the hearts of the people (15:1). Absalom was doing his "dirty work" for forty years. David, none the wiser, may have written some psalms during this time. Maybe some as a shepherd prior to his call by Samuel, we just don't know.

One of the reasons I like this psalm is in the early part of the psalm I underlined some "action" words, as I like to call them: *Trust* (37:3), *Delight* (37:4), *Commit* (37:5), *Rest* (37:7), *Cease* (37:8), *Wait* (37:9,34). Also, the powerful words of verses 23 and 24:

> The steps of a good man are ordered by the Lord, and He delights in his way. Though he fall, he shall not be utterly cast down; for the Lord upholds him with His hand. (Psalm 37:23-24) (NKJV)

What a great promise from God!

I think it is interesting how David words this warning, *Mark the blameless man, and observe the upright.* Who are your role models? Who do you look up to? What kind of testimony do they have? Why do you like them, and want to follow them? What kind of principles to they proclaim? Always remember that words are cheap, even more so today. Lying has become an art form. Look at their lives, their impact on the people around them. What is their "history".

Again, like I said earlier in the style of Solomon and here with David. The plus and the minus. Do this, don't do that. Right and wrong! The scary part is: It is your choice! When you choose to follow someone it is your choice, brother! You can't blame anyone else, so do your homework! Pay attention to that "still small voice" within you that will guide you on the right path! That Holy Spirit within the child of God will never lead you astray. You may be following someone down the wrong path with promises of things that only God can deliver. BUT, God says that is not the way. Don't be fooled by empty promises.

This is a great psalm to meditate on. There are a lot of truths that David is sharing with us. Ask God's Holy Spirit to open your heart to receive what God is trying to teach you here. You will see things that you had never seen before, assuming God is leading in your learning! Trust His guidance and THEN you will need to incorporate those teachings into your everyday life. Write them down, put them on the frig, practice them, pray over them and through them, till they become part of your "future!"

But the salvation of the righteous is from the Lord; He is their strength in the time of trouble. And the Lord shall help them and deliver them; He shall deliver them from the wicked, and save them, because they trust in Him. (Psalm 37:39-40) (NKJV)

Salvation is deliverance. I heard someone say once, "Saved from what?" Saved from an eternity in Hades. An eternity separated from God. David concludes this psalm with great comments on salvation. Let's take a look at some critical verses for the Old Testament:

> *Then Samuel took the horn of oil and anointed him in the midst of his brothers, **and the Spirit of the Lord** came upon David from that day forward. So, Samuel arose and went to Ramah (1 Samuel 16:13). (NKJV)*

Don't neglect to notice "from that day forward" that is unusual for the Old Testament. Now look:

> But the **Spirit of the Lord departed** from Saul, and a distressing spirit from the Lord troubled him. (1 Samuel 16:14). (NKJV)

These verses, back to back, illustrate the difference between the Old Testament and the New Testament. Thank God, we live in New Testament times. In the New Testament, the Holy Spirit is a "seal" of our salvation. It is a permanent reminder of our relationship with Almighty God. Look at these verses:

> For as many as are led by the **Spirit of God**, these are sons of God. For you did not receive the spirit of bondage again to fear, but you received the Spirit of adoption by which we cry, "Abba, Father." The Spirit himself bears witness with our spirit that we are children of God. (Romans 8:14-15). (NKJV)

That same Spirit that indwelt David indwells us today as children of God.

So, you ask, where was that Spirit the night David spied Bathsheba? He was there, but we as well as David can ignore Him. Discount His speaking to our hearts. Don't be too harsh on David. I am sure we have suffered the same results when we have failed to listen to God's Spirit. Look what David wrote in the 51st Psalm:

> Do not cast me away from Your presence, and do not take Your Holy Spirit from me. Restore to me the joy of Your salvation, and uphold me by Your generous Spirit. (Psalm 51:11-12). (NKJV)

David feared the same consequences as Saul. Do you remember his response when Nathan confronted David about his sin?

> So, David said to Nathan, "I have sinned against the Lord." (2 Samuel 12:13). (NKJV)

David confessed his sin and acknowledged his sin to God. Too many times our response is, "ignore it, it will go away."

David, from this point on, begins to slowly restore the joy of his salvation. I love this passage. Absalom has run David out of Jerusalem. David is running from his son who wants to kill him and become king. The priest followed him with the ark of God. Here is David's response:

> Then the king said to Zadok, "Carry the ark of God back into the city. **If I have found favor in the eyes of the Lord, He will bring me back and show me both it and His dwelling place.**" (2 Samuel 15:25). (NKJV)

I believe this was the beginning of David's repentance and restoring his fellowship with God the Father.

Don't overlook the final words of this psalm, *"Because they trust in Him."* Who trusts in Him? The righteous, the redeemed, the "saved". Those who have put their trust in the shed blood of God's Son on the cross of Calvary. What must I do to be saved? Pray, admit you are a sinner in need of a Savior! Look at these precious words from Romans:

> If you confess with your mouth the Lord Jesus and believe in your heart that God has raised Him from the dead, you will be saved. (Romans 10:9) (NKJV)

Let me finish with these words:

> For all the promises of God in Him are Yes, and in Him Amen, to the glory of God through us. Now He who establishes us with you in Christ and has anointed us is God, who also has sealed us and given us the Spirit in our hearts as a guarantee. (2 Corinthians 1:20-22). (NKJV)

David, A Man After God's Own Heart

L ong before God sought out David, Samuel spoke these words to Saul:

> *"But now your kingdom shall not continue. The Lord has sought for Himself a man after His own heart, and the Lord has commanded him to be commander over His people, because you have not kept what the Lord commanded you." (1 Samuel 13:14).* (NKJV)

Later in the New Testament, Paul, preaching in Antioch said this:

> *"And when He had removed him (Saul), He raised up for them David as king, to whom also He gave testimony and said, 'I have found David the son of Jesse, a man after My own heart, who will do all My will.'" (Acts 13:22)* (NKJV)

This has been a challenge, while also inspiring. I thought to walk with David through First and Second Samuel and see if I could discover why God would give David this title. I think one of the key things to keep in mind is to remember that David is just as human as you or me. He fell, he broke God's heart! He also repented and restored that fellowship with holy God. There are many lessons to learn from David. I hope this treatise will inspire, convict, encourage and bring you to a closer walk with our Heavenly Father.

Let's take a quick journey through David's journal and just be reminded of some things we will want to pray about, meditate on, and hopefully incorporate into our own lives. David has taught us many lessons, some good, some not so good. By taking a second look at these verses maybe we can piece together some truths to live by. The word of God will always inspire us. My Sunday School teacher is glad we are leaving the Old Testament and next month we will be in Galatians. There are so many riches in these stories in the Old Testament. I have said that what God teaches in the New Testament He illustrates in the Old Testament. The Old Testament is the foundation for the New.

We first meet David in First Samuel 16. He is a shepherd. God tells Samuel to go to Jesse's house, there you will find the next king. (16:1). He arrives at Jesse's home and asks to see his sons. Look at this verse:

> But the Lord said to Samuel, "Do not look at his appearance or at his physical stature, because I have refused him (Eliab). For the Lord does not see as man sees; for man looks at the outward appearance, but the Lord looks at the heart." (1 Samuel 16:7). (NKJV)

Our first, all important, principle. Eliab was the oldest and Samuel automatically said, "This must be the one." We see God's response.

I think it is interesting. After Samuel anointed David, David returned to the sheep. Here is another great principle I think we can learn. David ALWAYS waited on God's timing. Twice he had opportunity to kill Saul, he refused. It was God's call, not his. Later, David is summoned to Saul's court. David is to play soothing music for Saul. When he was not playing he returns to the fields.

Our first, of several, appearances of the Philistines, occurs next. David is in the field. Jesse summons him to take a lunch to his brothers on the battlefield. Here he meets Goliath. Just one simple verse here:

> Then all the assembly shall know that the Lord does not save with sword or spear; for the battle is the Lord's, and He will give you into our hands. (1 Samuel 17:47). (NKJV)

David's faith was in God not in our own strength. After this the people begin to praise David and ridicule Saul. After this battle David meets and befriends Jonathan. A friendship that will last long after Jonathan's death.

In chapter 31 of First Samuel Saul and Jonathan are slain in a battle against the Philistines at Gilboa. David was sent back to Ziklag prior to this battle. God was watching over David. Early in Second Samuel David writes and sings a psalm in memory of Saul and Jonathan.

We saw earlier that Samuel anointed David while he was a shepherd (1 Samuel 16:13). Later David would be anointed king of Hebron (2 Samuel 2:7) where he would rule for seven years. Eventually he would be anointed King of Israel. (2 Samuel 5:3)

Early in David's walk with God, David would "inquire of the Lord." (2 Samuel 2:1, 5:19, 5:23). It seems he got away from this. This had always helped David, a good habit for us to get into to as well. Just a reminder, you might want to look at Second Samuel Seven. Here is a great picture of the attitude we should have in our walk with God.

In Second Samuel, we see the story of Mephibosheth, Jonathan's son. David keeps a precious promise he made to his friend Jonathan! There are several "episodes" I have skipped, great pictures to help us understand God's fellowship with David. We have seen that David is said to be, "a man after God's own heart." We know also, that David broke God's heart one night when he was NOT where he was supposed to be. Then he tried to hide it, and eventually committed murder. Don't try to split hairs and say "he" didn't kill Uriah. In God's eye's it was David's sin.

There are several great lessons to learn from this episode in David's life. Prayerfully read through this story. Ask God to open your heart and reveal anything that stands between you and your fellowship with your heavenly Father. I went into detail about the difference between a "relationship" with God and the "fellowship" with our heavenly Father. I hope you will ponder those two and examine both your "relationship" (child of God), and your "fellowship" (your walk with God).

One of my favorite verses and great blessings that demonstrates God's grace comes after David's sin. The child that Bathsheba bore from David, as part of his consequence for this sin, the child would die. Here is David's response after the child dies:

> "But now he is dead; why should I fast? Can I bring him back again? I shall go to him, but he shall not return to me," (2 Samuel 12:23) (NKJV)

Think about that concept a minute! The grace was that Bathsheba had another son, his name was Solomon, the future king of Israel and the one God would use to build His temple. That is grace!

From chapter 13 of Second Samuel through the end of Second Samuel David is suffering the consequences of his sin. The judgment of God. From Amnon, Tamar, Absalom, Joab, At this point David writes his second psalm found in this narrative. Following the final victory over the Philistines.

Soon after the victory David acknowledges his "mighty men" in chapter 23. It doesn't say but I believe, because there is no mention of glory to God, God sends a plague on Israel. It lasts three days at which point David is told to build an altar to God. Here is another great verse:

> *Then the king said to Araunah, "No, but I will surely buy it from you for a price; nor will I offer burnt offerings to the Lord my God with that which costs me nothing." So, David bought the threshing floor and the oxen for fifty shekels of silver. (2 Samuel 24:24). (NKJV)*

So, how can we sum up our journey with David? The closer we can learn to walk with God the more blessed we will be. Don't miss this! Even walking close to God, we will stumble, we might wander off on the wrong path, God will simply remain at the crossroad where we left Him, until we return and renew our fellowship. Always keep that picture in your mind. Satan will do everything he can to break up that fellowship. Like the night David was not where he was supposed to be.

Each of us has a calling from God. When God created us in the womb He had a plan for our lives (Jeremiah 29:11-13). The greatest challenge and reward we could possibly have is to find that path, that plan and walk daily with God. Maybe when we stand before God, he might say, "Well done, thou good and faithful servant!"

Printed in the United States
By Bookmasters